A Culture of Ambiguity

Thomas Bauer

A Culture of Ambiguity

An Alternative History of Islam

Translated by
Hinrich Biesterfeldt and
Tricia Tunstall

Columbia University Press
New York

Columbia University Press
Publishers Since 1893
New York Chichester, West Sussex
cup.columbia.edu

Library of Congress Cataloging-in-Publication Data
Names: Bauer, Thomas, 1961 September 27– author. | Biesterfeldt, Hinrich, 1943– translator. | Tunstall, Tricia, translator.
Title: A culture of ambiguity : an alternative history of Islam / Thomas Bauer; translated by Hinrich Biesterfeldt and Tricia Tunstall.
Other titles: Kultur der Ambiguität. English
Description: New York : Columbia University Press, 2021. | Includes bibliographical references and index. | Translated from German.
Identifiers: LCCN 2020039638 (print) | LCCN 2020039639 (ebook) | ISBN 9780231170642 (hardback) | ISBN 9780231170659 (trade paperback) | ISBN 9780231553322 (ebook)
Subjects: LCSH: Religious tolerance—Islam. | Islam—20th century—Social aspects. | Islamic sociology. | Ambiguity.
Classification: LCC BP171.5 .B3813 2021 (print) | LCC BP171.5 (ebook) | DDC 297.09/04—dc23
LC record available at https://lccn.loc.gov/2020039638
LC ebook record available at https://lccn.loc.gov/2020039639

Cover image: Detail of a minbar from a mosque

Contents

Foreword *ix*

Introduction 1

Translators' Note 8

1. Cultural Ambiguity 9

Cultural Ambiguity, the Term 9

Ambiguity in Philosophy, Linguistics, Literary Criticism, and Literary History 12

Tolerance of Ambiguity in Psychology 16

Ambiguity in the Historical and Social Sciences 18

Forms of Cultural Ambiguity in Islam 20

2. Does God Speak in Textual Variants? 30

Crises and Domestication of Ambiguity 30

Ibn al-Jazarī's History of the Quranic Text 35

A Salafist History 40

The Inexhaustible Diversity of the Variant Readings 44

Diversity as Blessing 53

Diversity as an Offense 59
The "Postmodern" Tradition 69
3. Does God Speak Ambiguously? 74
The Inexhaustibility of the Quran 74
The Theologization of Islam 85
4. The Blessing of Dissent 94
Hadith as a Theory of Probability 94
The Theory of Probability in Islamic Law 103
The Gift of Ambiguity 121
5. The Islamization of Islam 129
6. Language: A Serious Business and a Game 151
Words with Opposite Meanings 151
Refinement and Piety 164
Ambiguity as Stigma 169
Training in Ambiguity 172
7. The Ambiguity of Sexual Desire 183
An Imposed—and Paradigmatic—Discourse 183
Western Sex and Its Ambiguities 185
The Near Eastern Plurality of Discourses 189
Sex and the Claim to Universality 199
The Cultural Hegemony of Western Discourse 201
8. The Serene Look at the World 214
The Perspectivality of Values 214
Politics with and Without Religion 216
The Ambiguity of the Stranger 236

Foreword

Forty or fifty years ago, Islam still enjoyed a fairly favorable image in the Western world, marred only marginally by the "oil shaykhs" who had provided, at least for German streets and highways, a series of pleasurably car-free Sundays. Westerners marveled at the ancient civilizations of the Islamic world and cherished the magic of Oriental fairy tales. Educated readers were familiar with Goethe's *West–Eastern Divan*, and operas occasionally staged *Der Barbier von Bagdad* by Peter Cornelius (without doubt, one of the wittiest German comic operas ever composed). However, there were only a few books in existence that offered a comprehensive account of the Islamic world and its history. Their authors were mostly professors who had devoted at least half their scholarly lives to the study of difficult Arabic, Persian, or Turkish texts, or weather-tanned travelers, diplomats, and journalists who had spent at least half their lives in Islamic countries.

Today the situation is almost entirely reversed. After the collapse of the Eastern bloc, "Islam" has successfully been established (beginning long before September 11, 2001) as a surrogate enemy. Not since the sermons of the Crusades has its image in Europe been as bad as it is today. It is true, of course, that the romantic *Arabian Nights* image also did not depict reality. But that image was closer to reality than the caricature developed in the last few decades.

The establishment of this image is accompanied by a miraculous proliferation of "experts" on Islam. The shelves of bookshops are crammed with books by authors who cannot decipher a single Arabic letter and whose contacts with the Islamic world are limited to an all-inclusive trip to Tunisia, but who feel entitled to explain to their readers "the essence of Islam." In view of this barrage of books, the effort expended for this book seems to be quite unfashionable. It was thanks to the initiative of two noble institutions that I was able to write it.

The first is the Institute for Advanced Study, Berlin, which allowed me, during the academic year 2006/2007, to spend the best year of my life, granting me the time to get acquainted with aspects of the Islamic civilizations that had heretofore remained marginal to my work. Here I met friends and colleagues who supplied me with fresh ideas and who put misrouted approaches on the right track; among these were Friedrich Wilhelm Graf, Thomas Hauschild, Almut Höfert, Christoph Möllers, Valeska von Rosen, Alain Schnapp, Suha Taji-Farouki, Muhammad S. Umar, and Andreas Voßkuhle.

The second institution is the Cluster of Excellence "Religion and Politics in the Cultures of Pre-modern and Modern Times" at the University of Münster, which—almost immediately following my year at Berlin's Institute for Advanced Study—offered me working conditions that allowed me to finish this book without much delay. I should like to name here Barbara Stollberg-Rilinger as a representative of all the colleagues whose encouragement and criticism have animated the completion of this book.

Finally, I would like to mention Hinrich Biesterfeldt, Norbert Oberauer, Thomas Birkel, and, again, Friedrich Wilhelm Graf, who have read the manuscript of my book, partly or entirely, and whose advice I have gratefully accepted (or stubbornly ignored).

At both the Institute for Advanced Study and the Cluster of Excellence, I was able to develop a theory that has its origins in a much older observation of mine. Originally, I had suspected that the contradictions that a reader of classical Islamic texts meets are not contradictions that their authors *failed to resolve.* Instead, they are contradictions that the authors *did not aspire to resolve* in the first place. Clearly, there are societies in which norms and values that are hardly compatible with each other may coexist side by side, without anyone insisting on the exclusive legitimacy of their respective norms and values, and sometimes even allowing for a peaceful coexistence of diverging norms and values in one and the same person. Members of such societies face the vague and equivocal aspects of life with equanimity, and do not so much pursue indisputable truths as remain content with seeking probable solutions. In these societies, equivocality is not only willingly accepted, but is even a welcome asset, in the sense that people derive pleasure from creating equivocality in literature and the arts.

In order to describe this phenomenon, I am making use of the concept of *tolerance of ambiguity*, a concept originally developed in psychology that has not yet found its place in cultural studies—although it must be stated that different societies and epochs are strongly characterized by the way people experience equivocality, vagueness, complexity, and plurality, and how they deal with these experiences. In certain times and places, people endeavor to obliterate as many ambiguities as possible, and to create a world of definiteness and of absolute truths. In other places and times, they are content merely to domesticate ambiguity. Even in these latter circumstances, the infinite possibilities for understanding and interpreting the world are reduced, but no attempt is made to eliminate them; rather, the goal is only to keep them limited, in order to be able to live with them. The resulting complexity is not distrusted, but gratefully accepted.

The consequences for society of these respective approaches are decisive. Religion, law and politics, literature and the arts, the ways that sex is dealt with, relations with friends, strangers, and minorities—there is scarcely an area of any society that is not significantly informed by the degree of tolerance of ambiguity practiced by its members. Therefore, it is one aim of this book to show that the experience of ambiguity, and the attitudes toward it, constitute a major field of research in cultural studies.

At the same time, this study is also, and primarily, a cultural history of Islam covering various aspects. A major focus is the contrast between the classical Islamic world, as shown by Arabic documents from Egypt to Iran between roughly 900 to 1500 CE, and the modern period, covering the last two centuries. Within this frame, I try to show how, in classical times, the areas of law and religion, language and literature, ideas about politics and sex, and contact with "the stranger" were characterized by an equanimous acceptance of complexity and ambiguity, and often by an exuberant pleasure in them. This high degree of tolerance of ambiguity vanished, however, and yielded to the *intolerance* of ambiguity that conspicuously marks the present time. Many Western observers of Islamic culture now profess to discern in this intolerance of ambiguity the true face of Islam—although all they see is their own reflection in the mirror. It will be one of the aims of this book to demonstrate that the West had a share in the development of this hostility against ambiguity. Therefore, this book also contains a piece of cultural history of the West and rectifies a number of judgments on "Islam as such" that the West has felt itself entitled to issue.

This account of cultural history builds upon certain theoretical premises; therefore, I have included a theoretical chapter after the introductory one. However, this should not deter the reader who is interested mainly in cultural history. The ensuing chapters move from the religious sphere to the secular; the connecting chapter 6 ("The Islamization of Islam") argues that Islamic cultures are not characterized by an inherently higher degree of religiosity than other cultures possess. If this study on the perception of complexity in the Islamic world contributes to a more acute understanding of the fact that Islam always signifies complexity, and that "Islam as such" does not exist, then this book has attained an important aim.

Since the first publication of the German original of this book, ten years have passed. During this period, some fields discussed in this book have been the object of intensive research, for example the fields of Islamic law and jurisprudence; other fields, such as Arabic literary history, have met with less interest. However, a consistent incorporation of the relevant publications that have appeared during this time would have resulted in further delay of the publication of this English version without leading to substantial changes in my arguments. Therefore, I have confined my revisions to correcting a few mistakes and updating some references in the notes. I also refrained from an extensive discussion of Shahab Ahmed's book *What Is Islam?*, with which this book has occasionally been compared, but I should like to refer the reader to Frank Griffel's detailed critical study of both books.[1] Griffel is also the author of an essay that, in several respects, develops arguments presented in the present book.[2] My recent essay on "Die Vereindeutigung der Welt" (Reducing the world to black and white), which has appeared in the same series as Griffel's essay, complements the ideas and arguments presented here concerning Western modernity, an aspect that this book addresses only in a rather general manner.[3]

Introduction

I am convinced that concepts such as absolute rightness, absolute accuracy, conclusive truth, etc., are phantoms which should not be admitted in any science.... This loosening of thought appears to me to be the greatest blessing which today's science has brought us. After all, the belief in one sole truth and the imagination to be its exclusive owner is the deepest root of all evil in the world.

—Max Born, *Von der Verantwortung des Naturwissenschaftlers*

Ambiguity and the history of Islamic culture: these topics have, at first sight, not much to do with each other. There seems to be no obvious reason for choosing the civilizations of Islam as a field of research in relation to the concept of ambiguity. This essay, however, will reveal in due course that it is *precisely* in the civilizations of Islam during the last few centuries that one may observe a transition from a relatively high tolerance of ambiguity and plurality to a sometimes extreme intolerance—a change which may have otherwise been hard to document so clearly, given that it has had such drastic consequences.

Moving from the past to the present, contemporary civilizations of Islam evidently witness their process of modernization as a process of annihilation of ambiguity. While scholars of the fourteenth century found the variant readings of the Quranic text enriching, the existence of these readings often constitutes a scandal for contemporary Muslims: where traditional exegetes celebrated the multiple possible interpretations of the Quran, most modern exegetes—whether Western or Eastern, fundamentalists or reformers—presume to know exactly what is the one and only meaning of a given Quranic passage. While in classical times, differences of opinion between scholars were seen, according to a well-known saying ascribed to the Prophet, as a blessing for the Muslim community, today all such differences constitute, for many, an evil to be eliminated. And while in earlier eras secular and religious political discourses happily existed side by side, today the notion is widely accepted that, when it comes to Islam, politics and religion are inextricably linked.

In contrast to the rigorous prudery that is steadily gaining ground in the Near East today, many classical scholars vied with one another in composing elegant (and sometimes somewhat frivolous) amatory verse. Arabic scholars of language and rhetoric collected polysemous words and analyzed stylistic instruments of ambiguity. Their centuries-old works are often the best theoretical expositions we have of linguistic ambiguity in eras preceding ours. Today, however, Western and Muslim scholars alike regard these works without understanding or interest; they interpret the classical cultivation of sophisticated polysemous expression as a sure sign of the decline of Islam.

It should be obvious, therefore, that the civilization of Arabic Islam is particularly suitable as the object of an essay on the relation between culture and ambiguity. It is equally evident that such an investigation will not only offer a new reading of the history of Islam, but will also tell us something about the modern Western world.

First and foremost, however, this is a book about *cultural ambiguity*. When we speak about ambiguity, we tend to think first of linguistic ambiguity—that is, expressions to which two or more different meanings can be attributed. Such ambiguities may occur by mistake (as in the newspaper headline "Alcoholics Getting Younger Every Day," or the phrase "eats shoots and leaves"), or they may be consciously formed, as in Karl Kraus's observation that the phrase "family ties" (*Familienbande*) has a tinge of truth in more than one way.[1]

Linguistic activity, however, is only *one* form of cultural activity and is by no means the only form that is subject to, or may be enriched by, ambiguity. Every mode of communicative action can be ambiguous in the same way a linguistic utterance can be, and this can happen intentionally or unintentionally. Foreign diplomacy, for example, could not exist without a cultivated ambiguity. Consider the telling moment during the visit of Pope Benedict XVI to Turkey on November 30, 2006, when he visited the Sultan Ahmet Mosque in Istanbul; there, in the midst of Muslim dignitaries, he remained in a posture that could be interpreted both as meditation and as prayer. But this does not sum up the complexity of his act, for even if one decides to resolve its principal ambiguity in favor of either prayer or meditation, we remain unsure of what it actually *means* when the Holy Father meditates, or prays, in a mosque.

Cultural ambiguity does not only appear in such scenes of public spectacle; it also permeates our everyday lives, although not always with the same degree of complexity. Our language, gestures, and signs are not unequivocal: actions must be interpreted, norms must be explained, and values that contradict each other must be reconciled or tolerated as coexisting. In short, hardly any moment of cultural acting is conceivable that does not call for some kind of disambiguation. By necessity, then, any cultural activity includes ambiguity. And since culture itself is the sum of the cultural activity of its members, it is by necessity a phenomenon involving a high degree of ambiguity. Cultural ambiguity is part of the human condition.

All cultures have to live with cultural ambiguity. Cultures differ, however, in how they deal with it. Ambiguity can be tolerated and consciously enacted through conventions of politeness and diplomacy, and through rites and works of art, thus performing important cultural functions. On the other hand, ambiguity can be avoided and opposed. In other words, cultures are different in relation to their *tolerance of ambiguity*. Cognitive psychologists have long researched the wide variation in tolerance of ambiguity among individuals. Tolerance of ambiguity, however, is an attribute not only of individuals but also of societies. Therefore, the investigation of cultural ambiguity and of differing degrees of tolerance of ambiguity among different societies is an important subject for cultural studies.

One of the aims of this book is to establish cultural ambiguity as an area of research in cultural studies. The potential usefulness of such research is exemplified here in a comparison between classical Islam, with its relatively high degree of tolerance of ambiguity, and modern Islam, with its much lower degree of tolerance. It will be shown that the way ambiguity is dealt with is one of the most important characteristics of a culture, and has a deep impact on many other aspects. Without a consideration of cultural ambiguity, many developments and dimensions of a particular culture cannot be properly understood.

Apart from having distinctly different attitudes toward ambiguity, people from different cultures have different ways of responding to it—just as they have different attitudes and responses in areas such as family, the strange versus the familiar, body and sex, illness and death. This is a universal phenomenon. Attitudes toward ambiguity manifest themselves in texts that either address the subject directly (for instance, treatises on the differences of opinions between scholars) or exhibit ambiguity themselves, consciously or unconsciously. In our study, these texts do not necessarily serve as sources for the history of ideas—that is, they are not read exclusively, and frequently not even primarily, for their ideas. Rather, they are analyzed as examples of a cultural practice, examples that will illuminate a culture's views and attitudes toward ambiguous phenomena. The role a text has played in the context of contemporary social practice; the way it presents itself to its audience; how it presents a fact or opinion; and what significance is given to which subject—we will consider all these aspects of a text to be as important as its specific contents.

The study of attitudes toward cultural ambiguity therefore constitutes a subject for historical anthropology, or, one might say, the history of mentalities. Such an approach seems to be gaining ground in Arabic and Islamic Studies;[2] it affords a way to study the history of Islam without being diverted by a Eurocentric view. Because we are focusing on human thinking, feeling, and acting, we can dispense with the writing of a coherent history—which is always in danger of evolving into a teleological view of history, that is, an attempt to answer the question of why Islamic civilizations have not followed the same course of development as Western ones. In the end, of course, this question cannot be avoided, even if this author is aware of its problematic nature, simply because Islam's image in the West has radically changed. After the collapse of the Eastern bloc, Islam was very successfully built up as a surrogate enemy. Today "Islam" is widely seen as a threat, and this feeling has almost eclipsed the former attitude of fascination.[3] This change makes it difficult to write about the Islamic world while granting to that world the right to its own history; the Western writer of this history will always be inclined to address contemporary questions directly linked to his historical object. He will consider important what is important to him and his contemporaries, and he will view Islamic history from this perspective.

In contrast, an approach guided by historical anthropology will be characterized by a consideration of what is important to the objects of research—that is, to the Muslim peoples themselves. Thus, the objects of research themselves will establish the priorities. It will be seen that when research takes seriously what the objects of research consider important, particularly meaningful answers to the questions of the current era will emerge.

Human beings and cultures differ from each other primarily in what they consider important—perhaps more in this area than in any other. Someone inquiring about phenomenon X in a given culture Y may receive an unsatisfactory answer, while at the same time culture Y offers innumerable answers to questions that are not asked. In this regard, the reader is invited to understand the subtitle of this book, "An Alternative History of Islam," in a double sense—as after all befits a book about ambiguity. The author does not actually intend to tell a different history of Islam; rather, the reader is asked to let Islam tell a different story. That story will bring into question some issues that we in our own culture are likely to take for granted. In fact, historical research that does not proceed in this way seems to me to have little value.

The question remains as to which period of Islamic history should be singled out for comparison with contemporary history. The usual Eurocentric choice would of course be the "Golden Age" of the early Abbasids, that is, the period of the caliph Hārūn ar-Rashīd, who reigned from 170–193 AH (786–809 AD), up to the reign of the caliph al-Mutawakkil (232–247/847–861). During this period, the central government was powerful; a rationalist theology had an important position; and Islam fulfilled its role—later decreed by the West as crucial for world history—of translating the heritage of the ancient Greeks and transmitting it to the Occident. Or perhaps one might choose the period of the Būyids (in Baghdad 334–447/945–1055), which has been designated by Adam Mez and Joel L. Kraemer as the "Renaissance of Islam"[4]—and quite rightly so, since the parallels in the history of mentalities between this period and the Western Renaissance period are striking. Almost certainly, the principal findings with regard to tolerance of ambiguity would have been the same whether the early Abbasids or the Būyids had been chosen as objects of investigation.

However, it is one of the aims of this book to bypass the rhetoric of the "Golden Age of Islam," which implies an ensuing period of stagnation and fall, and instead to present Islamic culture in its postformative period—in other words, the period when it was confronted with the modern era. If we look at Islamic history as a whole, the period of the Būyids and, even more so that of the early Abbasids, turn out to be formative times during which important features of (Sunni) Islam were not yet developed. Therefore, I have found it a sound decision to focus on *postformative* Islam along with contemporary Islam. This period may be divided into three major sections, conveniently named after three dynasties—even if we deal here with cultural, rather than political, phenomena. Those sections are as follows:

1. The period of the Seljuqs. In the fourth century after the Hijrah (the tenth century AD), the Islamic world appeared to turn inevitably Shiite. Particularly as a result of the westward expansion of the Turks, however, Sunni Islam began to gain new ground again. Therefore, one can speak of a *Sunni revival*, which scholars like to relate to the symbolic date 447/1055, because in this year the Sunni Seljuqid ruler Ṭughril Beg entered Baghdad and terminated the rule of the Shiite Būyids.

As always, however, the date and the appellation present only half the truth. For one thing, important steps toward the formation of a new Sunni society had already been taken in Būyid times. A scholar like al-Māwardī (364–450/974–1058), who late in his life happened to witness the entrance of the Seljuqs, must be counted as a protagonist of the *Sunni revival*, because his Quranic commentary and his handbook of public law were well-received—influential works that will also figure in this book. Secondly, the *Sunni revival* is not really a revival, insofar as the Sunni movement does not simply revivify old ideas, but in fact reinvents itself. Al-Māwardī's time is the period during which all the handbooks were written that develop older concepts into new syntheses.

It is these handbooks that shaped Sunni Islamic scholarship for centuries to come and that are often read in universities till today, in abridgments, commentaries, and adaptations. Someone interested in learning about the methodological principles of Islamic law (*uṣūl al-fiqh*) in their mature form would be well advised *not* to begin, as is often done, with the "Missive" (*ar-Risāla*) by ash-Shāfiʿī (150–204/767–820). It is true that this work is considered to be the founding charter of the discipline of Islamic jurisprudence, but in fact it is a wholly unfinished book in which almost all central issues of the *uṣūl al-fiqh* are not addressed at all.[5] One should rather study the handbook *al-Mahṣūl fī ʿilm al-uṣūl*, in which Fakhr ad-Dīn ar-Rāzī (543–606/1149–1209) achieved a synthesis of five great works of the preceding century, among them one by Abū Ḥāmid al-Ghazālī (450–606/1058–1111). This book had a direct or indirect impact on all later works that treat the methodology of jurisprudence, even up to the present day. And what holds true for this discipline is equally valid for other fields of scholarship.

2. The period of the Ayyūbids and the Mamluks. In the year 567/1171, Saladin (Ṣalāḥ ad-Dīn al-Ayyūbī) terminated the rule of the Shiite Fatimids in Egypt. Three years later, he ruled over Damascus, and in 583/1187 he liberated Jerusalem from the rule of the Crusaders. The return of Egypt to Sunnism, the termination of a long period of chaos and anarchy in Syria, and the unification of both countries under one rule, led Egypt and Syria toward an age of supreme flourishing—all this at a time when Mesopotamia was losing more and more political significance, and before the Mongol armies under Chengis Khan (in Baghdad 656/1258) and Timur (destruction of Baghdad in 803/1401) seized Baghdad. Therefore, the center of gravity in the Arab-Islamic world moved from Baghdad to Cairo and Damascus, and it was there that a long period of cultural continuity began—a period not broken by the transition from the rule of the Ayyūbids to that of the Mamluk sultans, which was based on a system of military slaves (648–922/1250–1517).

These three-and-a-half centuries form the basis of the "classical" subject matter of this book. In this period we will meet scholars who shaped its intellectual history, such as the poet and intellectual Ibn Nubātah (686–768/1287–1366); the specialist for different "readings" of the Quran, Ibn al-Jazarī (751–833/1350–1429); the greatest hadith scholar of the postformative period, Ibn Ḥajar al-ʿAsqalānī (773–852/1372–1449); and the polymath as-Suyūṭī (849–911/1445–1505).

3. The period of the Ottomans. In 922/1517, the Ottoman Sultan Selim conquered Cairo, thereby incorporating the Mamluk realm into the Ottoman Empire. The center of the Islamic world shifted toward Constantinople, a place outside of the Arab world. It was a painful turning point for Cairo and Damascus, which saw themselves demoted to provincial cities of an empire. Still, cultural and intellectual life in the Arab world continued largely unimpaired. It was only the confrontation with the West in the nineteenth century that constituted a decisive caesura in the history of the Islamic world. However, the Arabic scholarly literature of the Ottoman period has been studied only to a small extent, and the body of Arabic belles lettres of this period is virtually unknown. For the most part, Muslim authors' receptivity to the modern West has been described as an attempt of a few intellectuals to "modernize" their society. Such an approach is not really helpful for the purposes of this study; it is taken into account here only to a small degree, given the lack of advanced scholarship on this period.

This book, then, concentrates on the Arab-Islamic culture of Syria and Egypt in Ayyūbid and Mamluk times. The cultural precedents of Seljuq Baghdad and of the regions lying farther east will be given due consideration. The choice of the Ayyūbid and Mamluk dynasties as the object of study is not an artificial delimitation. This period is framed by two decisive turns of event; further, it was perceived by the people of the period as a continuum.

When, in what follows, I speak of "classical Islam," this should be understood to refer to Sunni Islam as shaped in Seljuq, Ayyūbid, and Mamluk times; I use the term "classical" because this culture remained viable in the centuries to come. I am aware that my use of the term is somewhat different from the way it is usually employed. But my purpose is to indicate that the object of this study is not all of precolonial Islam, but rather one representative culture among the ideological and regional varieties of Islam (albeit one dominant in many places for a long time). The diversity of Islam—even in the realm of the Mamluks, which also had Shiite subjects—cannot and will not be taken into consideration here. It may suffice to point out that the cultural ambiguity studied here, which will focus on the "orthodox" Islam of Sunni scholars, would be many times multiplied if all the ways of life and ways of thinking of all people in the premodern Islamic world were taken into account.

Similarly, modern Islam cannot be studied here in all its varieties. Therefore we focus, on the one hand, on the Salafist movements—often called fundamentalist—which hark back to the early times of Islam (and so have their own "Golden Age"), and, on the other hand, on the so-called reformists, who perhaps have a bigger audience in the West than in the Islamic world. The representatives of traditional Islam who are put on the defensive by these two movements are considered here only to a lesser degree (and they meet with more and more difficulties in being heard at all). Finally, Shiite Islam remains almost entirely outside the scope of this book.

In conclusion, a few technical remarks. First, about notes: the reader can rest assured that the notes given in this book indicate only sources and references, with occasional quotations of original passages of which the translations appear in the text. Thus the reader will not miss anything important if he or she prefers a relaxed reading, without the interruptions of continually tracking down references.

With regard to dates: A book that claims to entitle another culture to its own history must also give that culture the right to use its own dates. Therefore, all dates are given in a double form; the Islamic date is given first, followed by the corresponding date as measured in AD (though AH and AD are omitted from dates in parentheses). Only when whole centuries are indicated is the corresponding Islamic date omitted if there is no danger of misunderstanding.

TRANSLATORS' NOTE

If not indicated otherwise, all translations from Arabic, German, and French are our own, and have been checked with the author's version and the original. Translations from the Quran follow, with modifications, that of Arthur J. Arberry.

I
Cultural Ambiguity

The ambiguity that modern mentality finds difficult to tolerate, and modern institutions set out to annihilate (both of them drawing from this intention their awesome creative energy), reappears as the only force able to contain and defuse modernity's destructive, genocidal potential.

—Zygmunt Bauman, *Modernity and Ambivalence*

CULTURAL AMBIGUITY, THE TERM

Ambiguity has, until now, been used predominantly in the language sciences. However, when people confront the problem of multiple meanings, language is usually only one element among others. In fact, some situations containing multiple meanings make do entirely without language, as is shown by the example of Benedict XVI's "prayer" in the Blue Mosque. Therefore, it seems suitable to extend the term ambiguity to include all instances in which people produce or encounter multiple meanings, whether in the medium of language or in other communicative acts. That is why I use the term *cultural ambiguity*, which includes both language and nonlinguistic acts.

If one decides to extend the term *ambiguity* beyond linguistic actions, one is also bound to expand the term *meaning* in relation to the actions. We speak of linguistic ambiguity if one statement can be associated with two, or more, propositions. (In the popular example, "eats shoots and leaves," the words "shoots and leaves" may be understood either as nouns meaning "young plants and foliage," or as verbs meaning "fires shots and departs.") But the potential for ambiguity grows larger when we take into account nonlinguistic as well as linguistic acts at a cultural level. Ambiguity then appears whenever an action can be interpreted in different ways, according to different cultural patterns or social norms. Therefore, I define *cultural ambiguity* as follows:

We may talk of the phenomenon of cultural ambiguity if, over a period of time, two contrary, or at least competing, clearly differing meanings are associated with one and the same term, act, or object; or if a social group draws on contrary or strongly differing discourses for attributions of meaning to various realms of human life; or if one group simultaneously accepts different interpretations of a phenomenon, all of them entitled to equal validity.

It is important that the differing attributions of meaning or patterns of interpretation within a given group be observed *at the same time*. To offer an example: if the inhabitants of cultural category A in a city expect medical treatment from a magical healer, and the inhabitants of cultural category B in that city expect it from an academically trained physician, we have no phenomenon of cultural ambiguity before us, only a case of competing norms. Cultural ambiguity enters the picture only when a sufficiently large segment of the citizenry accepts both kinds of therapy as promising paths to recovery *at the same time*. Of course, the transition from side-by-side, competing norms to a generally accepted ambiguity of treatment is a fluid process. If only a few members of category B raise their voices against magic therapy, one may continue to talk of cultural ambiguity, because the rest of category B accepts both treatments at the same time. But if category B as a whole opposes magic, one can talk of cultural ambiguity only in a very restricted sense, namely in regard to that segment of the population which accepts both discourses at the same time.

We should also differentiate between a phenomenon of ambiguity that is merely transitional and one that is firmly grounded in a system of cultural attribution of meaning. Whenever a novel interpretation meets with an old one, a competitive relation between the two tends to emerge initially, and the two interpretations may show up side by side and simultaneously. For example, a photo published by J. Gerhards shows a street in a rural town near Gerolstein on May 1, 1939. In the photo, one sees a crucifix framed by two flags carrying the swastika.[1] At first sight, this looks like a case of cultural ambiguity; however, it could also be simply the overlapping of two patterns of interpretation as a consequence of competition between the two, with each aiming to crowd out the other. Such a competition may soon lead to a victorious outcome for one interpretive pattern and the disappearance of the other.

This scenario is also represented in two other photographs accompanying Gerhards's essay. Both show a classroom in a school of the Gerolstein region. The first photo, taken just at the time the Nazis seized power, shows a crucifix and a picture of the Virgin Mary on the wall. In the second photo, taken a few years later, both the crucifix and the picture of Mary are replaced by a picture of Hitler. Here, the elbowing out may have taken place without an intervening transition.[2]

In the world of traditional Islam, such competitions tended to take a different course; usually, they led sooner or later to compromises that either integrated the originally competing patterns of interpretation or left them to coexist. Basically, all of the important social systems of interpretation of the precolonial Near East are the results, wholly or partly, of this process of *making ambiguous*. Where phenomena of cultural ambiguity can be observed to last over a long period, one may always diagnose a high level of tolerance of ambiguity; social groups with a low level of ambiguity tolerance, on the other hand, tend to press for a speedy removal of competing interpretations.

Cultural ambiguity cannot be defined in the terms of *norm* and *deviation*. In the example given above, the therapeutic practice of "casting spells" constitutes, from our point of view, a deviation from the norm of academic-medical discourse. In the framework of magical discourse, however, it constitutes the norm. Cultural ambiguity is characterized precisely by the fact that mutually exclusive norms may be valid at the same time.

Tolerance of ambiguity must not be taken for *tolerance* in an ethical-social sense. Tolerance defined as "the general ability to accept any form of *being different or acting different* regarding opinions, background, sexuality, morals, religion, etc."[3] always presupposes a clear and unequivocal differentiation between one's own norms and the "other's" norms. Tolerance in this sense is one of several ways of reacting to an unequivocal situation, that is, a confrontation with interpretations, values, and norms that are different from one's own interpretations, values, and norms. One can either be open to letting the other interpretations stand side by side with one's own, or one can reject or even fight them. Psychologists have shown that a person's tendency toward one or another of these reactions depends on his or her level of ambiguity tolerance. However, we must make a clear distinction between social tolerance and tolerance of ambiguity.

Although there are obviously phenomena that may be better described by the term "cultural ambiguity" than by similar terms, the concept of ambiguity has not been widely employed in social sciences and historiography thus far; when it has been employed, moreover, it is usually not in the sense articulated above.

Therefore, it is worthwhile to take a look at those disciplines that have already produced more sustainable contributions to the study of cultural ambiguity.

AMBIGUITY IN PHILOSOPHY, LINGUISTICS, LITERARY CRITICISM, AND LITERARY HISTORY

In linguistics, ambiguity is defined as "a property of expressions in natural languages to which several interpretations can be attributed; and whose linguistic descriptors, whether lexical, semantic, or syntactic, characterize them in more than one way."[4] Thus, ambiguity is different from the complementary term "vagueness," insofar as the latter signifies pragmatic polysemy, or a quality of indeterminateness that escapes systematic description. To the examples of linguistic ambiguity given in the introduction one might add yet another aphorism by Karl Kraus, who writes that the world of the press may be characterized by the motto, "The bigger the boot, the bigger the heel."[5] This aphorism plays with the double meaning of German "Stiefel," "boot" and "idle prattle," and of "Absatz," "heel" and "sold copies" (compare the remark on *tawriyah*, "double entendre," p. 176).

Linguistic ambiguity as such is not yet an object of the study of cultural ambiguity. On the other hand, the study of cultural ambiguity inquires into how a society deals with linguistic ambiguity, that is, in terms of how it is presented and evaluated; how and when it is avoided or, conversely, sought; and whether it is a source of uneasiness or joy (and if so, when).

Since classical Arab-Islamic culture has dealt with linguistic ambiguity more than any other culture prior to or contemporary with it has done, this book will be concerned with the ways both learned and simple Arab people have dealt with linguistic ambiguity. We will trace serious scholarly endeavors to analyze ambiguity as a cause for unclear expression and faulty interpretation of texts; we will explore the manifold examples of pleasure in novel forms of linguistic ambiguity; and we will examine the vigorous wit and joy inherent in the production of sophisticated poems and prose pieces that are soaked with ambiguity. In the course of these examinations, a fundamental tendency of classical Arabic culture will become visible: its effort to domesticate, but not eliminate, ambiguity.

In this regard, the culture of Islam diverges conspicuously from mainstream Western traditions, whether of ancient classical or medieval times, which in many eras (although not all) rejected ambiguity. This phenomenon of rejection can be observed in the earliest instance of a theoretical approach to ambiguity, namely in Aristotle's employment of the word *amphibolia* as a term for (syntactical) ambiguity, which for him means a linguistic blemish.[6] Rejection of linguistic ambiguity as a violation of the principle of "clarity" of speech (*perspicuitas*) continued in the medieval Western world, only rarely complemented by more differentiated considerations.

However, that position apparently is not the original one within ancient Greek culture. Heracleitus uses ambiguity "as a means to render complexity, to join in one word several (contrary) aspects. In this way the word becomes a unity of a duality and thus corresponds to the world as a whole, which, comprising contraries, is homogenous."[7] Therefore, Aristotle's and the Stoics' negative regard for ambiguity, as simply a sign of human insufficiency, constitutes "a break with Heracleitus that is more radical than it is conceivable."[8]

Islamic culture, the Eastern heir to this ancient classical tradition, soon recognized that linguistic ambiguity not only may obstruct communication, but may also mean "compression, intensification, and abundance."[9] Medieval Europe, on the other hand, retained for the most part the negative attitude of antiquity. Wolfgang Ullrich goes so far as to say that in medieval Europe, "there was no real interest for the phenomenon of ambiguity anymore." While he potentially underestimates the complexity of medieval thought on ambiguity,[10] his assertion that "for around a thousand years, the concept of ambiguity did not yield any new aspects"[11] is also problematic in that it presupposes, as is not uncommon in the history of philosophy, a geography that limits the world at the borders of Europe. For it is exactly during these thousand years that Arab scholars of language and jurisprudence intensively reflected on homonymy and the stylistic uses of ambiguity.

In Europe, meanwhile, this era was not without progress in relation to the concept of ambiguity. Although it can be said that no paradigm-exploding insights into the problem of ambiguity were produced, almost all European countries developed new literary movements during this time that cultivated stylistic refinement and subtle play with language, and viewed ambiguous expressions and stunning *concetti* as enrichments of poetical expression and effect. This trend reached its apex in the beginning of the seventeenth century, when Luis de Góngora (1561–1627) in Spain, Giambattista Marino (1569–1625) in Italy, and John Donne (1572–1631) in England were active, and kindred literary movements arose in Germany and France. The works of these writers and their reception may be dissimilar, and the label "European baroque" may be problematic, but it cannot be denied that during this period, premodern European literature reached its peak with regard to tolerance of ambiguity, and, in its creative manipulation of the interpretive potential of language, finally attained the level which in Arabic literature had been standard for centuries.

The Age of Enlightenment soon put an end to this flourishing time. Pleasure with ambiguity is incompatible with the project of creating a radically clear language that helps to grasp and describe with ever more distinctness an allegedly unequivocal truth. Condorcet dreamed of a *langue universelle* whose precision would eliminate all errors and which "would be the means of giving to every object that comes within the reach of human intelligence, a rigor, and precision, that would facilitate the knowledge of truth, and render error almost impossible. Then would be the march of every science be as infallible as that of the mathematics, and the propositions of every system [would] acquire, as far as nature will admit, geometrical demonstration and certainty."[12]

With this new period, poetry ceased for a time to be a game played in partnership, with elegant and refined rules—a form of play with wisdom and language—and was demoted to the rank of a sober mediator of virtue and truth, tasked to express the feelings of the poet—that is, his *nature*—with as little borrowing from art as possible. Considered most praiseworthy were works that expressed "true feelings" in an "artless" manner. Since the poet was primarily supposed to express his own feelings, rather than eliciting those of his audience (as had been the goal in earlier times), poetry was confined to the small corner in which it has been kept until modern times. Thus, the nineteenth century was the absolute low point for the European tradition of rhetoric. We shall see that for the Arabic world, which adopted this Western trend in the second half of the nineteenth century, the results were devastating.[13]

But exactly when the Western theory of rhetoric had reached its nadir, there appeared philosophers, led by Friedrich Nietzsche,[14] who challenged the belief in the unequivocal nature of the world, and therefore also shook faith in the possibility of unequivocal language. In modern times, it has become a commonplace that equivocality is a necessary and ineradicable property of language and of the world. As soon as this fact is accepted, its positive aspects become visible, and we are able to see all that is possible only through ambiguity. Thus Merleau-Ponty can state that "Ambiguity is part of the essence of human existence, and everything that we live or think always has several meanings."[15]

The theologian John D. Caputo, in his "In Praise of Ambiguity," expresses himself with even more enthusiasm: "Whatever is important, valuable, significant is ambiguous—love and death, God and suffering, right and wrong, the past and the future. Just so, if something is unambiguously clear, transparently simple, is that not because its substance is spent, its future is over?"[16] Caputo is right in stressing the need to differentiate ambiguity from obscurity; as we shall see in our examples from Arabic literature, ambiguity is accompanied by precision and a strict method. Rather, ambiguity is "an excess of meaning, a multiplication of too many meanings, so that we find ourselves drawn in several directions at once."[17] Ambiguity undermines the certainty of an unequivocal attribution of meaning precisely by opening the way to a more adequate understanding of the complexity of the world. "Ambiguity is for me the condition that makes meaning possible by making pure and unambiguous meaning impossible."[18]

Even before the concept of ambiguity was revived in philosophy, it had taken its place in literary criticism. In 1930, the English poet and literary critic William Empson formulated the idea that a language cannot exist without ambiguity, saying: "In a sufficiently extended sense any prose statement could be called ambiguous."[19] Empson's extraordinary and inspired book, *Seven Types of Ambiguity*, paved the way for the concept of ambiguity to be accepted in literary criticism.

Empson's concept of ambiguity is very wide, comprising "any verbal nuance, however slight, which gives room for alternative reactions to the same piece of language."[20] For Empson, the complexity that results from ambiguity becomes no less than the criterion of literary quality. This position has been taken up and developed in many subsequent works on literary criticism,[21] and has also influenced the theory of fine arts.[22] Numerous literary works and other works of art have been studied from the viewpoint of ambiguity, and this viewpoint has shown validity even when the creator of a work of art has not aimed for ambiguity at all.[23]

For the purposes of this book, it will be less relevant to analyze the extent of ambiguity in selected works than to understand the treatment—almost always conscious in our case—of ambiguity in literary and other works of art, and therefore the position of ambiguity in the collective consciousness of the culture under review.

What I have said about the new approach of philosophers and literary critics should not give the impression that we live in a time of enhanced euphoria about ambiguity. Caputo, too, knows that he contradicts an established public opinion, and that he risks "the police of philosophy arriv[ing] to cart me off for my civil disobedience."[24] All the hype about ambiguity among artists, philosophers, and literary critics cannot conceal the fact that modernity, which has been characterized by a process of rationalization, is essentially against ambiguity. The steady rise of both bureaucracy and technology demands unified standards; any instance of ambiguity is viewed as a disturbance. Our awareness that ambiguity is inevitable is challenged by the continuing endeavors of computational linguistics to refine its strategy of eliminating ambiguity as much as possible.

The world of classical Islam accepted ambiguity as an inevitable part of human existence, something that has both good and bad aspects, and therefore can and must be observed and domesticated, but cannot and must not be eliminated. In contrast, the modern Western world exhibits a small ambiguity-friendly intellectual discourse, but a powerful mainstream culture that is hostile to ambiguity. This aspect of modernization has brought considerable devastation to the Islamic world.

TOLERANCE OF AMBIGUITY IN PSYCHOLOGY

In the 1940s, the German-American psychologist Else Frenkel-Brunswik observed that people who are not willing to admit emotional ambivalence also display, on the cognitive level, a high degree of intolerance of ambiguity. She concluded that this constitutes two varieties of personality, which she called "tolerance and intolerance of ambiguity"; she assumed that these represent "one of the basic variables in both the emotional and the cognitive orientation of a person toward life."[25] A personality intolerant of ambiguity has "a tendency to resort to black-white solutions, to arrive at premature closure as to valuative aspects, often at the neglect of reality, and to seek for unqualified and unambiguous over-all acceptance and rejection of other people."[26] In her fundamental article in 1949, Frenkel-Brunswik demonstrated a connection between racism and intolerance of ambiguity.[27] A year later, she contributed her findings to the (highly controversial) study on the "Authoritarian Personality," edited by Theodor W. Adorno and others.[28]

More recent studies of the connection between tolerance, or intolerance, of ambiguity, and other constituents of personality, show a significant positive correlation between intolerance of ambiguity on the one hand, and ethnocentrism, dogmatism, rigidity, and authoritarianism on the other.[29] For example, it can be stated that "dogmatism about one's religious beliefs (whatever they may be) should show a positive relationship with intolerance of ambiguity,"[30] and that people intolerant of ambiguity are inclined to endorse measures of censure.[31]

Frenkel-Brunswik's description of the personality intolerant of ambiguity has been replaced by more exact definitions, and questionnaires have been devised with the aim of a quantitative analysis of tolerance, or intolerance, of ambiguity. R. W. Norton, for one, defines intolerance of ambiguity as "a tendency to perceive or interpret information marked by vague, incomplete, fragmented, multiple, probable, unstructured, uncertain, inconsistent, contrary, contradictory, or unclear meanings as actual or potential sources of psychological discomfort or threat."[32] Extending this one-dimensional definition toward a two-dimensional theory, S. Budner and A. P. MacDonald assume that people with a high tolerance for ambiguity do not simply avoid unequivocal situations; they even seek equivocal ones: they "(a) seek out ambiguity, (b) enjoy ambiguity, and (c) excel in the performance of ambiguous tasks."[33]

In accordance with the two-dimensionality of his concept, Budner's definition also has two parts: "Intolerance of ambiguity may be defined as 'the tendency to perceive (i.e., interpret) ambiguous situations as sources of threat,' and tolerance of ambiguity as 'the tendency to perceive ambiguous situations as desirable.'"[34] His definition of an "ambiguous situation" shows how cultural ambiguity and the psychological concept of tolerance of ambiguity can be connected. Budner writes, "An ambiguous situation may be defined as one which cannot be adequately structured or categorized by the individual because of the lack of sufficient cues. It is possible to identify three such situations: a completely new situation in which there are no familiar cues, a complex situation in which there are a great number of cues to be taken into account, and a contradictory situation in which different elements or cues suggest different structures—in short, situations characterized by novelty, complexity, or insolubility."[35] If one compares the ambiguous situations described by Budner with the definition of cultural ambiguity given above, it becomes obvious that the second and third situations are exactly those in which people in societies with a high degree of tolerance of ambiguity will find themselves again and again. It may thus be assumed that, in a society which over a long period tolerated and even sought and enjoyed a high degree of cultural ambiguity, a significant number of people were psychologically tolerant of ambiguity.

It is not the aim of this book to make a contribution to "historical psychology"; considering the differences between the methods and objects of research of psychology, on the one hand, and the social sciences and history, on the other, one should beware of too hastily arriving at parallels. I think, however, that the hypotheses and findings of the study of ambiguity tolerance developed by the field of psychology can render an important contribution to the understanding of tolerance and intolerance with regard to cultural ambiguity in history. Therefore, we shall repeatedly refer to the contributions of psychology in this area.

AMBIGUITY IN THE HISTORICAL AND SOCIAL SCIENCES

The most important contribution of the social sciences to the problem of ambiguity was made by the sociologist Zygmunt Bauman, who shaped the term *ambivalence* as central to his sociological theory without, however, distinguishing it from the term *ambiguity*. When Bauman defines "ambivalence" as "the possibility of assigning an object or an event to more than one category,"[36] he comes very close to our concept of ambiguity. Here, however, the term ambivalence will not be employed in Bauman's sense (in our use of the term ambiguity), but as a psychological term that denotes the simultaneous existence of conflicting feelings, wishes, and thoughts. Ambivalence is a state of mind between hatred and love, proximity and distance, wanting and not wanting; it is a mental state of which one is often unaware, and which is far more difficult to interpret and solve than ambiguity. Such discomfort—something like feeling "not all right in oneself"—may in turn mean that ambiguous phenomena trigger discomfort. Thus ambivalence may be a cause of intolerance of ambiguity. This alone makes it imperative to distinguish between the two terms. Even if we do not follow Bauman's terminology, his work has supplied us with important insights into the phenomenon of ambiguity. These insights will be taken up in our chapter on alienation.

There are two other contributions of history and the social sciences, both quite different from that of Bauman, that should be mentioned here. One comes from Ross Brann, who has supplied his book on the Jewish poets of al-Andalus (the so-called Islamic Spain) with the subtitle "Cultural Ambiguity and Hebrew Poetry in Muslim Spain." Brann does not explicitly define the term *cultural ambiguity*, but he evidently understands the term as meaning the simultaneous coexistence of different ethnic and religious groups, the equivocal attributions of meaning given by members of these groups, and the life of one or more individuals in more than one group at the same time.[37]

This understanding of the term "ambiguity," it is true, includes only part of its meaning as it is used in this book; nonetheless, the phenomena described by Brann are of course highly relevant for our subject. I find particularly important the statement that the "ambiguity of values" that Brann identifies for the Jews who were attached to the courts in al-Andalus does not only result from the situation of the Jews within Arab-Islamic culture, nor only from Jewish religiosity.[38] Rather, Arab-Islamic culture itself was already shaped by such an "ambiguity of values," and this could be reemployed by the Jews, with little effort, for their own particular situation.

The role which linguistic ambiguity plays in culture is the central topic of Donald N. Levine's book *The Flight from Ambiguity.* Levine, a sociologist, worked for three years in the late 1950s with the Amharic people of Ethiopia, and developed a sense of the different ways in which cultures handle this ominous phenomenon of ambiguity. The misgivings that Western societies characteristically demonstrate when they meet with linguistic ambiguity (Levine quotes from Condorcet and Locke as chief witnesses) are, as he justly writes, part of Western "exceptionalism," the Western Sonderweg. "The movement against ambiguity led by Western intellectuals since the seventeenth century figures as a unique development in world history. There is nothing like it in any premodern culture known to me."[39] The remarkably different role of ambiguity in these cultures leads Levine to the question of what the function of ambiguity in a given culture is: "The fact that ambiguity was cultivated in so many forms in so many traditional cultures suggests that ambiguous expressions serve a number of social and cultural purposes. These purposes should be examined before one endorses without reservation the modern project of eradicating ambiguity."[40] Levine can refer here to his experience with the Amharic people, who prize linguistic ambiguity highly and who cultivate a poetic form they call "wax and gold," a figure of speech that has some similarity with the Arabic *tawriyah*, or "double entendre," and that may be considered nothing less than a way of life.[41] Levine contrasts this with conditions in the United States where, for all intents and purposes, an unequivocal and direct way of expression is demanded, and where poetry, "the last refuge of ambiguity," has only a low position.[42]

Levine differentiates between four cultural (1 and 2) and social (3 and 4) functions of linguistic ambiguity: (1) For one thing, it helps people to grasp complex phenomena more effectively than would an attempt to reduce them to clear and unequivocal terms. Levine speaks here of the "illuminative function" of ambiguity.[43] Closely connected with this is (2) the "expressive function" of ambiguity, which Levine describes as "expressivity through evocative allusions."[44] This function has been well described in the field of comparative literature.

In the social field, Levine assigns to ambiguity a (3) "protective function," according to which equivocal ways of expression can serve as a kind of self-protection.[45] While Levine stresses the potential of equivocal expression for cultivating a secret, for me the phenomenon of politeness seems to be of more importance.

Finally, Levine distinguishes (4) a "function of social bonding," saying that equivocal expression may help to create a feeling of social solidarity through the use of not too unequivocal symbols and modes of representation (which would lead to divisions in society) and through the ability to circumvent confrontations by avoiding starkly unequivocal positions.[46] Ambiguity not only facilitates adaptation to changed social conditions, but through its fourth function also remains an important element of modern politics.[47] In particular, the first part of Levine's inspiring book offers an important element of the theory of cultural ambiguity.

FORMS OF CULTURAL AMBIGUITY IN ISLAM

Research in cultural ambiguity inquires into the collective conscience of a social group that exhibits cultural ambiguity. It also inquires into the emotions triggered by phenomena of cultural ambiguity. Third, it studies the manifestations of cultural ambiguity themselves, which constitute the most essential material to be analyzed. This research then belongs to cultural history qua (historical) cultural sociology, to the history of mentalities, and to historical anthropology. Attempting a more precise internal differentiation between these disciplines may be helpful with regard to reflecting on the disciplines themselves, but it is not important for our purposes and will therefore not be pursued here.[48] Instead, we shall indicate a number of areas of Islamic culture in which phenomena of cultural ambiguity manifest themselves. Some of these will be presented in detail in later chapters.

Acceptance of a Plurality of Discourses

Cultural ambiguity occurs when different discourses exist side by side in a social group, and when these discourses simultaneously exert the power to set up norms which often are not mutually compatible and may even directly collide. What matters most is that this juxtaposition is accepted by many members of the social group, although there may be (and perhaps must be, in order to ensure the continuity of the distinct discourses) a few who reject the juxtaposition and would prefer the exclusive dominance of one of the discourses.

If such a group does not prevail in terminating the ambiguity, the juxtaposition of discourse may assume different forms. In an extreme case, the individual is free to choose which discourse he or she accepts as the norm for a given action.

In most cases, however, we may assume that informal mechanisms make certain decisions in certain situations more probable than others.

All important areas of classical Islam are basically the result of a compromise between discourses which were originally in mutually hostile opposition to each other. In an admittedly simplified way, one might say that Islam in its classical form has developed through a regular sequence of integrations of discourses, beginning with the accomplishment of ash-Shāfiʿī (150–204/767–820), whose aim it was to implement rational procedures in a jurisprudence which thus far had been oriented toward the tradition of the Prophet Muḥammad. Al-Ashʿarī (260–324/873–936) took a further decisive step in integrating rational methods of Greek philosophy with Islamic theology, without relinquishing the fundamental positions of the traditionists. Finally, al-Ghazālī (450–505/1058–1111) succeeded in incorporating the challenge (at times threatening) of Sufism into Islamic religion.

In all these cases, the compromise solutions have not resulted in the original positions being forgotten. Each solution merely constitutes the center of orientation around which a broad spectrum of positions continues to be constructed, which do not deny each other's right to exist; they compete with, and at the same time coexist with, each other.

Islamic law presents a particularly complex example of cultural ambiguity. Standing as it does between a transtemporal norm and the incalculable diversity of everyday life, law seems to be a field that contains a particularly rich potential for ambiguity. The inquiry into the relation between customary law and Islamic law, or the question of what role Islamic normativity plays in legal opinions, offers a wide field for research in ambiguity. A glance at a comprehensive collection of fatwas, such as the North African al-Wansharīsī's *al-Miʿyār al-muʿrib*, shows that entire areas of law exist largely without reference to normative Islamic texts. As such, they do not contradict any principles of Islamic law, because the principle of the common good, expressed by various terms (*istiḥsān*, *maṣāliḥ mursalah*), has itself become an element of legal theory.

Politics is another area which, in a sense, is equally a part of Islamic law. Whereas today it has become commonplace to say that in Islam one cannot divide state from religion, one finds in classical times not more than a handful of manuals and a number of brief chapters in legal compendia that treat the subjects of government and state from a religious perspective. On the other hand, there exists a vast number of poems praising the ruler. These poems certainly represent the discourse of government best known to the public; after all, they serve as a representation of the ruler. However, religion itself plays an entirely subordinate role in these poems.

A third and final discourse of government, extant in numerous works of advice to the ruler (*Fürstenspiegel*, mirror for princes), comprises a spectrum of texts that range from religiously oriented "admonishing" writings to works that display a completely nonreligious, utilitarian, not to say Machiavellian, attitude. Apparently there existed no mediating forum between these two discourses. The societal field of government may thus offer an example of an extreme case in which it was entirely up to an individual—in this case the ruler—to choose from divergent discourses.

A further example is the area of sex, where the commonly accepted social norm stands in strong contrast to the religious norm, a fact which may be more responsible than any other for the fractured relationship that many Muslims today have with their own history. And a last and culturally quite central area is society's image of the Muslim scholar. From the so-called Sunni revival in the eleventh century far into the Ottoman era, the ideal of the pious, devout scholar stood side by side with the ideal of the elegant, witty intellectual. It is small wonder that a large part of the secular literature produced in abundance by these scholars meets with total incomprehension on the part of their modern heirs.[49]

There is no doubt that Islamic theology itself constitutes an important object of our investigation. For the student of ambiguity, the normative texts themselves are of less interest than the question of which rivaling theological positions could exist side by side in which social, historical, and geographical frameworks. Since no relevant studies exist, and since this author's command of Islamic theology is limited, this formulation of suggested scholarly inquiry may suffice.

Acceptance of Divergent Interpretations

When as-Suyūṭī (849–911/1445–1505), a thoroughly arrogant and dogmatic master scholar, wrote a treatise on the Prophet Muḥammad's saying, "Difference of opinion is mercy for my community," he did not do it to show off his tolerance and openness for dialogue, but because this saying enabled him to capture one of the most important characteristics of classical Islam. Far from being dogmatically constricted, Muslim scholars developed a method of Quranic exegesis which endeavored to encompass the whole range of interpretations for each passage, instead of sticking with one exclusively valid interpretation. They developed a kind of "theory of probability" which allowed them to classify hadiths according to an elaborate and flexible framework of greater or lesser "authenticity," instead of subjecting them to the binary categorization of "right" or "wrong," as is the ideal of modern hadith scholarship. In Islamic law, whose most important fundamentals are the Quran and the hadith, we see a multiplication of the factors of unpredictability inherent in the interpretations of the two sources. In view of these principles, the difference of opinion does not appear as an evil that must be avoided, but as a constitutive element of the system.

Long before the discovery of ambiguity in modern times, Islam followed the idea that ambiguity is something unavoidable, with the idea that it opens new horizons. However, scholars of the theory of law were left with the task of curbing the excessive overgrowth of ambiguity and transferring it into a system that could be easily handled—a system that, for many centuries, guaranteed legal reliability to a large part of the Islamic world. In the end, this system, which was based on patiently negotiating between conflicts born of ambiguity, could not keep up with the tempo of the onslaught of the modern West, and either vanished or was replaced by a new dogmatic-ideological construction that, with its hostility toward ambiguity, could be made to fit with the modern West.

The consciousness of ambiguity in Islamic law has its parallels in many other areas of life in the precolonial Near East. There were authors who considered the idea of whether it is better to be poor or rich. Even if illness is something bad, does it not also have its good sides? Cannot stinginess sometimes be a virtue? Such questions were treated in works written since the third/ninth century on the "good and bad sides" of all conceivable objects; these works continued to be discussed in poetic debates and epigrammatic apologia well into the nineteenth century. All these texts nourished a consciousness of ambiguity which we may assume has permeated large sectors of the population for more than a thousand years.

Ambiguous Texts, Actions, and Places

Ambiguous texts, actions, and places originate when there is the potential to furnish them with divergent meanings. The ambiguous *text* par excellence is the Quran. While the Bible has been supplied with an apparatus of variant readings only by modern philologists, the Quran, according to the perspective of classical Islam, has been revealed together with its variant readings. These are not accidents of textual transmission, but genuine components of the text itself.

The same is true with regard to its incomprehensibility. While modern philology cannot but assume that between two different interpretations of a passage, at least one must be wrong, the Muslim exegete bases his work on the conviction that the incomprehensibility of some passages is an inevitable (because decreed by God) quality of the text—and this does not prevent him from pursuing his sober, scholarly job. Incomprehensibility is seen as a divine ruse that keeps inciting human interpreters to an ever-new occupation with the text, and gives them the opportunity to prove their knowledge and acumen. The traditional skepticism of Muslims about translations of the Quran is not to be explained by dogmatic narrow-mindedness; it is due to fear of the *loss of ambiguity* that every translation necessarily entails. Translations, therefore, can be regarded as valid only in the sense of an interpretation, not as texts equivalent with the original.

Ambiguity was realized and accepted not only in the fundamental religious texts, Quran and hadith, but also in secular fundamental texts of Arab-Islamic culture, that is, pre- and early Islamic poetry. In a culture with such a heritage of ambiguity, the potential offered by texts permeated by ambiguity must by necessity be realized and exploited. This in turn enables the production of ambiguous texts in their own right.

Later in this book, we will explore the vast abundance of texts which explode with ambiguity. Here we mention only the mystical texts and the poems praising the Prophet Muḥammad, which usually are not mystical, because, in addition to the ambiguous features furnished by the author himself, they function simultaneously in two discourses, the literary-aesthetic, and the religious. The recitation of a poem in praise of the Prophet is first of all an artistic act, namely the delivery of a text composed according to the rules of an Arabic literary discourse. At the same time, it is also a religious act, a prayer whose addressee is the Prophet himself. We know, for instance, that the writer an-Nawājī (788–859/1386–1455) gave his poems in praise of the Prophet to some friends who were going on the pilgrimage to Mecca, asking them to recite them "in the face of the Prophet" when they visited the shrine of the Prophet in Medina. When he himself performed the pilgrimage, an-Nawājī repeated this act in person. He also collected his poems in praise of the Prophet in a special volume, as well as in a divan.

In this divan, his poems in praise of the Prophet stand side by side with secular praise poems, wine poems, and erotic epigrams. Such proximity suggests that one may read the poems in praise of the Prophet not primarily as religious offerings but as aesthetic texts.[50]

Poems in praise of the Prophet thus display all the characteristics of aesthetic texts, and have these in common with secular texts. A secular praise poem usually begins with a *nasīb*, that is, a passage whose object is secular love. This feature was transferred to the poems in praise of the Prophet, and thus appeared a possible conflict with the idea of the praise of the Prophet as a religious act. Already an-Nawājī warned against introductions to poems in praise of the Prophet, asserting that they are too charged with eroticism,[51] and an-Nabhānī, a late Ottoman compiler of a four-volume collection of poems in praise of the Prophet, considered such introductions, with their use of amatory imagery, as actually improper. But he confessed that had he left out the poems with erotic introductions, he would have missed the best works. Thus we find in his collection a literary-aesthetic and a religious discourse in an almost completely uncomplicated side-by-side relationship, which for over a thousand years was characteristic of the whole Islamic world.

As for ambiguous *places*, a great number of examples are contained in the material collected by F. W. Hasluck between 1899 and 1916 in Greece and Turkey. One and the same place may be sacred for members of different religious communities, and every community may charge it with a different significance. Hasluck's study is also relevant because it shows that a culture of ambiguity existed also beneath the literate strata from which came all of the older material.[52]

Sacred places in Egypt were studied by Georg Stauth, who was able to demonstrate that a "dialogic encounter of Islam with the Pharaonic Egypt" occurred over and over in Egyptian history. The use of elements of Pharaonic architecture in mosques is not at all due to a search for cheap building materials; it was in fact "without necessity, rather arising from pride in the exotic beauty, seen as a wondrous enrichment from the times before Islam."[53] The Pharaonic relics integrated into Islamic sanctuaries "symbolize both the victory over old gloomy powers and the pride in a great past."[54] The resulting ambiguity represents, however, a scandal to fundamentalist circles.

Reflection Upon and Training in Ambiguity

Only a few years after Sībawayh (ca. 140–180/757–796) had composed the first "proper" Arabic book, in the sense of a work that was structured from beginning to end and considered to be conclusive (a work on grammar, of course), there appeared the first Arabic treatises on lexicography, which are still extant today. Among them are several collections of "words with contrary meanings," that is, words which simultaneously denote an object and its contrary. During the following centuries, more compilations of strange words appeared; such compilations were ever more voluminous and learned. It is a baffling fact about the Arabs that when they first began to approach scholarly matters, they had nothing more urgent to do than to reflect, of all problems, on that of ambiguity.

And this continued to be the case. In the third/ninth century, Muʿtazilite theologians discussed the problem of metaphors in the Quran. In 274/887, the Abbasid prince and poet Ibn al-Muʿtazz composed the epoch-making work on stylistics, *Kitāb al-Badīʿ*, in which he demonstrated that the style of the "New Poets," characterized by its wealth of metaphors, had its precursors in the Quran and in pre-Islamic poetry.

Almost at the same time, the chancellery member Qudāmah ibn Jaʿfar (died 337/958) wrote his work *Naqd ash-shiʿr* in order to show that poetics and stylistics can be considered on a scientific basis, just as grammar can. In the fourth/tenth century, the theologian and grammarian ar-Rummānī (296–384/909–994) confirmed the thesis that the Quran is inimitable by means of a stylistic analysis in which he demonstrated that metaphors serve not to obscure but to clarify statements.[55] In the 5th/11th century, ʿAbd al-Qāhir al-Jurjānī (died ca. 471/1078) composed one of the most intellectually rich books ever written on similes and metaphors.[56]

In the sixth/twelfth century, scholars working in Central Asia and writing in Arabic developed a theory of Arabic rhetoric, which was then standardized in as-Sakkākī's (555–626/1160–1229) *Miftāḥ al-ʿulūm* (Key to the sciences). This theory of rhetoric remains to the present day, and is, throughout the world, the one best elaborated and most firmly grounded in linguistics. Hundreds of adaptations of and commentaries upon this work found their way into the most remote villages of the Islamic world. Never before, and never since, has any population had at its disposal such an advanced rhetorical culture (and together with that, such a high consciousness of ambiguity) as did the people of the Islamic world between the seventh and nineteenth century of our era.[57] Western scholars, and also intellectuals of the Islamic world who were oriented toward the West, considered this to be a straying from the right path. Thus, the Scottish orientalist E. J. W. Gibb (1857–1901) fervently welcomed modern Turkey's banishing of the traditional theory of rhetoric and replacing it with the European linguistic disciplines (which were in fact deficient in comparison with the traditional theory).[58]

In the seventh/thirteenth century, the Egyptian author Ibn Abī l-Iṣbaʿ (died 654/1256) produced a handbook on Arabic stylistics, based on forty earlier works, that treated 125 different figures of style. A large number of these concerned instances of ambiguity. In the eighth/fourteenth century, the greatest master of the double entendre was the poet and member of the chancellery, Ibn Nubātah (686–768/1287–1366), who was active in Damascus. He was not interested in theory, but his student, friend (and, for a time, rival), aṣ-Ṣafadī (died 764/1363) took over this task and composed the first monograph in the world on double entendres.[59] In the ninth/fifteenth century, the aforementioned scholar as-Suyūṭī (who actually was not blessed with an acute sense of humor) composed a series of *maqāmah*s (witty narrative prose texts, often adorned with rhymes and pieces of poetry), in which scholars of various disciplines reported the erotic experiences of their wedding night, using the terms characteristic of their profession as double entendres.[60] In the tenth/sixteenth century, the Janissary Māmay ar-Rūmī, who had deserted the military in favor of poetry, advanced the art of the chronogram to its first apex. (A chronogram can be read as a normal text and, at the same time, if one adds together the numeric value of the letters used, as a date.) In the eleventh/seventeenth century, the Ottoman scholar Ḥusāmzādeh ar-Rūmī (1003–1081/1594–1670) wrote a treatise in which he demonstrated how every verse composed by the poet al-Mutanabbī in praise of the Egyptian ruler Kāfūr could also be read as defamation.[61] In the twelfth/eighteenth century, Christian-Arab writers participated for the first time in the literary art of the *badīʿiyyah*, which is not only a religious poem (for Muslims, a poem in praise of the Prophet), with all its accompanying ambiguity, but also an exemplification of the stylistic devices of rhetoric, including the practice of incorporating the terms of the specific stylistic means in the text itself. Roughly one hundred *badīʿiyyāt* were written between the fourteenth and twentieth centuries, constituting a surge in ambiguity in which a whole handful of social discourses intersected, and which are anathema to the Arabic intellectuals of the twentieth century and of today.

In the thirteenth/nineteenth century, the traditional culture of ambiguity reached a final climax with the Christian author Nāṣīf al-Yāzijī (1214–1287/1800–1871). The shaykh Nāṣīf composed one of the most amazing *badīʿiyyāt*, one conceived as transconfessional (and thus also religiously ambiguous). He wrote more artistically sophisticated chronograms than those of any other writer, and he authored easy-to-understand school textbooks on the standard theory of Arabic rhetoric.[62]

To summarize: throughout many centuries, hundreds of works on rhetoric were written, and thousands of poems and prose texts were composed by poets, scholars, merchants, craftsmen, and popular rhymesters, in which all conceivable sorts of ambiguity could be playfully bandied about. This continuous literary "ambiguity training" may have been a prerequisite for the acceptance of ambiguity in other areas of life.

Toward the end of the nineteenth century, all of this ended. The standard theory of Arabic rhetoric vanished from school curricula. Poetry was no longer allowed to be playful and permeated by ambiguity, but was supposed to express "true feelings in an unaffected manner." Arabs began to be ashamed of their own traditions. Even today, Arab intellectuals would like to erase from history a whole millennium (if not more than that) of Arabic literature.[63]

In the course of the twentieth century, a process began to occur which has often been falsely labeled "re-Islamization," but which is in truth a reinvention of Islam as an ideology, using the structures of Western ideologies, and which, after the decline of their civilizations, is understood by the Islamic world as the *only* alternative they can call their own. Like all ideologies, "Islamism" is intolerant, hostile to ambiguity, and totalitarian. Its proponents know the precise meaning of every Quranic passage; they know exactly which hadiths are valid and which ones are not. And they always arrive at the only, exclusively correct interpretation: divergent interpretations cannot but be mistakes.

The representatives of this ideology are also convinced that all spheres of human life must be subjected, totally and exclusively, to the rules of Islam—that is, the ideological system they consider to be Islam. Since the jurists of traditional Islam, like all jurists, have felt called upon to vent their opinions on everything and anything, the impression has arisen that this claim to all-comprehensiveness is an essential feature of Islam. It is not. This false impression leads so-called experts on Islam to look toward historical sources to find out what opportunities Islam as such has missed in its history, instead of realizing that what they perceive to be radical Islamism is actually a caricature of the West's own ideologization and disambiguation of the world.

There is a tragic aspect to this, in that the Western image of Islam, which locates the causes for all that is bad about Islam in its history, largely tallies with the fundamentalists' hatred of their own history, which they see as a continuous process of decline and decadence. They cite the phenomena of ambiguity described above precisely as proof of this view.

Among all the seemingly disparate modern-day developments mentioned here—the hostility toward rhetoric, the rejection of the indigenous literary tradition, the new sexual repression, a fundamentalist ideology that extends to visions of a totally Islamic state—there is apparently one common denominator: an instinctive, radical, and uncompromising hatred of ambiguity. This hatred which, in view of premodern Islam's fascination with ambiguity must by necessity end in self-hatred, is apparently one of the most relevant sources of what the Lebanese intellectual Samir Kassir, assassinated in 2005, has called "le malheur arabe."[64] Kassir was one of the few Arab intellectuals who doubted the validity of the concept of decline and decadence of the Islamic world over a period of a thousand years.

This concept, in fact, originates in the Western world. It has been taken entirely from the Orientalist discourse of the nineteenth century.[65] Further, intolerance of ambiguity in modern Islam is a phenomenon of modernity. If I may formulate my thesis in a very preliminary manner, this intolerance is the result of the displacement of a wholly ambivalent perception both of their own civilization, which during the era of European expansion proved to be militarily and commercially inferior, and also of the West, which is perceived at the same time as a destroyer and a harbinger of the future.

According to one of the theses of psychological research, such an ambivalent emotional worldview results in a strong intolerance of ambiguity. And this is intensified by the model of the West, whose history has been shaped by such intolerance over a long period, intensifying rather than diminishing since the Age of Enlightenment.

No matter how these ideas are judged, it seems to me that the subject of cultural ambiguity offers a potential for explanations of cultural, social, and political phenomena—a potential that thus far has not been fully realized.

2

Does God Speak in Textual Variants?

Whatever is important, valuable, significant is ambiguous—love and death, God and suffering, right and wrong, the past and the future.

—John D. Caputo, "In Praise of Ambiguity"

CRISES AND DOMESTICATION OF AMBIGUITY

Texts are polysemous, be it intentionally or unintentionally. Not even directions for the use of an appliance are safe from ambiguity. And even if their authors consciously attempt to avoid it (as we assume they want to do), it may happen that a working instruction does not clearly indicate into which socket a given plug goes. But technical appliances are not tolerant of ambiguity. They are not open to divergent interpretations of their working instructions, but work only if the plug occupies the *right* socket, whatever the wording of the instructions is.

A simple example should suffice to show possible outcomes. Let's imagine an appliance with a red socket and a green socket on the back. In order to operate the appliance, you have to stick the plug into the red socket. In the instructions we read: (1) "To connect the appliance, stick the plug into the red socket." This direction contains no ambiguity at all. Everyone who understands the words and can attach them to their corresponding objects will be able to interpret and apply it correctly.

Another version of the instructions, however, might read: (2) "To connect the appliance, stick the plug into the colored socket." Since there are two colored sockets, a red one and a green one, the direction is ambiguous. The user has no other possibility than to disambiguate it by checking the agreement of both interpretations with reality—that is, either studying the circuit layout of the appliance, or simply trying both sockets. Then it will turn out that the interpretation "green socket" is wrong, and the interpretation "red socket" is right. The result of the disambiguation of an equivocal passage in the instructions is always either wrong or right, and there remains only *one* right interpretation, while several wrong ones may exist. Finally, in a third version of instructions, we might read: (3) "To connect the appliance, stick the plug into the green socket." This is, again, a statement containing no ambiguity, but it does not agree with reality. If a reader follows this instruction, nothing happens (at best).

If we understand "true" in the sense of "agreeing with reality," then statement (1) is true and statement (3) is false. But what about statement (2)? It is certainly not false, since one is instructed to stick the plug in *a* colored socket. If we assume a simple opposition of "true" and "false," a statement that is not false should be necessarily true. But things are not that simple. Statement (2) contains, along with the right meaning, also the wrong one; it may, in fact, without being misunderstood, signify something false. If one is intent upon a sphere of truth that is distinctly separated from falsehood and contains nothing but what is true, then everything equivocal, everything that is perhaps (or only in one aspect) true, will be relegated to the sphere of the false.

Thus, *unambiguity* becomes the *criterion for truth*. This concept is central to the philosophy of Enlightenment. René Descartes makes it a fundamental maxim: "Consequently I may stipulate as a general rule that everything which is true is that which I perceive as quite clear and distinct."[1] For Descartes, only that is true which can be perceived *clare et distincte*, and only that clear perception can be considered as distinct which "is separate and different from all other perceptions to such a degree that it does not contain anything else than what is clear."[2] Everything that is not "clear and distinct" does not allow for a judgement.[3]

Descartes may not explicitly refer to the interpretation of polysemous texts, but it is not difficult to calculate the consequences of the triumph of Cartesian thinking for the status of normative texts with a claim to truth. Religious texts—those with which we are here primarily concerned—are much closer to literary texts than to factual texts. Now, literary texts display a much higher density of ambiguity than do texts containing technical instructions. More importantly, their ambiguity is *intended*, since *polyvalence* is indeed a criterion that distinguishes literary from factual texts.[4] We may put aside for the moment the question of whether the polyvalence of religious texts is a matter of intention—most classical scholars are of the opinion that this polyvalence definitely applies to the Quran.

A later chapter will deal with the kinds of strategies that were developed to solve this conflict on a level of interpretation. At this point I would like to present a much more fundamental problem, and that is the unequivocality of the *text as an entity itself.* Ambiguity does not start with the assumption that a text allows for different interpretations, but with the fact that next to a reading A of a text, a reading B exists which also can lay a claim to correctness. At this stage, it is irrelevant whether reading B entails a different interpretation from that of reading A—it is sufficient that reading B takes a different route to the same interpretation. If, however, a tradition of "enlightenment" understands unequivocality of the interpretation of the text as a criterion of truth, it is all the more interesting to see how the equivocality of the *text itself* is dealt with.

In texts that have been transmitted in manuscript form and/or orally, such a textual ambiguity is quite inevitable. As is well known, the Old and New Testaments offer particularly telling examples of texts allowing for many variant readings, particularly as all of them were subject to complicated processes of redaction and canonization. It is not as well known that this holds equally true for the Quran, albeit to a lesser degree. Therefore we would like to dwell for a moment on the history of the Quranic text and of the Quranic readings—not in order to add one more theory to the recently thriving discussions of the early history of the Quranic text, but because the history of the Quranic text gives an ideal example of the process of a *domestication of ambiguity* resulting from a *crisis of ambiguity.*

Such a process is typically characterized by the following stages: (1) There is initially a surplus of ambiguity, for different reasons, which leads (2) to a crisis. This crisis causes (3) a procedure of disambiguation aiming at a reduction of ambiguity, reinterpreting the text in such a way as to narrow down the surplus of ambiguity—a procedure that usually involves several steps. Disambiguation, however, will not be followed through to its end, because a total elimination of ambiguity would be perceived as a loss. At the end of the process, therefore, there appears not total unambiguity but a certain amount of ambiguity that has become open to assessment, and thus socially manageable. The next step (4) is that this *domesticated ambiguity* will be accepted as an established cultural element, affirmed by ever-newly enacted cultural procedures, and integrated into cultural consciousness.

After a long period of a stable acceptance of ambiguity, the challenge of Western modernity led to a new crisis. The demand for coming up with unambiguous texts—and for promoting totally consistent ideologies and conceptions, assuming unequivocal positions, constantly attuning social behavior to stable norms, and submitting to the process of growing bureaucracy and technology—led to an ambivalent position toward a tradition that tolerated ambiguity. This resulted in three different reactions. Traditionalist circles kept more or less firmly to the traditional position, tolerance of ambiguity, and tried to defend it by minimizing its elements of ambiguity. But it was exactly this defensive attitude that strengthened the impression that traditionalism was nothing but hopelessly, obdurately holding on to old times which, in the battle "between tradition and modernity," were doomed to vanish anyway.

The two other reactions were, in contrast, informed by intolerance of ambiguity. This intolerance was due, on the one hand, to the ambivalence felt toward tradition, and, on the other hand, to an adaptation to the modern West. The modern West had, after all, confronted the Islamic world first in areas that were particularly intolerant of ambiguity (technology and the military complex, economy and bureaucracy) and operated in the political-ideological dispute with clear-cut ideologies.

The turn from a traditional position, tolerant of ambiguity, to a modern one intolerant of ambiguity can happen in two quite different ways. One way is a more or less complete acceptance of the Western position; in the extreme form of this position, the only function of the indigenous Islamic heritage is to paint the global Western modernity with some local color. Seen from this perspective, the traditional position appears to be the result of a millennium of decay and paralysis which prevented the development of the Islamic world in the direction taken by the Western world, and which now has to be overcome with the help of the West.

The second course of reaction is that of fundamentalism. It uses genuinely Islamic elements, preferably from its early history, in order to create an ideology, shaped after the model of Western ideologies, which is to a large extent free from ambiguity. Here the traditional position is seen as the result of a millennium of decay and of alienation from the ideals of the first Islamic community; the humiliation of Islam by the West has become evident for everyone and must be overcome by a reversion to the ideals of Islam's earliest period.

These two positions, the Western liberal and the fundamentalist, have something in common: they look at their own history with highly ambivalent feelings, often even with manifest hatred. This emotional ambivalence results in an intolerance of ambiguity which corresponds with elements of Western modernity that are intolerant of ambiguity, and thus is much more able to communicate with Western positions—be it in the person of a pro-Western intellectual or an Islamist manipulating the political discourse of the West—than is the traditional position.

This means that the relation between modern Islam's fundamental positions and its history is different from the way in which it is commonly presented. Most often, the various fundamental positions of modern Islam are presented as gradual deviations from a norm defined by Western modernity. According to this model, there are, to begin with, the liberal Muslims who make accommodations with modernity; the traditional Muslims who more or less tolerate modernity; and, at the extreme end, there are the fundamentalists who reject modernity. A diagram would look like this:

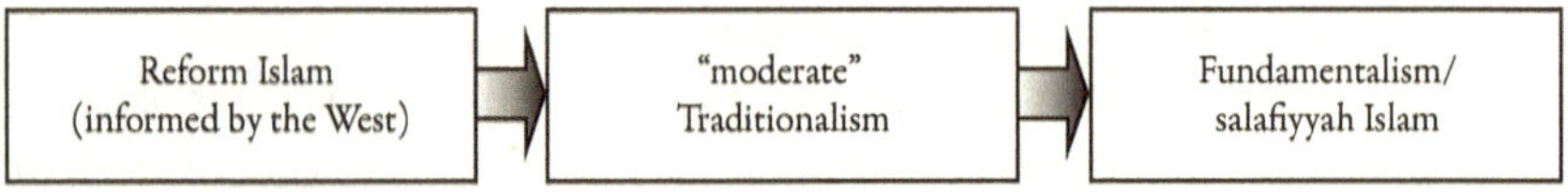

However, the evidence of truth for this diagram is slim. For one thing, it does not show a historical sequence; for another, it does not reflect on the question of whether Western modernity is valid as a normative position that defines all other positions as deviations. In point of fact, in a global context, the attitude of Western modernity toward ambiguity presents an exception, not a norm: "The movement against ambiguity led by Western intellectuals since the seventeenth century figures as a unique development in world history. There is nothing like it in any premodern culture known to me."[5]

Considering these principles, the above diagram should be modified as follows:

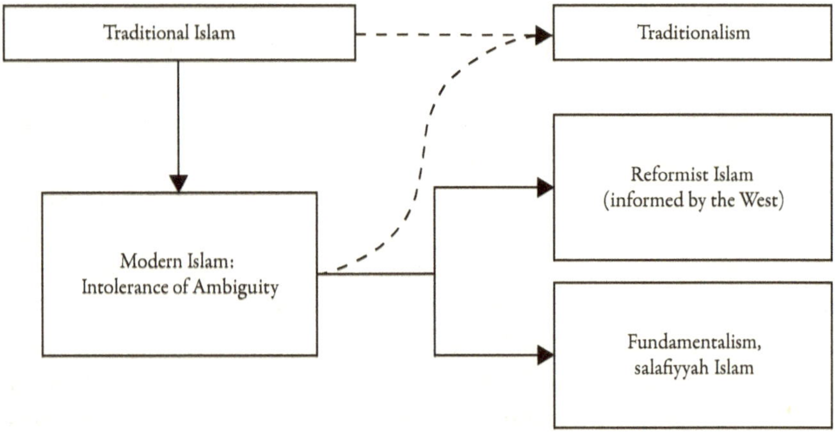

It is obvious that this diagram, too, like all such simplifying diagrams, cannot do justice to reality with its many transitions and intermediate positions. However, it avoids the kind of false conclusions produced by the perspective of the first diagram. To take a particularly blatant example: during the rule of the Taliban in Afghanistan, Western media constantly expressed the opinion that the Taliban wanted to take Afghanistan "back to the Middle Ages," since among their measures were the stoning of adulterers and the prohibition against listening to music. This statement corresponds exactly to figure 3.1, according to which fundamentalism constitutes an excessive form of traditionalism. It must be stated, however, that during the historical period that in Europe is, unfortunately, called the Middle Ages, neither was music forbidden nor were adulterers stoned in Balkh and Herat. It is true that there existed manuals of Islamic law containing a paragraph on the stoning of adulterers, but the enactment of that law was at the same time made impossible by a number of further regulations. And it is true that certain legal scholars issued a fatwa against music, but they were overruled by a larger faction of muftis who declared music as something accepted by God. These ambiguities—laws that were not implementable and legal opinions that were inextricably contradictory—in fact provided a good way to live for centuries (indeed, some observers have remarked that the Afghans could not fare better than returning to the "Middle Ages").

In the confrontation with modernity, such a seemingly lax handling of the law seems to be no longer tolerable. There remain two ways out, both of them intolerant of ambiguity: the modern Western one, which wants to have the inconvenient regulations abolished, or the fundamentalist one, which wants them implemented. These two positions may be contradictory, but on a higher level they are closely related, because they both originate from an attitude of antitraditionalism and of hostility to ambiguity.

The history of the Quranic text—and the acceptance, or nonacceptance, of variant readings of the Quran—offer a particularly telling example of this model, because the varying attitudes toward the multiform versions of the text are quite characteristic of different periods and different ideological positions. Therefore, we intend to tell the story of Islam's coming to grips with ambiguity in the context of an authoritative classical author confronted with modern Salafist and reformist positions.

IBN AL-JAZARĪ'S HISTORY OF THE QURANIC TEXT

The Quranic discipline of the "readings" (*ʿilm al-qirāʾāt*) deals with the variant readings of the Quranic text that are transmitted. This scholarly discipline joins the practice of Quranic recitation—the audible, aesthetically formed presentation of the Quran. The text has been revealed as one to be orally recited, and has been dealt with as such throughout Islamic history;[6] not only is the Quran treated orally in its ritual context, but in addition, the transmission of the text itself takes place orally, with the written text serving merely as an aid to memory.

Many of the prosodic characteristics of Quranic recitation escape notation; this art has been transmitted by direct contact between teacher and student until the present day, and cannot be replaced completely by cassettes or CDs or the internet. One who wants to train to become a professional Quran reciter must look for a teacher from whom he hears a specific way of recitation and so learns to recite that way, as has been done for centuries. Each teacher, in turn, authorizes his pupil to transmit the text that way. Thus they continue in a chain of transmission that goes back to one of the early Quran reciters, who lived in the second/eighth century. Since these early Quran reciters have their knowledge from oral transmission, which in the final analysis goes back to the Prophet himself, the oral tradition not only safeguards the preservation of textual items which were never specifically put down in writing, but also constitutes a spiritual link to the Prophet, and beyond him, to the Divine Speech.

However, the texts which are credited to the early Quran reciters are not identical; they differ from one another. Most differences concern the prosody, but the number of variant readings of vowels and consonants is not insignificant. Every "reading" (*qirā'ah*, pl. *qirā'āt*) is understood as one particular version of the whole Quranic text, in the tradition of one of the early Quran readers. Since the slightly different versions of these first readers are learned and then transmitted by their students, the next generation must also be taken into consideration. Thus one may speak of a reading "ʿĀṣim in the transmission (*riwāyah*) by Ḥafṣ," or, more briefly, "Ḥafṣ from ʿĀṣim," meaning that version of the Quranic recitation which goes back to Ḥafṣ b. Sulaymān al-Kūfī (died 180/796), who in turn transmitted it from ʿĀṣim b. Abī n-Najūd (died 127/745). At the same time, one can speak of a *qirā'ah* in the sense of a single passage that has varying readings in different versions. This word then corresponds with our term "variant reading," and the juxtaposition of variant readings is actually comparable with the critical apparatus of a text edition that contains the variant readings of the text in different traditions. We shall see that it is not only the way of presentation that is different, but also the ontological status of the variant readings.

Western research into the Quran that deals with works about *qirā'āt* has been almost exclusively interested in the question of how they furnish us with useful material for the reconstruction of the "original" Quranic text. Western scholars, whose work is based on an understanding of the text that is informed by the Classical and Christian traditions, have not only failed to pay attention to the oral tradition, but have also widely ignored the two Quranic disciplines that are closely attached to the oral form of the Quran, that is, the discipline of beautiful recitation (*ʿilm at-tajwīd*) and the aforementioned *ʿilm al-qirāʾāt*. Navid Kermani is clearly right when he states: "A scholarship that is not based on the Occidental concept of writing but refers only to the oral and ritual character of its holy 'scripture,' and depends moreover on the oral transmission of its findings, must almost inevitably be neglected or even dismissed as irrelevant by Western research."[7]

Consequently, most Western introductions into the Quran present the *qirāʾāt* in a way that is simplistic, if not outright mistaken. In most instances one reads that there are seven "canonical" readings, among which that of "Ḥafṣ from ʿĀṣim" is the most widely used. Sometimes it is mentioned that three more readings beyond the original seven are accepted as "canonical," and that all other traditions are rejected as *shādhdh* (irregular, noncanonical). This is not completely wrong and certainly conforms to the knowledge of most educated Muslims. However, a closer study of the classical works on the Quranic readings would reveal a substantially more differentiated picture; most notably, it would show that the *qirāʾāt* constitute more than a piece of folklore (an area to which modern science likes to relegate everything ritual or ambiguous). Rather, the discipline of the Quranic readings has led to an intensive reflection on the nature of the Quran which, over the centuries, has shaped Muslim understanding of this text much more strongly than the theological debates on its being created in time or not.

When a modern scholar in either the Western or the Muslim world wants to inquire into the Islamic understanding of the Quran, he will not hesitate to base his studies entirely and exclusively on the debates of the theologians—despite the fact that in Islam speculative theology (*kalām*) did not have the status it enjoyed in the Occident, and despite the fact that throughout Islamic history many more scholars of the *qirāʾāt* than *kalām* scholars were trained and active in the Islamic countries. Most modern authors who write about the Islamic concept of the Quran have not realized that the works on *ʿilm al-qirāʾāt* have developed an ontology of the Quran that is clearly different from the ontology of the theologians, and is in fact much more representative and characteristic of Islamic culture (once it had finished with the controversy over the createdness or uncreatedness of the Quran).

Among the numerous works on the readings of the Quran, the one by the Damascene scholar Ibn al-Jazarī (751–833/1350–1429), *an-Nashr fī l-qirāʾāt al-ʿashr*, has a prominent position. There exist many older works on this subject, but because of Ibn al-Jazarī's skillful choice of material and his conscientious methodology, his book remains indispensable. Above all, it has shaped the discipline of Quranic readings over many centuries, and it counts as a standard reference until today. Therefore, it is used here as a basis for an outline of the traditional position, even though most statements presented here are to be found in many other works both older and newer.[8] This chapter is meant to provide not a reconstruction of the historical truth but the reconstruction of a cultural practice, in this case an academic discourse on the Quranic readings. Hence, we direct our attention not only to the facts presented, but also to the mode of presentation, that is, the importance the author attributes to his various subjects, the space that certain discussions occupy, and the evaluations that the author reveals both consciously and unconsciously.

Ibn al-Jazarī was probably more familiar than anyone else with the older literature on his subject. He had recourse to more than sixty source works. His high valuation of oral transmission is typical for a Quran reader; he proudly states to have read these source works in the presence of authoritative scholars who, in turn, had received their authority to transmit them from still older scholars. Thus a chain emerges which ultimately goes back to the original author.[9] This scholarly practice parallels the ritual oral transmission of the Quranic text in its variant readings, which link the Quran reader in his turn with the Prophet in an uninterrupted chain.

In the beginning of his work, Ibn al-Jazarī quotes hadiths on the significance of the Quran readers ("The most noble members of my community are the bearers of the Quran"), and, after thus praising his own profession, goes on to stress the significance of oral transmission.[10] God, he says, has distinguished the Islamic community in contrast to all other communities through His order to learn the Holy Scripture by heart.[11] He then offers a short survey of the history of the Quranic text, which agrees with the accounts given in other Islamic texts and, to a large degree, with Western studies, but which also accentuates his own main points: right at the beginning, he stresses the primarily oral tradition of the Quranic text. Just as the Prophet had recited the text orally, so, too, was its transmission based at first on oral tradition. Ibn al-Jazarī does not mention the reports, particularly frequently cited in Western accounts, that Quranic texts were written on materials such as palm leaves, pieces of leather, shards, or the scapulae of sheep and goats.[12] He is right in this regard, because such brief, fragmentary notes were not likely to be of much use for the final form of the Quran.[13] Instead, he gives a list of the companions of the Prophet who knew the Quran partly or wholly by heart.[14]

According to both the Islamic and the established Western view, it was the first caliph Abū Bakr (reigned 11–13/632–634) who commissioned the first complete written copy of the Quran; this was accomplished by the Prophet's secretary, Zayd b. Thābit. This Quranic collection apparently did not have the function of eliminating ambiguity, but served as a kind of backup copy seen as necessary by Abū Bakr after numerous authorities on the Quran had lost their lives in the seditious wars after the Prophet's death. This copy of the Quran was bequeathed to ʿUmar after Abū Bakr's death, and after ʿUmar to his daughter Ḥafṣah, thus treated as a piece of private property. All this is related by Ibn al-Jazarī with extreme concision and without giving testimonies from the hadith. He seems to see the sole relevance of this first collection as lying in its being the principal source for the subsequent recension produced under ʿUthmān. Since there is no indication that Abū Bakr's collection ever achieved public effectiveness, this assessment is probably correct.[15]

The recension under ʿUthmān, which Ibn al-Jazarī dates at 30/650–651, was caused by a crisis of ambiguity in a positively classical form. Ibn al-Jazarī reports that the general Ḥudhayfah, who had conquered Armenia and Ādharbāyjān, noticed how the "inhabitants were in disagreement over the Quran, and one said to the other, 'My version is more correct than yours!'"[16] Alarmed by the prospect that the Muslims would fall into quarrel and schism, as had the Jews and Christians before them, Ḥudhayfah hurried to the caliph ʿUthmān, who took prompt measures. He obtained from Ḥafṣah the Quranic codex that had been written by Zayd b. Thābit on the order of Abū Bakr, and ordered four men (among them once again Zayd b. Thābit) to copy the text of this codex and to use as a guideline, in cases of doubt, the Arabic dialect of the Quraysh, the Prophet's tribe. These copies were then sent to Basra, Kūfah, Damascus, Mecca, the Yemen, and the province of Baḥrayn (eastern Arabia). One copy remained in Medina and one in the possession of the caliph.

The "committee" appointed by ʿUthmān clearly did little more than copy the collection that Abū Bakr had commissioned, and remove possible differences in dialect.[17] The fact that the copies produced by the committee were sent to the most important garrison headquarters of the empire as exemplary codices is proof that ʿUthmān's measure can be interpreted as an act of *disambiguation* caused by a *crisis of ambiguity*, a crisis that might have developed into a serious threat to the unity of the nascent Islamic community. This is also the way that Ibn al-Jazarī, whose account we have followed closely, presents ʿUthmān's initiative.

Again, the concision of his presentation is striking; it would hardly have exceeded Abū Bakr's version had he not attached a long list of the readers in the garrison headquarters who, on the basis of the ʿUthmānic text, were the first to recite the Quran—and who are important for the reciters of the Quran as a final link of the oral chains of transmission. At the same time, Ibn al-Jazarī refrains from presenting traditional accounts of the origin of the ʿUthmānic text that are divergent and less credible.[18] In addition, the account of the crisis of ambiguity which occasioned ʿUthmān's recension could have involved much more color and vividness, on the basis of hadith material. "It went so far," a hadith quoted by as-Suyūṭī has it, "that the boys quarreled with their teachers."[19] Since for Ibn al-Jazarī ʿUthmān's measure of disambiguation constituted merely an episode in the history of the Quran recitation—moreover, one that by no means is limited to a disambiguating function, as we shall see—such accounts would have had nothing of importance to contribute.

A SALAFIST HISTORY

At this point we want to interrupt Ibn al-Jazarī's account and compare it with a text of a modern author, that of the Saudi scholar Ibn ʿUthaymīn (1347–1421/1929–2001) who was one of the most renowned representatives of Wahhabi-Salafist thought. For his students, this influential author wrote a brief introduction to the Quranic sciences under the title *Uṣūl fī t-tafsīr* (Fundamentals of Quranic exegesis). This book not only is available in print, but also can be viewed on various internet sites.[20]

One of its chapters deals with the process of collecting and putting into writing the text of the Quran. It tells the same story that we have heard in Ibn al-Jazarī's version; it is based on the same sources, and takes roughly the same amount of space. And yet it is not exactly the same story as before.

While Ibn al-Jazarī shows no interest in early written recordings of Quranic passages, Ibn ʿUthaymīn assigns to these recordings a higher status; according to his formulation, in the times of the Prophet one "has relied *more* on memory than on writing."[21] Ibn al-Jazarī had written that one had "relied on memory, *not* on writing." In this passage, Ibn ʿUthaymīn introduces the tradition of writing of Quranic passages on palm leaves, pieces of leather, bones, etc., a practice Ibn al-Jazarī had held to be dispensable.

The account of Abū Bakr's collection of the Quran takes more space in Ibn ʿUthaymīn's book than in Ibn al-Jazarī's, although Ibn ʿUthaymīn has little more of substance to offer. Surprisingly, despite the brevity of his whole account, the report on the writing on palm leaves is taken up for a second time! There are various reasons why Ibn ʿUthaymīn may have quoted a hadith according to which ʿAlī praised Abū Bakr for his services to the codification of the Quran. But it is clear that he is eager to stress the early written recording of the Quran—obviously unaware that the "palm leaves" story does not serve to strengthen trust in the transmission of the Quranic text and to highlight Abū Bakr's initiative. Whether Ibn ʿUthaymīn wants to counter Western doubts about the authenticity of the Quranic text; whether he has begun to believe, perhaps unwittingly, in the idea that even in ancient Arabic conditions, scripturality is more reliable than orality and may therefore be better able to vouch for truth—in any case, he is obviously keen to demonstrate the significance of a written recording of the Quranic text at an early stage.

Next, Ibn ʿUthaymīn allots a great deal more space to ʿUthmān's standardization project than does Ibn al-Jazarī, and presents it from a totally different perspective. For one thing, Ibn ʿUthaymīn fixes the account, without inserting a "circa," in the year 25/645–646, five years earlier than the dating of Ibn al-Jazarī and of most of the other Islamic sources.[22] More strikingly, he sees the differences of opinion that brought about the ʿUthmānic recension as referring solely to the written form of the Quran. While Ibn al-Jazarī refers only vaguely to a conflict about the right "reading" (*qirāʾah*), Ibn ʿUthaymīn knows positively that "the cause of people's differences of opinion about the correct reading has to do with the differences between the folia (*ṣuḥuf*) that were in the hands of the Prophet's companions. Therefore, ʿUthmān gave an order to gather these *ṣuḥuf* in one single codex." However, as the hadith quoted by Ibn ʿUthaymīn shows, the *ṣuḥuf* ʿUthmān orders to "have gathered" are not divergent Quranic texts in the hands of several companions of the Prophet, but only those folia that were in the possession of Ḥafṣah and were returned to her after having being copied.

Thus, compared to the established tradition, Ibn ʿUthaymīn's account conveys a wrong impression in two respects. First, the written word is again awarded an unduly prominent position. The Arabic alphabet differentiates between various letters only by means of punctuation. These diacritical dots, however, were not yet widely used in the era under discussion. Without such dots and without additional signs for short vowels, Arabic writing leaves open so many possibilities of reading and interpreting words that no one would have been able to settle a dispute over the "correct text" solely on the basis of the written version, without a parallel (in fact a *primary*) oral tradition. It is true that the written version of the Quranic text could have served as an aid to memory and thus helped to prevent the insertion of explanatory additions, the substitution of unfamiliar words by better known ones, and omissions and changes of the order of words. It could also have helped to fix the overall arrangement of the text. But if its oral transmission had not been known, its exact wording could not be ascertained with sufficient accuracy. For Ibn ʿUthaymīn, however, the oral tradition is no longer an issue. On the contrary, variant texts are ascribed to variant written versions to be found already in the codices of the Prophet's companions—although on the preceding page, he credits some of these companions with transmitting the Quranic text orally.

Second, Ibn ʿUthaymīn's suggestion that the ʿUthmānic recension of the Quranic text consisted of converting many different texts into one homogeneous text is a further distortion of the traditional view. Ibn al-Jazarī and most of the older sources depict ʿUthmān's project merely as a revised edition of Abū Bakr's Quran. Further, in addition to this Quranic recension, there existed a few others, among which those of Ubayy and of Ibn Masʿūd are well attested. These collections differed mainly in their different arrangements of the suras and a few textual variants. The literature on the variant readings transmits the arrangements of the suras in these recensions, as well as numerous variants between them.[23] ʿUthmān's recension is apparently distinguished by the fact that among three or a few more competing recensions (which certainly went along with an oral tradition), it gives a dominant position to one specific recension, namely that of the secretary of the Prophet, Zayd b. Thābit.

As for Ibn ʿUthaymīn, he devotes almost half of his chapter to ʿUthmān's project of unification, and wants to give it as much significance as he possibly can. Among other testimonies, he cites a hadith (one with a conspicuously pro-Sunni tendency) stating that ʿAlī had approved of ʿUthmān's project. Ibn ʿUthaymīn then presents a hadith that relates an eyewitness report of the burning of divergent codices, which ʿUthmān allegedly had decreed in order to enforce a uniform text.[24] He writes, "Muṣʿab b. Saʿd reports: 'I saw how people arrived in droves when ʿUthmān ordered to have the Quran codices burned, and they liked it.'" He further writes, "No one among them disapproved of this act, one of the good deeds of the caliph ʿUthmān that are acknowledged unanimously by the Muslims."[25]

Ibn ʿUthaymīn ends his chapter with fulsome praise for the achievement of ʿUthmān through whose unification of the Quranic text "the Muslims attained the greatest possible good, in the sense that the Muslim community was united, spoke with one voice, and was imbued by the feeling of brotherhood, while at the same time [ʿUthmān] fended off a huge evil, namely the schism of the community and difference of opinion, which sows the seeds of hatred and enmity! And so as it was then, it remained until today: Unanimously the Muslims acknowledge the Quran and transmit it, widely and uninterruptedly, each time a young Muslim receives it from an older one. The hands of the corrupters could not abuse it, and the base intentions of the dissenters could not extinguish it!

Therefore praise be to God, the lord of the heavens, the lord of the earth, the lord of the worlds."[26]

It is amazing how different stories construed on the basis of the same material can be! On the one hand we have the account of Ibn al-Jazarī, which is firmly established in the tradition of his discipline, that is transmitted in both oral and in written form from the masters of the discipline, and thoroughly pondered by the author himself. If one does not want to reject outright the Islamic version of the origin of the Quranic text, one is bound to admit that Ibn al-Jazarī's account offers the most plausible version of the relation between the written and orally transmitted Quranic text. Western scholarship, however, following the Western mode of text analysis, draws on numerous reports that deal with the early written recordings of Quranic texts, while largely neglecting the oral history of the text offered by readers of the Quran. It is instructive to note that this is the approach taken by Ibn ʿUthaymīn, for whom the written tradition stands at the center of attention.

Still more instructive is the different degree of relevance both authors attribute to ʿUthmān's recension. For Ibn ʿUthaymīn, ʿUthmān had not only initiated the examination of an existing collection of the Quran, privileging it over other collections, but had also created a uniform collection to begin with. This unification appears in the exposition of the Saudi legal scholar primarily as a *political* act that constituted the unity of the Muslims altogether and for all times—a *single* Quranic text establishes the *unity* of all Muslims who withstand all challenges by enemies as, by extension, does their text.

In an era when the Islamic world is divided in internal quarrels and has become a pawn in the hands of diverse powers, this representative of the Wahhabi doctrine of *tawḥīd*, according to which other Islamic orientations (e.g., the Shiites) are branded again and again as heretics, announces, in his description of the collection of the Quran, a clear political message of "unity"—whatever is meant by that.

Thus, in his introduction to Quranic exegesis, Ibn ʿUthaymīn plainly reacts to modern Western discourses; this is shown in his selection of the elements he finds essential—precisely those which, superficially viewed, are most closely compatible with a modern Western understanding of texts. Thus the praise of God at the end of the chapter, which would have a strange effect had it appeared in a similar position in Ibn al-Jazarī's writing, makes the impression of an ideological affirmation rather than the continuation of a religious tradition.

A comparison between what the texts *omit* puts in even stronger relief the contrast between Ibn al-Jazarī's classical version and Ibn ʿUthaymīn's modern one. Ibn al-Jazarī, in his brief account of the history of the Quranic text, skips whatever he deems superfluous or of no special interest to him, for instance the administrative measures taken to enforce the ʿUthmānic recension. Ibn ʿUthaymīn, in his abridged account of the textual history, gives an incorrect impression of the status of the Quranic text after ʿUthmān's redaction.

The Saudi author does not mention even a word about the fact that ʿUthmān's exemplary codex contained only the *rasm*, i.e. the Quranic text in its consonantal form. This text does not make use of the diacritical dots that differentiate between otherwise identical letters. Thus, in the beginning and in the middle of words the consonants *b*, *t*, *th*, *n*, and *y* appear only in the form of a small hook (ـٮـ). In punctuated writing, however, they are differentiated by dots beneath and above the basic sign (ـيـ ـنـ ـثـ ـتـ ـبـ). In the ʿUthmānic *rasm* the dots are missing, along with the signs to indicate the short vowels *a*, *i*, and *u*, and the gemination of a consonant. Therefore, this reduced form of writing in many places allows for a great number of varying options of pronunciation. Only the oral tradition can add flesh to the bones of the ʿUthmānic *rasm*, which in its turn may stabilize the oral tradition.

A uniform *rasm* is thus far from guaranteeing a uniform Quranic text. Such a text would have existed only if the oral tradition had also been uniform—but this was not the case! Ibn ʿUthaymīn withholds this story. For him, the history of the Quranic text *ends* with the ʿUthmānic recension. For Ibn al-Jazarī, the interesting part of history of the Quranic text *begins* with that initiative.

Ibn ʿUthaymīn's unequivocal enthusiasm for unity goes so far as to suppress a central tenet of the Islamic dogma of the Quran. If someone had confronted Ibn ʿUthaymīn with this omission, he would probably have had to concede that there exist several different accepted Quranic readings. The fact that he keeps silent about this issue in an introduction to the Quranic sciences nicely illustrates the irony that the Salafists' attempt to get to the true roots of the prehistoric "righteous ancestors" (from whose ranks, after all, the oldest transmitters of the Quranic readings arose) leads not to the "true" tradition, but to an ideology that strives to prove itself as being compatible with modern Western ways of thinking—and by doing so, leads to an abandonment of its own tradition.

THE INEXHAUSTIBLE DIVERSITY OF THE VARIANT READINGS

In order to present ʿUthmān's project of standardization as something definite—which it was not, because the ʿUthmānic consonantal text remained open to variant ways of readings—Ibn ʿUthaymīn withholds their existence. The phenomenon of variant readings is mentioned in most other modern Islamic and non-Islamic introductions to the Quran. However, there is one central feature of Ibn al-Jazarī's account that I have not encountered in modern works on the history of the Quranic text and its variant readings, namely his notion that the work that was commissioned by ʿUthmān both removes ambiguity and at the same time makes new room for ambiguity.

A close reading of Ibn al-Jazarī's *Nashr* yields the puzzling observation that in this book, the ʿUthmānic recension is by no means presented as a *pure* project of disambiguation. It is true that Ibn al-Jazarī's version shows the ʿUthmānic redaction as a standardization caused by a crisis of ambiguity; but the *disambiguation* of the Quranic text goes hand in hand with an *ambiguation*. And this ambiguation is so important to Ibn al-Jazarī that he deals with it extensively in two places.[27]

In order to understand his account it may be reemphasized that the ʿUthmānic Quran gave only the *rasm* of the text, which presented an ambiguous portrait and which could be recited correctly only if the reader already knew the text.

Indeed, greater accuracy of the text to be recited would have been achievable, since diacritical signs were known since pre-Islamic times and can be found, for instance, in the Arabic text of a Greek-Arabic papyrus from the year 22/643 (i.e., prior to the ʿUthmānic recension of the Quran).[28] Thus it would have been highly possible to render the Quranic text with more precision and consistency than was done. According to Ibn al-Jazarī, this foregoing of further precision was intentional. To be sure, the ʿUthmānic *rasm* was drawn up on the basis of the last oral recitation delivered by the Prophet in the last year of his life. But quite deliberately, the text was not furnished with diacritical dots and vowel signs. On the contrary: "These codices [commissioned by ʿUthmān] were all *stripped of* diacritical dots and vowel signs to leave them open to every faithfully transmitted reading that is unobjectionably transmitted, that has a way of recitation traceable to the Prophet—one relied, *nota bene*, on memory [the oral tradition], and not on mere written information—and that is one of the seven *aḥruf* to which the Prophet refers in his saying 'The Quran was revealed in seven *aḥruf*.'"[29]

It is difficult to determine what the word *ḥarf* (in its plural form *aḥruf*) signifies here. Its basic meaning is "edge, brink." In trying to interpret *ḥarf* in this context, scholars have come up with dozens of suggestions that Ibn al-Jazarī discusses later at length. In this passage, however, the fairly well-attested saying of the Prophet about the "seven *aḥruf*" serves first of all as a justification of the diversity of the Quranic text. Since clearly the Prophet could recite only *one* version of the text in his last recitation, and yet various versions going back to him were circulating, the diacritical dots and vowel signs had to be omitted "so that the codex permits a reading that was unobjectionably transmitted from the Prophet, without being identical with his last recitation. Instead, they (the Quran scholars) vacated (*akhlaw*) the codices of diacritical dots and vowel signs, in order to let *one single written record* refer to *both readings* that are transmitted, heard, and recited, in exactly the same way that *one single expression* may refer to *two meanings* which are understood and comprehended."[30]

Such formulations make it clear that the plurality of the Quranic text was not at all viewed by the classical authors as a makeshift, an involuntary stopover, as it were, on its way to a uniform text, a stopgap with which we are stuck due to adverse circumstances. Many modern authors ascribe the plurality of readings to the deficiencies of the Arabic writing.[31] They overlook the fact that texts that are scripturally transmitted over long periods, in writing systems that are more complete than the Arabic one, generally exhibit far more variant readings than the Quran. This can be observed in classical Greek, Latin, Middle High German, and other texts. In contrast, pre-Islamic poetry is an example of a literary tradition transmitted over a long period of time exclusively or predominantly in oral form, and yet arrived in fairly trustworthy shape in the scriptural culture—where it was further enriched by new variant readings. Ibn al-Jazarī perceives no relation between the deficient writing of the *rasm* and the existence of textual variants, although he is keenly aware of the fact that oral transmission, too, may generate variant readings and mistakes. The science of the *qirāʾāt* must of necessity exist, because in the course of generations during which the Quran was transmitted by capable and not-so-capable readers, mistakes crept in and more and more variant readings developed. It is now the task of the *qirāʾāt* scholars to separate the good transmissions from the bad ones.[32] But this procedure is not valid for the early generations. The "ultimate submission" (*al-ʿarḍah al-akhīrah*),[33] that is, the Prophet's last recitation of the Quran in his year of death, has not led to the establishment of a text without variant readings—which is not necessarily a matter of regret.

The somewhat radical tool of abrogation (*naskh*) has proven useful for the elimination of contradictions between Quranic verses respective of Prophetic actions; according to this convention, Quranic verses revealed later, or sayings and acts issued later by the Prophet, invalidate earlier such instances if there is no way to reconcile both versions.[34] The "ultimate submission" only standardizes the extent and arrangement of the Quran—the latter also at the cost of previous "versions"—but does not abrogate the various current older readings. Therefore, the normative codex has to remain without diacritic dots, in order to preserve the variety of the readings transmitted by the Prophet's companions.

Still, an observer firmly rooted in the modern Western way of thinking is liable to suspect that the theory of the Quranic readings serves, in the end, only to justify a plurality of traditions that cannot, after all, be revoked, and constitutes an attempt to hush up, as it were, an occupational accident. This assumption might be countered, however, by the observation that the variant readings differ most conspicuously on the phonetic level, in terms of assimilation, vowel inflection, velarization, the execution of the glottal stop, etc., all of which give each of the *qirāʾāt* a clearly discernible, specific character that points to an early provenance. But whatever the ultimate truth behind the existence of this or that variant or reading may be, there remains primarily one significant and eventually unsurmountable gap between the two approaches. The modern observer *knows* that there must have existed a single, consistent urtext, which was corrupted in the course of its transmission and which may be recovered, to a certain extent, by applying the historical-critical method. The traditional Muslim scholar *knows* that total unambiguity is something that contradicts human nature, and gratefully accepts the divine gift of a plural Quran text whose exact boundaries are open and which offers him a chance to master a task and a test. This is what makes Ibn al-Jazarī's text replete with joy at the rich variety of the holy text and with pride regarding the science that enables the cultivation and domestication of that variety. And it is for this reason that his text is completely free from Ibn ʿUthaymīn's apologetic undertone and bashful twisting of the historical facts.

In between these two scholars, there must have been a process of revaluation of plurality. Unfortunately, there has never been an investigation of the Ottoman period in this regard, as far as I know, but it is probable that plurality was almost never as enthusiastically enacted as it was in the Mamluk period, the time of Ibn al-Jazarī.

This shows in his position regarding the so-called Seven Canonical Readings, in which he clearly exceeds what appears to contemporary traditionalists as an established plurality (and is thus a thorn in the side of modern Salafists and liberals). In a Western introductory work, the conception of the readings that prevails in today's traditionalist Islamic thought is characterized as follows:

> The present Islamic tradition has acknowledged seven such readings as "canonical," that is, valid. This reveals a characteristic feature of Islam as such, namely its quite amazing capability to accommodate the principle of plurality, at the same time, however, delimitating this practice in a way that avoids tendencies of schism. Hence one should stress the greatly remarkable fact that the text of

> God's revealed word is by no means fixed unambiguously but admits, within a precisely defined frame, variant readings and hence variant interpretations.[35]

This fact is remarkable especially if one approaches Islam with the prejudices that prevail today. For Ibn al-Jazarī, the existence of variants—in a frame that was by no means *precisely*, but only *approximately*, defined—was an obvious fact, and the delimitation of the "Seven Readings" posed an annoyance to him. The idea of recognizing as authoritative just seven out of the many readings originates with the Baghdadian scholar Ibn Mujāhid (245–324/859–936), who was the first author to write a comparative study of the Quranic readings in which the attempt was made to canonize those "Seven." With Ibn Mujāhid's project the endeavors to standardize the Quranic text reached their climax for the time being. For modern authors, this endeavor of attaining greater homogeneity appears to be only too conceivable, and therefore it is tempting to attribute motives to Ibn Mujāhid that may be conceivable from a modern point of view, but not in the context of his period and culture. Compare, for instance, what A. T. Welch writes in the *Encyclopaedia of Islam*: "His aim was to restrict the number of acceptable readings, accept only those based on a fairly uniform consonantal text, renounce the attempts of some scholars to achieve absolute uniformity (something which he realized was impossible), and at least ameliorate if not bring to an end the rivalry among scholars, each of whom claimed to possess the one correct reading."[36]

While the first two statements are simply a description of what Ibn Mujāhid did, the two latter points seem to be due to an idea of the author who, as a matter of course, adopts a position that most of us today would feel to be normal for his historical object. Thus, he supposes that the existence of several traditions inevitably calls for standardization, and that different scholars who have divergent traditions will necessarily claim to be in sole possession of the right one. But nowhere do the Arabic sources in which the topic of the "Seven" is extensively discussed contain a call for complete standardization of the text, or the claim of a scholar to be in exclusive possession of the right tradition.[37] A. T. Welch's assumptions that the scholars of the time all claimed to possess "the one correct reading" are thus a typical example of an undue generalization of our present way of thinking, which it is evidently difficult not to regard as universal. It is nowhere borne in mind that the real reason for Ibn Mujāhid's project may be that a reader of the Quran can corroborate the correctness of his tradition only through the completeness and good quality of the chain of its transmission.

This criterion is suitably used to give more weight to the tradition, but cannot be used to *invalidate* and thereby *eliminate* other, equally legitimate, traditions.

For this reason alone, the allegations of scholars that they possess the one and only true tradition is absurd. Furthermore, such scholars do not take into consideration that some people might not find it at all desirable to have only one tradition. Finally, it is a misjudgment of the mentality of a traditional Muslim scholar to assume that he would have been proud of possessing the allegedly sole true tradition. Rather, one may assume that the pride of a Quran reader would consist in the knowledge of a neglected Quranic reading, unknown to other readers, quite as the legal scholars were proud of their dissenting opinions within the orbit of their school of jurisprudence.

These observations should make it clear that the quest for a stricter systematization, and hence a greater degree of standardization, did not originate from the assertions by many scholars that each of them was in possession of *the one sole* true reading. Rather, it originated from scholars' assertions that they had *another* correct reading available. The surplus of ambiguity that had thus developed did not concern the problem of the *true* tradition, but simply confronted the discipline of the Quranic readings with a complexity that had become unmanageable. This is how Christopher Melchert interprets the Arabic documents that discuss the necessity to put a stop to the accumulation of readings and to alleviate the arduousness of Quranic studies.[38]

Ibn al-Jazarī's account points in the same direction. First, he resolutely takes sides against all those who want to fix the canon of the readings according to Ibn Mujāhid's "Seven." Here he has the support of a large tradition; the restriction to exactly seven readings had never found common acceptance.[39] Only the erroneous equation of the seven *aḥruf* with the seven readings selected by Ibn Mujāhid ("for which only ignorant laymen fall")[40] has secured a greater popularity for his preference. According to Ibn al-Jazarī, the number of the readings in which the Quran was revealed, and which in their entirety correspond to the seven *aḥruf*, is in fact much greater, and even inexhaustibly great: "The seven readings known today, respectively ten or thirteen of them, are only a fraction of a plenitude, only drops in an ocean, compared to the readings which were known in the first generations of Islam."[41] The number of transmitters growing from generation to generation, their varied competence, and a certain negligence sneaking into the discipline eventually necessitated a stricter examination of the tradition and a separation of authentic from inauthentic material. Ibn al-Jazarī writes that the first author to collect the Quranic readings in a book was Ibn Qutaybah (died 276/889). In addition to the seven readings, he incorporated twenty-five further readings.[42] Other authors have compiled books on twenty and more readings. Abū l-Qāsim al-Hudhalī, who died around 465/1072, traversed the whole Islamic world and assembled fifty readings in 1,459 traditions from 365 shaykhs.[43] And still 150 years later, Abū l-Qāsim ʿĪsā ibn ʿAbd al-ʿAzīz al-Iskandarī (died 629/1231) was able to collect close to seven thousand traditions on diverse readings.[44]

Such collections, which inevitably contain well-attested along with dubious material, confirm Melchert's thesis that a kind of endeavor to alleviate the arduousness of Quran scholarship was the motive behind Ibn Mujāhid's attempt to reduce its complexity. On the one hand, a restriction to seven readings furnishes the reader of the Quran, or a group of people listening to its recitation, with a reading of high authority, and at the same time allows the cultivation of the customary plural tradition—albeit in a reduced manner. On the other hand, the selection of just seven readings was bound to meet with reservations. At an early stage, three further readings were added to the seven, and Ibn al-Jazarī does not tire of denouncing the restriction to seven as a sign of ignorance and intellectual laziness. Many scholars, he writes, have only studied the *Taysīr* (a handbook on the Seven Readings by ad-Dānī, died 444/1053) and the *Shāṭibiyyah* (a didactic poem, based on the *Taysīr*, by ash-Shāṭibī, 538–590/1144–1194) and think that they know the accepted readings, "indeed, many of them even call those readings which do not go back to the seven readers 'isolated/far-fetched' (*shādhdh*), although much of what does not figure in the *Shāṭibiyyah* and the *Taysīr*, and originates from sources other than the Seven, is more correct (*aṣaḥḥ*) than much of what is presented in these two works."[45]

While Ibn al-Jazarī vehemently fights against the restriction to those Seven, and spends a great amount of energy in proving that the "Three after the Seven" are at least a match for the Seven in every respect, this does not mean that he wants to expand the canon of the Seven to one of Ten. For him, the restriction to ten readings remains a less-than-ideal solution determined by technical reasons. Even the ten readings in no way represent the full scope of the trustworthy tradition, let alone exhaust the sum of the seven *aḥruf*. He approvingly quotes Abū Ṭālib al-Makkī, who stated "that leading scholars mention in their books more than seventy transmitters who have a higher rank and a greater value than those seven."[46] After this, Ibn al-Jazarī selects from Makkī and other sources no less than thirty variant readings for passages from the quite brief first surah, and presents them with part of them diverging from the Seven even in their consonantal text, but all agreeing throughout with the criteria that are valid for acceptable readings.[47]

The list shows that the transmission and examination of the numerous extant readings soon reach the limits of practicality, and that a limitation becomes inevitable. However, even those readings that were not transmitted with the same degree of reliability as the Ten possess, and which thus may contain false material along with correct passages, have correct variant readings that are not transmitted elsewhere. Because of their barely separable mixture of correct and hardly probable material, these "isolated" (*shawādhdh*, singular *shādhdh*) readings are to be excluded from ritual practice, but continue to be cultivated in the Quranic sciences. The border between the commonly accepted and the *shawādhdh* readings is an open one, which has to be drawn solely for practical exigencies with reasonable strictness. Basically, however, in order to arrive at a conclusive judgment on the reliability of a variant reading (which by its nature is always only a judgment of probability), one would have to determine the entire transmission of that one reading. This is the basis for Ibn al-Jazarī's famous definition of an acceptable reading (*qirāʾah*, here in the sense of the reading of a certain Quranic passage). The author introduces this definition with a lengthy passage in rhymed prose in order to highlight its significance, and then proceeds:

> Every reading which (1) conforms to the rules of Arabic grammar—even if their correctness is a matter of debate—and which (albeit possibly)—(2) matches one of the ʿUthmānic exemplars, and (3) whose chain of transmission is flawless, is an irreproachable reading which is not to be rejected or censured. It belongs to the seven *aḥruf* in which the Quran was revealed. It must be accepted, whether or not it originates with the Seven Imams or the Ten or with another one of the recognized Imams. If one of the three principles is missing, one talks (depending on the reliability of the given tradition) of a "weak," an "isolated," or an "invalid" tradition, no matter whether it goes back to one of the Seven or to a previous transmitter.[48]

In a manner similar to that of Ibn Ḥajar al-ʿAsqalānī in the hadith sciences, who calls for the critical application of methods his discipline has developed for seemingly established text corpora,[49] Ibn al-Jazarī reviews the entire scholarly discipline of Quranic readings from its foundations and picks to pieces the notion of a stable stock of seven "canonical" readings. He does not use the dichotomy between *mashhūr* (widely known, accepted) and *shādhdh* (isolated)—the term "canonical" used in Western scholarship is a transfer from the discourse on the biblical canon to the Quran, and is hardly appropriate to the different characters of the two text corpora. Instead, the author divides the Quranic tradition into four degrees of trustworthiness: from *ṣaḥīḥ* (valid), *ḍaʿīf* (weak), and *shādhdh* (isolated), to *bāṭil* (void). This division shows, first of all, that the readings cannot be classified according to categories such as "right" or "wrong," but only according to various levels of probability of correctness. Therefore, this fourfold schema (which was evidently transferred from the hadith sciences to the discipline of the Quranic readings) should not be understood as a strict division between four neatly separate categories. In what follows Ibn al-Jazarī's exposé, it is not taken up again. Rather, those four terms constitute only demarcations on a continuous scale of probability that extends from "indubitably valid" to "indubitably void," a scale on which every reading (respectively every hadith) may be placed at a precise point on or between the marks. Only the limited "accuracy of measurement" of the sciences of tradition prevents a greater degree of precision.

On such a scale, an acceptable reading is not at all bound to attain a degree of a hundred percent. This would be the case only if it were transmitted as *mutawātir*, that is, handed down by so many people in all generations that any error is completely ruled out. If one would claim a *mutawātir* tradition for every well-attested tradition, one would have to dispense with many good readings.[50] This also means that among the seven or ten commonly accepted readings, there are quite a number that are established not with certainty, but only with a high probability.

The probable validity of a given reading depends almost exclusively on the criterion of the quality of the transmission, that is, the reliability and number of the transmitters. The two other criteria—(1) and (2)—are downplayed by Ibn al-Jazarī as much as possible. Thus it is by no means imperative that a reading be regarded as correct Arabic by all grammarians, or that its notation exactly match that of the first exemplar.[51] The trustworthiness of a reading is guided not by the letter—which can only curb rampant growth—or an abstract norm, but by the dependability of the social interaction. In other words, a given reading is only as trustworthy as the persons who have transmitted it, and therefore complete certainty is a rare thing.

Up to now, the idea of the Quranic text presents itself as follows: This text has been revealed in seven *aḥruf* of which the readings which have "survived" until now are only a small part, and the exact relation between the *aḥruf* and the readings is left undecided. One may know the Quran, conceived horizontally, in its entirety, but, conceived vertically, one does not know all the readings that are part of the Quranic revelation. The divine word is abundance and variety which man may never fully grasp. Since this is so, man is compelled to compromise, and to take those readings whose transmission may be regarded, according to human reason, as largely valid as a basis for the ritual Quran recitation, and, conversely, to cultivate the other readings whose reliability is less attested, but which may well contain genuine readings in the scholarly discourse. The fixation of one sole reading would be to willfully abandon a part of the Quranic revelation that over the centuries has remained a fairly uncontested heritage of the community. Once the reflection on the Quranic text has reached this level, a further standardization can only be viewed as a loss.

DIVERSITY AS BLESSING

What is the reason for God to reveal a text whose wording, let alone whose semantic wealth, man is unable to completely fathom? The answer given by the Islamic tradition, with which Ibn al-Jazarī deals at length, is unequivocal: The diversity of the *qirā'āt* is meant to be *takhfīfan 'ani l-ummah wa-tahwīnan 'alā ahl hādhihī l-millah* (an easing of burden for the community and relieving for this people).[52] Ibn al-Jazarī quotes several variants of a hadith according to which the Prophet initially receives an order from the angel Gabriel to recite the Quran in one single *ḥarf*. The Prophet, however, points out that this kind of compressed revelation would overtax his community. So Gabriel returns with the order to recite the Quran not in one *ḥarf*, but in two. Muḥammad still considers this as too taxing a demand for his people; finally the order is given: "God has ordered you to recite the Quran to your community in seven *aḥruf*; following whichever *ḥarf* in their recitation, they will always do the right thing."[53] Thus the variant readings constitute a divine blessing that does not burden man with an additional duty. It is therefore acceptable that parts of the text are hidden in the "isolated" readings of the seven *aḥruf*,[54] and even that certain parts of the text are totally unknown to man.

But, in fact, what are the seven *aḥruf*, which according to general consent are different from the seven variant readings established by Ibn Mujāhid?[55] There is hardly another Quranic term that has met with so many different interpretations. In his *Itqān*, as-Suyūṭī writes of forty different attempts at interpretation; however, the more plausible of these may be reduced to two basic patterns. One group of exegetes holds that the seven *aḥruf* represent different Arabic dialects; the other group interprets them as different textual species, kinds of statements, legal categories, or combinations of these.

In addition, many scholars do not consider the number seven to be a precise figure, but as a metonymy of "many." Ibn al-Jazarī himself rejects interpretations belonging to the second category, because the pertinent *aḥādīth* show rather clearly that the *aḥruf* represent primarily phenomena concerning the sound, not the contents of the text. But he finds the interpretations of the first category equally problematic, because there is a sound tradition relating a dispute between two companions of the Prophet, both belonging to the tribe of Quraysh, about variant readings, who, supposing that *ḥarf* would mean a tribal dialect, would have had no occasion for quarrel in the first place.

Dissatisfied with the existing attempts at interpretation, Ibn al-Jazarī has pondered this problem, as he writes, for more than thirty years.[56] The solution at which he finally arrives is a structuralist one. This may surprise a modern Western reader; however, those familiar with the indigenous theory of Arabic grammar will be aware of the frequent use of generative-structuralist methods in grammar. Following the lead of this theory of grammar, Ibn al-Jazarī develops a "generative theory of the Quranic readings." He notices that all variant readings of the Quran, including the isolated, weak, and rejected readings, as well as the commonly acknowledged ones, may be reduced to seven generative ways of transformation.

They are:

	Substitution or elision of short vowels	Substitution of a consonant or a long vowel	Substitution of a character of the unpunctuated *rasm*	Semantic change
1	+	–	–	–
2	+	–	–	+
3		+	–	+ (necessarily)
4			+	–
5			+	+
6	pre- or postposition			
7	addition or omission			

(1) The substitution or elision of a sign of a short vowel that does not entail a semantic change. Thus, seven of the ten *qirāʾāt* read the word for "avarice" in Q 4:34 and 57:24 as *bukhl*, and three as *bakhal*, with no semantic difference. (Ibn al-Jazarī knows of two more variant readings.)

(2) The same as in 1, but resulting in semantic change: For instance, all readers of Q 2:37 have *fa-talaqqā Ādamu min rabbihī kalimātin* (then Adam received words from his Lord), whereas al-Kisāʾī has (grammatically fairly unwieldy): *fa-talaqqā Ādama min rabbihī kalimātun* (then words of his Lord hit Adam).

(3) Substitution of the punctuation of a letter by another one while the *rasm* remains the same, resulting in semantic change—for instance, in Q 2:259, which has "look at the bones as *we raise* (*nunshizuhā*) (ننشزها) / *resurrect from the dead* (*nunshiruhā*) (ننشرها) and then cover them with flesh"; each *qirāʾah* of the two is supported by five of the ten.

(4) Substitution of a character of the *rasm* by another one without ensuing semantic change, as in the word for "straight path" in Q 1:7, where Yaʿqūb and a transmitter from Ibn Kathīr read *sirāṭ* (سراط) instead of the usual *ṣirāṭ* (صراط) (and where Ibn al-Jazarī mentions a further reading, *zirāṭ* (زراط).[57]

(5) The same as in 4, but resulting in semantic change. As one example, Ibn al-Jazarī presents Q 62:9, where all ten readers have *fa-sʿaw* (فاسعوا) *ilā dhikri llāh* (then run to the invocation of God). However, the reading of the Prophet's companion Abū l-ʿĀliyah, which has not found its way into the list of ten, has *fa-mḍū* (فامضوا) (then go on).

(6) Pre- or postposition, e.g., in Q 9:111, where seven of the ten have "they kill and are killed" and three "they are killed and they kill."

(7) The swearing clause, Q 92:3: *wa-**mā khalaqa** dh-dhakara wa-l-unthā* (by that which has created the male and the female!) appears in the readings of the Prophet's companion Abū d-Dardāʾ and probably also of Ibn Masʿūd; these do not tally with ʿUthmān's *rasm* as *wa-dh-dhakari wa-l-unthā* (by the male and the female!), omitting the two words given above in bold.[58]

Thus God reveals a Quranic text consisting of an abundance of textual variance that can be generated by means of seven rules. The trustworthiness of the variant readings must be assessed from case to case. This variance, however, does not negate the validity of the text. The fact that for the majority of the Sunni Muslims, the Quran constitutes God's uncreated word, does not necessitate the uniformity of the text and hence its semantic uniformity. God is tolerant of ambiguity.

It is admittedly conceivable that plurality (meaning a tolerance that leaves the truth claim of the text untouched) can reach its limit (in the event of variant readings being significantly different and yet each being regarded by some as probably correct) and lead to irresolvable contradictions. But this does not happen. "Rather, the variety of the Quranic readings is a variety of diversity and difference, not a variety of contradiction and incompatibility, which cannot exist in God's word."[59] This is in fact the only factual concession required by Ibn al-Jazarī's concept of the Quran as a divine text. Ibn al-Jazarī ascertains three types of differences:

(1) The wording may be different, but the meaning is the same (see the examples *bukhl* and *ṣirāṭ*, given above).

(2) A different wording results in different meanings, which converge, however, in one and the same idea: see the example, given above, of *nunshiru/nunshizu*, where the bones are raised and composed at the same time, as well as resurrected to life, or the example in Q 1:4 which in one reading calls God the one who "has the power (*mālik*) over the day of judgement" and in another reading uses the phrase "the ruler (*malik*) of the day of judgement." For Ibn al-Jazarī, the important thing is not the question of right or wrong meaning or which one is closer to the truth, but rather the question "has God included both meanings in the two variant readings."[60]

(3) If the different meanings do not converge in one and the same idea, the alleged contradictions may be resolved at a higher level. Q 12:110, for instance, talks of the apostles of ancient peoples who delivered the message of God's oneness, but met with deaf ears. They almost believed "that they were taken as liars" (*annahum qad kudhdhibū*, as five of the ten readers have it), or "that they tell lies," that is, that the message they are meant to deliver is a lie (*annahum qad kudhibū*, as the other five have it). In this case as well, the two variants do not result in contradictory meanings, but rather present two possible aspects of the situation: The apostles realize that their audience does not believe them, and begin to doubt their own message.

One could—and this is what modern scholarship chooses to do—consider the existence of two variant readings as a nuisance to be remedied, and try to determine, using philological and historical-critical methods, the "true" reading. But in view of the fact that in any case, there exist no texts without variant readings, one may also "domesticate" the plurality of the variant readings by critically examining the textual transmission—and then envisaging the advantages resulting from the assumption that several readings remain which are true and correct to the same degree. Ibn al-Jazarī has compiled a list of such advantages, which opens a new horizon for anyone who moves beyond the dogma that a single, uniform text is the only true one. Ibn al-Jazarī names eight aspects, which will be outlined here in a slightly different order:[61]

(1) *Facilitation*. Lack of variants is something unnatural. Man, that variant creature, cannot sustain the pressure of variantless definiteness. The *aḥādīth* quoted above have made it clear that the incorporation of variant readings in the revealed text was meant to facilitate the task of its transmitters and of its audience.

(2) *Concision*. To say much with few words is an Arabic stylistic ideal that also shapes the scholarly style of authors such as Ibn al-Jazarī—to the

chagrin of their modern readers, who would sometimes wish for greater elaboration. Notably in the Quran, with its numerous elliptical passages, scholars of Arabic rhetoric have discovered a particularly high degree of "concise brevity" (*ījāz*). How, asks Ibn al-Jazarī, could brevity be achieved more effectively than by allocating different meanings to different readings? That God acts both as *mālik* and as *malik* over the day of judgment, that the bones of the dead are composed and resurrected to life at the same time, that the messengers realized their audience did not believe them and therefore began on their own accord to doubt the truth of their message—all this might be expressed in distinct phrases and sentences, but a higher degree of concision is gained by incorporating the vertical dimension of language; that is, by distributing the variant aspects among variant readings of a single passage and thus creating, as it were, a hypertext.

(3) *Mnemotechnical aid*. In addition, concision allows for easier memorization and transmission, particularly since all variant readings are based on one and the same *rasm*.

(4) *Incentive and performance test*. Although at first sight, textual variation presents a kind of facilitation, it also constitutes a challenge, since the variety that allows one to cope with a variety of life situations demands, in itself, a variety of interpretations. Thus "the members of this community strive to progress as far as possible in their endeavor to realize the meanings of these variant readings, to deduce the wisdoms and legal judgements toward which each single passage points, and to distil the concealed secrets and hidden intimations"[62]—and through such striving, they enable themselves to gain a greater amount of divine reward.

(5) *Stimulus of scholarly activities*. The activity of "facilitation," which is made possible by the plurality of the text, is primarily meant as an adaptation to the *conditio humana*, but not as a license to take liberties with the text. On the contrary, precisely because the plurality of the text is a reflection of the plurality of the *conditio humana*, the text contains many more subtle nuances of meaning than does a uniform text. Consequently, according to Ibn al-Jazarī, facilitation of such a text demands the exploration of the wording of every single passage, the examination of every single form, the investigation into the criteria of correctness, the mastering of the art of recitation, the attention to every vowel and its nuance of articulation, etc.—and all this with a thoroughness and precision the like of which no other community demands—another proof of the superiority of Islam over other communities.[63] Here, ambiguity presents itself as a divine grace.

(6) *"Miraculous filiation."* There is a further sign of divine grace which can be found in the idea that every reciter of the Quran who transmits it in one of its

many readings is a link in a chain which goes back to God Himself. This idea, grounded in the primarily oral transmission of the Quran, is not as alien to modern secular times as it may seem at first sight. The poet and novelist Werner Bergengruen speaks with great emotion of a "chain of transmission" of utmost brevity (that is, as always aspired to by transmitters of hadith), between him and Goethe:

> In the year 1935 I met in Vienna an elderly lady from Bohemia who, as a young girl, had made the acquaintance in a spa—perhaps this happened in Karlsbad or Marienbad, but my memory is not quite certain—of a lady, very much advanced in years, who was Ulrike von Levetzow. It is a strange thought for me that the hand which I pressed and kissed had been clasped by Ulrike's hand, a hand which had been held by Goethe's hand. So then between the handshake which he gave and that which I received there was—miraculous filiation!—only one link.[64]

(7) The fact that the oral transmission of the Quran, along with its cultivation of the variant readings, continued through all centuries and in all quarters of the world is a sign of God's presence.

(8) *Proof of the truth.* Adrian Brockett has examined the question whether variant readings may be traced back to early attempts to interpret incomprehensible Quranic passages in a better or more ideologically acceptable way. A close comparison of two readings led him to the conclusion "that the readings found in these transmissions are most likely not of exegetical origin, or at least did not arise out of crucial exegetical dispute. They are therefore of the utmost value for the textual history of the Quran."[65]

If one does not want to resort to general conspiracy theories, as it has become fashionable to do in Western writing on the Quran, one would actually have to concede that Quranic readers succeeded remarkably well in eliminating readings fabricated from exegetical zealousness or theological partiality. The remaining readings still offer a plurality of interpretative options; they are, however, in some way mutually compatible. For Ibn al-Jazarī, this compatibility is "a tremendous proof and clear evidence" for the truth of the text. Still, consistency as a criterion of truth is different for Ibn al-Jazarī than it is for Descartes; it is not a matter of recognizing something as true *valde clare & distincte* (quite clearly and distinctly), but a matter of whether, *despite all this difference and diversity* (*maʿa kathrat hādhā l-ikhtilāf wa-tanawwuʿihī*),[66] something can be interpreted as true without irresolvable contradictions. Thus, only diversity and ambiguity allow for consistency as a criterion of truth.

DIVERSITY AS AN OFFENSE

What is left of that in the modern age? One might say, in a few words: a marginalized tradition, often misunderstood, and a great unease.

On the one hand, the tradition of the Quranic readings (which is still carried on and to whose discipline even some academic chairs are devoted)[67] has reclaimed, thanks to modern techniques of communication, some of the terrain it had lost precisely because of those techniques. The internet offers informative pages on the *qirāʾāt*,[68] and under *islamweb.net* one can read the Quranic text in the fourteen versions of Ibn Mujāhid's seven *qirāʾāt*, with the divergences from the reading of the "Ḥafṣ-from-ʿĀṣim" tradition marked in color. In addition, one can download audio files containing partial recitations of the Quran in 22 traditions. A completion of this corpus is in process.[69]

On the other hand, the introduction of printing dealt a severe blow to the idea of the plurality of the *qirāʾāt*. The year 1344/1925 saw the printing of the Quran in the reading "Ḥafṣ-from-ʿĀṣim." Nöldeke observes, "This edition does not do justice to the original diversity of the Quran, although that diversity is still theoretically recognized."[70] This edition has soon gained acceptance in the whole Islamic world (apart from the Maghreb, whose Quran editions in Maghribī script follow the reading of "Warsh-from-Nāfiʿ"). The worldwide success of the "Ḥafṣ-from-ʿĀṣim" reading is thus due merely to historical coincidence, and not to distinctive differences from other readings. Its triumph marks the culmination and the provisional endpoint of the standardization of the Quranic text in the twentieth century.

At the same time, the concept of the Quranic readings itself came under fire. Whereas Ibn al-Jazarī had to struggle against attempts to reduce the number of accepted Quranic readings to seven, now the existence of even a few such readings is generally questioned. Initially, it was Arab intellectuals oriented toward the West who attacked the idea of a plurality of Quranic texts. Ṭāhā Ḥusayn, for instance, the Egyptian author and cultural policy maker (1307–1393/1889–1973), was an early critic of the traditional concept of *qirāʾāt* and an eager advocate of a cultural Westernization of Egypt, persistently arguing against the uncritical acceptance of his own religious and literary cultural heritage. Even today, Ṭāhā Ḥusayn is regarded by liberal, secular, nationalistic Arabs as a heroic fighter for progress and modernization, and remains, notwithstanding a few minor criticisms, a symbolic figure of the first rank. In several respects, his case anticipates that of Naṣr Ḥāmid Abū Zayd: both thinkers had to undergo an inquisitorial investigation of their publications by the religious establishment—which did not, however, defend the subtle and sophisticated approaches of the classical scholars so much as insist on a much more rigid version of the tradition. Even in the time of Ṭāhā Ḥusayn, the religious elite had been pushed into a defensive position that had ceased to allow for the old tolerance of ambiguity:

> Ṭāhā Ḥusayn knew how this propagation of the necessity for scepticism was bound to be received. The spirit of free enquiry, meticulous scrutiny and admission of limitation of knowledge which characterized much of the classical learning . . . was long dead. Neither the common readers nor the leading dignitaries were equipped to distinguish between doubt and denial, scepticism and atheism, dissent and treason. *Yaqīn*, sure knowledge, is one of the cardinal blessings which faith brings to a believer. Hence the uproar which met the book, and the variety and virulence of the religious, moral and patriotic accusations it stirred.[71]

This scandalizing book, which appeared slightly revised and mitigated, under the title *Fī l-adab al-jāhilī* (On pre-Islamic literature) in 1927, did not necessarily deserve the attention it got, because its central claim—that the entire pre-Islamic Arabic poetry constitutes a forgery from later times—was doomed to collapse shortly. Al-Nowaihi writes, "In modern Arabic scholarship, it would be difficult to find a hypothesis more implausible than that advanced by Ṭāhā Ḥusayn in his *fī 'l- 'adab al-jāhilī.* Yet it may be wondered whether any other book, written by a contemporary Arab, has had a comparable influence in changing the fundamental attitude of the Arab intelligentsia towards their classical literature and history."[72] But the skepticism that Ṭāhā Ḥusayn applied not only to the venerable literary heritage, but also to the Quran, contemporaneous with ancient Arabic poetry, was felt as a more general provocation. In his arguments, he explicitly labeled himself a Cartesian, asserting that only in following the method of Descartes could one arrive at the truth. His method, he claimed, was therefore the criterion of modernity.[73]

No matter how well the Egyptian scholar had understood Descartes, it is well-nigh inevitable that the traditional concept of the *qirā'āt* would fall victim to such an approach. Ṭāhā Ḥusayn deals with the Quranic variant readings primarily in order to demonstrate that different Arabic dialects existed in pre-Islamic times; he offers this as a proof that ancient Arabic poetry, which does not feature these differences, cannot be authentic. All the elements of this argument are false or superfluous. Both early Arab philologists and old Arabic inscriptions bear witness to the existence of different ancient Arabic dialects. Ancient Arabic poetry is written, as has been known for a long time, in a transtribal koine, which is why differences in dialect manifest themselves only occasionally (but by no means never). Finally, the view that the variant readings of the Quran trace back to differences in dialect is only one among several, and certainly does not apply to variant readings such as *nunshiruhā/nunshizuhā*.

Unimpressed by these facts, Ṭāhā Ḥusayn firmly asserts:

> The Qur'an readers from different tribes had scarcely accepted the Qur'an, which (originally) had been recited in one sole linguistic form and one single dialect—namely that of the Quraysh tribe—, that there originated multiple readings (*qirā'āt*), and a host of dialect forms infiltrated the text. . . .
>
> This place calls for an excursus, since many religious authorities understand this issue in a way that suggests that the tradition of the Seven Readings (*qirā'āt*) goes back, in a breadth and completeness (*mutawātir*) that precludes any error, to the Prophet himself, who in turn was inspired by Gabriel. Therefore, they say, anyone disavowing these readings is, without any doubt, an unbeliever. In support of their allegation, however, they can present no other proof but that of the Prophet's sayings, recorded in the authoritative hadith collections: "The Qur'an was revealed in seven *aḥruf*."
>
> The truth is, however, that these seven readings are not in the least part of the revelation, and that someone who denies their validity is not an infidel, nor a sinner, nor a defier of religion. Rather, the origin of these readings lies in the differences of dialects, and everybody is free to discuss them, to reject those and accept these, much as they were in fact discussed (already at an earlier period) and contested, and were mutually accused of error, although, as far as we know, never a Muslim would have accused a fellow-Muslim of unbelief.[74]

It is interesting to see how much the "Cartesian method," as it appears in Ṭāhā Ḥusayn's programmatic introduction, differs from his own actual procedure. In his introduction, he suggests that to follow Descartes means first and foremost to renounce all prejudices and partiality, and to accept all results arrived at through strict scholarly procedures, even if those results are contradictory to the ones one actually wanted to find. In his own investigation, however, Ṭāhā

Ḥusayn remains considerably short of this standard. Rather, he picks and chooses only those traditions and facts that suit his own preconceptions.

Nevertheless, there is a trace of Cartesianism in the author's procedures of which he himself may not have been conscious. That is to say, for Ṭāhā Ḥusayn the world and history represent two different claims to truth. Anyone who denies the validity of the Quranic readings is, according to Ḥusayn, deemed by "religious authorities" as being "without doubt" an unbeliever, he says (although he himself acknowledges the fact that no one stating a dissenting opinion on the *qirāʾāt* was ever declared a heretic), and discussions of the different readings represent for him, as they do for A. T. Welch, discussions of the *sole*, exclusively true reading. Because he thinks only in certainties, not in probabilities, it is difficult for him to conceive that Ibn al-Jazarī, in his *Nashr* does not posit a "broad and uninterrupted transmission, excluding error" (*tawātur*) as a condition for an accepted reading. It is difficult for him to imagine that the Quran was revealed in more than one *qirāʾah*.

If one single and unambiguous truth always exists in opposition to a large field of error, then every conviction is bound to be true or false. Since the author holds *this* conviction to be true, he can introduce the statement of his views on the relation between the *qirāʾāt* and revelation with the formula *wa-l-ḥaqq an . . .* (However, the truth is . . .). A classical scholar like Ibn al-Jazarī, dealing with a problematic and controversial question, would have never said, let alone written, such a statement.

One cannot escape the observation that Ṭāhā Ḥusayn's level of argument is far below that of Ibn al-Jazarī. According to the latter, only "ignorant laymen" would believe that the Quranic readings were identical with the seven *aḥruf*. Ṭāhā Ḥusayn follows aṭ-Ṭabarī's opinion that six of the seven *aḥruf* were rendered superfluous by the ʿUthmānic Quran text (which is seen as constituting one *ḥarf* of these *aḥruf*, and claiming exclusive validity). This interpretation comes closest to Ṭāhā Ḥusayn's own opinion, since the God-given plurality that the hadith on the *aḥruf* is originally meant to express leads in the end, after six of the seven *aḥruf* are abolished, to a single reading free of ambiguity. It is also telling that Ṭāhā Ḥusayn does not even address the problem of dissenting opinions on the interpretation of the seven *aḥruf*. So much for the openness and impartiality of "Cartesian" scholarship.

The critique leveled against the concept of the *qirāʾāt* by Ṭāhā Ḥusayn, the self-appointed Cartesian, may carry little weight. But the fundamental doubt about the traditional conception of the Quranic readings could not, at some point, be dismissed—not because that conception had proven flawed or had been refuted, but simply because it contradicts a Western understanding of revelatory texts.

Thus it is no great wonder that one encounters the same objections in the camp exactly opposite that of Ṭāhā Ḥusayn. The antipode to this Egyptian secularist and nationalist, who views the Arab world (or at least Egypt) as part of the Mediterranean culture and is a champion of a thorough Westernization, is his younger contemporary, the Indian Sayyid Abū l-Aʿlā Mawdūdī (1321–1399/1903–1979), the leading mastermind of political Islam, whose ideas strongly shape Islamism until today. For Mawdūdī, Islam is an integral ideological system, on a par with the Western ideologies, and meant to take their place. For him, progress means not imitation of the West but a rolling back of Western influence.

His most comprehensive work is a commentary on the Quran in six volumes,[75] the first of which, published in 1949, begins with an introduction to Quran interpretation which in purpose and contents clearly harks back to that of the aforementioned Saudi Ibn ʿUthaymīn, and which is also available in independent English and Arabic translations.[76] In contrast to Ibn ʿUthaymīn, who puts the greatest stress on ʿUthmān's establishment of a standardized Quranic text, Mawdūdī emphasizes the fact that the Quranic text in today's form was already fixed at the Prophet's death (so much so that one wonders what role remained for Abū Bakr and ʿUthmān). He mentions the story of the palm stalk, and states, with more definite conviction than I have encountered in any other author, the undeniable "historical fact" that "whenever a surah was revealed, the Prophet gathered his copyists around him, dictated its text to them meticulously and told them which place among the other surahs it was supposed to take. . . . Therefore it is a historical fact that the collection of the Qur'an was completed on exactly that day in which the revelation itself was concluded."[77]

The Quran edition commissioned by Abū Bakr thus represents, for Mawdūdī, the authoritative version of the text. However, since the Quranic text continued to be recited differently in different Arabic dialects, although it was revealed in only one dialect (that of the Quraysh), ʿUthmān deemed it advisable to send copies of Abū Bakr's standard version into the garrisons of the Islamic army. The minimal role that Mawdūdī assigns to ʿUthmān in the history of the Quranic text seems to consist of prohibiting recitations in dialects other than that of the Quraysh. Apparently Mawdūdī (who, by the way, did not enjoy a solid scholarly education, as did most other Islamic reformists) refers here to the well-known old scholarly position that the seven *aḥruf* were seven (or more) Arabic dialects in which the Quran was recited. These dialectical recitations were abolished by ʿUthmān—or thus one must presumably understand Mawdūdī.

This squarely contradicts the accepted position on the seven *aḥruf*; the well-known hadith states not that the Quran was revealed in one single *ḥarf* and then recited by Arabs in seven different ways, but originally in seven (or more) different *aḥruf*. As is shown by Mawdūdī's position on the revelation of the Quran solely in the dialect of the Quraysh, the idea of a plural revelation of the text is as alien for Mawdūdī as it is for Ṭāhā Ḥusayn. The authenticity of the Quran, writes Mawdūdī, is demonstrated precisely in its permanent lack of variant readings:

> The Qur'an, as we have it today, is exactly identical with the edition that was prepared by command of Abū Bakr and whose copies were, by command of ʿUthmān, officially sent to various cities and provinces. Some copies of this original edition of the Qur'an are extant until today. Anyone who has the remotest doubts about the authenticity of the Qur'anic text is free to remove them by buying a copy from some bookseller, say, in West Africa, and then asking a *ḥāfiẓ* [someone knowing the Qur'an by heart], say, from Java,[78] to recite the text by heart. Now we ask him to compare both versions with each other and with former versions of the Qur'an from all the centuries since ʿUthmān's times—and if he discovers a single difference between them, be it a sole letter or a sole syllable, then let him proclaim his discovery to the whole world.[79]

These are the words of someone who has clearly never heard of the discipline of the *qirāʾāt*. Consider, for instance, his comparison of a text printed in West Africa that follows the reading of "Warsh from Nāfiʿ" with a text printed in, say, Java, that follows the reading of "Ḥafṣ from ʿĀṣim." The comparison reveals a serious textual variant as early as the eighth verse of the second surah, a variant concerning more than just one syllable (or, as the Arabic translation of Mawdūdī has it, "merely a short vowel (*ḥarakah*)." ʿĀṣim reads, in Q 2:9: "they [the unbelievers] deceive only themselves (*yakhdaʿūna*)," whereas Nāfiʿ reads: "they only try to deceive themselves (*yukhādiʿūna*);" in the following verse, ʿĀṣim reads: "They will receive a painful punishment because of the lie they tell (*yakdhibūna*)," whereas Nāfiʿ reads: ". . . because of what they tell to be a lie (*yukadhdhibūna*) [namely the divine message]." A philologist could try to find out which of the two variant readings is more plausible, and what accident might have led to the existence of the other reading. He could argue that *yukhādiʿūna* is a textual corruption caused by the same form a few words before, at the beginning of the verse. Therefore, he might continue, it is probable that the original text had *yakhdaʿūna*. A classical Arabic philologist dealing with pre-Islamic poetry principally would have proceeded in the same way. Alternatively, one following the classical doctrine of the *qirāʾāt* might consider the existence of two well-documented readings as an enrichment, because God, through variant readings of His word, can open up new aspects of the text.

But what one feasibly cannot do is to deny the very existence of these variants, as does Mawdūdī. His ignorance is so blatant that a revised English version of his text (the editor of which remains unknown) contains an extended inserted passage on the Quranic readings, "since their existence has led to the misunderstanding that the Qur'anic text has not remained intact."[80]

This passage begins with an exposition of the history of Arabic writing and its initially defective character, at first apparently using the philological method of assuming that such variant readings have their origin in an "urtext" that was corrupted in some places. But then the explanation takes a turn toward Ibn al-Jazarī's argument, brings in his definition of an acceptable reading, and discusses the semantic gain offered by the acceptance of different readings. All these points of discussion now parade merrily side by side, and it does not become evident to the reader why the existence of variant readings should impair the authenticity of the text, or, if all readings go back to the Prophet, what should have been the effect of the lack of diacritical dots in the early manuscripts. So this well-meaning correction in Mawdūdī's exposition shows a curious vacillation between a modern Western approach and an awkward conjuring of traditional clichés.

It is remarkable that the ideological position of an author hardly seems to influence his stand on the *qirāʾāt*. On the contrary, it becomes evident that the Salafist Wahhabi Ibn ʿUthaymīn, the Western-oriented intellectual Ṭāhā Ḥusayn, and the political Islamist Mawdūdī all have a similar stance on the diversity of variant readings. This has the cumulative effect of suppressing the *qirāʾāt* entirely, either by simply denying their existence or by minimizing them as an insignificant, marginal phenomenon.

The reason for this common position of the three authors then does not derive from an approach to Islam or to the Islamic tradition that for each of them is originally quite different, but from the constant presence of a discussion partner, sometimes visible, sometimes not, that is Western modernity. Western thought can, and must, admit that a historical account such as that of the Bible displays variant readings, but it cannot admit this for a text which claims to be divine speech, as the Quran does.

By renouncing one's own traditional positions, only in order to be compatible with modern prejudices, one has exposed a wing which Christian critics of Islam promptly attacked. A lively discussion about the problem of Quranic variant readings began to take place between two websites: http://answering-islam.org.uk, one of the most important anti-Islamic propaganda panels run by Christian evangelical missionaries, and its Islamic counterpart, http:// www.islamic-awareness.org.

One of the authors on the "prosecution's" side is Samuel Green, who attacks the widely attested claim that the truth of the Quran is vouchsafed by the absence of variant readings. The quotation to which he refers probably goes back to Mawdūdī's text; he frames it as follows: "No other book in the world can match the Qur'an. . . . The astonishing fact about this book of ALLAH is that it has remained unchanged, even to a dot, over the last fourteen hundred years. . . . No variation of text can be found in it. You can check this for yourself by listening to the recitation of Muslims from different parts of the world."[81] Do Muslims of our days really have to make it so easy for their enemies? With great relish and the air of a muckraker unveiling heretofore hidden secrets, Green quotes from texts presenting illustrations of Quran copies that follow different variant readings, or that indicate them in the margin. For Green, this is proof that the deniers of variant readings are convicted of lying and at the same time it is proven: "Since the Qur'an, both in its written text and in its oral transmission, shows variant readings, it is not superior to the Bible." Note that Green does not doubt the claim that the absence of variant readings guarantees authenticity; he is merely satisfied to point to the variant readings and to refute his opponents' claim to superiority. No wonder, then, that the three authors who respond to Green adduce the far greater margin of variant readings in the New Testament as an argument:

> So, by applying the standards of the Christian missionary Samuel Green, we should reject the New Testament as a "superior Holy Book" because there is not a single sentence in it that is uniform. Oh! we also forgot to mention that according to the great Church tradition, we have the Bibles of the Protestant Church, Roman Catholic Church, Anglican Church, Greek Orthodox Church, Coptic Church, Ethiopic Church and Syriac Church. They contain different numbers of books and God knows best how many variants one is expected to see in them. So, our question now is which variants and the books in the Bible are inspired by God? And what is the evidence for it?[82]

—which is then answered by a Christian voice that endeavors to play down the variant readings in the New Testament.[83]

One more quite elaborate pamphlet is presented by John Gilchrist, and it is mentioned here only because it quotes (secondhand) Ibn al-Jazarī's definition of acceptable Quranic readings. Gilchrist comments on this with the statement: "This statement shows how impossible it was to define the seven different readings."[84] Indeed, once one has relinquished Ibn al-Jazarī's idea that the wealth of divine revelation may be limited, at best, but never exhausted, then all attempts to gain as much as possible from this revelation must be construed as inability to achieve unambiguity.

The replies of the Muslims on the site "Islamic Awareness" render the traditional position objectively, but they concentrate exclusively on making plausible the authenticity of the *qirāʾāt*. Their main argument is that these readings are *mutawātir*, that is, transmitted from the Prophet in a broad and uninterrupted manner that excludes any error.[85] Forced back into a position of mere self-justification and defense, no Muslim author apparently dares to celebrate the diversity of variant readings as a gain.

For Muslims who parry the attacks of Christian missionaries, too, the evidence of the *qirāʾāt* seems to be an embarrassing fact. And so it is inevitable that a school of Sunni Islam thought has arisen that does not deny, conceal, or downplay the existence of variant readings, but simply refutes their validity. This is the position of the scholars of the Pakistani Institute of Islamic Sciences, al-Mawrid, in Lahore.[86] The founder of this institution, Javed Al Ghamidi (born 1951) is a leading voice of Islamic reformation, heard far beyond the borders of Pakistan. In his youth, he was closely connected with Mawdūdī, but in the seventies he turned away from those ideas and to a nontraditionalist Islam, oriented toward modern views.

His student, the Quranic exegete Shehzad Saleem, has written an extensive text on the collection and transmission of the Quran that in the final analysis represents a scholarly vindication of Mawdūdī's radical position: "The Qur'an, as we have it today, is word for word identical with the one that was revealed to the Prophet Muḥammad. It was put together during his lifetime in book form and learnt by heart by his companions, and it was transmitted both in oral and written form to subsequent generations. The quality of this tradition is so impressive that the flawlessness of the Qur'anic text is an undisputable reality."[87]

Saleem's argument takes its cue from Quranic passages in which God announces to the Prophet that He will reveal the Quran in segments, up to the completion of His revelation (e.g., Q 25:32; 20:113–114; 87:1–18; 75::16–19; 87:18). Since these Quranic passages contradict the Quranic text traditions ascribed to Abū Bakr and ʿUthmān, Saleem writes, the latter must be rejected, since the Quran has a greater authority than the hadith.[88] One might object that the Quranic passages quoted by Saleem were also known to the classical Muslim scholars, who did not perceive them as in contradiction to the redactional measures of the caliphs. However, Saleem is addressing not the classical scholars but the Western Orientalists:

> It is only because they neglected the testimony of the Qur'an and insisted on the validity of such spurious reports that it could happen that the collection of the Qur'an became the object of the Orientalists' serious and severe criticism. . . .
>
> If the material that the Muslims want to adduce in order to prove the authenticity of their scripture leads to dubious results, they are facing a really difficult task, since their non-Muslim disputants who honestly search for truth have available an ostensibly legitimate argument to reject the Qur'an as the unchanged word of God.[89]

The hadith on the seven *aḥruf* is rejected because it is incomprehensible, writes Saleem, and because it appears to be, in its most probable meaning, namely that the *aḥruf* denote different dialects, contrary to reason: "How is one supposed to accept the fact that the Almighty Himself has revealed the various accents and ways of pronunciation?"[90] Next, the Quranic passage Q 75:18 ("So, when We recite it, follow thou its recitation") is interpreted as evidence for the fact that the Quran was brought forth in only one reading. Ultimately, he writes, this is shown to be obvious by the fact that all over the world only one reading is customary, and this matches the "ultimate presentation." The reading "Warsh from Nāfiʿ," prevailing in North Africa, is disputed away by simply declaring North Africa to be an insignificant, marginal stretch of geography. The historical coincidence that the "Ḥafṣ from ʿĀṣim" reading traveled on the coattails of the Ottoman Empire (and eventually, thanks to printing technology, gained a position of virtual monopoly) now becomes a proof of this reading's authenticity:

> The entire Islamic *ummah* is in agreement about reading the Qur'an in one sole form. Only a few North African countries take exception to this. That range of variations is so insignificant that they should not be accorded any validity. These regions of the African continent are not even part of the mainstream of

> the Islamic *ummah* that the companions of the Prophet conquered during the reign of the Right-Guided caliphs. The only complete version of the Qur'an, which in all central regions of the Islamic world since the times of the Prophet is commonly used, is the *qirā'ah 'āmmah* (the general reading), and that is precisely the version that was recited by the Prophet when the revelation of the Qur'an was completed.[91]

According to Saleem, this reading was falsely called "Ḥafṣ from ʿĀṣim," but must actually be called "the universal reading." Where the divergent readings differ from this "universal" reading also in terms of contents, they turn out to be contradictory, and therefore wrong. After all, the Quran was revealed as a *mutawātir* text, whereas the readings refer to different chains of transmitters (which technically can function only in this way) some of whom, what is more, are regarded as unreliable in the collections of transmitters' biographies. "This analysis clearly shows that the variant readings that can be found in the Qur'an commentaries and that are read and memorized in religious schools are in no way to be accepted. Be it that they originate in the stubborn insistence of some transmitters on the first recitation of the Qur'an or constitute interpretive endeavors of the Prophet's companions . . . , be it that they were fabricated, like the 'Satanic Verses,' in order to bring the Qur'an into miscredit, it remains a mystery, never perhaps to be solved. That much seems to be certain that they do not have to do anything with the Quranic text."[92]

Saleem's argumentation runs roughly thus: on the one hand, there cannot possibly exist a plurality of readings—if only for the reason that this would provide a target for non-Muslims—and on the other hand, there does exist a version of the Quran, widely used and printed, which must be the only correct one. Therefore, he concludes, traditions that do not support this view are wrong. It is a peculiar experience to see an open and reasonable school of modern Islam trying to come to terms with the Western episteme and yet falling far behind the position reached by Islamic thinkers five hundred years ago.

THE "POSTMODERN" TRADITION

The classical Islamic exposition of the Quranic readings, as represented by Ibn al-Jazarī, proceeds from the simple assumption that the divine word, as it enters human history, cannot be a text without variants. Rather, God has made the variants to be elements of His own revelation. The concept presents difficulties only if one believes that God must have revealed a uniform text, without variant readings, and that such readings must therefore have originated through human mistakes. This belief is based on a common philological fallacy, namely the seductive belief in a single urtext for which philologists almost inevitably fall in their editorial work, unless substantial signs suggest that the author of a work himself has generated it in different versions.

Poets of all times and cultures have often reworked their writings over and over, and have presented them in different versions. Still, the primary philological impetus, hard to suppress, is to reconstruct any work that is not explicitly the autograph manuscript on the basis of the manuscript tradition, with its many variant readings, as the one and only true original version, the *propria verba* of the author himself—with the tacit implication that he or she spoke them either only once, or again and again in the same version.

More often than not, such an original version never existed. What existed was a sequence of different reworkings and revisions of a text. In the course of its transmission, the text has been enriched by further variant readings that often can no longer be distinguished from variant readings generated by the author.

What prevents us from assuming such a plurality of urtexts for the Quran? To begin with, many variant readings can be convincingly explained with the help of common textual-critical methods. Consider for instance the reading *nunshiruhā (*as opposed to *nunshizuhā* in Q 2:259, mentioned above), which can be explained by dropping a diacritical dot in the written form. This yields a *lectio facilior*, a reading that is easier to understand (and therefore suspect). Text-critical considerations, then, unmistakably support the reading of an original *nunshizuhā*.

However, this does not begin to contradict the theology of the *qirāʾāt*, which views the existence of variant readings as an adaptation necessary for human beings, who are creatures of variation. This theology also allows the apparently secondary reading, *nunshiruhā*, to be a part of the revelation, even while the *nunshizuhā* reading retains its validity, since variant readings are meant to complement and illuminate each other. Since the reading *nunshiruhā* contributes a semantic nuance worth considering, welcoming it means that the Quran is in fact enriched. God's ruse consists in anticipating potential textual variants that may occur in the early period of a textual tradition, as part of the revelation itself—and beyond them, many more variant readings that will be forgotten in the course of time, or will live on in the shadows as parts of dubious *shawādhdh* traditions. God, then, takes variant readings into account, and is the first to reveal them. A simple examination of the tradition is all that is required to determine whether or not a given reading may be traced back to the companions of the Prophet (and thus to the Prophet himself) and is part of this revelation.

Human fallibility is bound to come into the picture, making it impossible to decide such cases with absolute certainty. But precisely by granting man this fallibility—the inability to preserve a text without variants—it has become a part of God's plan and finds its proper position by conceding to man the right to make judgments on the basis of probability, and granting him the privilege to strive for approximating the truth and thus earning divine reward.

In accepting variant readings as equally valid ones, the Quran is not the same as a text with its critical apparatus of variant readings. Such an apparatus informs us of the history of the text, but is not part of it; the text is intact and continuous as it stands, and can exist on its own, according to the decisions and methods of its editor. In the case of the Quran, the variant readings do not offer "background information" but constitute part of the text itself. The Quran is not one continuous text, because each written or recited portion is not able to include the vertical dimension, written or spoken, of the variant readings.

Exploring this dimension, we arrive first at the accepted readings of the Ten Readers, then to well-documented readings, and eventually to ever more dubious deviants from the text. This shows the Quran to be a nondefinite, or open, text. Ibn al-Jazarī's understanding of the text of verse 4 of surah 1 may be schematized as follows:

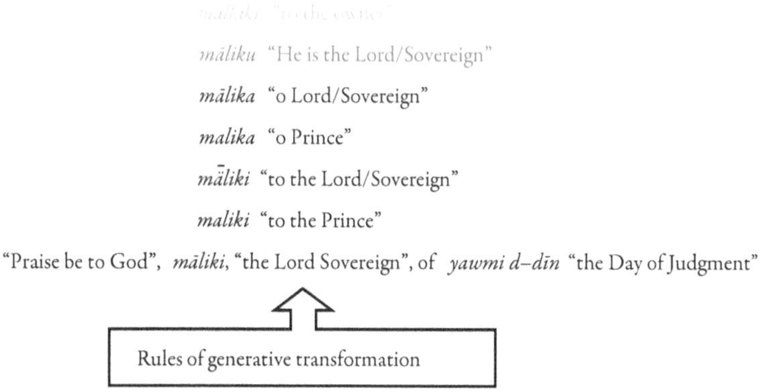

In this passage, four among the Ten Readers—ʿĀṣim among them—read *māliki yawmi d-dīn* (to the Lord/Sovereign of the Day of Judgment); the reading of the majority of the Ten Readers, *maliki yawmi d-dīn* (the Prince of the Day of Judgment) remains widely unknown. But Ibn al-Jazarī discusses further readings that meet his criteria. In one of these, for example, *mālika* appears instead of *māliki*. Here the noun stands in the accusative case of the address (O Lord . . . !). Ibn al-Jazarī comments, "A beautiful *qirāʾah*!"[93] The variant reading *maliki* also appears in the accusative: *malika* (O Prince . . . !). In the reading of ʿAlī the noun *malik* changes to the verb *malaka*, which means "to possess, to command, to be king of" (*malaka yawma d-dīn*). Another variant uses *malki* instead of *maliki*, apparently without a semantic shift.[94] The variant reading of *māliki* and *māliki* is purely phonetic. Another variant puts the noun into the nominative and alters the syntax of the whole passage: *māliku yawma d-dīn* (He is the Lord on the Day of Judgment). The consonantal form of the text is even affected by the variants *mallāki*, meaning "the owner," and *malīki* (the king), but both, Ibn al-Jazarī writes, are backed by analogical reasoning.[95]

All these variant readings belong, with different probabilities, to the seven *aḥruf*, and may well be genuine constituents of the divine revelation—but with most of these this cannot be pronounced with certainty. The continuous Quranic text is open to supplementation by the added dimensions of these variants. The very mechanism that generates further variant readings is itself counted as a component of the text.

This shows that Ibn al-Jazarī sees the Quran as a plural, open, hypertextually structured text whose semantic range never can be completely exhausted, but demands from its listeners and readers a new textual endeavor. Such an endeavor never leads toward absolute definiteness—and this concept, intrinsic to the classical Quranic disciplines, is incompatible with the modern Cartesian way of thought. But it is, in a way, *postmodern*. Is it possible, then, that the Islamic sciences in general, having left behind the rationalism of the Muʿtazilah, are essentially postmodern?

Western thought and its allies in the Islamic world are not tiring of demands that Islam return to the rationalism of the Muʿtazilah (that is, back into the third/ninth century) and build on it, bypassing all centuries since then to arrive finally to modern times. Muslims' hatred of their own history, internalized since the times of colonialism and consistently blocking a clear view of their own achievements in Ayyubid, Mamluk, and Ottoman times, also obstructs their view of the postmodern elements of these achievements—which emerge as much more up to date than the crude modernity to which Muslims of *all* shades have subscribed. Ever since the nineteenth century, the Islamic world has fixed its rabbit gaze on the snake of modernity, in the futile wish to become the snake itself. Therefore, accesses to Islam that are inspired by certain insights of postmodern thought seem to be beyond its horizon—even though its own tradition (albeit in the version of the postformative period, disdained up until now), offers a broad avenue to proceed.

But the concepts of the traditional sciences apparently have become incomprehensible to a great part—indeed the active and visible part—of the Islamic intelligentsia. It becomes clear that the problem is not that traditional, "medieval" Islam and its contemporary "fundamentalist" proponents are opposed to the forces of modernization, liberalization, and enlightenment. Rather, it is that fundamentalists and reformers alike, under the banner of the Western episteme, wage a war against their own culture. The opponents are not medieval versus modern times; it is the modern insistence on unambiguity versus the postmodern potential of the Islamic postformative tradition.

3
Does God Speak Ambiguously?

For there are some secret places in the Holy Scriptures into which God has not wished us to penetrate more deeply and, if we try to do so, then the deeper we go, the darker and darker it becomes, by which means we are led to acknowledge the unsearchable majesty of the divine wisdom, and the weakness of the human mind.

—Erasmus of Rotterdam, *De libero arbitrio*

THE INEXHAUSTIBILITY OF THE QURAN

The preceding chapter's account of Ibn al-Jazarī's manual has shown that classical scholars were convinced that the abundance of variation in the Quranic text was intended by God. They even saw in this abundance a particular sign of His grace, since the wealth of variant readings was intended as a relief for mankind, as well as an incentive to occupy oneself with the sacred text. In addition, the nonlinear structure that the Quranic text gains by the vertical polyphony of its various readings permits one to enrich certain passages through a plurality of meanings that complement and illuminate each other, without the necessity to augment the linear text itself.

If the semantic variety is perceived initially as an enrichment on the level of textual form, before the actual interpretation of the text begins, one will view a plurality of possible interpretations as a further enrichment. Ibn al-Jazarī provides a classical formulation for this:

> Ever since early times, the scholars of this community never stopped (and will never stop) deducing from the Quran (juridical) indications, arguments, proofs, insights, and so on, which earlier scholars had not yet realized, without exhausting it for future scholars. Rather, the Quran is a vast ocean in which one never reaches ground or is stopped by a shore. This is why this community is not in need of a further prophet after this one—God bless him and grant him salvation—as was the case with earlier peoples whose prophets were always supposed to pass judgment according to the rules of their writings and to lead man towards his salvation in this world and the next.[1]

Anyone who follows current discussions in and about Islam cannot help but be perplexed by Ibn al-Jazarī's formulation since it squarely contradicts the stance of present-day Islam. Today, a common opinion is that the Quran does not offer allowance for interpretation because it constitutes the uncreated word of God. This, the argument goes on, is the greatest obstacle on the path toward a "modernization" of Islam. This view is held not only by non-Muslims but also by Muslim reformers like Naṣr Ḥāmid Abū Zayd, who has devoted much of his thought to this problem.

From a Christian point of view, a good formulation of this position is voiced by the scholar of Islamic studies and Jesuit Father Christian Troll, who pointed out in an interview on Islam that with the advent of Christ for Christians, the revelation is completed, just as for Muslims, the completion of revelation came about with the advent of the Quran. Since the Quran, however, is a text which is "believed . . . word for word" (which arguably implies that it is to be interpreted literally), it cannot be viewed historically:

> The Roman catechism tells us that although the revelation is not completed, its content is not totally exhausted. . . . The great difference between this and Islam lies in the fact that at the center of the Christian faith stands not a text, but a person: Jesus Christ. This faith says that God . . . has decided to become a human being. Nothing greater and more conclusive can be predicated of God. Therefore, beyond this truth of faith, nothing new can be said. But this truth needs to be understood ever more profoundly. . . . The history of the Church is also a history of growing into the secret of God.

For Muslims, Troll says, the challenge posed by the end of revelation "is still more radical, because they, unlike us Christians, base themselves on a belief in the idea of a text as divine word for word, formulated in the seventh century and possessing unchanging validity for all times to come. How can one combine this belief with the universality of Islam, with the mission to reach all human beings and cultures, and with a mentality that strives to be open to the future?"[2]

The two texts, Ibn al-Jazarī's and Troll's, show astounding parallels. For Ibn al-Jazarī, the revelation is complete, but its contents are not exhausted because the semantic abundance of the Quran is inexhaustible. Each generation discovers something new in the Quran that preceding generations were not aware of, and for future generations, there still remains much to be discovered. If this is not a "mentality that strives to be open to the future," what is it?

For Ibn al-Jazarī, history is a "history of growing into the secret of God," as Christian Troll describes the Catholic position. The main difference between the two positions, indeed the sole difference, consists in the question of whether the medium of revelation has an influence on the range of interpretation—and if so, what kind of influence. It is not at all obvious that a text necessarily offers less range of interpretation than does the normative life of a person. Further, it can also be said that the life of Jesus is accessible only through texts, and that in Islam, too, the living model of a person, the life of the prophet Muḥammad, possesses normative power.

In contrast to Troll's point of view, Ibn al-Jazarī considers the mundane way of the life of a prophet to be temporal. Therefore, God sent a new prophet to each of the peoples again and again, as updates, as it were, on the divine revelation. Only the sending down of the Quran prevailed over this temporal and cultural conditionality. By virtue of its semantic wealth, the Quran is open to the future. The range of its interpretation, says Ibn al-Jazarī, makes a single prophecy for all times superfluous. This presupposes that the Quranic message harbors a plurality of meanings—that God speaks ambiguously. For Ibn al-Jazarī, this was self-evident.

In contemporary times, it is equally self-evident that a normative text must be unequivocal. Anyone today who believes in a text revealed to man by God will also presume that this text is unequivocal—an assumption that would not be shared by one who asserts that the Quran is uninterpretable. The entire argument must then look like this:

Premise (1): According to the prevalent Sunni-Islamic understanding, the Quranic text is the uncreated word of God.

Premise (2): God speaks unequivocally.

Conclusion: Every verse of the Quran has only one single correct meaning, which does not admit any interpretive margin, and therefore cannot be adjusted to changing temporal conditions.

If premise (2) is dropped, the conclusion also disappears. That is, the ontological status of the Quran according to the respective theology *in no way* affects the possibility of interpretation, since all meanings that are conceivable and reasonable at different times have already been incorporated in the text by God, even if not all of them have been perceived at various points in history. Therefore, independent of whether the Quran is seen as uncreated or created, one can extract from it a multiplicity of interpretations—a multiplicity that has its limits only in the postulate of consistency (lit., of containing no mutual contradictions), as the preceding chapter has shown.

Premise (2) is an idea of Cartesian modernity; the insistence on a single meaning for each Quranic passage, solely correct at all times, is a result of the *modernization* of Islam. Through the acceptance of premise (2), "Islam has made it into modernity," while simultaneously losing the flexibility to cope with the problems of modernity. From this perspective, the action of a person seems to offer a broader range of interpretations.

For scholars of classical Islam, the situation was exactly the reverse. This is documented by an intriguing hadith that as-Suyūṭī presents in his compendium on the Quranic disciplines, *al-Itqān fī ʿulūm al-Qurʾān*. This handbook, the most important of its kind to this day, contains a chapter on polysemy in the Quran (*al-wujūh wa-n-naẓāʾir*). Here the reader encounters a historical report on ʿAlī, who was fighting the rebellious Khārijites. He was approached by Ibn ʿAbbās, who declared that he was ready to meet the Khārijites and to convince them, with the help of the Quran. "O commander of the believers," said Ibn ʿAbbās, "I know the book of Allah better than they. After all, it was revealed among my family." "Yes," ʿAlī replied, "but the Quran contains many aspects of meaning (*wujūh*). Instead, conduct your controversy with them on the basis of the exemplary actions of the Prophet (*sunan*). From these they will not be able to escape."[3]

For the protagonists of this hadith—and hence also for as-Suyūṭī, who quotes it approvingly—the living example of the Prophet is far more unequivocal than the sacred text, which is open to different interpretations. Even if this assumption has never stopped Muslims from conducting arguments on the basis of the Quran, we can safely posit that the notion of the sunna as a more stable basis for proof than the Quran was prevalent in wide sections of premodern Islam. This gives us a glimpse into a classical commentary on the Quran. Let us take as an example a particularly difficult Quranic passage at the beginning of sura 79. This text, originating in the first Meccan period[4] (i.e., the beginning of the Prophet's preaching of the Quran), starts with a series of oath formulas that is followed by a description of the Last Judgment. Such oath formulas[5] display a very archaic vocabulary; in addition, the things by which the oaths are sworn are frequently named by adjectives that describe them but do not denote them. In a comparable form, this is also a stylistic device used in the contemporaneous poetry in ancient Arabic.[6] The large extant corpus of ancient Arabic poetry, however, almost always permits inclusion of the thing meant by that substitute word, whereas this is quite often not the case with the Quranic oaths.

In Arthur J. Arberry's translation, which tries to render the Quran in a form that gives at least an impression of the sound of the original, the beginning of the sura is given like this (I am also including the Arabic text; in order to achieve an acoustic suggestion of the sound of the original, one must articulate the *-an* which concludes a colon as *-ā*):

1	*wa-n-nāziʿāti gharqan*	By those that pluck out vehemently
2	*wa-n-nāshiṭāti nashṭan*	and those that draw out violently,
3	*wa-s-sābiḥāti sabḥan*	by those that swim serenely
4	*fa-s-sābiqāti sabqan*	and those that outstrip suddenly
5	*fa-l-mudabbirāti amran*	by those that direct an affair!

Admittedly, although Arberry's translation sounds good, much of it remains incomprehensible. But it is precisely this method of translation that gives a good impression of the original—which in this passage is no more comprehensible than is Arberry's translation. Even if his translation has not always hit on the right meaning, it has the incontestable merit that it does not strive to appear more comprehensible than the original. The German translation by Rudi Paret (1901–1983) is quite different, in that it claims to try to understand the Quran as it was understood in the period of its revelation. It fails, however, to arrive at a plausible version of the five introductory verses of sura 79. In complete disregard of the linguistic shape of the passage, this version presents the following brackets-and-question-marks-studded monstrosity—which is certainly not the way it was perceived during the period of the Quran's revelation. "1 By those who (in flinging the bowstring) fully stretch it (?) (or: who extract [?] by force [from the humans their soul] out of [their body]; or [if not angels, but horses are meant:] who vehemently tug at the reins), 2 who are extremely brisk 3 and rush off like wildfire (?) (lit., [with all fours] row [actually: swim]) 4 who overtake (all others) 5 and know how to manage an affair (?)."

It is clear that Paret, an experienced philologist, does not suggest that the text is comprehensible. He offers several interpretive options and includes four question marks. But he, too, is convinced that only one of these interpretations is the correct one.

This understanding has become so natural for us in contemporary times that we read a classical commentary using the same premise. Let us again take as an example the commentary of an "orthodox" author who does not reveal any Sufi or esoteric leanings and is accessible on today's traditionalist websites: the commentary on the Quran of the Shāfiʿite legal scholar al-Māwardī (364–450/974–1058), who worked in Baghdad. Only his explanation of verse 4 is given here:

For *fa-s-sābiqāti sabqan* there are five interpretations:

(1) The angels are meant, who overtake the satans when they deliver God's revelation to the prophets. This is maintained by ʿAlī and Masrūq; al-Ḥasan opines that they are before them with the faith.
(2) The stars are meant, of which one overtakes the other. This is maintained by Qatādah.
(3) Death is meant, which overtakes the souls, as Mujāhid maintains.
(4) The souls are meant, of which one overtakes the other, when at death it leaves the body. That is maintained by ar-Rabīʿ.
(5) ʿAṭāʾ maintains that the passage talks of horses.There is also a *sixth possible interpretation*, namely that the "ones that overtake each other" are the souls that arrive at Paradise or the infernal Fire before their bodies do.

It is striking that al-Māwardī puts the different interpretive options side by side, and does not introduce a hierarchy or give his own preference. In fact, his whole, relatively comprehensive work, only rarely contains an instance of his own opinion, in the sense of judging one interpretation more probable or more farfetched than another. This holds true not only for his work but also for the majority of the classical Quran commentaries. Still more rarely does an author go so far as al-Māwardī does, to enumerate the different possible interpretations.

Most interpretive options adduced by al-Māwardī refer back to older authorities—which were by no means limited to *as-salaf aṣ-ṣāliḥ*, "the righteous ancestors" invoked by today's Salafists. Sometimes, al-Māwardī quotes the opinions of his teacher. It is striking that he introduces his passage by saying that there are five interpretive options, but at the end adds a sixth one as worth considering. This practice is frequent throughout his entire commentary; he often adds, as an afterthought to a list of already existing interpretations, the words "and there is yet another possible interpretation." Doubtless, these "extra" options constitute interpretations offered by al-Māwardī himself. Therefore he does not subsume them under the already existing interpretations indicated by the headline "for this there exist *n* interpretations."

Here we see that the theory of the inexhaustible interpretive wealth of the Quran, formulated by Ibn al-Jazarī, among others, is confirmed in the practice of an "orthodox" Quran commentator who has no misgivings about adding the results of his own reflections to the older traditions. (This would be only natural for Sufi Quran commentators—to whose numbers al-Māwardī does not belong.) It is true that Quran commentators who confine themselves to explaining the Quran through hadith passages (*tafsīr bi-l-maʾthūr*), or through brief works that present only one possible interpretation, do not display this kind of interpretive procedure. We must assume, nevertheless, that these authors share the basic epistemological assumption of their time, according to which any interpretation may claim only probability and not certainty, and the probable correctness of an interpretation does not categorically exclude another interpretation. This is evidenced by the fact that al-Māwardī does not attempt to posit his own interpretation as the only correct one, in contrast to the other ones. For him, it is merely an additional interpretation that might also be applicable.

In this regard, al-Māwardī acts as a perfect exegete should, if one applies what as-Suyūṭī says in his chapter on *al-wujūh wa-n-naẓāʾir.* Here as-Suyūṭī quotes the hadith: "Nobody can claim perfect understanding before he has grasped many *wujūh* (aspects of meaning) in the Quran." This hadith, the author goes on, is explained as follows: "This means that when someone encounters a linguistic expression that can be perceived with different meanings, he will not confine himself to one meaning, but will perceive it in its different meanings, as long as they do not contradict each other." Resonating with the theory of Quranic readings as *simultaneously* correct, if they are well transmitted and free from mutual contradiction, as-Suyūṭī's words express the conviction that different meanings may coexist as simultaneously valid ones, as long as they do not ostensibly contradict each other. Therefore it is possible, and indeed not improbable, that in the Quranic verse 79:4 angels *as well as* stars, etc., are meant. In his commentary *al-Kashshāf*, az-Zamakhsharī has beautifully demonstrated how one can consistently relate all four verses, respectively, to angels, horses, stars, and souls.[7]

If one accepts this assumption about the plurality of Quranic readings, one will perceive in the interpretive variety of the Quran no deficiency, but rather an enrichment. When classical commentators put several interpretive options (on occasion, relatively abstruse ones) side by side without commentary, they are simply following this principle of the possibility of parallel truths. From the nineteenth century on, the Western world ceased to understand this principle. Instead, the lists of meanings in the Quranic commentaries were held to be "scholastic" quibbles, signs of submissiveness to authority, or indications of the fact that the commentators were unable to understand the Quran.

The impression that the classical Quran commentators were submissive to authority is probably due to the fact that, on the one hand, they were convinced of the simultaneous possibility of the truth of different interpretations and the potential inexhaustibility of the text, but on the other hand, they almost never (if they were not Sufis or esoterics) attempted to go substantially beyond the interpretations that were transmitted from older authorities.

This conservative approach can again best be explained as an effort to *domesticate ambiguity*. The best one could do was to collect and keep interpretations that were already articulated, and to economize with these old interpretations as long as no novel interpretation seemed to be necessary. There is also a progressive aspect to this approach, since any other approach would have had the potential to stir up an ambiguity crisis, and it seemed preferable to cultivate ambiguity than to let it proliferate uncontrolled. The cultures of the Islamic world were shaped, perhaps more than any other cultures, by texts and the commentaries and interpretations upon them. Not only religious texts but also secular works were commented on; for example, the secular ancient Arabic poems and later literary works like al-Mutanabbī's poems and the *Maqāmahs* of al-Ḥarīrī. In general, there was an awareness of what could, by *in*terpretation of a text, gotten *out* of it. Aṣ-Ṣafadī warns against excessive interpretation of a text: "If someone really wanted to interpret the *Muʿallaqah* of Imraʾalqays (a pre-Islamic poem about love and heroism) as an elegy on a cat or a love poem to an elephant, he would certainly find ways and means."[8]

In the context of premodern times, in which living conditions changed only gradually, this attitude favored a good coexistence of stability and plurality. When living conditions began to change rapidly in the nineteenth century, this balance was challenged by a culture that demanded unequivocal answers and did not want to accept the simultaneous coexistence of different truths. The consciousness of the plural truth of the sacred text came increasingly close to vanishing. The old, differing interpretations were no longer considered as simultaneously valid alternatives, but rather as different attempts to find the only correct interpretation. And the best solution appeared to lie in having only one interpretation.

Thus the Salafist Ibn ʿUthaymīn knows of only one interpretation of Q 79:4, which runs as follows:

> *Fa-s-sābiqāti sabqan* means the angels who in precipitate obedience to God—He is mighty and exalted—execute His order. Therefore the angels are faster and stronger in obeying God's orders than are the human beings. God—He is exalted—says when He describes the angels of the hellfire: "And over [the fire] are harsh, terrible angels who disobey not God in what He commands them and do what they are commanded." (Q 66:6) And the Exalted and Mighty says also: "And those who are with Him wax not too proud to do Him service, neither grow weary, glorifying Him by night and in the daytime and never failing." (Q 21:19–20) Due to their strength and power to execute God's orders—He is mighty and exalted—the angels overtake God's order of what He orders, and they are not disobedient against what He orders and do what He decrees.[9]

This commentary might astonish those who believe that modern Muslim fundamentalists, especially Salafists, orient themselves toward Islamic tradition. While classical commentators of all sorts naturally quote the transmitted interpretations of the ancestors (*as-salaf*)—at least among others—and, as a rule, several different ones, the Salafi Ibn ʿUthaymīn, unique among the commentators, does not quote any *salaf.* He refrains from putting several interpretive options side by side, or even considering that there may exist several forms of interpretation; he knows of only one. And this one is an interpretation that the classical commentaries themselves do *not* know!

Admittedly, the interpretation that the "overtaking ones" are angels is a common one, and the question of whom the angels overtake, and in what respect, finds different answers (al-Māwardī quotes two of them). Ibn ʿUthaymīn's answer, however, is not to be found in the usual commentaries, neither in those that concentrate on the collection of exegetical hadiths[10] nor in Ibn Kathīr, whose classical commentary is the one most widely used by today's fundamentalists. It is not to be found even in the commentary of Ibn al-Jawzī, who as a Ḥanbalite is a member of the legal school from which the ideology of the Salafists originated. Ibn al-Jawzī knows only of the following three interpretations, all of which he can trace back to one of the "ancestors": "First interpretation: The angels are meant. There are three opinions on what that signifies. (1): They overtake the satans when they deliver God's revelation to the prophets. This is maintained by ʿAlī and Masrūq. (2): They overtake the believers with the believers' spirit in Paradise. This is maintained by Mujāhid and Abū Rawq. (3): They overtake man with the faith, as al-Ḥasan maintained."[11]

This shows that the interpretation of the "traditionalist" Ibn ʿUthaymīn is made without recourse to tradition. Instead, he quotes two Quranic verses that also happen to refer to angels. His method is guided by the principle of the "interpretation of the Quran by means of the Quran."

As-Suyūṭī has shown in his chapter on *al-wujūh wa-n-naẓāʾir* that it is precisely because of the miraculous properties of the Quran that one and the same word can have quite different meanings, to a degree that exceeds the homonymy of everyday language. He implies that caution is advised against assigning to a word in context *x* the same meaning that it has in context *y*.

But Ibn ʿUthaymīn's interpretation is even more risky, for the word *sābiqāt* (or merely the root *s-b-q*, which is the actual object of explanation) does not even figure in the two passages the author has mobilized for his interpretation. Ibn ʿUthaymīn has done nothing but pick two Quranic passages that talk of angels in a manner that seems to him equally plausible for the interpretation of Q 79:4. It is probably no coincidence that this interpretation lends itself more to moral exhortation than do most classical interpretations.

Ibn ʿUthaymīn's thought is clearly not irrational or reactionary. He follows the rational tenets of Cartesian modernity and bases his thinking on the absence of mutual contradictions in normative texts. He believes that only *one* interpretation can be true, and is convinced that since he knows how to use reason, he knows this interpretation, even if he disregards the tradition.

The objection that it is not modern and enlightened to believe in angels and other supernatural beings does not hold. First, it is not correct historically, and second, the issue is not so much *what* is believed in as *how* something is believed in.[12] And Ibn ʿUthaymīns's belief that he is able, by his own hermeneutical effort, to achieve the only true and possible interpretation is a modern belief. Consequently, his interpretation is conceptually different from the traditional interpretations.

As a result, the Salafist movement is not traditionalist. As far as I can see, the traditionalists themselves have thus far done little to counter the Salafist fervor. Unlike Ibn ʿUthaymīn, they continue to cultivate the interpretive plurality of the old authorities; yet they seem to have lost, to a great extent, their traditional epistemological foundations. Without these foundations, an interpretation can only be either right or wrong, and only one interpretation can be right. In this respect, modern traditionalism is not too far from modernist trends.

The most important difference is that for a traditionalist today, it is scarcely conceivable that the right interpretation would not be documented in the tradition, for this would mean that God has kept His community deceived for over a thousand years. The nearest way out of this dilemma is to choose from the old interpretations one that is approved by a high authority, and to declare it to be probably the right one. Thus the modernization of Islam's epistemological foundations actually complicates the adaptation of pertinent statements to the problems of modernity. The result is what is commonly—and not without justification—perceived as ossification and dogmatism. This ossification occurs because the belief in the preordained ambiguity of the divine word has been given up; preceding generations are perceived as walking in error, and an interpretation not yet known to them is explained as being the right one.

If one does not entertain these scruples around ambiguity, as many modernists do, the tradition turns out to be nothing but a burden one has to shed, because in searching for the one true meaning, one no longer needs the many different interpretations, a great number of which appear to be improbable anyway. The Pakistani reformist Muslim Khalid Zaheer, a student of the reformer Islahi, writes: "Islahi always said that every Qur'anic verse has, on the basis of its formulation and its context, only one correct meaning. For me, this means that the opinion, held by many exegetes, that there are different, and often contradictory, options to interpret a verse, is not correct. For when the Almighty intends to say something, he does so in a clear way. His sayings denote something unequivocal. As a rule, He would insist that a given verse has only one meaning."[13]

For Zaheer, to put different and often mutually contradictory interpretations side by side is not acceptable. And since such coexistence has become meaningless even for many traditionalists, this statement, in the present situation, is nothing but consequent. The students of Islahi who argue this way, it is true, are not able to solve the problem of the perennial validity of the Quran, since the sole valid meaning would have to have been valid in the past too—even though this meaning was not necessarily known or understood.

Non-Muslims frequently suggest to Muslims a *historicization* of the Quranic text, meaning an interpretation of the Quran within the context of the historical situation in which it was revealed. However, this offers only an apparent solution, because again, only one single meaning is acknowledged as the right one—in this case, the meaning of the text at the historical point of its revelation. From this meaning (if it can be discovered with sufficient certainty at all) a timeless "core" is then distilled, and applied to situations of the present time. This method unites two characteristic features better than any other. For one, it is highly *manipulative*, that is, it is not difficult to always distill that "core" that one wants to hear. It opens the door to *ittibāʿ al-hawā* (following one's own whim), which Muslim scholars have always tried to avoid. Secondly, it is extremely *reductive*, since it not only insists on one sole possible meaning, but also constricts this meaning to a certain historical moment, and thus hollows out the semantic potential of the text more than do other comparably monolithic approaches.

On the other hand, if one presumes that religious texts present a timeless semantic potential, one can draw a comparison with literary texts. It may be highly interesting for a student of English literature to know how the audience of the Globe Theater understood Shakespeare's *Romeo and Juliet.* For the present-day theatergoer, however, this question is irrelevant. The environment, the consciousness, the range of private feelings, the ways to love—all this is totally different from Shakespeare's times. Yet *Romeo and Juliet* displays sufficient semantic relevance for present-day theatergoers to challenge them intellectually and stir them emotionally, even if the meanings they bring to it often have little to do with the meanings which Shakespeare's audience associated with it.

One should not go too far in presenting analogies with literary texts. But it should be pointed out that texts to which one ascribes a timeless semantic potential cannot be reduced to the meaning they had for their first audience. The constriction of a historical-critical interpretation of the Quran would never allow for a Sufi interpretation, since at the time of the revelation of the Quran, there existed nothing resembling the later mystical movement.

In general, it must be stated that a Quranic exegesis oriented toward the premises of the modern West is, *as such*, no more open and more tolerant of ambiguity than a traditional one. Modern approaches to interpretation call for "openness" not in order to *join* traditional approaches but to *replace* them, and since they lay a claim to exclusive truth, they are more susceptible to ideology than are traditional methods. To grant the Quranic text a timeless semantic potential and a semantic plurality, as the classical scholars did (which did not always necessarily have an impact on their demeanor)—this may be the only possible way to overcome the time-conditioned situation of Quranic exegesis.

THE THEOLOGIZATION OF ISLAM

There is no consistent discipline regarding "the science of the Quran" in classical Islam. Rather, there are several disciplines that deal entirely or partially with the Quran, each of which selects a different object of investigation and a different methodological approach to the Quran. Nevertheless, it makes sense to speak of the *ʿulūm al-Qurʾān*, the Quranic disciplines, in the plural; this is due to the

Cairene scholar az-Zarkashī (745–794/1344–1392), who assembled the relevant disciplines in a compendium called "The demonstration of the Quranic sciences" (*al-Burhān fī ʿulūm al-Qurʾān*). Still broader dissemination was achieved by as-Suyūṭī with his work "The perfection of the Quranic sciences" (*al-Itqān fī ʿulūm al-Qurʾān*, already quoted a number of times), which strongly relies on az-Zarkashī's work.

At first glance, we can find in these handbooks[14] many sections based on the science of tradition, that is, the knowledge of hadith. These sections deal with the exterior conditions—the historical background and the social situation—that were the causes for revelation of the various Quranic verses; contrary to popular prejudice, these are interpreted by the exegetes in the light of their historicity. Historical and text-critical approaches are employed in the sections on the history and form of the Quranic text.

Further chapters refer to the disciplines of Quranic readings and recitation. An extensive linguistic section follows. Lexicographical chapters deal with dialectical expressions and foreign words in the Quran, among other topics, and also with polysemous and even incomprehensible expressions. The Quranic exegesis described in the following sections obtains its methods, to a large extent, from legal methodology (*uṣūl al-fiqh*), whose origins are in turn linguistics and rhetoric. Finally, we find purely rhetorical and stylistic chapters, followed by some sections that defy further systematization (for instance, the inimitability of the Quran, persons alluded to but not named, peculiarities and salvific qualities of single verses, script, types of Quran commentaries, and indications of which ones are the most well-known).

This is the horizon of the classical science of the Quran, which rests in equal degrees upon historical, linguistic, rhetorical, stylistic, and juridical-exegetical methods. One discipline that we would first expect in such a handbook is completely missing in this list: theology. Quite demonstrably, for as-Suyūṭī and his contemporaries, theology has little to contribute to the understanding of the Quran.

It is important to recognize that the Arabic term *kalam*, which we translate here as "theology," is not congruent with our modern understanding of the academic discipline of theology. The discipline of *kalam* focuses on the dogmatic theology of God, His attributes, His revelation (which, as God's "speech," is one of His attributes), His creation and the position of man in it, and (here in particular) the question of predestination.

It is obvious that the tenets of the theologians' dogma are derived from the Quran, or are buttressed by arguments from the Quran and tradition. It is equally obvious that the theologians make statements based on the ontological status of the Quran; in other words, they make use of the insights of the Quranic disciplines. In contrast, most scholars who dealt with Quranic exegesis did not see themselves as "theologians." In biographical collections, they are presented sometimes specifically as *mufassir* (exegete of the Quran), and more frequently by reference to their original scholarly disciplines, that is, as scholars of law, linguistics, or hadith; sometimes simply as "scholars" (*ʿulamāʾ*)—but hardly ever as theologians who strove for an understanding of the right belief (a concept that did not count as a problem of Quranic exegesis). Consequently, these scholars did not attempt to derive from the Quran a comprehensive dogmatic system of Islam, a system that would exceed the scope of the basic truths of the Islamic faith as formulated by the *kalam* scholars.

In fact, the archetype of the scholar of the classical period is not the theologian but the jurist. Jurists, when they acted as judges, may have had occasion to issue decisions on theological questions—for instance, in the case of Ibn Taymiyyah (661–728/1263–1328), whose radically Ḥanbalite zeal endangered the social peace, whereupon he was accused of anthropomorphic heresy and taken to jail. In this case, the *ʿulamāʾ* used theological arguments, but they would not have formed the idea that all their activities took place under the roof of theology. The modern concept of theology as a scholarly reflection on faith and its forms of expression would have appeared strange to them, since they viewed their activity as legal scholars and linguists, and not as a theological one, and often, probably, not even as an expressly religious one. The exegetical procedures, after all, are largely independent from the nature of the texts to be interpreted.

The respective approach and epistemological aims of theologians are substantially different from those of legal scholars. Jurists are not out to explore the *truths* of the faith; they are expected to pass judgment according to probability. A telling example of the irritations that may be caused by a theological insistence on unequivocal truths can be seen in the work on variant readings by Ibn al-Jazarī. For Quran readers, every reading of a passage in which the transmission is sound, and which does not clearly contradict the rules of grammar and the ʿUthmānic codices, is seen as acceptable and therefore as part and parcel of the "seven *aḥruf*." What is the case, however, with variant readings whose transmission is not so well attested, but which might still be correct? Ibn al-Jazarī writes:

> If it is not established that a reading belongs to the seven *aḥruf*, can one definitely conclude that it does *not* belong to the seven *aḥruf*? The great majority is of the opinion that a definitive conclusion on this is not necessary. Whether or not a reading belongs to the seven *aḥruf*, these scholars hold, is not a question about which we are bound to have certain knowledge. We agree with

> this view, and Makkī, with his statement "How evil acts he who rejects (such a view)!," points in the same direction. Some theologians (*ahl al-kalām*), however, thought that it was necessary to definitively conclude that a reading does not belong to the seven *aḥruf*; some among them even went so far as to decide that he who does not regard the *basmalah*—except in the sura "The Ant"—as part of the Quranic text commits a sin. Others decided that to the contrary, he who regards it (always) as part of the Quranic text commits a sin. They thought, to wit, that the Quran leaves no space for individual endeavors to arrive at a right decision (*ijtihād*), and that therefore it is necessary to know for certain that a given reading is to be rejected. In fact, however, it is right that *both opinions are simultaneously true* (*ḥaqq*), and that the *basmalah* in some *qirāʾāt* constitutes a verse of the Quran, to wit, in the reading of those who see the *basmalah* as a separator between surahs, but that it does not constitute a Quranic verse for those who do not ascribe that function to the *basmalah*. God knows best.[15]

This passage shows that for Ibn al-Jazarī, the Quran is an open text. The single readings apply, or they do not, and this happens with varying probability. The readings that are accepted by the broad majority are correct to such a high degree of probability that one may assuredly rely on them. However, one cannot absolutely know whether the readings that are not so well attested are as correct as the former ones, that is, whether or not they constitute a part of the seven *aḥruf* in which God has revealed the Quran.

Muslim theologians and legal scholars differentiate between *definitive knowledge* (*ʿilm qaṭʿī*) and *hypothetical knowledge* (*ʿilm ẓannī*). Definitive knowledge belongs in the domain of the theologians. An article of faith cannot be probably true; it is either true or false. A theologian issuing a statement such as "Probably there is only one God" would not have made much of a career.

It is not easy to arrive at statements of certainty that do not allow for doubt, especially in a discipline that is based on tradition. But for the reader of the Quran, it simply is not necessary to have certain knowledge about the admissibility of a reading to the seven *aḥruf*. On the contrary, as Ibn al-Jazarī points out in another passage,[16] it is meritorious work to take pains to determine the credibility of a given reading. However, the theologians to whom Ibn al-Jazarī refers here view the problem differently. For them, it is indeed necessary to possess definitive knowledge about the question of what belongs to the Quranic text and what does not, since for the Quran a "personal endeavor" (*ijtihād*) is not possible. In the example presented above, their approach amounts to questioning the accepted readings.

Basmalah means the formula *bi-smi llāhi r-raḥmāni r-raḥīm* (in the name of God, the Merciful, the Compassionate) which introduces every Quranic sura (except the ninth) and which is found, in one place, in the middle of a sura ("The Ants," Q 27:30). In some readings, the introductory *basmalah* is counted as a part of the Quranic text; in others, it is not. For Ibn al-Jazarī, this does not pose a problem. In some good readings the *basmalah* is part of the Quranic text and in others it is not, therefore it is logically *both* part and not part of the Quranic text. Both propositions are for him equally *true*.

Thus there are things that can very well be true and whose opposites can also be true. The fact that there were theologians who had decidedly opposite opinions demonstrates that the insistence on one single truth, in the present-day sense, did exist in Ibn al-Jazarī's time. However, the society in which he lived, informed and shaped by a tolerance of ambiguity, was capable of containing such claims and pointing out their limitations. In the view of Ibn al-Jazarī, those theologians, insisting on a single truth, had clearly transgressed these limitations.

Today, an argument such as that of Ibn al-Jazarī would meet with incomprehension. The multiplicity of classical approaches to the religion of Islam—based on analyses of tradition, law, aesthetics, culture—yields more and more to the approach of theology. In classical Islam, many questions of religion were asked not only by theologians but also by legal scholars, linguists, philologists, historians, and Sufis, and were answered according to the specific methods of each discipline. All approaches were considered collectively relevant for religion, without being assigned to "theology" as an independent science of religious faith. The claims to truth brought to bear by the respective disciplines were accordingly diverse.

In religion today (at least in its interior perspective), the sole authority of theology reigns. So people put theological questions to Islam and expect theological answers. The hosts of so-called critics of Islam constantly demand *theological* answers to problems that have little or nothing to do with theology (and, more often than not, even with Islam), and leave no choice to Muslims but to push forward with the theologization of their religion. The innumerable interreligious conferences and papers bringing together Muslim representatives and Christian theologians inadvertently foster this tendency; after all, in such contexts, one expects to hear statements from Muslims that match Christian theological patterns of thought. Many brief publications on Islam, in the form of pocketbooks or books on the religions of the world, largely concentrate on the content and practice of Islamic faith (i.e., "What do Muslims believe?"). Even the intra-Islamic discussion of methods—frequently constricted to the dichotomy of reformist vs. fundamentalist—is often conducted along the lines of Western patterns.

This theologization has changed Islam profoundly. Traditional answers that were often not theological, in a strict sense, suddenly appear to be instances of an ossified dogmatism, since their original ontological foundations have disappeared and been replaced by those of theology. Based on this new foundation, the old answers appear to constitute a dogma, and to display a claim to truth and exclusivity that they did not originally possess. Since they now enter the stage with a claim to truth, they can be countered only by according opposite standpoints parading equally dogmatic aspirations. Thus we see theological controversies arising that were never seen in classical times.

The position of Islam on the translation of the Quran shows how, seen from the perspective of Islam's theologization, a traditional position can be misunderstood, and how Islam is implied to have held positions that are quite different from its original ones. According to a current and widely held opinion, translating the Quran is not allowed. Even scholars of Islamic Studies talk of a veritable "prohibition of translation."[17] The following text may serve as a typical demonstration of this concept of "prohibition of translation." Typically, it contains the word "theology," respectively "theologians," no less than three times:

> For many centuries, the Quran was not allowed to be translated into another language, because the dogma of Islamic theology on the 'inimitability' of the Quran was interpreted by Muslim theologians to mean that a Quran was supposed to exist only in the form of its original revelation.
>
> A translation, they said, would never be equal to the ur-text, and therefore would not be an actual Quran. According to the opinion of Muslim theology the language of the Quran is perfect in every respect. It is the most beautiful Arabic, and the text shows insuperable harmony and perfection.... Only in more recent times—particularly in the past three or four decades—the ban on translation has been relaxed. Today, for missionary purposes, numerous translations of the Quran are published, financed for the most part by Saudi Arabia.[18]

Indeed, it is correct to state that a translation is never equivalent to its urtext. This holds not only for the Quran, but also for the poems of Shelley. The supposed "inimitability" of the Quran, however, is not due to a "dogma" but to the interpretation of certain Quranic verses which say that the unbelievers are incapable of producing something like this Quran (Q 2:23–24; 10:38; 11:13; 17:88; 52:33–34). This "rendering-incapable-of-the-unbelievers" (*iʿjāz*) is to be regarded as an authenticating miracle through which the prophet Muḥammad has confirmed his divine message. This is in fact a theological consideration, and to believe in the divine message of the Prophet is indeed a dogma of Islam. But it is hardly a dogma to be asked to look for the corroborating miracle in the *language* of the Quran. In the usual catechisms, there is no word of it. And from the beginning, there were other interpretations, for instance the theory of *ṣarfah* (preventing/turning away) according to which the unbelievers' incapacity to produce something like the Quran is ascribed to the fact that God Himself has prevented or diverted them from doing so.

Nevertheless, the thesis of the inimitability of the Quranic style has gained wide acceptance. However, its most important propagator, ʿAbd-al-Qāhir al-Jurjānī, was no theologian, but a grammarian, a scholar of rhetoric and of literature, and his method was that of linguistics, rhetoric, and literary esthetics. He achieved groundbreaking results in these fields. But he has not proclaimed theological dogmas. At any rate, reading al-Jurjānī (a German translation is available)[19] makes it clear that the Quran has an aesthetic dimension[20] and that one cannot translate it without losing part of this dimension.

But *not to be able* does not mean *not to be allowed*. What is the matter with the alleged prohibition of translation? First, it is notable that during the entire premodern history of Islam, there is no known case of somebody being convicted or even accused of translating the Quran. The prohibition, clearly, didn't have much clout.

We are helped by the Quran commentary of az-Zamakhsharī (467–538/1075–1144), who was a major authority for many centuries, and who developed the following theological argument in his commentary on Q 14:4: The Quran, he writes, says that every prophet was sent to his community using its proper language. Muḥammad, on the other hand, was sent not only to the Arabs, but to all mankind (Q 7:158). How does that square with the fact that the message was only revealed in Arabic, but not in the other languages of mankind? Zamakhsharī's answer is: Had God revealed His message in more than one language, He would have been compelled to reveal it in *all* other languages (because a "representative choice" would have been out of question). This would have led to an excess of diversity.

To use our own terminology: the revelation in only one language is a sort of divine domestication of ambiguity. If the divine message is revealed in only one language, then naturally it should be in the language of its prophet, because his community is closest to him and its members understand him most clearly. A revelation in languages other than Arabic is not necessary, because there are translators who take on this task and, "as is the case now," Zamakhsharī writes, forward the meanings of the Quran to all peoples. Thus all people can understand the meanings of the Quran, even though not all people can participate in the exegesis of the primary Arabic text.[21]

Az-Zamakhsharī does not discuss the pros and cons of translations of the Quran. For him, living in Central Asia and working as an author of one of the oldest multilingual dictionaries of the Islamic world, translations of the Quran are an everyday reality. Indeed, they serve the solution of the theological problem of a message addressed to *all* peoples, but revealed only in *one* language.[22]

If translations of the Holy Book in Islam have less significance than in Christianity, the reason for this must be sought elsewhere, rather than in theology. The reason lies, as mentioned above, in literary aesthetics, and first and foremost in a kind of exegesis, trained in juridical methodology, that does not aim at unequivocal truths but strives for an interpretive spectrum scaled along different degrees of probability. According to this kind of exegesis, the Quran is, to repeat Ibn al-Jazarī's words, "a vast ocean in which one never touches ground or is stopped by a shore." A translation cannot be as unfathomable and shoreless as the original text. The translator has to make a choice. In the words of Hans-Georg Gadamer, "he must state clearly how he understands. But since he is always in the position of not really being able to express all the dimensions of his text, he must make a constant renunciation. Every translation that takes its task seriously is at once clearer and flatter than the original."[23] The translator cannot render *fa-s-sābiqāti sabqan* in six ways at the same time. Six meanings, more than one of which may be right, can be simultaneously preserved only by a commentator (who might not be aware of a seventh meaning that may be equally right). A translation, in contrast to a commentary, is always *disambiguating.* If the ambiguity of a text is viewed as its essential component, any translation will result in a text substantially reduced in dimension.

The Quranic passages that are relevant for Islamic law present this problem in a particularly urgent way, since these passages, too, display a spectrum of possible interpretations. It is the task of the legal exegetes to translate this spectrum, by disambiguation, into concrete juridical regulations. But should the legal exegete base his work on a Persian translation, his point of departure would be a text for which the translator had already performed the job of disambiguation. The translator may strive to retain the meaning of the text, "but since it must be understood within a new language world, it must establish its validity within it in a new way. Thus every translation is at the same time an interpretation. We can even say that the translation is the culmination of the interpretation that the translator has made of the words given him."[24]

In this sense, only in the original version is interpretive openness preserved. It is significant to note that no regime in the Islamic world has ever succeeded in enforcing an "authoritative" translation of the Quran from above, although such an exploitation of religion by the state must always have been attractive. It is a highly appreciable achievement of the middle class in the Islamic world to have prevented such a usurpation of religion by politics. In Western Christianity, the defensive attitude against a translation of the Bible (already translated into Latin) into the vernacular languages was aimed at preserving a monopoly of power over the text. In this case, translation constituted an act of emancipation. Similarly, in the Islamic world, the content of the Quran was made accessible to people who had no command of Arabic, by way of interlinear versions and translations of Quran commentaries (aṭ-Ṭabarī's monumental commentary was already translated into Persian and Turkish by the tenth century AD).[25] By keeping to the Arabic original text for ritual and law, in the interest of retaining its aesthetic value and its range of ambiguity, the authority over the text remained with the middle class, from which came the reciters, readers, commentators of the Quran, and the legal scholars. In this case, the emancipatory act consisted in the defense of the text's aesthetic values and also its potential for ambiguity. In recent times, no "relaxation of the ban" has happened, as the quotation above suggests. Rather, translations of the Quran are now used for ideological aims, such as proselytization, and used by states and organizations to enforce their own interpretation of the Quran.

To summarize: A prohibition on translating the Quran never existed. There were translations and explications of the text available in many languages. Muslim scholars never intended to withhold the Holy Book from people or to "stultify" the population. However, the classical Islamic world was aware that translation means reduction. First of all, there is a loss of its aesthetic dimension, which was seen as a crucial characteristic of the divine text (differently from Christianity). Secondly, the translated text suffers a reduction of ambiguity and forfeits part of the semantic potential of the original. The translation is more one-dimensional, and thus ideologically more open to manipulation, than the original; it makes a stronger claim to truth than does the commentary, which is able to present a multitude of interpretations side by side. What Zygmunt Bauman has formulated in another context holds also true in this instance: "As they stand together, and because they stand together and cannot but remain in each other's company (as no one has the right to stand alone; on its own, each one is a lie), each interpretation cancels the rest. Between themselves, they provide what each one separately denies and hides: the impossibility of fathoming the full depth of the multilayered world of meanings."[26]

4
The Blessing of Dissent

Unanimity of opinion may be fitting for a church, for the frightened or dazzled victims of some . . . myth, or for the weak and willing followers of some tyrant; variety of opinion is a feature necessary for objective knowledge; and a method that encourages variety is also the only method that is compatible with a humanistic outlook.

—Paul K. Feyerabend, *Problems of Empiricism*

HADITH AS A THEORY OF PROBABILITY

The Quran is God's speech. This makes it the highest-ranking source of Islamic law. But although Ibn al-Jazarī holds that the meanings contained in it are infinite, its volume is not. The most current calculation comes up with 6,236 verses. Very few of them, however, deal with legally relevant topics. The number of these *āyāt al-aḥkām* (verses which may be relevant for legal judgments) is calculated at between two hundred and five hundred. Thus, the Quran is a highly important but also very limited source of law. Even questions about ritual are frequently not addressed. Anyone who would attempt to determine, solely on the basis of the Quran, when and how often a Muslim is supposed to perform his prayer, would not get very far. The Quran *does* contain some passages on prayer, but nothing on how often, when, and in what manner it should be performed. The daily five prayers, common all over Islam, are not mentioned;

instead, there is a remark on a "night prayer," which—as is well known—is not practiced.[1]

The same applies to another pillar of Islamic life, the pilgrimage. One can read in the Quran *that* it is obligatory, but without the tradition of the Prophet's practice, no one would know *how* it is to be performed. Other areas of Islamic life are even less documented in the Quran. Its sparse statements on the prohibition of usury do not begin to constitute a trade law. The statement "The judgment is God's alone" (Q 6:57; 12:40, 67) has never been utilized as a basis for politics (except, perhaps, by the Khārijites in the first/seventh century), until today's Islamists took it up. Their spectacular attempts to reimplement ancient Islamic penal law cannot hide the fact that the vast majority of what constitutes penal law in our societies, and the whole of injury law, are nowhere addressed in the Quran. In this context, press releases stating that this or that country applies the Sharia law, with the Quran as the sole legal code, are somewhat absurd.

As these examples show, the Quran as a giver of norms for Islamic law is widely insufficient. Therefore, there were—and there are—few attempts to do without the exemplary practice of the Prophet—the sunna. Shiism is no exception to this, even if it uses source texts other than the ones used by the Sunnis. The sunna, of course, is available not directly, but only via the tradition of the sayings and acts of the Prophet, his companions, and their successors. A report on such a saying or such an act is called *ḥadīth*. (Its correct plural form is *aḥādīth*, but the word has become so familiar in English usage that I employ the usual English plural form *hadiths*). A hadith consists of two parts. The actual text (*matn*) is introduced by the *isnād*, (chain of transmission), naming the people who have transmitted the hadith through the generations, from the Prophet up to the respective author (we have seen that Quranic readings also have such an *isnād*). In addition to the single report, hadith also signifies the sum of all traditions. The scholarly disciplines that deal with the hadith are called *ʿulūm al-ḥadīth*.

Although the hadith tradition is even more important than the Quran for the formation of Islam and particularly Islamic law, I deal with it here only briefly, because much of what has been said about the Quran and the Quranic disciplines also applies to the hadith tradition and the classical hadith disciplines. In many respects, the analogy between these two areas is quite astounding; it confirms once again the observation that there exists a principle—namely, the domestication of ambiguity coupled with the greatest possible theoretical openness—that guides all Islamic disciplines.

First of all, the hadith corpus is a corpus with open margins. This is relevant to the question of how many *aḥādīth al-aḥkām* there are, that is, how many hadiths containing legally relevant material. While for the Quran the number of such verses, *āyāt al-aḥkām*, varies between two and five hundred, the calculations of the number of *aḥādīth al-aḥkām* range from eight hundred to seven thousand.[2]

The wide variation in these estimates is due primarily to the fact that there is no single book in which all valid hadiths are listed. Instead, there was an early phase during which the transmission of hadiths happened orally, and written records were meant primarily for personal purposes; then, from the eighth century on, hadiths were systematically collected and compiled in larger compendia. However, it was inevitable that among the hundreds of thousands of hadiths in circulation, many of them—indeed, the conspicuously greater part—turned out to be unreliable, if not forged. Therefore, during the ninth century, collectors of hadith, foremost of all al-Bukhārī (194–256/810–870) and Muslim (ca. 202–261/817–875), began to establish strict criteria for admitting a hadith into their collections. This meant that hadiths considered well-attested by other compilers did not figure in their books, and that whole areas of topics were insufficiently represented. Instead of putting an end to the production of hadith collections (which had not been the intention of those two compilers), their work stimulated the publication of further collections, each of which presented their own claim to authenticity.

Basically, all significant steps in the formative phase of the hadith disciplines may be explained along the lines of *crisis of ambiguity* and *domestication of ambiguity*. To begin with, al-Bukhārī and Muslim aimed to select from the mass of circulating hadiths those that could most likely count as *ṣaḥīḥ* (correct, valid). It is said that al-Bukhārī chose his 7,397 hadiths (including repetitions) from a total of 600,000.[3] The works of al-Bukhārī and Muslim are known under the title *Ṣaḥīḥ al-Bukhārī* and *Ṣaḥīḥ Muslim*, and often combined in the Arabic dual form as *aṣ-Ṣaḥīḥān* (the two *ṣaḥīḥ*-works). They do not, however, intend to replace all other hadiths. On the contrary, in the introductions to the chapters of his collection, al-Bukhārī does not abstain from quoting hadiths with clearly fragmentary *isnād*s.

The emergence of further hadith collections that presented themselves with a decided claim to authority led to a further surplus of ambiguity.

Finally, according to tradition, four collections were settled upon as those that should be granted—after the *Ṣaḥīḥān*—the greatest authority.[4] These make up the six works that in Western scholarship are always referred to as the "canonical" hadith works. However, it remained highly controversial which books should belong to these "Six Books" (*al-kutub as-sittah*). In particular, the collection of Ibn Mājah was often denied the right to belong to the circle of the "Six."

Many would have liked to see works from the pre-Bukhārī era in that position, such as Mālik's *Muwaṭṭaʾ* or Ibn Ḥanbal's *Musnad*.

The parallels to the situation of the Quranic readings are obvious. Again, an excessive complexity had to be reined in, and again, there was an attempt to reduce it, not to *one* reading, or, respectively, *one* hadith collection, but to several accepted ones. And in both processes, such a reduction is still clearly much too simplistic.

In the hadith disciplines, the privileged status given to the "Six Books" had almost no consequences at first. There was only unanimity on granting the *Ṣaḥīḥān* a special status. But even the question of which of the two *Ṣaḥīḥ* works should be given precedence had no unanimous answer. While al-Bukhārī's *Ṣaḥīḥ* is by common consent currently considered the most reliable book after the Quran, for a long time, authorities working in North Africa have preferred Muslim's work, which is much more neatly arranged. Authors of the Mamluk era, however, never quoted the other four works with greater frequency than the pre-Bukhārī hadith collections mentioned before, or the later collections by aṭ-Ṭabarānī (260–360/873–971). In the end, authors of Mamluk and Ottoman times continued to collect hadiths from all kinds of works and to transmit hadiths from oral tradition.

Evidently, the four hadith collections that, together with the *Ṣaḥīḥān*, formed the "Six Books" played no greater role in the everyday practice of hadith scholars than did other collections. The reason for this was that this or that hadith collection did not enjoy a status of greater or smaller reliability as a corpus, but only this or that single hadith did. Here, too, the parallel situation to that of the Quranic readings is evident. The reading of a certain passage is not accepted as particularly reliable just because its wording appears thus in the collected readings of such-and-such a reader. Rather, it is seen as reliable because it is transmitted by many authorities in a reliable way. The collected readings of such-and-such a reader derives its authority from the fact that all of them, or most of them, are incontestably reliable. Thus, the *Ṣaḥīḥ* works of al-Bukhārī and Muslim, as such, are not actually *ṣaḥīḥ*. Rather, they derive their authority from the fact that they contain only hadiths that deserve the predicate *ṣaḥīḥ*.

Therefore, it seems to me too simple to speak of a "canon" of "Six Books." A professional hadith scholar will not be impressed by the fact that a hadith is part of Ibn Mājah's collection. Rather, he will apply his own criteria, and will not hesitate to give more authority to a hadith from the pre-Bukhārī collection of Ibn Abī Shaybah, or from aṭ-Ṭabarānī's *Great Muʿjam* (collected after the "Six Books"), than to a report contained in Ibn Mājah's collection. Thus the "Six Books," except for the two *Ṣaḥīḥ* works, do not have a special status of authority which would principally single them out from the range of qualitatively high-value hadith collections. Instead, the idea to select six books ahead of many others merely serves to reduce complexity. It enables the nonprofessional, in particular, to have at his or her disposal a fairly reliable corpus of hadiths that covers a wide thematic range. It is not the respective collection that counts as reliable or not, but only the single hadith that has to be examined from case to case. Again, we can think of the parallel situation in the Quranic readings, whose confinement to seven or ten readings was nothing but a manner of reducing complexity. The criteria of quality were stricter for the Quranic readings, however, so we might rather compare the seven or ten Quranic readings to the two *Ṣaḥīḥ* works, and compare the remaining four books to a reading such as one by Ḥasan al-Baṣrī that, concerning reliability, was positioned after the "ten readings."

The scholars of the ninth century endeavored to create a selection as reliable as possible from the vast mass of circulating hadiths. These endeavors mark the beginning of a discipline that developed ever more subtle methods of identifying genuine hadiths and revealing forgeries. One work that became a standard of this discipline—the "theory of hadith criticism" one might call it (in Arabic it is usually called the "discipline of the terminology of the hadith scholars")—was a book by the Damascene hadith scholar Ibn aṣ-Ṣalāḥ ash-Shahrazūrī (577–643/1181–1243) that was commented on and adapted countless times. Ibn Ḥajar al-ʿAsqalānī (773–852/1372–1449) composed a book (*an-Nukat*) that lucidly criticizes this earlier work, and is even more voluminous. Finally, Ibn Ḥajar himself presented a brief general exposition of the discipline (*Nukhbat al-fikar*), which became as popular as Ibn aṣ-Ṣalāḥ's previous work. These are just a few of the dozens of works written over the course of centuries.

The most important criteria according to which a tradition is examined are:

(1) The point of origin of a tradition: Does the hadith date back to the Prophet himself, or to one of his companions, or to a person belonging to the subsequent generation(s)?
(2) The uninterruptedness of a tradition: Has every transmitter named in the *isnād* heard the report immediately from the transmitter named before him, or is there a gap?
(3) The quality of the transmitters: Are they upright people with good memories? Is their reliability perhaps impaired by partiality, addiction to drink, senile dementia, etc.?
(4) The manner of transmission: Has the transmitter heard the hadith from his teacher? Has he read it to him, alone or in a group; has he simply copied it? Or can the manner of transmission not be ascertained?

(5) The consistency of content: Does the text make sense, and is it congruent with other traditions, similarly or equally reliable?
(6) The breadth of transmission: How many persons transmit the hadith in every step of transmission?

The best mark that a single hadith may receive is *ṣaḥīḥ li-dhātihī* (per se valid). According to Ibn Ḥajar, a hadith is *ṣaḥīḥ li-dhātihī* if it is transmitted in an uninterrupted chain (*muttaṣil as-sanad*) by exclusively honest (*ʿadl*) people capable of completely precise reporting (*tāmm aḍ-ḍabṭ*); if it does not reveal a hidden defect (*ghayr muʿallal*, i.e., a defect that only appears when comparison is made with other chains of transmitters); and if it does not contradict a tradition that is still more reliable (*lā shādhdh*).[5] If a hadith shows a small defect that can be mended through parallel hadiths, it is still *ṣaḥīḥ*, but no longer "per se" (as such). If a small defect in a hadith cannot be remedied, the hadith receives the mark *ḥasan* (good), again divided into "good per se" or not. Alongside these four categories of acceptable (*maqbūl*) hadiths are a large group of unacceptable ones (*mardūd*) that show greater defects, such as a gap in the chain of transmitters, a link regarded as unreliable, or the existence of a contradictory tradition with better credentials. For each sort of defect there is a specific term. Such hadiths are still collected and transmitted because the fact that they are, *with a high probability*, not authentic does not mean that they are *by necessity* not authentic. They still retain, therefore, a certain informational value, and may be used for edifying purposes, if not for establishing judicial decisions.

The assignment of hadiths to one of these categories is a highly difficult affair, and it is little wonder that many hadiths are the subject of controversial discussion. These discussions still continue, even after centuries. The example of Ibn Ḥajar al-ʿAsqalānī, certainly the most significant hadith scholar of his era, shows how self-assuredly scholars of the postformative era could deal with older material. In spite of all the difficulties of the discipline of hadith, Ibn Ḥajar has a high opinion of its efficacy.

This can be seen, for instance, in his response to the case of al-Ḥākim an-Nīsābūrī (321–474/933–1014), a scholar who had composed a work with the title *al-Mustadrak ʿalā ṣ-Ṣaḥīḥayn* (Supplement to the two *Ṣaḥīḥ* works). Its point of departure was the realization that there were numerous hadiths that did deserve the mark "valid" but had not found their place in the collections of al-Bukhārī and Muslim. Al-Ḥākim claimed to have assembled such hadiths in his *Mustadrak*. At first, the work was seen as indispensable, because its numerous good hadiths supplemented, in many respects, the material collected in other hadith collections. But it soon came to cause offense, as it became clear that many of his hadiths were not *ṣaḥīḥ* at all; some were not even qualified to pass as *ḥasan*. So what was to be done?

The author on hadith theory Ibn aṣ-Ṣalāḥ thought of a highly practical solution. Since the *Mustadrak* had thrown together hadiths of different qualities, all of them should be considered *ḥasan*. Ibn Ḥajar, however, could not bring himself to accept such well-meant fiddling, which would lead to the voluntary relinquishing of a number of perfectly valid hadiths. Some argued that in view of the length of time that had elapsed since the Prophet, it was no longer possible to establish with precision whether any hadith was *ṣaḥīḥ* or not. Ibn Ḥajar countered this position with a brisk scientific optimism. If the methods of the theory of hadith criticism were meticulously applied, he maintained, it would still be possible to discover hadiths that qualify as valid, even if they had not formerly been recognized as such.

Thus the process of recognizing hadiths as *ṣaḥīḥ* (Arabic *taṣḥīḥ*) had not come to an end with the generation of al-Bukhārī and Muslim, but remained possible at any time: "The gate of *taṣḥīḥ* is open!" writes Ibn Ḥajar.[6] This is evidence that, as late as the fifteenth century, there was no trace of an ossification of Islam or an uncritical imitation of the ancients.

Instead of blindly following an older but imperfect authority like al-Ḥākim an-Nīsābūrī, Ibn Ḥajar demands an examination of each single hadith with the new and refined instruments of his generation, in order to allocate it to one of the categories of reliability. These categories are by no means rigid and homogenous. A given hadith is not simply *ṣaḥīḥ* or *ḥasan*; it is so to a greater or lesser degree. The terms *ṣaḥīḥ* (correct, valid), *ḥasan* (good), and *ḍaʿīf* (weak) are not absolute measures; they merely mark points on a continuous scale of probability. The criteria needed for judging the reliability of a hadith do not lead to definite knowledge of its authenticity; they allow only for inferring its greater or smaller *probability* of authenticity (*ghalabat aẓ-ẓann*).[7] Therefore, within each category there exist gradations (*tafāwut*)—even within the category *ṣaḥīḥ*.

In fact, the act of judging a hadith is the result, so to speak, of a multiplication of probabilities. The question of whether a hadith is transmitted without gaps can be answered only with more or less probability. The fact that transmitter B has known transmitter A, who comes before him in the chain of transmission, does not exclude the possibility that there was a further transmitter between A and B who was not mentioned—that there exists, in fact, a "hidden defect." In all other criteria for ascertaining the quality of a hadith, we are faced with comparable difficulties. The greatest factor of instability lies in the evaluation of the individual transmitter, for this can only be ascertained on the basis of reports, and these reports are afflicted with the same uncertainties as are the hadiths themselves. Further, the evaluation of a transmitter is frequently worded in a way that is itself in need of interpretation. A representative entry in a biographical dictionary of transmitters is the following; it, too, is taken from a work of Ibn Ḥajar al-ʿAsqalānī:

> Al-Ḥusayn ibn ʿAbdallāh ibn ʿUbaydallāh ibn ʿAbbās ibn ʿAbd al-Muṭṭalib al-Hāshimī al-Madanī: He reports from Rabīʿah ibn ʿIbād who has met with the Prophet, from ʿIkrimah and from Umm Yūnus, the servant of Ibn ʿAbbās. From him in turn reported Hishām ibn ʿUrwah, Ibn Jurayj . . . , and others. Al-Athram reports that Aḥmad [ibn Ḥanbal] has said: "One finds with him inacceptable things." Ibn Abī Khaythamah reported that [Yaḥyā] Ibn Maʿīn has judged: "[He is] weak (*ḍaʿīf*)." Ibn abī Maryam, however, reports from Yaḥyā: "Nothing can be said against him, one notes down his hadiths." Al-Bukhārī remarks that ʿAlī [ibn al-Madīnī] has said: "I have not taken his hadiths into account and neither has Aḥmad [ibn Ḥanbal]." Abū Zurʿah is of the opinion: "Not a strong authority," and Abū Ḥātim: "Weak, but I prefer him to Ḥusayn ibn Qays. One can note down his hadiths, but not argue on their basis." Al-Jūzjānī is of the opinion: "One does not deal with his hadiths." An-Nasāʾī judges: "Not to be taken into regard," and in another passage, "Not reliable." . . . Ibn ʿAdī is of the opinion: "His hadiths resemble each other. He belongs to those whose hadiths are noted down. Among all his hadiths I have not found one which was inacceptable to a greater degree." Ibn Saʿd states: "He died in 140 or 141 [around 758]. He transmitted numerous hadiths, but I have not witnessed that one has argued on their basis." I can add . . . that al-Bukhārī says that he was suspected to be a Manichaean (*zindīq*). Al-Ājurrī reports from Abū Dāwūd: "ʿĀṣim ibn ʿUbaydallāh has a higher position than him." . . . Ibn Hibbān claims: "He turns around the components of a personal name in the *isnād* and inserts a name in hadiths which skip the companions of the Prophet [in the *isnād*]."[8]

Despite all this, hadiths transmitted by him made it into Ibn Mājah's collection, one of the "Six Books" (albeit the most controversial). At any rate, this much is clear: a hadith whose *isnād* contains this al-Ḥusayn ibn ʿAbdallāh is no longer *ṣaḥīḥ*. But is it still *ḥasan*? Can it be deemed valid if the same text exists with a different chain of transmitters? Can it be used, at the very least, to complement hadiths that are better transmitted? Does the diverse judgment this transmitter has received from the older authorities allow for a decisive judgment?

In the view of the classical Muslim hadith scholars, at least, that last question can clearly be answered in the negative. A critical investigation into the text and the *isnād* of a hadith cannot yield more than an approximate determination of what degree of probability would allow for an assumption of authenticity. This holds true even for single hadiths transmitted in the best manner, because according to the classical theory of hadith, the criterion for *ṣaḥīḥ* provides a very high probability of the authenticity of a tradition, but not absolute certainty.

At best, such certainty can be reached if one goes beyond the consideration of the hadith itself and finds that a report was transmitted from the beginning and through all subsequent periods of history by so many people that an error or a conspiracy can be excluded. Only then is the mark of 100 percent on the scale of probability attained, because only such a "broad transmission"—the Arabic term is *mutawātir*—provides not just probability, but certainty. In this "broad transmission," the quality of the single tradition eventually does not matter any-more (i.e., *mutawātir* hadiths do not have to be *ṣaḥīḥ*), only the large mass of the tradition. Just as no one in his right mind would doubt that China exists, even if he never visited it and knows no one completely trustworthy who has visited it, so *mutawātir* hadiths do not allow any doubts about their authenticity, solely on the basis of the large scale of their transmission.

This is a point on which the Muslim scholars of classical times largely agree with each other, but here unanimity ends. Even the question of how many ways a report has to be transmitted, in order to count as *mutawātir*, is controversial. Are four enough? Must they be at least seventy? Both these and many other numbers are mentioned, but Ibn Ḥajar is certainly right when he insists that determining a minimum number is incompatible with the system: there is no reasonable justification for deciding that *n* parallel traditions should indicate certainty, but not *n*-1 or *n*+1. The number of parallel traditions must simply amount to so many that all doubt is dispelled, and that cannot be indicated by exact numbers.[9]

But which hadiths are *mutawātir*? How many are there, anyway? Again, we encounter great controversy. Ibn aṣ-Ṣalāḥ was of the opinion that a *mutawātir* tradition was a rare thing, and not even the word of the Prophet, transmitted in numerous ways, for instance "Who fabricates a lie about me is assured of a place in Hell" (which after all is supposed to create a foundation of belief in the institution of hadith), is a candidate for *mutawātir*. This attitude—and the even more extreme position that no hadith whatsoever, but only the Quran, meets the criteria of *mutawātir* transmission—were firmly rejected by Ibn Ḥajar, although he was not willing to commit himself to a definite number.[10] Thus, the somewhat paradoxical conclusion remains that *mutawātir* transmissions guarantee certainty, but that one can determine only with more or less probability whether a text in fact complies with the criteria of *mutawātir*.

Let us resume: to establish an Islamic ethics or an Islamic law solely on the basis of the Quran is hardly possible. The lacunas left by the Quran are too large, and the range of possible interpretations offered by its texts is too great. As a supplement, multitudinous materials, in the form of disparate traditions from the Prophet and his primeval community, offered themselves. However, this material was not only contradictory, but also, to a considerable degree, susceptible to error, manipulation, and plain forgery, well-meant or malevolent. Early on, therefore, Muslim scholars developed critical methods that made it possible, if not to remove, at least to domesticate the uncontrolled growth of the hadith tradition. Marco Schöller rightly states: "In spite of the ideological and sectarian tendencies . . . it remains a striking feature to what a large degree the Muslim scholars were capable of continually keeping the whole tradition of hadith under rigorous scrutiny and thus keeping it relatively homogeneous."[11]

To be sure, the hadith scholars did not claim to command with absolute certainty. Rather, Islamic hadith criticism is a method based on rational criteria that permit the sorting of hadiths according to the probability of their authenticity. The degree of that probability depends on the applicability of a hadith. Thus, a hadith that forms the basis of a legal proposition is bound to have a far higher probability of authenticity than one that is used to admonish the believers in a sermon. The assignment of hadiths to specific categories of probability is the result of a discussion between professionals that is not concluded, and that can be taken up again with professional arguments at any time. The classical Islamic system of hadith thus allows the effective utilization of the tradition of the primeval community for the formation of contemporary society, while at the same time suspending, to a great extent, the claim to absolute truth.

Again, we see that uncertainty and contradictoriness are not eradicated but *domesticated*, in the form of a theory of probability. A suspension of truth throughout centuries in the interest of a theory of probabilities presupposes a high tolerance of ambiguity, as was noted by the creator of this term when she writes: "Intolerance of ambiguity must further be related to a reluctance to think in terms of probabilities and a preference to escape into whatever seems to be definite and therefore safe."[12]

THE THEORY OF PROBABILITY IN ISLAMIC LAW

As a rule, Islamic law is characterized as a *religious* law or even as a *divine* law. But such a characterization is misleading, because it absolutizes this one, religious, aspect of the Islamic law and conveys the impression that there is not another, secular, aspect. At first glance, the everyday practice of a judge in the classical Arab world does not yield much religious material. He is supposed to take what is relevant for him as applicable law from one of the usual handbooks of his legal school. If he is a member of the Shāfiʿite school, he might use one of the numerous commentaries on the *Mukhtaṣar al-Muzanī.* This brief survey of Shāfiʿite legal doctrines, written by al-Muzanī (175–264/792–877) not only goes back to one of the students of the school's founder, ash-Shāfiʿī (150–204/767–820), but also is so brief (and therefore so open to interpretation) that it has offered itself for longer commentaries that amplify and update it. Such a book does not look much different from a commentary on the regulations of a legal culture with statute law. The judge issues his verdict on the basis of precisely such a manmade legal handbook. In doing so, he applies a legal doctrine that in principle is not different from that of a Western legal system. Ultimately, his verdict is a fallible human act. It has no sacral character whatsoever and cannot claim a higher divine legitimation.

But there is also a religious aspect to Islamic law. Two text corpora from which legal norms are derived have a religious nature, namely the Quran, as God's word, and the hadith tradition that leads to the knowledge of the sunna of the Prophet. Furthermore, Islamic law deals not only with the social relations between persons but also with ritual; in this it is not different from Roman law. More significant is the status of jurisprudence as a religious discipline that has the task of exploring the divine world order. This order, established by God, is the Sharia. It is misleading to translate the word *sharīʿah* as "Islamic law"; this term must be strictly distinguished both from Islamic law as a legal discipline (*fiqh*) and from the legal propositions (*aḥkām*) collected in the books on legal applications (*furūʿ* works). It is true that these works claim to comprise legal applications that largely, and with a high probability, match the divine order of the Sharia; however, they do not *constitute* the Sharia, which in its totality is not accessible to man—not even with a high degree of certainty. Thus there exists no book in which "*the* Sharia" is laid down. In the seventeenth century, Ḥājjī Khalīfah composed a comprehensive catalog of books. He mentions 187 legal works. None of them has the word *sharīʿah* in its title.[13]

The Sharia is, first of all, the sum of God's judgments on human acts. Such a judgment is called *ḥukm* (in the plural form, *aḥkām*). This term, which is central for Islamic law, is often mistakenly translated as "legal prescription" or "mandatory legal application." But it is not these—or, at most, it is these only in second place. In the first place, according to the classical definition, *ḥukm* denotes nothing but "text" (*khiṭāb*) or the "divine speech" (*kalām*) that is connected with human acts, that is, is "attached" to them.[14] Every human act is judged by God in a certain way—either as a duty or as a forbidden act, as desirable or to be refrained from, or as unrestrictedly tolerated. Precisely this judgment is a *ḥukm*. According to the opinion of many religious scholars, these divine *aḥkām* are firmly established from the beginning (i.e., since the time of the revelation, according to some scholars, even since the creation of the world), independent of whether a person commits such an act or not. In a sense, these judgments are a part of the divine world order. And it is the task of the Muslim legal scholar to explore this order.

How, then, does one track down these *aḥkām*? In order to answer this question, the discipline of *uṣūl al-fiqh* (roots of the law) has been developed. We shall use here the term "methodology of law" for the Arabic term *uṣūl*. This discipline originated in debates on the question of what Islamic law in general would have to build upon. During the first two centuries of Islam, there soon evolved local traditions of rather different natures. In Medina, the local legal tradition was seen as more important than the tradition of hadith going back to the Prophet. From this Medinan tradition, practiced by Mālik ibn Anas (died 179/796) and his followers, evolved the Mālikite legal school. In Iraq, "individual judgment" (*raʾy*) was held to be more important than the Prophetical tradition. Here, the Ḥanafite legal school, based on Abū Ḥanīfah (80–150/699–767), originated. It is probable, though difficult to prove, that some material from Roman law was inherited. The establishment of the Prophetic hadith as the second source of law after the Quran, and the discussion of the relation between the two, was the achievement of ash-Shāfiʿī, who later became, as did Mālik ibn Anas and Abū Ḥanīfah, the authority and eponym of a legal school. The eponym of the fourth legal school, Aḥmad ibn Ḥanbal, was not a legal scholar but was the protagonist of a pious movement based on the hadith tradition. Only later did his followers constitute a "real" legal school, the Ḥanbalite—not least in the debate with the Shāfiʿite theory of law.

This early period was characterized by intense discussions about how to define the principles of law; at the same time, voluminous compendia of law were compiled. It was then the task of legal methodologists of subsequent centuries to arrive at a minimal consensus about Islamic methodology of law on the one hand, and, on the other hand, to explain and legitimize the differences in the commonly practiced legal prescriptions. In a first formative period, whose end may be dated in the year of ash-Shāfiʿī's death, 204/820, there had been a dispute about what could actually constitute a source of jurisprudence. This was followed by a second formative period, spanning the time of the so-called Sunni revival, in which the logical, epistemological, and linguistic foundations of the legal theory were broadened and systematized. This process was led by scholars like Abū l-Ḥusayn al-Baṣrī (died 436/1044), a representative of the theological line of the Muʿtazilah; al-Juwaynī (419–478/1028–1085), the "Imām of the two Holy Sites" (i.e., Mecca and Medina); and his pupil al-Ghazālī (450–505/1058–1111), who in today's Western thought has the reputation of being a philosophy-averse theologian, but whose work *al-Mustaṣfā*, saturated with philosophical concepts and methods, contributed substantially to the incorporation of Greek philosophy, in particular logic, into Islamic legal methodology. These three scholars were authors of influential compendia of *uṣūl al-fiqh* that had not previously existed in this form.

It was Fakhr ad-Dīn ar-Rāzī (544–606/1149–1209) who, on the basis of these and other works, compiled a *summa* of legal methodology that constituted its authoritative reference work for many centuries to come. Ar-Rāzī (the man from Rayy; Rayy is today a suburb of Tehran) was a truly universal scholar whose writings contributed significantly not only to jurisprudence but also to philosophy, theology, rhetoric, and the linguistic sciences. His brilliant, eccentric (and highly popular) Quran commentary was mocked as containing everything in the world, but no commentary.[15] This author's magnum opus on legal methodology not only carries the title "the result" (*al-Maḥṣūl*—which nicely rhymes with *uṣūl*), but also, in fact, represents the sum of the preceding extensive discussions on the foundations of Islamic law. No future author on the theory of law should be able to bypass this work, and if there exists a book that concludes the formative period of Islamic legal theory, it is ar-Rāzī's *Maḥṣūl*, and by no means the *Risālah* (the Epistle) of ash-Shāfiʿī.

To emphasize this fact is not trivial. According to an ideology common to Eastern and Western thought and inherited from European colonialism, the Islamic world entered a stage of decline and torpor, if not of general stupidity, from the tenth or eleventh century onward. Therefore, the adherents of this theory of decline (which will be addressed further in chapters to follow) did not deem it the least bit necessary to read works from this period. It is no coincidence that ar-Rāzī's *Maḥṣūl*—a work of which numerous manuscripts, commentaries, and excerpts are extant—was published in print only in 1977! Some contemporary Muslim experts of Islamic law are still followers of the theory of decline and almost never quote from a legal work of the postformative period.

They are content to accept the Western position, authoritatively formulated by Joseph Schacht, according to which Islamic law had found its conclusive formulation with ash-Shāfiʿī in the beginning of the ninth century. But this is definitely not the case,[16] and Naṣr Ḥāmid Abū Zayd is certainly wrong in believing that once one is done with ash-Shāfiʿī, one has taken care of the entirety of Islamic law.[17] The opposite is true. The theoretical foundations of the methodology of Islamic law were laid in the eleventh and twelfth centuries, and a scholar who wants to deal with classical Islamic law must start here and leave behind the infatuation with "the beginnings" that has dominated Islamic Studies until recently.

In the context of this brief presentation we would like to focus on a later work—not, however, on ar-Rāzī's monumental *summa*, but on a slim Mālikite book on legal methodology, written by Abū l-Qāsim Ibn Juzayy al-Kalbī (born 693/1294 in Granada, killed in the battle at Rio Salado in 741/1340) and clearly following the model of ar-Rāzī. The booklet has the title *Taqrīb al-wuṣūl ilā ʿilm al-uṣūl* (Expedient to arrive swiftly at the methodology of law). It was meant to serve as a primer for one of Ibn Juzayy's sons (who later on became a secretary to the famous traveler Ibn Baṭṭūṭah) and is thus better suited than the lengthy compendia of other scholars to offer a concise outline of the classical *uṣūl al-fiqh*.

Now how does one find out, according to classical legal methodology, about the *aḥkām*, the divine judgment on the human actions? First, of course, by consulting the Quran and the hadith tradition. But what one finds here are not the *aḥkām* themselves, but only *references to the aḥkām*. These pointers (*dalīl*, pl. *adilla*) are only quite rarely unambiguous, and even those that present themselves on first sight as definite, reveal, under close scrutiny, their deviousness.

To quote an example that Ibn Juzayy also mentions in his book: the Quran says (Q 5:3) *ḥurrimat ʿalaykumū l-maytatu* (Forbidden to you is carrion). This looks quite definite, and Rudi Paret, in his translation of the Quran, did not have problems with the passage. He translates: "Forbidden to you is (the eating of) meat of carrion." But "the eating of meat" does not figure in the Arabic text. There, it is written only *that* carrion is forbidden. It does not say which *action* in relation to these animals is forbidden. In fact, some scholars maintain that this Quranic passage is not clear and thus does not permit the drawing of conclusions from it. The majority, however, holds that context and common usage suggest that the eating of carrion is meant. But this is not the conclusive answer to all questions. What about the fur of carrion? This question will be discussed later in detail, but here it is already clear that the Quranic passage is far from furnishing us with a *ḥukm*; it constitutes only a *dalīl*, a pointer toward a possible divine judgment.

Thus, to investigate the *aḥkām*, one must start from such a *dalīl* and build, by *logical thinking* on the one hand and *linguistic exegesis* on the other, a hypothesis about the divine judgments which is probably valid. The rules to be followed are exactly those of the discipline of *uṣūl al-fiqh*, that is, the methodology of legal reasoning.

Ibn Juzayy's ambition is to present a particularly logical and well-structured description of this science. He starts his work, therefore, with a first principal section about logic and the theory of knowledge, in which he deals with the potentials and limits of human cognition, syllogisms, definitions, proofs etc. It is especially in relation to the discipline of logic that the Greek heritage became an integral part of Islamic culture in this period. This section also shows clearly that there was no opposition between rationalists and legal scholars (which is already evident from the fact that the philosopher Ibn Rushd/Averroes wrote significant books on Mālikite law, along with his philosophical works). This theory of law represents the discipline of logic—as Ibn Juzayy himself emphasizes—as the one most profoundly based on both tradition and reason, and it is therefore not only the most difficult science but, as he remarks not without some vanity, the noblest one.

More important than the first principal section is the second one, which deals with linguistic foundations. On the background of his own period, Ibn Juzayy's account is decidedly modern, because he is able to make use of the insights of the great linguistic scholars of the East, among them ar-Rāzī. Starting from these, Ibn Juzayy bases his thoughts on a model of linguistic communication and demonstrates that one must consider the meaning of an expression from three different perspectives. First, one may investigate the lexical meaning (*waḍʿ*); second, the meaning with which the *speaker uses* the expression (*istiʿmāl*); and third, the meaning the *hearer ascribes to* (*ḥaml*) the expression—that is to say, "independently from whether the hearer understands or misses what is meant." This shows that Ibn Juzayy explicitly includes the possibility of misunderstanding, and thus provides a model to describe a crucial feature of Islamic law.

It is therefore imperative that a legal scholar has detailed knowledge of the linguistic disciplines that enable him to judge how a given expression in the Quran or a hadith should probably be understood. In doing so, he should (according to the usual understanding and that of Ibn Juzayy as well) follow the more probable opinion, defined as the one that involves less effort of interpretation. Thus, if nothing suggests that an expression should be understood as a specific one, it must be understood as a general one. If nothing indicates that an expression should be understood in a metaphorical sense, it must be taken with its usual meaning.[18]

After these two sections, which deal with the *How* of gaining knowledge of divine law, Ibn Juzayy proceeds in his third principal section to the *What*, that is, the divine judgments on human actions, the *aḥkām*, that judge them according to the categories obligatory, recommended, allowed, reprehensible, and forbidden.

The fourth principal section of Ibn Juzayy's work treats the four well-known "sources" of Islamic jurisprudence; more precisely, the sources from which the legal scholar takes the indications of Islamic law, namely the Quran, the sunna, the legal consensus, and the deduction by analogy. Ibn Juzayy, as a Mālikite, includes as a fifth source the consensus of the Medinan scholars in the early period of Islam.

The fifth and last principal section of Ibn Juzayy's work establishes the connection between theory and practice. For instance, the author addresses the question of which conditions must be fulfilled by a *mujtahid*, that is, someone who is capable of elaborating his own legal opinion on the basis of the principles presented heretofore.

The last chapter of this section, and so the last chapter of the whole book, is titled "Reasons for differences of opinion among legal scholars." As Ibn Juzayy writes, he is the first author who has clearly arranged these reasons, and an interest in these differences of opinion is eminently useful for everyone dealing with Islamic law. As a matter of fact, the "difference of opinion" (*ikhtilāf* or *khilāf*) is a further pivotal concept of Islamic jurisprudence. This is because the legal scholar assumes, in the model of linguistic communication, the position of the *hearer*. He is perforce confined to the role of forming his own *opinion* on what the speaker (God, His Prophet) may have intended to say, without being able to know with definite certainty what was meant. Thus, a person facing the divine law has only *hypothetical* knowledge on almost all issues, and it is inevitable that different scholars arrive at different opinions, and that hence differences of opinion arise.

Such a difference of opinion is by no means a sort of "occupational hazard" in the finding of justice, but it is an integral part of justice which not only has to be tolerated, but also must be considered as necessary. If our human knowledge of the divine order is limited by necessity, it is indispensable that different opinions on a given problem be assembled—if we want to be sure that the right one is among them. This last chapter of Ibn Juzayy's book is by no means meant to eliminate such differences of opinion, but is meant to show and explain the possible reasons for the occurrence of different opinions.

It is not reasonable to debate the epistemological foundations of *ikhtilāf*, difference of opinion, without giving a pertinent example. We return therefore to the problem cited above, concerning the permissibility of using the fur of carrion, by using current legal compendia and going into more detail. In this analysis, some of the most important reasons for the occurrence of *ikhtilāf* will become apparent.

The starting point of the discussion is the prohibition of carrion, of blood, and of pork in verse 3 of the fifth surah of the Quran. At first sight, the wording seems to be clear: "Forbidden to you is carrion." The natural interpretation is that the verse refers to a dietary prescription that forbids the eating of animals that have died due to an illness or accident, not by *ḥalāl* slaughtering (*dhakāʾ*) or in a hunt. The problem, however, is that the verse does not mention eating; it only prohibits carrion, without indicating precisely what one must not do with carrion. Abū l-Ḥasan al-Karkhī (260–340/873–952), head of the Ḥanafites, pointed out that one cannot prohibit objects, but only actions on objects. Therefore, statements such as "Forbidden to you is carrion" or, in an almost identical formulation, "Forbidden to you are your mothers" (Q 4:23) cannot be utilized as evidence. On the one hand, not all conceivable actions with relation to carrion and to mothers can be prohibited; on the other hand, it is also not possible to posit one specific action as being more probably prohibited than another. And finally, one would have to assume that if one could, in fact, posit a specific action, the same action would have to be posited concerning carrion and mothers, given the parallel formulation of both Quranic passages.[19]

In his skepticism, al-Karkhī stands virtually alone. The generally accepted opinion advocates that such passages should be supplemented according to everyday usage, that it is prohibited to marry mothers and to eat carrion, but not to remove carrion. But what about the skin of carrion? Is it allowed, say, to make a water container out of the skin of a goat one has found dead this morning? May one use a sheep's fur as a rug, even a prayer rug, if the sheep has not been slaughtered according to the *ḥalāl* regulations? The Quranic passage clearly does not help us answer this question. Fortunately, the Quran is not the only authority that furnishes us with a *dalīl* for the *ḥukm*. In addition to this passage, we can have recourse to a number of hadiths, the most important four of which are assembled in the following table showing the *dalāʾil* for this problem:

Is it allowed to use the skin of carrion?
Dalīl 1: Q 5: 3: "Forbidden to you is carrion." (*ḥurrimat ʿalaykumū l-maytatu*)
Dalīl 2: Ḥadīth Maymūnah: "Why do you not use its skin?" (*a-fa-lā ntafaʿtum bi-jildihā?*)
Dalīl 3: Ḥadīth Ibn ʿUkaym: "Do not use skin or sinews of carrion." (*lā tanaffaʿū mina l-maytati bi-ihābin wa-lā ʿaṣabin*)
Dalīl 4: Ḥadīth, transmitted from Ibn ʿAbbās: "Every skin which is tanned becomes pure." (*ayyumā ihābin dubigha fa-qad ṭahura*)
Dalīl 5: Ḥadīth: "Tanning of a skin is equal to its slaughtering, according to the *ḥalāl* regulations" (*dibāghu l-adīmi dhakātuhū*)

The first hadith, that of Maymūnah, apparently presents the perfect solution to the problem. It reports that the Prophet Muḥammad, upon seeing a dead sheep, had asked his last wife Maymūnah: "Why do you not use its skin?" When hearing the answer that that sheep died by itself, he replied: "It is only prohibited to eat it."[20] This hadith meets the highest criteria of trustworthiness to count as *ṣaḥīḥ* (valid); it is transmitted in both hadith collections called *aṣ-Ṣaḥīḥ* and in most other recognized collections. Thus the problem seems to have been solved; in fact, az-Zuhrī (around 50–124/670–742), who himself transmits the hadith in the second generation from the companion of the Prophet, Ibn ʿAbbās, judges it as a basis for the unconditional acceptability of using the skin of carrion. The Egyptian scholar al-Layth (94–175/713–791), who cannot be subsumed under a specific legal school, subscribes to the same opinion.[21] And yet it remains a minority vote. This is because the Maymūnah-hadith is not the only one on this topic: one Ibn ʿUkaym has it that the Prophet, shortly before his death, wrote a letter to the tribe of Juhaynah—the exact references vary between versions—saying: "Do not use skin or sinews of carrion." This is a clear statement, but it is in contradiction to the Maymūnah-hadith! This is a case of "contradictoriness of indication," the most frequent form of difference of opinion, according to Ibn Juzayy and others.

How to solve such a contradiction? The options are as follows:

(1) *Abrogation.* A Quranic passage revealed later than another Quranic passage may abrogate, that is invalidate, the earlier one. The same holds true for

two hadiths. However, only a Quranic passage can abrogate a hadith; a hadith cannot abrogate a Quranic passage. The question whether one can state a case of abrogation is a further source of difference of opinion. In our case, the state of affairs seems to be rather clear. Since Muḥammad's letter to the Juhaynah tribe is supposed to have been written shortly before his death, this hadith probably postdates the Maymūnah-hadith and would thus abrogate it. For scholars of the classical period, however, abrogation is only a makeshift procedure to which one takes recourse only when other ways of solution are blocked. And in our case, there do exist such other ways.

(2) *Hadith criticism*. The two hadiths are not of equal quality. While the Maymūnah-hadith shows an immaculate chain of transmission, the purported letter to the Juhaynah tribe shows a number of flaws. To begin with, there are discrepancies in the *isnād*, and the date at which the letter is supposed to have been written differs in the various versions. First and foremost, it is not clear whether the transmitter Ibn ʿUkaym was a companion of the Prophet at all, and even if so, whether he had not learned about the contents of the letter indirectly via his tribal companions, as one version has it. If this is so, the hadith belongs to the category of *mursal*, meaning that there is a missing link between the first transmitter and the person who heard the hadith from the Prophet. A further important source of difference of opinion is the difficult issue of how to weigh hadiths on the basis of the probability of their authenticity.

(3) *Simultaneous application of contradictory indications*. According to the classical scholars, this is the royal road that should be followed when it seems that two indications contradict each other. Instead of inconsiderately ignoring a Quranic passage or a hadith, even if it is not quite reliably transmitted, one should investigate ways to make use of both indications. Frequently, this is done by assuming that one *dalīl* is *specified* (*makhṣūṣ*) by the other one. We must examine whether we have before us a specification (*takhṣīṣ*) or not—this, again, constituting a source of many differences of opinion. In our case at hand, such a *takhṣīṣ* succeeds in one direction with the help of a further hadith, and in the other direction by utilizing Arabic lexicography.

The hadith most legal scholars use to solve that contradiction is distinguished by the predicate "valid." It runs thus: "Every skin which is being tanned becomes pure." The word used for "skin" here is *ihāb*, as used in the Ibn ʿUkaym-hadith. The lexicographers say that this word only denotes *untanned* skin, whereas the word *jild*, used in the Maymūnah-hadith, means both untreated skin and tanned leather. So here appears the solution: the Ibn ʿUkaym-hadith can be utilized to explain the Quranic passage open to question by considering it a prohibition of using *untanned* skin. Skin becomes pure by tanning, and thus the Maymūnah-hadith retains its validity: "Why do you not use the—tanned—skin?"

Most legal scholars have decided in favor of this solution. Exceptions to this position are the extreme points of view of az-Zuhrī and al-Layth, on the one hand, who permit the use of the skin of carrion in general, and of Aḥmad b. Ḥanbal, on the other, who persists in the general validity of Q 5:3 and rejects the specification according to the hadith on tanning.[22] The great majority of legal scholars, however, are of the opinion that the skins of carrion are impure as long as they are not tanned, but become pure by tanning, and may be used in this state without hesitation.

But this is not the end of the problem. As a matter of fact, only at this point are legal scholars confronted with actual challenges. This is because the hadith on tanning that introduces the concept of *purity* creates a new level of problems. If the process of tanning procures *purity*, the question necessarily arises whether this process does not also render utilizable the skins of animals that are principally impure.

The most radical affirmation of this consequence comes from Abū Yūsuf (113–182/731–798), a student of Abū Ḥanīfah and the first chief qāḍī of Baghdad. For him, the hadith on tanning is absolutely and generally valid, and also admits the use of pigskin. Well-known scholars like the Ẓāhirite Abū Dāwūd (200–270/815–884) and the important Mālikite teacher Saḥnūn (160–240/776–854) transmit this opinion.[23] They all insist on the general validity of the hadith on tanning, while Abū Yūsuf's teacher Abū Ḥanīfah and other scholars make an exception for the pig, on the grounds that it may not be used as a living animal.[24] In this case, the principal usability of the animal is what counts, not its purity or impurity. According to this opinion, the tanned skin of dogs may be used, because dogs are as impure as pigs, but their functions as watchdog or shepherd dog are explicitly approved of.

Ash-Shāfiʿī is a representative of the most prevalent opinion, which proceeds on the assumption that tanning applied to pure animals—and only these—removes the accidental impurity caused by their death, but does not apply to the essential impurity of pigs and dogs.

However, even if one restricts one's interpretation to pure animals, problems remain. According to the opinion of the majority, the Quranic passage deals with the *consumption* of animals; that is, it refers to animals that can, or may, be eaten. There are animals such as horses and mules that are admittedly pure, but fall into the category of "prohibited to eat." These animals, when slaughtered, do not become edible. But will their skin become utilizable by tanning? Those legal scholars who ascribe general validity (*ʿumūm*) to the hadith on tanning have no difficulty with this question. Abū Ḥanīfah adduces the hadith: "Tanning of a skin is equal to slaughtering according to the *ḥalāl* regulations." Regardless of whether the animal is edible or not, he says, its skin acquires the same purity as the meat of an edible animal by slaughtering according to the *ḥalāl* regulations.

Abū Thawr (died 240/854), who is regarded occasionally as a Shāfiʿite, but more frequently as the founder of his own school, takes this hadith as the basis of an argument that precisely counters the former one: the hadith, he says, matches the effect of slaughtering with that of tanning. Therefore, it must be inferred that where slaughtering has no effect—that is, with inedible animals—tanning, too, has no effect. In addition, Abū Thawr adduces a hadith according to which it is forbidden to settle oneself on the fur of predators.[25] Here we are amid the field of analogical reasoning (*qiyās*), which is an important source of legal reasoning, but also a constant wellspring of differences of opinion.

It is remarkable that these differences of opinion are not at all congruent with the legal schools. Arguments of legal scholars that do not belong to a still-existing school are in fact taken into consideration, and, on the other hand, divergent opinions are voiced even within one and the same legal school. In our example, it is the Mālikiyyah that shows a broad spectrum of opinions. This may be due to insecurity about the position of the eponymous head of this school, Mālik b. Anas; he is credited with different opinions that moreover contradict other early authorities, such as Saḥnūn. All in all, it seems that Mālik had an intermediate position, according to which tanned skins of carrion may be used in principle, but do not attain complete purity and therefore are not apt to serve as receptacles of liquids. On the question of whether they may be used as prayer carpets, the opinions ascribed to Mālik diverge.[26] In later times, the Mālikiyyah has approximated the position of the Shāfiʿiyyah, as it has often done.

The following table assembles, in a simplified manner, the various most prevalent positions. It can be observed that almost all positions that may, in some way, be sensibly taken are represented, not only in Ibn Juzayy's times, but already in the eighth and ninth centuries, during which the authorities named in the left column worked.

Which of these positions is the valid one? It is true that within the legal schools, one of the positions is dominant from case to case. This does not mean, however, that this position would be the exclusively valid one; only that, in the opinion of its representatives, it is more probably true than the other positions. This may also be noted in the terminology of the authors, most of whom say that their position is "more valid" (*aṣaḥḥ*) than that of the others. But they do not maintain, even when they propose their opinion with utter conviction, that they are the sole holders of truth.

	Untanned	Tanned			
		Pure Animals		Impure Animals	
		Edible	Inedible	Dog	Pig
Az-Zuhrī (died 742)	yes	yes			
Ibn Ḥanbal (died 855)	no	no	no	no	no
Abū Yūsuf (died 798)	no	yes	yes	yes	yes
Abū Ḥanīfah (died 767)	no	yes	yes	yes	no
Ash-Shâfiʿī (died 820)	no	yes	yes	no	no
Abū Thawr (died 854)	no	yes	no	no	no
Mālik (died 796)	no	outwards			

What degree of truth claim is implied in juridical discussions is instructively shown in the treatment of our "skin problem" by the Mālikite Ibn ʿAbd al-Barr (368–463/978–1071). To the hadith "Every skin which is tanned becomes pure," he devotes a very detailed discussion that for us seems to be a bit superfluous. He states that the reference to skins that become pure by tanning is meant to connote skins that are not pure originally, since it would be meaningless to say of pure skins that they become pure by tanning; they are pure from the beginning. What Ibn ʿAbd al-Barr intends to express by this laborious statement becomes clear in the following sentence: "The knowledge of this comes to us nearly necessarily."[27] The term "necessary knowledge" (*ʿilm ḍarūrī*) or "certain knowledge" (*ʿilm yaqīnī*) is central to Islamic thought. Certainty that cannot be reasonably doubted comes to us primarily through empirical experience, or through irrefutable logical proof. Theologians generally assert that their central dogmas constitute certain knowledge, and base this on proofs that are evident to everyone's reasoning, for instance the fact that there must exist a creator from whom being originates.

Jurists whose knowledge of the divine order derives exclusively from transmitted texts lay claim to certain knowledge much more rarely. This is because the premise for deriving certain knowledge from the tradition, that is the Quran and hadith, is only valid if the tradition itself leaves no doubt about its authenticity (what is called *mutawātir*). Such certainty, however, is established only for the Quran itself and for relatively few hadiths (the latter, however, not enjoying a general consensus). But even an unequivocally authentic tradition leads us toward certainty only if it makes a statement, in clear and unambiguous words, that is in no need of further interpretation. Such a statement is called *naṣṣ*. The Quranic verse "Forbidden to you is carrion" requires interpretation, and thus is not a *naṣṣ*; therefore, it cannot lead to certain knowledge, but only to "hypothetical knowledge" (*ʿilm ẓannī*), its complementary term.

Ibn ʿAbd al-Barr's logical proof, which he derives from the hadith on tanning, serves to build a basis for further considerations that offer as great a certainty as possible. The wording of that basis is: the hadith talks about *impure* skins that become pure by tanning. For Ibn ʿAbd al-Barr, this conclusion is as trivial as it is for us. Still, he does not want to do without this statement, because it offers *nearly* (!) certain knowledge. It can be seen that the bars to attaining certain knowledge are very high.

The same applies to the term *naṣṣ*, the unambiguous indication that does not allow any room for interpretation. Its complementary term is *dalīl*, meaning "guide, indicator" which also points toward an issue, but in a manner that leads only toward hypothetical knowledge. Now for Ibn ʿAbd al-Barr, the hadith on tanning contains both a *naṣṣ* and a *dalīl*. The *naṣṣ* is: the purity of the skin comes about by tanning. This is the obvious meaning one can derive from the hadith without further interpretation. But from this, Ibn ʿAbd al-Barr continues, one may gain the following *dalīl*: the skins of carrion, when they are not tanned, are impure and consequently forbidden.[28] Thus the hadith on tanning already yields a contradiction with regard to the statement of the Maymūnah-hadith, and it is not necessary to adduce the controversial hadith of Ibn ʿUkaym. The subsequent arguments of Ibn ʿAbd al-Barr follow the ways already described. At any rate, his reasoning shows very clearly how much classical authors on Islamic law are aware of the limitations of their possible knowledge, how they lay claim only to "almost certain knowledge" even of evident issues, and how they have developed a subtle terminology which reveals a certain skepticism with regard to gaining knowledge.

A result of this skepticism is a necessarily open-ended discourse. Since no interpretation may claim certainty, competing interpretations can never be conclusively discounted, and possible new interpretations may not be rejected out of hand. Therefore, none of the opinions on the problem of tanning mentioned above may be predicated as the correct one or as being refuted, let alone un-Islamic, even if any legal scholar of today would hardly support az-Zuhrī's opinion. Since this is the situation, the identical questions that have been discussed hundreds of times in handbooks, commentaries, and collections of opinions are treated over and over again. By no means is a legal opinion (fatwa) written only on issues arising for the first time. In all periods of history, there are fatwas dealing with problems that one would expect to have been solved long ago. It would not be difficult, for example, to collect dozens of fatwas from all centuries on the prohibition of wine, and our question of tanning continues to be treated by Ibn ʿUthaymīn, among others, who in his fatwa unreservedly appropriates the Shāfiʿite position.[29]

If we meet with a self-confident legal scholar who discounts an opponent's opinion as absurd, and claims to hold the only right position, we always have to evaluate such a statement against the background of the theory of knowledge discussed above. In contrast to a theologian whose tenets claim to be irrefutably true, legal scholars maintain only that it is more probable that their judgments agree with the divine judgment.

But can a state be run on the basis of such an undogmatic law? In fact, it turns out to be a source of possible problems that the legal scholar has a dual task: as a representative of religious scholarship, he must investigate the divine order (for the most part, however, attaining only judgments on probabilities); at the same time, he has a responsibility to help shape the social life of the members of a secular community and to arrive at unambiguous judgments. To put it in Islamic terminology: in his position as an Islamic legal scholar, the jurist attempts to find the *ḥukm*, that is, the divine judgment upon a human action, and as a secular judge he is obliged to issue a *ḥukm*, a binding judicial decision. So we have on one side the one *ḥukm* of God, and on the other side the expectation from the mufti and the judge to issue a definite *ḥukm*. In between, there is the realm of ambiguity, through which the legal scholar, with the help of the criteria of probability, has to find his way. On the one hand, there is the question of how God positions Himself in view of the different interpretations of His order; on the other, the question of how legal scholars, with their plurality of possible interpretations, accommodate the demand for judicial certainty.

The question of the relationship between the judgments of the jurists and the divine judgments is discussed in the controversy around the statement "Every *mujtahid* hits (the right spot)" (*kull mujtahid muṣīb*). A *mujtahid* is a legal scholar who is qualified to find justice by using his own interpretation of the legal sources. If a legal question arises that cannot be decided upon with certainty, and two scholars arrive at two different judgments, both of them still "hit" upon the divine *ḥukm*. Many Ḥanafites and Shāfiʿites held this opinion.[30] Others, however, took exception to the notion that the divine *ḥukm* is realized only through the judgment of the *mujtahid*—a consequence of the position just outlined. They assumed instead that the divine judgments of human actions are fixed all along. Thus, only one *mujtahid* "hits" the divine judgment;

the others do not. But the *mujtahid* who misses cannot be forced to acknowledge the right aim. His false judgment will not be counted as a sin—on the contrary, he is assured of receiving divine recompense for his endeavors. The one who hits upon the right answer receives a double recompense. The layman who is not qualified for *ijtihād* is obliged to follow the *mujtahid* in any case, because he cannot decide himself who is right. However, he is bound to choose the *mujtahid* who is available and best qualified, and, if there are competing fatwas, to follow the one by the better *mujtahid*, not the one whose opinion suits him better.[31]

Regardless of whether one considers different *aḥkām* as being simultaneously right, or insists that only one *ḥukm* is right, but in practice ascribes to the wrong judgment the same validity as to the right one—the relation between the *one* divine order, on the one hand, and the multiplicity of the options of interpretation, on the other, is arrived at by a *suspension of the truth*. Realizing that, in all questions of the *furūʿ*, and at all times, truth is dependent on the learning and acumen of the legal scholars, and since none of them can lay claim to infallibility, there will never be a definite solution, and all questions will have to be posed and answered again and again.

In this model, the will of God and the multiplicity of interpretations are quite compatible. But it is more difficult to solve the problem of how the multiplicity of learned interpretations can be aligned with the need for unambiguous and consistent rules with regard to persons subjected to juridical procedure.

Initially, a solution presented itself that exactly followed the principle of reduction of complexity we have already observed in the privileging of the "seven Quranic readings" or the "Six Books" of the hadith tradition. In the interest of practical applicability, the number of maintainable opinions had to be reduced. This happened first in the legal schools. While in the printed version of al-Māwardī's detailed legal compendium, the topic of the use of the organs of carrion—skin, sinews, bones, horns—contains around twenty pages,[32] Māwardī's younger contemporary ash-Shīrāzī (393–476/1003–1083), in his handbook on Shāfiʿite law, presents only the Shāfiʿite position: "The skin of every animal which by decease has become impure becomes pure by tanning, except dogs and pigs."[33] The six divergent positions of our table are not mentioned, because in this handbook only the discussions within the author's legal school are represented. However, even within one legal school, divergent positions are on the agenda. Ash-Shīrāzī continues his discussion by expounding upon the problem of whether skins that have become pure by tanning may be sold. It is interesting to note that ash-Shāfiʿī himself has changed his position regarding this issue. And there is complete discord among authors on the question of whether the hair of deceased persons is to be classified as pure or impure. Here, ash-Shīrāzī is compelled to present three different lines of argumentation, which lead to five different positions.[34]

But it can be done more briefly, too. Al-Māwardī has reduced the 4,000 pages of his *Ḥāwī* to a sort of crib sheet of cues of Shāfiʿite law. In this text, titled *al-Iqnāʿ* (The contenting), only one sentence is retained from our initial problem—and that sentence answers a certain question we have not addressed so far. The sentence is: "If the skin of carrion is tanned by bark from dodonaea or acacias or substances which have a comparable effect, like gallnut, it becomes pure."[35] In this treatise, controversies are mentioned only rarely. But we should not be misled: behind the forty pages of the *Iqnāʿ* there are still the 4,000 pages of the *Ḥāwī*. It is easy to learn forty pages by heart, and one can without difficulty recall al-Māwardī's formulation of the prevalent legal opinion in the Shāfiʿite school, and at the same time remember the more detailed treatment of the subject matter in class. Since the training of the judges was based essentially on such concise handbooks on the *furūʿ* and their commentaries, we may assume that the actual court sentence seldom deviated from them. Thus, a fairly high degree of legal certainty evolved, which made the administration of the law predictable and ensured that, for example, a trader from Syria, which was dominantly under Shāfiʿite jurisdiction, could expect to be treated in Tunis according to common Mālikite mercantile law, and not be surprised by exegetical feats of an overambitious jurist.

Restricting the number of Sunni legal schools to four (we have seen that, in the ninth century, there were more), and letting those schools privilege certain legal opinions as dominant school opinions thus constituted necessary procedures to make justice calculable and applicable transregionally. But for centuries, further restriction of the legal plurality continued to be seen as undesirable. On the contrary, in the Ayyūbid and Mamluk period, the pride of this legal plurality in the form of four Sunni legal schools reached a summit that also found its expression in architecture, namely in the form of mosques or madrasahs with four iwans (estrades), to each of which one of the four legal schools is assigned. A particularly beautiful example is the mosque and madrasah of Sultan Hasan in Cairo. In this period, even in smaller towns, four chief qadis from each legal school were appointed. The sultan in Cairo, or his Damascene deputy, assembled all four chief qadis around him for every important occasion. Toward the end of this period, as-Suyūṭī wrote his treatise on the praise of the difference of opinions, which will engage us in the next section.

It is quite probable that, during this time, a balance was achieved between the acceptance of a plurality of legal opinions and the need for a functioning, largely homogenous juridical procedure, a balance that showed the highest degree of functionality at all levels of society.

For a long time, Western scholarship has not recognized this achievement, let alone appreciated it. Joseph Schacht held that the formative period of Islamic jurisprudence had already ended with ash-Shāfiʿī—who did not even leave behind a finished legal methodology. In this period, Schacht believed, the "door of *ijtihād*" had been closed, thus initiating a time of stagnation and decline—an idea that has had wide currency ever since Schacht, in the Islamic world as well as among Western scholars. Meanwhile, it has become established, that before the Ottoman period, there was no "closing of the door of *ijtihād*"[36] and, for that matter, no "closing of the door of *taṣḥīḥ*"—that is, the retrieval of flawless hadiths (see p. 100). The only matter of discussion has been the extent to which *ijtihād* may be practiced without staggering the basis of the legal system. Can there exist an "absolute *mujtahid*," that is, someone who is qualified to alter the basis laid by the founding fathers of the legal schools? Indeed, as-Suyūṭī himself, the panegyrist of the *madhhab* system, laid claim to this rank. But for most scholars, the stability of the system remained more important than the unpredictable ambition of individual and self-appointed "absolute *mujtahids*." On the question of the day-to-day development of the law, the problem of *ijtihād* was never controversial. The works on the methodology of law always contain sections on the prerequisites of *ijtihād*, which for them is the normal situation, while mere "imitation," *taqlīd*, is permissible only under closely limited conditions.

So if an author argues for the "opening of the door of *ijtihād*"—and, in fact, the existence of the purported "closing of the door of *ijtihād*" is attested almost exclusively by authors who plead for something they think is its "opening"—then one can always expect a person with a greater amount of reforming zeal. It is understandable that such a reforming zeal has arisen precisely in the dispute with the Western world, and equally natural is the fact that some apologists of *ijtihād* do not strive for a greater variety of opinions, but seek instead the enforcement of an exclusive position that had not been accepted so far.

Characteristically, the attempt to modernize Islamic law has initially taken a seemingly backward course. By the end of the nineteenth century, the Islamic civil code in the Ottoman Empire was implemented. This so-called *mecelle* became valid in 1877, and partially remained the law in the successor states of the Ottoman Empire up to the Second World War. This meant a standardization that conformed to all modern requirements. However, it is obvious that such a codification of Islamic law totally misses its essence. What a perversion of Islamic law the *mecelle* represents can be seen in the fact that, for the first time in the Islamic world, Jews and Christians were also subject to Islamic prescriptions of the civil code. Even today, Islamic states confine themselves, as a rule, to considering the Sharia as only *one* source of their (set) law.

THE GIFT OF AMBIGUITY

With the help of the following chart, let us summarize how in the theory of the *uṣūl al-fiqh* an accumulation of probabilities leads to a legal judgment. We have not yet taken into account "consensus" and "analogical reasoning" as sources of law, nor have we included further sources, such as common welfare, which are implemented in different ways according to different legal schools. But even if we restrict ourselves to the Quran and hadith as sources of law, a complex tableau emerges.

First of all, neither textual corpus is transmitted without variant readings. While the Quranic readings that are transmitted with the highest degree of probability (i.e., the Seven or the Ten) display relatively few variant readings that are juridically relevant,[37] hadiths similar in content are often transmitted in very different textual form. For example, there is a tradition of the Maymūnah-hadith mentioned above ("Why do you not use its skin?") that has the supplement ". . . after you have tanned it"—which, if one could accept its authenticity, would lead, of course, to a much swifter solution of the problem.[38]

For the transmission of the hadith, this question of authenticity presents the greatest problem. In order to solve it, we are again dependent on traditions for establishing how reliable each transmitter is—which in turn may be more or less reliable.

In the next instance, the text of the Quran and the hadith are to be interpreted linguistically. The classical treatises on the *uṣūl* devote the most space to this linguistic exegesis. Their analytical instrument is philology, which had attained a supreme level of sophistication in the discipline of rhetoric, had anticipated innumerable insights of modern linguistics as early as the twelfth century, and offered the most convincing solutions to many problems, such as the definition of the metaphor. It is evident that such problems, as well as the exegesis of content, can only be tackled with a *certain degree* of probability, and never definitely.

Eventually, the question emerges of how to proceed if two indications contradict one another. In this "assessment of probability" (*tarjīḥ*), the jurist has to decide whether a *dalīl* is sufficiently well transmitted and sufficiently unambiguous to lead

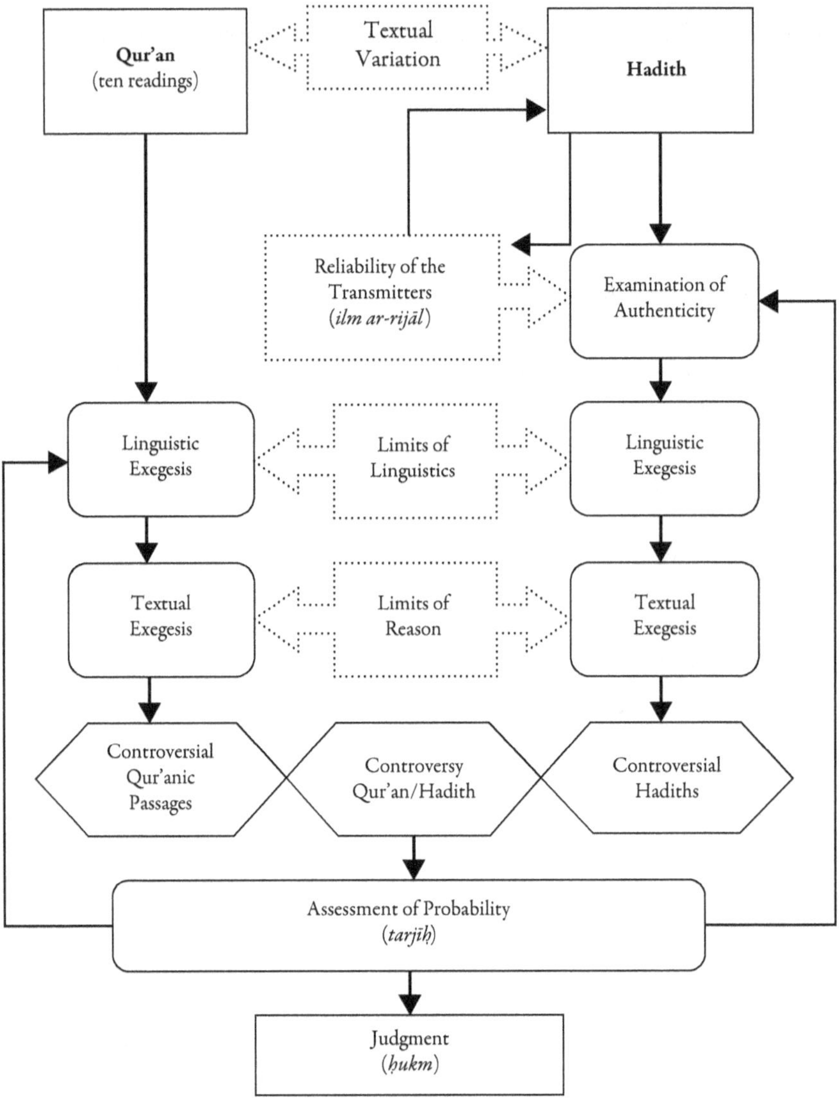

to certain knowledge, and, if this is not the case, how to proceed on the basis of contradictory indications. He then has to decide whether those contradictions may be reconciled with one another (for instance, by applying both indications, if one of them is understood as a specification of the other, as the tanning problem allowed); whether one passage must be understood as abrogated; or whether perhaps a proof on the basis of analogy must be rejected as less probable.[39] The final judgment on the issue is by the *mujtahid*, a judgment that ideally agrees with the divine *ḥukm*, but in the great majority of instances is confronted with competing judgments of other jurists. Thus a difference of opinion, *ikhtilāf*, arises.

According to classical theory, differences of opinion (*ikhtilāfāt*) are an indispensable part of the law, which on the one hand is based on the divine order of law, and on the other hand materializes as manmade law. As in the case of the field of different Quranic readings, which, according to classical conception, are an essential part of the Quranic text, one may find this plurality annoying or conceive of it as an enrichment. After what we have said so far, it comes as no surprise that modern authors tend to have the former reaction, while classical authors mostly appear to be followers of the latter position.

The Egyptian master scholar as-Suyūṭī (849–911/1445–1505) has devoted a specific treatise to this topic, *Jazīl al-mawāhib fī ikhtilāf al-madhāhib* (The generous gift: on the difference of opinion of the legal schools). As-Suyūṭī engaged in elaborate self-justifications, and was a man who saw himself as an absolute *mujtahid*—and even as a *mujaddid* of the tenth century, for there exists a hadith from the Prophet Muḥammad saying that at the beginning of every new Islamic century a "renewer" (*mujaddid*) of Islam will be sent forth. Since as-Suyūṭī was convinced that he qualified as such, due to his achievements, and since his biographical dates fit, he came to the conclusion that he was precisely this *mujaddid*. Be that as it may, he is not a marginal "liberal" figure who sings the praises of plurality, but a thoroughly "orthodox" religious scholar.

For his argument, he uses a hadith in which the Prophet asks his people to first search the Quran; then, if they do not find an indication in it, the Prophet's sunna (example); and next, what the companions of the Prophet have said; because "my companions are like the stars in the sky: you are rightly guided to whomever you may turn, while the difference of opinions among my companions is a mercy for you" (*wa-khtilāfu aṣḥābī lakum raḥmatun*).[40]

As-Suyūṭī was too good a hadith scholar not to know that this hadith was open to question, and the fundamentalists of our days are charging an open door when they go up in arms about the authenticity of this hadith—or its variant, even more popular (and even less well attested), *ikhtilāfu ummatī raḥmatun* (The difference of opinion within my community is a mercy).[41] For as-Suyūṭī does not endeavor in the slightest to discuss this hadith under the aspect of hadith criticism; instead, he intends to arrive at good reasons for the tenet—and this is his core thesis—that indeed "the difference of opinion between the legal schools constitutes in this religious community a great mercy and a huge advantage."[42]

First of all, as-Suyūṭī mentions several cases from the early period of Islam in which certain authorities *consciously* refrain from the opportunity of a disambiguation. For instance, this incident:

> I heard Mālik b. Anas [died in 179/796 in Medina] say the following: "When the caliph al-Manṣūr [reigned 136–158/754–775] performed the pilgrimage, he said to me: 'I have decided to give an order to have the writings composed by you copied and have sent one copy to every Muslim garrison town. I shall order all people to act according to the rules laid down in them and not to turn toward other rules.' I replied: 'O commander of the Muslims, don't do that! The people have already taken cognizance of different opinions and have heard different traditions and transmit different reports. So every group keeps to what has reached it first and they adhere to that from among all the different opinions of people. Let then the inhabitants of all regions keep to what they have chosen for themselves!' "[43]

Whatever historical truth this tradition contains, it says nothing less than that Mālik b. Anas, the leading figure of the Medinan legal scholars (and from whom the legal school named after him would emerge), consciously turns down the opportunity to make his legal doctrine the basis of a law that would be authoritative for the whole empire. We remember: ʿUthmān is said to have consciously refrained from using orthographical signs in his Quran redaction that would have rendered impossible variant readings of the text. Similarly, a father figure of Islamic law is quoted as a principal witness for the conscious and desired plurality of legal opinions.

In what follows, as-Suyūṭī's discussion of his core thesis moves in ways that remind us of Ibn al-Jazarī's argument that allows the multiplicity of possible interpretations of the Quran to render further prophecy unnecessary. As-Suyūṭī also argues that the former prophets had brought to their respective communities a single and very constricted law that had offered no choice and thus, one may infer, outlived its usefulness. However, writes as-Suyūṭī, the divine order (*sharīʿah*) of Islam is "easy and generous," to be observed in the "Seven *aḥruf*," the possibility of abrogation, the option to choose between two procedures in certain cases, and, in particular, the positive assessment of the *ikhtilāf*:[44]

> This being so, the schools in their diversity may be viewed as several '*sharīʿahs*' which are all prescribed in this one *sharīʿah*, and this one *sharīʿah* is as a number of different *sharīʿahs*, all of which the Prophet brought with him when he was sent down. . . . [This fact distinguishes the Prophet as against all other

> prophets] insofar as every one of them was sent with only one *ḥukm* (for every issue), while he—God bless him and grant him salvation—for every single issue brought several *aḥkām* that are equally valid as offering a basis for a judgment and enforcing it, *aḥkām* that legitimize everyone who upholds them [i.e., "every *mujtahid* hits (the right spot)"] and grant him recompense and right guidance.[45]

This summarizes as-Suyūṭī's "gift" of plurality. In modern times, his position is no longer met with great enthusiasm. The contemporary need for unambiguousness cannot be brought into accordance with the plurality of the legal schools. Unambiguousness may only be attained where truth rules. The old paradigm of probability was: there exists truth. It may be manifold ("every *mujtahid* hits [the right spot]") or not, but since we are incapable of knowing it, our action, within the framework of an assessment of the plausibility of our decisions, is justified in any case. This paradigm is no longer valid.

This suspension of truth could equally offer a basis for a democratization of Islamic law. But the development tends in another direction. This can be studied with the Salafist scholar Ibn ʿUthaymīn, who has already voiced his opinion as a Quran interpreter. There is also a text by him on the subject of *ikhtilāf* that, thanks to the Internet and an English translation, has found wide dissemination. It is titled "The Difference of Opinion Between Scholars: Their Causes and Our Position in Regard of Them" and begins with a subtle intertextual reference to the hadith (not generally accepted) saying "The difference of opinion is a mercy for our community." In Ibn ʿUthaymīn's text, we read: "It is a mercy of God—He is hallowed and exalted—for this community that in the fundamentals of religion and their basic sources, there is no difference of opinion."[46] In fact, this is the classical opinion as far as fundamental tenets of belief are concerned. But Ibn ʿUthaymīn's optimistic certitude exceeds that position by far. The Prophet, he writes, has delivered a message of explicitness so sufficient that it is in no need of subsequent clarification. The Prophet has been sent in order to proclaim right guidance and the religion of truth, and this excludes error and false religion in every meaning of expression.[47]

Since right guidance is clear and unambiguous, and since no religious and trustworthy person would intentionally contradict what the Quran and the sunna say, differences of opinion must *always* result from an error (*khaṭaʾ*). This radically changes the status of the law, as opposed to its status in the classical system. How far-reaching a change this is can be seen through a comparison between the lists of "causes of the *ikhtilāf*" in Ibn Juzayy and in Ibn ʿUthaymīn.

The fiftieth subchapter of Ibn Juzayy's introduction to legal methodology—in a sense, his crowning conclusion—consists of a list of sixteen possible causes for differences of opinion. Some of them have been mentioned already in our discussion of the animal skin problem. According to Ibn Juzayy, the most important cause is "contradictoriness of the indications."[48] (2) is "lack of knowledge of an indication" (that is, as a rule, lack of knowledge of a pertinent hadith), followed by (3), a "difference of opinion on the valid kind of transmission of the hadith." Then come two causes (4 and 5) referring to different principles of legal methodology between schools; next (6) is differences of opinion due to different Quranic readings. Further causes of differences of opinion originate from different possibilities for grammatical interpretation of a linguistic expression (7 and 8); from divergent interpretations of homonymous expressions (9); and from divergent understandings of whether a given expression is general or specified (10), veridical or tropical (11), complete or needing supplementation (12). Cause (13) concerns the question of "whether a *ḥukm* is abrogated or not." The last three causes have to do with questions of whether an order or an interdiction should be understood as obligatory or recommended, and whether an act of the Prophet is tantamount to an obligatory order, or is only a recommendation, or in fact indicates only that the act is permissible.

Ibn ʿUthaymīn's list of causes for differences of opinion is much briefer. Many of the exegetical procedures that were common knowledge of classical legal scholars are rejected by the Salafist Ibn ʿUthaymīn, since he postulates the principal clarity of all Quran and hadith texts. These would be sufficient to solve all questions without resorting to complicated analogical proofs. His position, which is centered on hadith, can also be seen in the fact that six out of the seven causes he names concern the hadith tradition. Since for Ibn ʿUthaymīn, methods of finding justice that deviate from those of the Salafists constitute heresy, he is not compelled to address differences of opinion due to differences of legal methodology.

The main difference between Ibn ʿUthaymīn's approach and a classical approach like Ibn Juzayy's is the former's fundamental conviction that in every case, only *one* interpretation is right and hence all others must be wrong. This difference is clear even in the language of the authors. Ibn Juzayy explicitly ascribes only one cause—"lack of knowledge of an indication"—to human failure. In all other cases, two positions simply stand side by side, either of which can be held, depending on the case. Ibn ʿUthaymīn, on the contrary, always sets the wrong positions in opposition to the only right one. Accordingly, he formulates the "lack of knowledge of an indicator" (his cause no. 1) as follows: "The first reason is the fact that a person who holds the divergent opinion and is wrong in his judgment has not received an indication."[49] One should, however, render the word *dalīl* in Salafist texts as "proof" (as the English internet version has it). To be sure, this translation is not correct (the Arabic equivalent to "proof" is *burhān*, a term also used in the works on *uṣūl*), but it acknowledges the changed understanding.

This terminology is pursued by Ibn ʿUthaymīn. Ibn Juzayy treats abrogation, as he treats most of his points, as a pro-and-con weighing of arguments. For Ibn ʿUthaymīn, the question of whether abrogation exists in a given case can only arise if somebody *does not know* that there exists an abrogating passage. Similarly, *dalāʾil* that contradict each other do not exist for him; there is only the erroneous supposition that a contradiction exists.[50] It is not true that "every *mujtahid* hits (the right spot)"; only one hits. Therefore, the opinion held by an author is not designated, as in the classical texts, as *al-arjaḥ* (the more probable one) or *al-aṣaḥḥ* (the more valid one), but as *aṣ-ṣawāb* (the correct one).[51] The apodictic statement has replaced the comparative form of the classical texts.

It is obvious that in this system in general, whenever the ruling opinions of the different legal schools are at variance, only one opinion can be the right one. Since none of the established legal schools can be right everywhere and always, and since it is a sin to diverge from the true guidance even though one knows better, the principal Salafist assumption holds that adherence to a legal school is nothing but sacrilege and heresy.

Therefore, this modern Islamic theory of law is often called *lā madhhabiyyah*, "antischool movement." In fundamentalist circles, this movement has often replaced a former affiliation to the Ḥanbalite school (and its Wahhabi offshoot) and has gained such a degree of popularity that one might even call it a new legal school—if this designation would not contradict its own self-concept. It is not the aim of this movement to be put side by side with the other legal schools; the aim is to delegitimize their claim to a nonexclusive truth by laying claim to the exclusivity of truth. A traditional scholar like the Syrian shaykh Muḥammad Saʿīd Ramaḍān al-Būṭī (1929–2013) is not wrong when he calls the *lā madhhabiyyah* "the most dangerous heresy that threatens the Islamic *sharīʿah*."[52]

It may be observed that Salafist texts such as the treatise by the Saudi author Ibn ʿUthaymīn, on the difference of legal opinions, create an initial impression of being very traditionalist—especially for a Western observer—since they deal with topics and problems that have been treated in Islamic scholarly literature for centuries and that are removed, as far as is conceivable, from current discussions in Western modernity. But a closer look reveals that they constitute an almost unimaginably drastic break with tradition, because all traditional presuppositions are being discarded. The *ḥukm* of classical Islamic law, regarding the overwhelming majority of its cases that do not allow for complete certainty, always contains an element of ambiguity. Even if some *ḥukm* may claim to have a degree of, say, 99 percent probability (and scarcely any can do that), it still retains that one percent probability of the dissenting opinion. The Salafist position of the *lā madhhabiyyah* is the kind of reform that is based on an *intolerance of ambiguity*. Thus, it must be understood as the most radical attempt so far to *modernize* the Islamic law.

The Ḥanbalite school emerged from the dispute with the theological rationalist movement of the Muʿtazilah, and as such was originally a theological movement; only in a second step did it become a legal school. This tendency has gained complete prevalence, through the catalyst of Western rationalist modernity, in its stepchild, the *lā madhhabiyyah*. A legal school that—according to human criteria—searches for the most adequate judgment has developed into a search for truth that perceives as intolerable the plurality of possible truths implied by the ambiguity of the normative texts. Thus, the Salafiyyah is representative of the general tendency toward the "theologization of Islam," which in turn is a reaction to the demand of the modern West to achieve ideological unambiguity.

5
The Islamization of Islam

Christianity destroyed for us the whole harvest of ancient civilization, and later it also destroyed for us the whole harvest of Mohammedan *civilization. The wonderful culture of the Moors in Spain, which was fundamentally nearer to* us *and appealed more to our senses and tastes than that of Rome and Greece,* was trampled down . . . *because it had to thank noble and manly instincts for its origin—because it said yes to life, even to the rare and refined luxuriousness of Moorish life!*

—Friedrich Nietzsche, *The Antichrist*

When people talk about the Islamic world, we almost always encounter the emphatic assertion that there is no separation between the religious and the secular spheres—indeed, that there is no secular sphere, because Islam permeates and regulates all areas of life. Probably no other prejudice concerning Islam has had a more devastating effect than this one. In Europe, the separation between the worldly and the religious—or, more precisely, the emancipation of the worldly from the domination of the religious—is held to be the most important precondition for modernity. To assert that such a distinction not only has never been known in Islamic history, but also is wholly alien from the essence of Islam—this means that Islam is essentially incompatible with modernity. According to this view, Islam thus remains in the Middle Ages in perpetuity, since "throughout the Middle Ages, religion remained man's primary interest."[1] It is easy to imagine the consequences of this conviction for the West's contact with Muslims and the Islamic world.

It is not so difficult to disprove this prejudice. As would be natural, there have existed areas free from religion in Islamic culture; people *would* differentiate between religious and worldly matters; and many of those people would be principally interested in things other than religion. But before we can draw conclusions from these commonplace observations, we must check some circular arguments and unravel some knots of prejudice.

One such pivotal knot is the term "Islamic culture." As Almut Höfert has observed, when people speak of the civilizations of the ancient world, they identify "among others, mostly the following five: Europe, India, China, Japan, and Islam. It is striking that among these civilizations, only Islam is not designated by a geographical term, but receives its denomination from a religion. This fact which, like the paradigm of civilization, goes back to the nineteenth century, turns out to be a fundamental conceptual obstacle."[2] It can be shown that in the course of the nineteenth century, there was a growing intensification of the "Islamization of Islam,"[3] first in Europe and then in the Near East,[4] with curious consequences. The word "Islam" serves both as a term for a religion with an established set of religious norms, and as a term for a culture that is not at all coextensive with the former. For one thing, the "culture of Islam" was the culture of many members of other religions. Until the end of the First World War, a large part of the population of what is today Turkey was non-Muslim. Second, many areas of life that are definitely not affiliated with religion are termed "Islamic." A great number of the objects exhibited in our museums of Islamic art belong to the secular sphere of life, but hardly anyone seems to object when, in an exhibition of "Islamic art," we can observe a jug with figured motifs and then move on to a cabinet displaying a wine goblet listed in the catalog as "Islamic metalwork."[5] And yet to talk of an "Islamic wine goblet" is as reasonable as to talk of "Christian adultery."

Whole areas of secular life are sacralized by terming them "Islamic," which in turn blurs the differences among Near Eastern societies. For example, some speak unthinkingly of "Islamic medicine," ignoring the fact that medicine in the cultures of the Near East constituted a separate subsystem of society. It had its own experts, whose knowledge was committed exclusively to the standards of its own discipline. Theologians or other religious experts had no say in it. When a patient or his relatives asked a scientifically trained doctor for help, they expected the patient to be treated according to the commonly recognized standards of

Galenic humoral pathology as developed by Arab, Persian, and Indian physicians, and to receive the respective therapy and medicaments. This kind of medicine did not possess anything "Islamic," in the sense of a religious system of norms.

At the same time, something like "Islamic" medicine—that is, the so-called medicine of the Prophet (*aṭ-ṭibb an-nabawī*) did exist, for the Prophet Muḥammad himself is said to have taken care of the health of his community. There are numerous traditions, most of them not too trustworthy, that report on the Prophet administering dietetic advice to healthy and sick people.[6] This "Medicine of the Prophet" was collected by hadith scholars—not professional physicians—and apparently played a role in everyday practice that is comparable to medieval Western medicine à la Hildegard of Bingen. Someone who consulted a professional physician did not expect a honey recipe in the style of the Prophet, but rather a phlebotomy or medicaments according to the serious standards of humoral pathology. Finally, a third sort of "Islamic" medicine might be named, which is treatment by amulets, talismans, prayers, spells, and magical practices. This form of therapy also found its written form in books by authors other than proper physicians or established religious scholars—even if, time and again, they stole their authoritative names.[7] This is another wholly distinct discourse that was neither accepted (let alone practiced) by physicians nor approved by most religious scholars.

Thus there exist three discourses, by and large independent from each other, on sicknesses and their therapy: a scientific one that has nothing to do with the religion of Islam; a pious one based on traditions that go back to the Prophet ("Medicine of the Prophet") and may have been popular, but was not seriously considered by the medical establishment; and a magical one that made use of Islamic formulas but was not accepted by real physicians or serious religious scholars. In the greater part of this scientific community, apparently not even a notable tolerance of ambiguity has existed.

Hence we see the consequences of the term "Islamic medicine": the plurality of Near Eastern discourses on medicine is negated; the totally *areligious* discourse on scientific medicine, coupled with the adjective "Islamic," acquires a meaning that is inappropriate and misleading, given that it is the least "Islamic" of the three discourses; and the existence of a firmly established social subsystem of "medicine" is veiled.

As a matter of fact, the existence of a medical discourse responsible only to its own norms seems to be a serious imposition for Western scholars, acceptable only if followed by a great "But." Martin Plessner, a historian of the sciences in the Islamic world, writes:

> The medical works of Isaac Israeli and Maimonides are in no way different from the works of Islamic authors.... Science was perhaps the one cultural area that was least accessible to "Islamization." Moreover, the continued and undiminished hostility of official orthodoxy against the ancient sciences remained as characteristic of Islam as it was of Christianity until deep into the Middle Ages, and of orthodox Jewry to the very threshold of our present time. Knowledge not founded on revelation and tradition was deemed not only to be irrelevant but to be the first step on the path to heresy.[8]

Another Orientalist speaks of a "struggle between the religious and the secular powers."[9] He notes that an author (probably a hadith scholar) dedicated a work on the medicine of the Prophet to Sultan Bāyezīd II, and takes this fact as proof "that even here, toward the end of the fifteenth century, Galenic medicine found itself in the clasp of the medicine of the Prophet."[10] Neither author wants to acknowledge that in the classical Islamic world, there existed a juxtaposition of discourses that stayed relatively independent from one another, with each retaining its own system of norms. If one does not want to perceive the autonomy of different discourses, and deems the "Islamic" discourse the actual one (since it has to do with an "Islamic" culture), then the existence of a nonreligious discourse is bound to appear dubious.

Secular medicine is then viewed as a sort of pocket of resistance to religion ("least accessible to 'Islamization'") or as engaged in permanent strife against religion ("struggle," "clasp"). Such views correspond with the imagination of Orientalists who try to depict a society totally dominated by religion, rather than one with an everyday reality in which secular scientific medicine existed as an undisputed autonomous discourse. When pious patients carried their trust in God so far that they refused medical treatment (a behavior also found today in the Western world), or when hadith scholars preferred the medical wisdom of the Prophet to all secular science, those instances did not invalidate the autonomy and significance of the scientific medical discourse. It stands to reason that some individuals may have felt tensions between pious belief and secular learning. But this did not affect the juxtaposition of a religious, a "magical," and a secular medical discourse, independent from each other.

The actual position of scientific medicine in everyday practice may be better documented by works on *ḥisbah*, which deal with concrete individual cases. These works consist of instructions to the *muḥtasib*, the "supervisor of the markets," whose principal job was trade control. This office was filled mostly by legal officials, and was mostly understood as a religious office. A typical *ḥisbah* work was written by an Egyptian *muḥtasib* from the 8th/14th century, Ibn Bassām,[11] who begins his chapter on the physicians with the following words:

> The head and authority of the medical profession should be someone who has great respect and possesses an unsurpassable professional experience. He should pledge irrevocably to demand from all his fellow-physicians that they be in command of what the doctor Yūḥannā b. Māsawayh has laid out in his book *Examination of the Physician*. Those that he finds to be complying with all these requirements, chapter by chapter, he should admit to their occupation, but should tell them that he has been nice to them, since he has not asked from them everything that Galen demands in his *Examination of the Physician*—for hardly any physician masters all of this. Those who do not comply with these requirements, the examiner should keep from this occupation and tell them to go on with their studies and keep to their books before he lets them treat patients, because that would mean great harm to them. . . . The chief physician should also read to his colleagues what Hippocrates has stipulated for himself and the other physicians and what he has pledged them to . . . [then follows the Hippocratic oath].[12]

After that we find purely professional rules—for instance, to have complete medical equipment ready, to convene a consultation among colleagues in complicated cases, and so on. All the norms that the *muḥtasib* is supposed to impose on the physicians are taken from professional medical discourse, whose basis is without question the Galenic medicine. The chief physician is supposed to have authority and experience, and the criterion of medical competence is nothing but professional ability. An authoritative text to be used for exams is a work of the Christian physician Ibn Māsawayh (died 243/857), which is apparently a revised and abbreviated version of a work by the pagan physician Galen (129–216 AD);[13] our author did not want to overwhelm beginners with this extensive text. All the advice and admonitions follow from the requirements of the medical profession. The only ethical statement of the text is the Hippocratic oath (Hippocrates died around 370 BC), which is quoted in full. Thus medical discourse derives even its ethical basis from its own practice; a fourteenth-century Muslim *muḥtasib* is asked to obligate the physicians according to the ethical principles of a pre-Christian pagan! It is somewhat odd here to continue speaking of an "Islamic" medicine.

The whole terminological misery is possible only because, in "Islamic" culture, the relation between religion and society was different from premodern history in Europe, and because this relation cannot be characterized by the terms used to describe the nature of Western modernity. The problem is twofold:

The first problem is that for every topic, there is also something or the other that is "Islamic." There exists, in fact, an "Islamic medicine" in the full—religious—sense of the term. But since the term "Islamic" denotes, on the one hand, the system of norms of the religion of Islam, and, on the other hand, the whole culture, "Islamic medicine" in the first sense is not at all identical with "Islamic medicine" in the second. Indeed, it represents only a comparably insignificant area, which was only rarely taken seriously by the experts on the social subsystem of medicine.

The second problem is that religion itself was differentiated in a highly complex manner (although this is perhaps a misleading way of expression, since all terms and formulations with which one attempts to describe the relation between religion and the world are shaped by the European experience; when they are deployed for the culture of the Near East, they inevitably result in a biased perspective). In other words: The Near Eastern societies in Islamic history present not only a high degree of division of labor,[14] but also a differentiation of societal subsystems, which can be found in comparable measure in Europe only in the modern period. This differentiation does not necessarily follow the same lines as in modern-day Europe. Most importantly, in the Near East, the religious/secular dichotomy plays a smaller role—not because religion is so omnipresent there, but because religion is not managed and defined by an ecclesiastical hierarchy; rather, in every partial system it assumes its own distinct function and therefore does not exist as a socially all-embracing system of "religion."

It is true that the Islamic world was always aware of the difference between *dīn* (religion) and *dunyā* (world), but the conflict situation is different from the one in Europe. Here, law, politics, medicine, literature, etc. can differentiate themselves as independent subsystems of the society only after they have emancipated themselves from the supremacy of the churches and the religiosity organized by them. The dichotomy between religion and the world is fundamental here. The Islamic world, in contrast, does not have churches that command the right to define the field of religion. Therefore, the development follows the converse direction. The urban cultures of the Orient retain the ancient standards to a high degree, and develop them, after less than a century of an Arabic transformation, toward ever-higher levels of complexity. This leads to an ever-increasing division of labor and social differentiation. Here, religion is not primarily an independent agent, but a factor that in every one of the different partial systems is construed and formed according to its own particular manner, without the construction and forming of religion prevailing over the other respective partial systems.

From this development results the following: the single partial systems are easily and clearly perceived. There is the law, Sufism, theology, hadith, medicine, literature, etc.—each of them equipped with its own standards, experts, and discourses. Religion plays a highly diverse role in each of these fields. It is central in theology (*kalām*), which inquires into truth; it is central in the hadith culture in a quite different form, namely as a pious tradition of the texts of the first generation of the Muslim community; it supplies the normative foundations for the law, whose experts, however, display a far more worldly bearing than the theologians and the hadith scholars, and employ a set of nonreligious discourses such as logic and rhetoric; it is irrelevant for scholarly medicine; and it plays almost no role for the men of letters. So each partial system of society has, in a sense, its own religion, while, on the other hand, a social partial system of religion *itself* is not easy to discover. We would most likely look for it in everyday religious cults—with the imams (leaders of the prayer), the muezzins, and the preachers. In this way, we would come closest to European perceptions of religion; after all, there is no question that these represent religious officeholders. But they occupy posts that are low paying; they have next to no influence on the intellectual strata; and they cannot constitute a genuine and authoritative religious discourse.

It is at this point that a further calamitous fallacy of Western interpreters of Islam sets in: *the* Islam, as a religion, was nowhere to be found. Religious elements, however, were to be found in quite diverse areas of society. Western interpreters imported from their own culture the fundamental belief in a religious sphere that is opposed to a worldly sphere. They ascribed every field that was covered by a fine layer of religious dust, be it ever so thin, to the religious sphere, and then declared the culture that bore the name "Islamic" as religious to the core. However, the kinds of references to religion maintained by jurists, theologians, Sufis, and preachers are totally diverse, and their relation to the worldly side of life is shaped more by the norms of their respective sphere of activity than by an alleged religious/worldly dichotomy.

The Western approach was different. To begin with, everything that revealed a remote relation to religion, however diverse in nature, was unequivocally booked under "religion." The whole culture was then named "Islamic" and counted as the archetype of a culture dominated to the core by religion. Then followed the final step: when Western interpreters had arrived at designating Islamic culture as religious to the core, they proceeded to do away with the remnants that did not readily conform to this approach. Everything in the Islamic world that was not obviously religious was either nevertheless sweepingly designated as "Islamic," for instance art and medicine, or seen as peripheral, for instance literature and music. In places where discourses of piety appeared next to less pious or even wholly secular ones, the nonpious discourses were seen as deviations from a norm—while of course the pious-religious discourse was seen as the one exclusively establishing the norm. So the entire Islamic culture can be described in the words of G. E. von Grunebaum as follows:

> Islam aims at comprehending life in its totality. It posits the ideal of a life in which, from the cradle to the grave, not a single moment is spent out of tune with or merely unprovided for by religious ruling. This distinction between important actions and unimportant detail of daily routine loses much of its meaning when every step is thought of as prescribed by divine ordinance. Profane and sacred no longer denote the area withdrawn from, and the area subject to, religious supervision. No sphere is left in which our doings are inconsequential for our fate in the hereafter. The relevance of our failings will vary according to their moral and social significance, but nowhere shall we find a no-man's land to which religion does not lay claim.[15]

This passage may, in fact, approximately describe the attitude of Ḥanbalī hadith scholars living in the Damascene suburb of Ṣāliḥiyyah. However, the author is not talking about pious transmitters of hadith, but about the Islamic world in general. The description given by von Grunebaum is nothing but an absurd caricature that has as much to do with the real life in Islamic societies as the monastic ideal of the Carthusian monks had to do with the everyday life of a Catholic Boston businessman. This fantasy Islam, depicted by von Grunebaum as a general law and a lived practice, existed before the nineteenth century, if at all, in a small pious minority, and exists today primarily in the imagination of Western Orientalists and radical Salafists. The mere fact that pious people who cherish such a comprehensive understanding of Islam have existed, and still exist, should not result in privileging the discourse of piety over other discourses.

To say it even more clearly: Historians of the Islamic world distort reality if they take religious discourses *a priori* as more important and more correct than nonreligious ones, or, should religious and nonreligious discourses contradict each other, if they consider the religious discourse as the norm and the nonreligious one as a deviation from it, only because we designate the culture being investigated as "Islamic" and base our view on the supposed religious saturation of this culture. Instead, we should always start our investigation with the question of what significance a given discourse possessed for which social stratum. It will then become evident that the old, pious *ʿulamāʾ* are credited with a privilege of discourse of which, in their own lifetimes, they would never had dared to dream. As the epigraph of this chapter has it, Nietzsche was fascinated by Islamic culture because he thought it owed its origins to the "noble and manly instincts"[16] which did not succumb to petty piety. Regarding this point, at the very least, he had a greater understanding of Islamic culture than many a contemporary expert on Islam.

In contemporary times, the "Islamization of Islam" has had an impact upon institutions that occupy themselves with the culture of the Near East. Few German and American universities have the discipline of "Arabic Studies." But that does not mean one cannot study Arabic or get a PhD in Arabic literature in other universities. These simply offer such courses under the name "Islamic Studies," which of course suggests that the preoccupation with literature is less relevant than the preoccupation with theology.

In English Studies, after all, one would not be expected to get a PhD on the doctrine of the sacraments of the Anglican Church. Since the label "Islamic Studies" implies that one is bound to pursue those studies in the sense of the religion of Islam, there is also an implication that other topics—such as literature, once a significant focus of Arabic Studies in Germany—are marginalized.

The marginalization of literature in today's view of "Oriental" history is striking. While in Arabic and Persian culture, poetry and artistic prose enjoyed a central focus of interest in all periods, and while literary discourse was by far the most important one for many areas of public and private life, contemporary experts on the region frequently believe they can manage without knowledge of the literatures and can simply skip the numerous poems interspersed in historical works and even in Quran commentaries. They are seduced into doing so, perhaps unconsciously, on the basis of a conclusion by analogy with our contemporary situation, where important matters are seldom treated in the form of literature, let alone in that of poems.

It is overlooked that, in the cultures of the Near East, things were quite different. This tendency to ignore literature is strengthened by the fact that by far the largest part of Arabic, Persian, and Turkish poetry is completely secular, and that it not only ignores religious norms but also downright contradicts them. Since supposedly there is nothing secular in Islam, nonreligious literature is ignored or discounted, against all evidence, as marginal.

But the frivolous poems of, say, Abū Nuwās were not sold under the counter. On the contrary, they were part of the cultural syllabus of the intellectuals, and not only those who worked in the secular area. Religious scholars as well, such as Ibn Ḥajar al-ʿAsqalānī, the greatest hadith scholar of the postformative era, wrote poems and frequently published them in various collections. Religious poems figure among these, but the subject of profane love in all its forms dominates by far.[17] Modern scholarship, however, has suppressed this secular aspect of Ibn Ḥajar's work so thoroughly that not even the author of the article on Ibn Ḥajar in the *Encyclopedia of Arabic Literature* took cognizance of this scholar's literary works.[18]

The "Islamization of Islam" not only blocks from view the nonreligious areas of life in the Islamic world, but also distorts the image of fields more likely to be assigned to the religious sphere. The primary example of this is Islamic law, which is regarded as a well-nigh ideal specimen of religious law. Many observers even go beyond calling the Islamic law "religious," speaking instead of a "sacred" or "holy" law, although Muslim jurists never used such terms. Still, labeling the law "religious" does not tell us anything about the judicial system, even if many who do so believe they have arrived at a characterization of its essence. From such a procedure follow false, or at best nonsensical, statements like the one asserting that Islamic law is the sum of Allah's commandments.[19] This "Islamization of the Islamic law" follows the same strategies we see in other areas. These strategies consist of (1) concentrating attention on the early period, (2) ignoring the nonreligious elements or downplaying their significance, and (3) designating all elements, no matter how religiously they are determined, as "Islamic," thus suggesting the religious nature even of elements whose religious character is not evident to the observer.

It is true that the ultimate foundation of Islamic law is of an unquestionable religious nature. There exists a divine order, namely divine judgments of the human acts; the attempt to approach this order through the exegesis of Islamic documents is the justification of the jurists' business.

Equally important, however, is the fact that since the end of the formative period (at the latest, since the middle of the fifth/eleventh century), the juridical system in the core countries of Islam presents itself as a distinct social subsystem with a conspicuous inside–outside differentiation, in which clearly definable problems are approached in a systematically specific manner, by following a systematically specific method and theory. The juridical system employs a highly complex technical terminology, which belongs only to this system and is defined in specialized dictionaries of juridical terms. A work with the neat title *Ṭilbat al-ṭalabah* (What students want) by Najm ad-Dīn an-Nasafī (died 537/1142) explains more than 1,500 terms with which a student of Ḥanafite law should be acquainted.[20] Scholars of juridical theory also differentiate theoretically between the general (*lughawī*) and terminological (*iṣṭilāḥī*) usage of terms.

The postformative system of Islamic law is the result of a process of differentiation, after which knowledge of religious traditions (hadith) emerged as an independent discipline; later on, in the view of jurisprudence (*fiqh*), it acquired the status of an ancillary discipline. From then on, legal scholars (*fuqahāʾ*, sing. *faqīh*) do not have to transmit hadith in order to be regarded as jurists. It is remarkable that jurists who are still active in both fields, *fiqh* and hadith, maintain the differentiation as follows: in their capacity as jurists, they call on the hadith texts that are applied in the standard texts of their respective legal school (*madhhab*), while in their capacity as hadith scholars, they also know and transmit other hadith texts, often with divergent contents. This means that they differentiate between their roles as hadith scholar and *faqīh*.

The separation between theology and jurisprudence is still more definite. The jurist is not responsible for the truths of religious belief, but he draws upon his fallible reason in order to arrive at judgments that cannot claim certainty. The area of religious dogma is, to a large degree, outside his responsibility. Vice versa, theologians cannot interfere in the affairs of the jurists. Again, it becomes obvious that the legal system in the Islamic world does not constitute a partial system of a superordinate system of "religion."

This is not affected by the fact that Islamic law, like Roman law, also regulates the ritual, that is, as the Roman jurist Ulpianus says in his famous definition of jurisprudence, *divinarum atque humanarum rerum notitia* (the knowledge of the divine and human things). Islamic legal manuals start with chapters on ritual purity and the four ritual duties (prayer, *zakāt* due, fasting, pilgrimage) and related topics (funerals, slaughtering, and sacrifices). These chapters are defined under the term *ʿibādāt* (religious observances) and are often explicitly marked as different from the following chapters on *muʿāmalāt* (social interactions), such as the laws of marriage, commerce, inheritance, procedures, contracts, and endowments, to name the most important ones. This shows that already the outline of legal manuals keeps religious and secular affairs separate and apart. The religious sphere is treated comprehensively only insofar as it is accessible to juridical regulation. This has been repeatedly criticized by Western observers, since one might reasonably expect religious, even divine law to also include statements on the interior relation of man to God.[21]

In fact, such statements exist in great number. They are not to be found, however, with the jurists, but in an overwhelmingly rich literature on piety, in books on *az-zuhd wa-r-raqāʾiq* (asceticism and heartrending admonitions), in Sufism, and with some theologians. Jurisprudence declares itself definitely not responsible for piety. Even for filling the position of a judge, piety (let alone an ascetic attitude) was not seen as a desirable or even necessary qualification. In a study of several manuals on the office of the qadi, Irene Schneider could point to only a few occasional remarks according to which the judge was supposed to be "god-fearing and honest." Instead of accepting the fact that this is all there is to it, she concludes that the small number of indications of the allegedly postulated religiosity of the judge is due to "the orientation towards religion [being] such an obvious fact that the available texts offer only few pieces of expressis verbis evidence."[22] To me, it seems far more self-evident that a qadi is supposed to be *honest* rather than be *religious*—and I am fairly confident that the authors of books on the office of the qadi did not view it much differently.

But Muslim authors may write what they want. The preconception of an "integral understanding of the world"[23] in a completely religious culture will always grant Western authors the right to fantasize for themselves a culture completely imbued by religion and to maintain—against all textual evidence—that "the religiosity of the judge and hence the religion as fundament of life" constituted a principal condition for the office of the judge in the Islamic world.[24]

A cross-check is instructive. A book on the office of the sermonizer—the first of its kind, one that the author composed in conscious reference to the works on the office of the judge—presents a wholly different job profile. In the very first paragraph, we read that the sermonizer must be "impeccable in his religious convictions." Not enough: his whole life should be oriented toward God: "When he gets up, he gets up for God, when he sits down, he sits down for God, when he moves, he does it for God, and when he rests, he does it again for Him."[25] This is how a Western observer imagines a religious Islamic personality, and this is the way an Islamic observer expects a sermonizer to be. If such an abandonment to God is not explicitly asked of judges, then it is not because it would be natural—that would be much more the case with sermonizers, after all—but simply because it was not expected from judges. The same view of the sermonizers was presented by the transmitters of the Quran. The author of a manual for Quran readers deems it the single most important requirement that the instruction in the reading of the Quran is conducted, both for teachers and students, "for the purpose of attaining God's contentment."[26] After this, there follow admonitions not to have one's eyes on worldly gain or a successful career and fame, and all this is buttressed by numerous Prophetic sayings.

It is hard to conceive of a greater difference between this work and the sober and professional handbooks for judges. The idea of a personality wholly shaped by religious perspectives did in fact exist in the classical Islamic world, and it found its considerable expression in the prolific literature on pious themes. But it did not constitute an ideal for the whole of society. The authors knew how to differentiate. A judge should be "devout," but only in the sense of "an honest man." There is no inquisition into his religious convictions. He should be mindful of attaining the respect of his fellow beings in worldly matters, but he should not forsake them; piety is not a job-related virtue. Opposite to this professional profile, we have that actually religious ideal of the sermonizer and the Quran reader. Here, where piety is indeed an obvious prerequisite, we see the plausible image of a thoroughly pious person that is supposed to be a model for the office holder. To be sure, this is not a general conception of man, valid for the whole of society, but a distinguishing mark of officeholders in the field of religion. Judges are not part of this field.

In fact, among the offices of Islamic jurisprudence, that of the judge is the one that has the least to do with religion. While the mufti is also supposed to issue legal opinions on areas of ritual law, the qadi is hardly ever concerned with that. Court proceedings almost always deal with "social affairs" and are not considered as religious acts. The author whose study on handbooks for judges has been quoted above states, in another context, that in reading ash-Shāfiʿī, who firmly speaks out against the holding of court proceedings in mosques, we may "discern a novel tendency to separate between a sacred and a profane—here juridical—area. Secular affairs, such as judicial proceedings, are segregated from religious service."[27]

Generally, an Islamic judge does not have a quality that, according to common Western ideas of religion, would designate him as a religious functionary—even if, in administrative terminology, the office of the judge belongs to the *waẓāʾif dīniyyah*, the "religious offices." His legitimation is due to the fact that he is installed by the state, and furthermore due to his scholarship and the respect that he is able to gain from the people of his judicial district. Piety, admittedly a widely appreciated virtue, cannot enhance this respect to a greater degree than it does for a person in other professions unrelated to the quality. Piety is not a specific feature of the judge. Quite the contrary—we observe again and again how the pious fought tooth and nail against accepting the office of qadi. To act as a judge and to remain sinless at the same time demanded superhuman strength. And finally, it is a horrible idea for a pious person to receive his salary from the state whose revenue consists, for the greater part, of non-Islamic taxes.[28]

Rather, the habitus of a judge in a leading position is that of a scholar who is proud of his knowledge and acumen, who has learned with older important scholars, and who completely masters the relevant literature. Whoever wants to be held in esteem holds an opinion on a number of legal issues, dissenting from the established position. More tokens of his belonging to the elite may be urbane proficiencies such as literary flair and the talent to write good poems; another token may be an ascetic detachment from the world, but that is by no means a privileged one.[29]

An Islamic judge does not have religious legitimation. He has no priestly privileges, no sacramental functions, no transcendental abilities, no influence on the salvation of his customers, no magical prowess, no supernatural knowledge. The court case is not a religious ritual, the venue of trial is not a sacred place. The judge issues his sentence not on the basis of a sacred text, that is, the Quran or hadith collections, but on that of established juridical handbooks, together with their commentaries as applicable in the given period. His statements are based, it is true, on Quranic and hadith texts, but also on rational procedures such as linguistic interpretation and logical proofs, as they are beaten into all law students (except those of the Ḥanbalī school) in the introductory chapters of the works on the theory of law. But for many areas of day-to-day judicial proceedings, these handbooks do not reveal much.

It is here that fatwa collections step in, compilations of legal decisions from which judges can find their bearings on the fundamental anthropological constant of quarrels between neighbors on molestation by noise or smell, or on the manifold problems arising from fruit trees in the neighbor's garden.[30] The legal opinions and decisions of older jurists recorded in these collections rest mostly on very general principles such as the avoidance of harm. There is no direct deduction from the word of God or the Prophet, and this is not considered a deficit. Such court rulings do not contain anything *religious*. In its legal doctrines and its findings of justice, the Islamic law hardly differs from Western legal traditions.

It is not to be denied that Islamic law contains essential religious elements. But it should be clear that labeling it as religious law, and hence as part of religion, leads to a distorted picture. Rather, Islamic law is the product of a legal system that contains both religious and nonreligious elements (as do, incidentally, most legal systems of the world, including the Western post-Enlightenment one). What is more important than the religious or nonreligious nature of specific areas of this legal system is the fact that, as a whole, it constitutes a clearly delimitable subsystem of the societies of the postformative Islamic world, one that follows its own rules and is characterized by a specific professionality. In recent years, it has increasingly become the main concern of scholarship in this field to study those rules and that professionalism. On the other hand, there still remains an older tradition of research and a tendency, primarily prevalent among the nonacademic public, to describe Islamic law as thoroughly religious and hence an irrational phenomenon. Such law—if it is not entirely denied qualification as "law"[31]—is supposed to appear archaic and strange in order to facilitate the presentation of Islam as an opposite pole to (Western) modernity.

In conclusion, still another strategy of the "Islamization of Islam" that has been mentioned before should be analyzed. When both a religious and a nonreligious discourse exist in a given social sector, the religious one will always be considered the norm, while the nonreligious one will either be judged as a deviation or remain unnoticed. This perspective even enters religion itself: where different religious movements and ways of thought exist side by side (that is, practically everywhere), each time the most radical, pious, bigoted, and intolerant variety will be considered as the norm, while all the other variant forms will count as deviations or remain unnoticed. An example of this is the statement by Martin Plessner, quoted above, according to which "the continued and undiminished hostility of official orthodoxy against the ancient sciences remained as characteristic of Islam as it was of Christianity until deep into the Middle Ages."[32] Plessner refers to two sources. The first one is the foreword to an edition of a philosophic-theological Utopian novel by the physician Ibn an-Nafīs. However, the passage quoted by Plessner contains almost precisely the opposite of what he makes of it. We read here that the "hostility of some sectors of Islamic orthodoxy, and the Ḥanbalī school in particular, towards the 'sciences of the ancients' was but one aspect of the intellectual life of the sixth/twelfth and the seventh/thirteenth century."[33] Clearly the authors say: not *the* orthodoxy, but only "some sectors," this being just *one* sector among many. We may rather observe, the authors Meyerhof and Schacht go on to write, "how highly the educated Muslims in the Ayyūbid and the Mamlūk period regarded the medical profession," and even if anti-Christian emotions may have arisen due to the Crusades, this has not affected the general positive attitude toward medicine as a principally non-Islamic science. In particular, "educated people, including the specialists in Islamic religious sciences, as a rule held aloof [from a negative attitude]. There were religious scholars who took an interest in philosophy and medicine, and medical men who were active in the field of religious scholarship."[34] Still, the authors write, there remained a perceptible tension between both areas, exemplified in the littérateur and philosopher ʿIzz ad-Dīn al-Irbilī (died 660/1262) whose private lectures on philosophy and the "sciences of the ancients" (i.e., the Greeks) were attended by Sunnis, Shiites, Jews, Christians, and unbelievers alike. Although he is said to have repented on his deathbed, ʿIzz ad-Dīn was an absolute freethinker. The entries devoted to him in the biographical dictionaries of his time and of later periods are full of praise for a brilliant mind and an inventive poet, despite his entirely un-Islamic worldview and way of life—he did not perform the prayers, and nor did he pay attention to the regulations of cultic purity.[35] Even the Ḥanbalite al-Yūnīnī has only words of praise for him, tactfully passing over ʿIzz ad-Dīn's lack of religion. Only one of his biographers has negative things to say about him, and that is Ibn Kathīr (died 774/1373), one of the most narrow-minded bigots in the intellectual history of Islam—a fact that has helped him attain great popularity these days. His Quran commentary of small originality is nowadays distributed by Saudi publishers in great numbers, and enjoys a great reputation especially with Salafist readers.

Thus Meyerhof and Schacht say that medicine and the "Greek" sciences were held in high esteem by scholars, including religious scholars, and that these disciplines met with opposition only from a few scholars, particularly Ḥanbalites, but that this antagonism had no lasting influence upon the flowering of those sciences. Even a decidedly areligious freethinker such as al-Irbilī was highly appreciated—with one single, and unsurprising, exception—by all learned authors, even Ḥanbalites.

It is hardly conceivable, then, how Plessner can base his statement that there was a "continued and undiminished hostility of official orthodoxy against the ancient sciences" on this wholly realistic and well-balanced presentation by Meyerhof and Schacht. Plessner's second reference offers more material, namely from Ignaz Goldziher's treatise published by the Prussian Academy of the Sciences in 1916 under the title *Stellung der alten islamischen Orthodoxie zu den antiken Wissenschaften* (The position of early Islamic orthodoxy regarding the ancient sciences).[36] In this treatise, Goldziher has collected a large part of what can be found in the statements of Islamic scholars who held a critical view of science. The motives for their opposition to the "Greek" sciences are quite heterogeneous. Some pious Sunnis, for instance, are afraid of contagion with heretical opinions concerning the eternity of the world, if they get into too intensive a contact with philosophy. But it was precisely the rationalistic theologians (*mutakallimūn*) who showed themselves to be outright adversaries of logic, since "in their rationalist efforts they dismissed the syllogistic rules of the methods of demonstrative proof."[37] Evidently we are witnessing here a controversy about the meaning of particular sciences, a dispute which cannot be reduced to the simple dichotomy of "rationalists" and "orthodoxy."

Goldziher goes on to deal extensively with opponents of logic. He even presents an edition of an Arabic text on the refutation of logic in order to substantiate his assertion that the Islamic "orthodoxy" is hostile toward this discipline that was taken over from the Greeks, and that the logician "does not belong to the favorites of orthodoxy."[38] Even if Goldziher is bound to quote several positive statements of undoubtedly "orthodox" scholars, he then hastens to dive into a treatise directed against logic, which he presents as an example of the general way of thought in Islam. This text, written by the hadith scholar Ibn aṣ-Ṣalāḥ (died 643/1243) is, according to Goldziher, "the explicit expression of the views in Ibn aṣ-Ṣalāḥ's time that shaped the orthodoxy of large parts of the Islamic world."[39]

This is an odd pronouncement, because precisely "in his time" (i.e., the seventh/thirteenth century) we witness the composition of numerous introductions to the methodology of jurisprudence (*uṣūl al-fiqh*). The authors were scholars of all four legal schools. The works of the three great schools, the Shāfiʿites, Ḥanafites, and Mālikites all contain, at all times, more or less detailed presentations of logical procedures to arrive at a proof, sometimes in the form of specific chapters, sometimes in the course of the chapter on deduction by analogy (*qiyās*). The latter is the way followed by al-Māwardī in his fundamental work on the methodology of jurisprudence.[40] According to Goldziher's terminology we would have to label al-Māwardī as "unorthodox." But in another passage of Goldziher's treatise, al-Māwardī is quoted as an authority for the position of hostility of the "orthodoxy" toward the "Greek" sciences, on the basis of the assertion (no doubt correct) that the Prophetic sayings in favor of attaining knowledge refer only to religious knowledge.[41] This way, the great al-Māwardī comes out to be orthodox and not orthodox at the same time!

Of course, logic has always been—and remains in our time—an established element of the curriculum of the Islamic universities. For this reason, introductions to this discipline have always been composed, as well as didactic poems (to make them more memorizable, or retrievable, for the student). As recently as in a work by ash-Shawkānī (died 1250/1832), logic appears without any reservation as a basic discipline of the Islamic sciences, followed by recommendations of suitable works for the beginner.[42] Now, if thousands of religious scholars have, for centuries, drilled hundreds of thousands of students in the discipline of logic, as developed by pagan Greeks, how can one talk of an opposition of the orthodoxy to logic? Toward the very end of his treatise, Goldziher admits the fact that "this logic-bashing attitude of the fanatics has eventually not prevailed in the curriculum of Islamic theology."[43] And this is not only true for logic: "The same phenomenon can be observed in the other branches of the *ʿulūm al-awāʾil* [the "sciences of the ancients," i.e., the Greeks], a proof of the well-known fact that the *theoretical* protests and desires of biased theologians in Islam could not disrupt the formation of *reality*."[44] How true, but what a chaos of terminology! Throughout Goldziher's treatise, the opponents of "the ancient sciences" are labeled, as the title announces, as "orthodox." But in the end, there remain only a few "fanatics" and "biased theologians" who *could not prevail*! One has to savor this volte-face slowly: The "orthodoxy" is hostilely minded toward the sciences of Greek origin, which, however, does not influence the "formation of reality"—which in turn leads to the conclusion that reality in the Islamic world is *unorthodox*!

In speaking of an "Islamic orthodoxy," Goldziher subsumes under that term people he subsequently calls "bigots" and (somewhat exaggeratedly) "fanatics," who were in no way able to influence reality. In this, he commits two mistakes. For one, he overlooks the basic fact of a *plurality* of discourses in the Islamic world, which was stabilized by a prevailingly high tolerance of ambiguity—even if, from time to time, dogmatic scholars turned up to aim poisonous barbs at people with dissenting opinions. Secondly, Goldziher privileges as "orthodox" precisely those discourses that are particularly intransigent and hostile to compromise and that look especially reactionary, fundamentalist, and "medieval" to modern eyes. In the end, however, he has to admit that these discourses do not constitute a majority. In light of the envisaged plurality of classical Islam, it is not legitimate to talk of an "Islamic orthodoxy," unless one uses this term in a very broad way. If such a problematic term is used at all, it should first be applied to movements that form the majority and "shape reality"—and to these the abominable enemies of logic simply do not belong.

Thus Plessner's contention of a "continued and undiminished hostility of official orthodoxy against the ancient sciences" becomes invalid. It is based on nothing but a backhanded attempt to equate a small group of exceptionally scrupulous pious people, mostly of Ḥanbalite provenance, with *the Islamic orthodoxy*. In this context, one will have to stop arguing that Islamic scholars are responsible for the slow development of the natural sciences in the Islamic world. As often as not, the answer to this problem is to be found in the West—an answer, that is, to the question of why it was here and only here, and from a certain point in history onward, that there arose an urgent need for scientific knowledge. It is not the fault of Islamic scholarship that such a need did not equally develop in the Islamic world.

The "Islamization of Islam" not only leads to wrong notions of the history of the Islamic world, but also contributes to the distortion of the Western view of today's Islamic world, a distortion that is on the one hand planned and politically favored, and that on the other hand follows its own dynamics and escapes control.

Some Muslims, it is true, have themselves fallen victim to the process of the "Islamization of Islam" and adhere to ideas of an integral Islamic society. But even the most fundamentalist Islamists are pushed by motives that are beyond religion. Thus, the members of the Palestinian Ḥamās are driven not only by the vision of an Islamic state, but also (and mostly first) by nationalistic fervor. Western media, however, never fail to furnish Ḥamās with the epithet "radical-Islamic," thus reducing this movement to a religious one. "Holy warriors" (a Western term) who fight for a "theocracy" (a term harking back to Augustine's *civitas Dei*), hoping to die a martyr's death in order to be rewarded with paradisiacal virgins, are in fact not suitable partners for negotiations. Consequently, Western media like to show sequences from farewell videos taken of suicide assassins, videos that apparently support this view. The *political* communiqués, much more numerous, which even the most extremist organizations publish in great numbers and which make use of political arguments in a quite rational manner, remain ignored because they would require a discursive dispute. While Basque and Corsican separatists, who for a long time were responsible for the overwhelming majority of terror attacks in Europe, are granted a political agenda and political dispute over their demands, Islamism is being stylized as an irrational and demonic threat that renders any rational argument impossible.

For this is the difference between the two forms of fanaticism: *Political* fanaticism is a pursuit of political aims that exceeds an acceptable limit—aims, however, that can be rationally comprehended in principle. One will disapprove of the fact that a Basque or a Corsican advocates for the independence of his homeland and kills for this aim. But it is an aim that in principle does not exclude rational argumentation. Negotiations may frequently break down, but they are not *a priori* hopeless. *Religious* fanaticism is a wholly different thing. It is principally irrational, more a psychological disturbance than an ideological aberration, and it eludes any reasonable control. Therefore the aims of religious fanatics cannot be communicated, and religious fanatics cannot be partners in a discussion of their aims. According to this argument, it appears evident that one cannot negotiate with Islamist organizations and that their political arguments are obviously bound to be faked, so that one is not obliged to discuss them. One can observe here the same mechanism at work which led to the "alienation" of the Islamic world in colonialist discourse. The other is simply the stranger who is not open to our rationalist arguments and is discounted as a dialogue partner. That means he cannot be an acting subject, but only a passive object of his acting. Both in the colonialist discourse of the past and the political discourse of the present, the "Islamization of Islam" is the main instrument by which the adversary is alienated.

The situation in Iraq after the U.S. attack in 2003 offers plenty of illustrative material for the devastations wreaked by this strategy. Even before the war, the regime around George W. Bush justified its attack against Iraq via international law by claiming that Saddam Hussein was a supporter of Islamist terror and was associated with al-Qaida. Though it is hard to top this level of absurdity, the claim was believed by many, because it fit the image of an Islamic world dominated, or at least infiltrated, by Islamist fanatics. So the war was sold as a "war against terror," although, as soon became evident, it grew to be a war *for* terror.

When the Iraqis started to fight back against the tortures and murders of the occupying forces, any show of opposition was denounced as "Islamist terror." No difference was made between the raging of al-Qaida and the nationalist opposition. The courageous politician and manager Jürgen Todenhöfer examined the total mendacity of this propaganda at the scene of battle, where he came to the remarkable conclusion that there were more *Christian* fighters than al-Qaida terrorists active in the Iraqi resistance.[45] In the end, he too concluded that the right way to deal with the phenomenon of Islamist violence was not an irrational demonization of the adversaries, but an argument addressing their *political* motives: "Has not the anti-terror politics of the West in the last years been so utterly unsuccessful precisely because most politicians have never concerned themselves with the phenomenon of terrorism? The Baker-Hamilton report states, with some sarcasm, that in the United States one knows almost everything about the explosive devices employed against the troops. However, about the persons who fire them and about their motives, next to nothing is known."[46]

And how could it be otherwise, if the alienation of the Islamic world as a religious monster, closed to any rational argumentation, makes political dispute appear hopeless? Todenhöfer is not part of this game, and proposes instead a thesis that is in clear contrast to the Western "terror" discourse but sounds quite plausible and could constitute a basis for a constructive policy: "The main cause of terrorism is . . . the feeling of total hopelessness about being able to use legal means to remove a situation felt to be utterly unjust. Against this kind of terrorism, only a strategy that unites rigor with justice can be effective."[47]

A precondition for this is to allow that the adversary is accessible to rational political argumentation. But that is precisely what the anti-Islamic polemics of our day deny. Not only that. From the very beginning, the "Islamization of Islam" was a policy guideline of the U.S. occupying forces in Iraq. Iraq is a country whose power structures after the collapse of the Abbasid rule are shaped by families, clans, and tribes to a higher degree than in the Levant or in Egypt. This is because, along with the decline of the great cities of Mesopotamia, Bedouin tribes made strong gains in power. It is not by chance that the dialect of the Muslims of Baghdad is typologically a Bedouin dialect.[48] The complicated web of power of clans and tribes which derive their identity, if at all, only in the second instance from their membership in a religious community did not vanish under Republican rule. The U.S. occupiers, however, attempted to restructure the Iraqi people entirely along religious parameters—perhaps even from sheer ignorance of ideological victims to the concept of the "Islamization of Islam." The consequences of this policy were terror, civil war, forced displacement, and "ethnic cleansing." Todenhöfer quotes a Shiite resistance fighter assessing this development: "An important factor in the current interior problems of Iraq consists in the fact that, after the invasion, the USA distributed power according to religious affiliations. It was part of the U.S. program to enhance the conflict between Sunnis and Shiites, which before had not existed in this sharpness, in order to split the country."[49] The elections of 2004 fully oriented themselves to this policy of religious segregation. A Christian resistance fighter is quoted as saying: "Really free elections would only happen after the withdrawal of the Americans. . . . In the elections of 2004, not even the names of the candidates, 'for reasons of security,' were made public. The voters had no other choice than to decide according to religious or ethnic affiliation."[50]

The U.S. attack of Iraq witnessed the strategy of "Islamization of Islam" in at least three contexts. First of all, the "Islamization" of Saddam Hussein served as a pretext for war. Next, the entire, extremely heterogeneous, resistance to the brutal occupation policy of the United States was "Islamized" as Islamist terror, a measure that foreclosed any possibility of rationally discussing the causes and aims of that resistance. And finally, the whole country was "Islamized" by reducing its inhabitants to members of one of the religious denominations of Islam. The whole political system now oriented itself along these religious structures. In this way, the vision of a quintessentially religious world of Islam has finally come true. Iraq, having once grown into the most secular Arabic state by adopting Western political models, was now rendered (by a Western state) an Islamic state with religious denominations that had never existed in this form in premodern times. Partly caught in the ideology of the "Islamization of Islam," and partly consciously exploiting it, the U.S. occupying forces substantially contributed to the Islamization and confessionalization of Iraq, and at the same time opened a new field of operation to Islamist terrorism. In light of the bloody consequences of the "Islamization of Islam," it appears to me not a purely academic question as to whether it is really meaningful to talk of an "Islamic culture," or whether one should perhaps consider prompting a more differentiated perception of the Islamic world by a *terminological de-Islamization* of this culture.

Let us summarize: the image of an Islamic society that is completely pervaded by religion is a caricature—one that perfectly fits, however, into the colonialist discourse and can be mobilized today in many ways to serve political purposes. Ironically, with this image of Islam, the West confirms the ideology of

Islamism for which this kind of Islam represents its purest embodiment. The following procedures of the "Islamization of Islam" to create this image of an "Islamic Islam" ("Islamic" in a religious sense, on the one hand, and in a cultural sense, on the other) can be observed:

(1) By using the term "Islamic" (Islamic culture, medicine, art, literature), a religious identity is suggested for areas that have little or nothing to do with religion.
(2) Nonreligious discourses are declared to be atypical, or unimportant for Islamic culture, or ignored altogether. The same applies for nonreligious elements in areas in which religious elements play a discernible role (e.g., law).
(3) If a given area displays several discourses, that which most easily matches Western ideas of religion is considered to be the most representative, without its social position being examined.
(4) If a religious and a nonreligious discourse exist side by side, the religious one is considered as a norm and the other one as a deviation.
(5) If various religious discourses exist side by side, the one that is most "conservative," according to Western standards, is considered as the "orthodox" norm most applicable to the "essence" of Islam.

In these ways, the ambiguities and pluralities in the Islamic world are rendered invisible, and a monolithic Islamic-religious culture is construed which then confronts the modern Western culture as something quite strange and antagonistic. The observer who prevails over those five mechanisms working for the "Islamization of Islam" will discover a culture that is astonishingly "normal," as will be further shown in the chapter on state and government. Such a "normal" culture should consequently be dealt with in a "normal" way—that is, at least according to the standards valid for the West in negotiating with countries of the non-Islamic world. If, for instance, the West justifies its joint ventures with Russia and China with the argument that close economic and cultural cooperation with these states will eventually lead to a stronger democratization of these countries, then this argument should apply also to Iran and Palestine. Once the mechanism of the "Islamization of Islam" is exposed, it will be difficult to justify the treatment of the Islamic world according to standards different from those for non-Islamic areas.

6
Language

A Serious Business and a Game

People talk the most incomprehensibly
when their language is meant to serve nothing but
to make themselves comprehensible.

—Karl Kraus, *Beim Wort genommen*

WORDS WITH OPPOSITE MEANINGS

In the Arab-Islamic world, the juxtaposition of secular and religious discourses as described in the previous chapter is not the *result* of a protracted development, but it is its *starting point*. In fact, Arab culture has two roots (if one disregards Roman–Greek and Iranian antiquity). One is indeed a religious one, Islam, represented by the Quran and the actions of the Prophet. The other root, however, is a secular one, namely ancient Arabic poetry. Each is *equally significant*, and each triggered a comparably large measure of cultural energy in the first centuries of Arab-Islamic culture. However, as a result of the "Islamization of Islam" described in the previous chapter, the secular root of the Arab-Islamic culture received less and less attention over the course of the twentieth century. Most works published today on the origin and early times of Islam make no mention of it.

Ancient Arabic poetry may be a cumbersome subject, but without taking it into cognizance, no understanding of the history of early Islam is possible. The image of the Arab desert tribes incited to religious fervor by Muḥammad's preaching—much cultivated by present-day's accounts—cannot be maintained when one considers the cultural conditions of the Arab peninsula at Muḥammad's time. In fact, the course of the Islamic raids may be read in pre-Islamic poetry. The Arabs were then a divided people, wedged between the two great powers of East Rome and Persia, and dependent on both in manifold ways. There had been several attempts made at unifying Arabs. Imraʾalqays, the son of the founder of the Lakhmid dynasty, calls himself "King of all Arabs" in an Arabic inscription dated 328 AD.[1] Toward the end of the fifth and in the beginning of the sixth century, all the Arab tribes were widely unified, but their power ended up disintegrating as well. Still the political fervor of the Arab leaders did not cease. Pre-Islamic Arabic poetry offers lively testimony for this, for instance when the poet and leader of the Taghlib tribe, ʿAmr b. Kulthūm, hurls defiance at the Lakhmid prince ʿAmr b. Hind (reigned 554–570), the Arab vassal of the Sassanid king, issuing, in his *Muʿallaqah* poem, a declaration of war which culminates in the verses: "The prince may want to subject the people to abasement—but we are not willing to be humiliated! We have filled the mainland until it became too tight for us, and some day we shall fill the surface of the sea with ships!"[2] The threat to fill the seas with battleships—remarkable for a "Bedouin" of the central Arabian highlands—was doomed to stay unaccomplished for some time to come, because the Arab tribes' loyalties to competing superpowers were too strong to allow them a coherent course of action. Consequently, the Arabs of the seventh century were observers of, rather than actors in, the theater of war in which Romans, Persians, Ethiopians, and Yemenites performed. The advent of Islam altered the situation considerably. By accepting Islam, the Arabs were in possession of their own, Arabic Holy Scripture, and a "modern"—that is, a monotheistic—religion, which was neither Jewish nor identical with any of the diverse Christian schools that rivaled one another. Now it was possible for the Arabs to revoke the old, religiously based loyalties, to conduct a common Arab agenda under the banner of Islam, and to confront the old superpowers as an independent force. Only after the Islamization of the Arabs, partially by force, could the program formulated by ʿAmr b. Kulthūm and other pre-Islamic poets be put into practice. Thus the religion of Islam did not *cause* the campaigns of conquest; it only *made them possible.*

The historical moment was favorable, and the success was sweeping. Within a few decades, large parts of East Rome and the entire Persian Empire became part of an empire that, in its early stage, presented itself as an Arab successor to the ancient empires. The conquerors were not interested in the conversion of the non-Arab population—quite the contrary. Anyone who wanted to become a Muslim had to be affiliated with an Arab tribe as a "client": one had to become an *Arab* before being allowed to become a *Muslim*. This alone shows that religious fanaticism can hardly have been the driving force behind the raids of conquest.

In view of the premodern structures of communication and administration, the tempo with which the newly conquered empire developed into an *Arab* empire was breathtaking. In the decade between 690 and 700, barely fifty years after the death of the Prophet, the caliph ʿAbd al-Malik had already implemented comprehensive administrative and monetary reforms. For this, an efficient administration was indispensable. Such a thing apparently still existed in the East of the Roman Empire and in the Sassanian Empire, while the imperial administration in the Western part of the former Imperium Romanum had collapsed long before. In this area, almost no coins were struck anymore; in the East Roman and Sassanian realms, coins continued to be available. The Arabs first took over without change both the Greek and Persian administration and the ancient coins, whose forms they changed only slightly. There followed a period of experiments, until under ʿAbd al-Malik, the coins were completely Arabized and Islamized, and Arabic was introduced as the official language in all offices of the now-huge empire.

ʿAbd al-Malik's reforms are among the most successful ones in history. Within a few years, the coinage was aligned to a new standard, and minting facilities from Turkmenistan to North Africa struck gold and silver coins that displayed only writing and no images, something that had never existed before. This was only possible due to a smoothly functioning administration. The astounding efficiency with which this reform was carried through shows that the old administrative and economic structures in East Rome (in contrast to West Rome) and in Persia had weathered the storms of Late Antiquity, that the Arab takeover had not put them out of business, and that the relevant clerks who were not Arabs actively supported the Arabization.[3]

Even more amazing than ʿAbd al-Malik's monetary reform is the transition from Greek and Persian to Arabic as the official language. It is not possible to change the official language of a state "just like that." As the example of modern states shows, the creation of a standard language requires intensive planning in several phases:[4]

(1) It must be decided on what basis the written language should have its origin. As a rule, that decision is made in favor of a dialect that is particularly prevalent or prestigious. Arabic was divided into several dialects; however, one

could fall back on the language of poetry, which already possessed a high degree of standardization.

(2) The language has to be standardized and shaped according to norms. The former happened speedily; early Quran manuscripts and papyri, however, show that the later norms of orthography, and in part those of grammar, gained currency only gradually.[5] A fixed norm in written form can apparently be observed only in the grammar of Arabic by Sībawayh (died around 177/793), a hundred years after ʿAbd al-Malik's reforms.

(3) Even if a suitable writing system has been found and has gained currency, and the dialectal differences are negotiated by a homogeneous standard language (all of these being quite improbable processes), a given language still does not yet possess the vocabulary necessary to match the requirements of an efficient administration. Therefore, an extension of the vocabulary is the next important step. But even an elaborate and homogeneous lexicon is not sufficient. Forms for documents and charters have to be devised that are applicable in all regions in a comparable manner.

(4) This norm has to be implemented in the community of speakers. Before the first written schoolbooks existed, in the beginning of the ninth century, instruction must have been primarily oral and on the basis of learning by doing—with noteworthy results even in these modes.

(5) The fully developed standard language requires cultivation, a task undertaken by multitudes of linguistic scholars from the beginning of the eighth century onward.

The difficulties of such a process can be observed very well in sub-Saharan Africa. Very few of the indigenous languages in this region can be regarded as more or less fully developed standard languages,[6] first among them Swahili and Hausa. Not by chance, these are languages that adopted Arabic writing, even before the colonial era. Most other language areas are still dependent on English or French as languages of administration—a remarkable testimony to the failure of colonialism in this domain.

It is startling to note that the military success of the Arabs has occupied the interest of many historians, while the Arabization of the administration, which is actually a much more amazing achievement, is hardly ever taken into account. But the Arab empire was founded at least as much on the basis of the pen as of the sword. In Europe, the replacement of Latin as the language of administration by the various vernacular languages took many centuries, with consistent languages of administration gaining acceptance only in the eighteenth and nineteenth centuries. What in Europe required a millennium needed only a few decades in the Arab empire of the Umayyads. By the end of the seventh century, the entire administration of the empire, from the Atlantic Ocean to the Indus, used a homogeneous written language that not only had standardized forms for documents but also soon produced, in the person of the administrative officer ʿAbd al-Ḥamīd al-Kātib (around 66–132/685–750), an authority who was able to compose letters with supreme stylistic mastery, furnishing an aesthetic model for centuries to come. Scarcely a hundred years after the death of the Prophet, the Arabs had succeeded in establishing throughout their whole empire a homogeneous, functioning, and, moreover, an aesthetically shaped language of administration. Of all the wonders of Arab-Islamic conquest, this is perhaps the greatest.

All this would not have been possible had the Arabs not done the necessary preparatory work in pre-Islamic times. Although their material culture was by no means as primitive as prejudice would have it, the fact remains that pre-Islamic Arab culture was first and foremost a *culture of language*. From around 500 AD at the latest, poetry in Arabia had attained the level of a highly sophisticated art that in its complexity and artistic refinement surpassed the poetry of the ancient civilizations. For Arabian tribes, poetry was the most important medium for communicating their interests. But early on, we also encounter poems (often quite long) whose purpose is mainly artistic.[7] The linguistic difficulty of these poems, which were not easily comprehensible even at the time of their composition, testifies to a highly developed language consciousness.

The Quran, itself a stylistically demanding text, was revealed in a milieu in which people were used to linguistic works of art that often required a more detailed explanation in order to be understood. It is much less striking than often assumed, therefore, that over long periods, the Quran not only suggests an aesthetic reception, but also contains passages that we must assume were in need of a commentary even for the contemporaneous listener.

But this factor, which for contemporaneous listeners increased the appeal of the texts, gradually evolved to become a problem. The focal places of the new and fast-evolving Islamic culture were in the cities outside Arabia, and those who maintained this culture and were their carriers, often of Iranian or Aramaic origin, were no longer familiar with the language and literary tradition of the ancient Arabs. So they were not able to readily understand either the ancient Arabic poems or the Quran, let alone to speak the Arabic of these texts.

The emergence of an Arab empire, and eventually an Arab-Islamic culture, would not have been possible had they not been able to cope with this linguistic problem. But the Arabs were successful in precisely this area. In a strikingly short time, a linguistic science developed, almost from nothing, that outdistanced everything existing in this field—be it in India or in Greek–Roman antiquity—and became one of the fundamental disciplines of Islamic scholarship. In fact, the first "real" Arabic book, which has no further title than simply *Kitāb Sībawayh* (Sībawayh's book), is the first Arabic text conceived in a form that fully corresponds to our ideas of a book as a fixed, consciously structured, extensive text between two covers. The norms Sībawayh used for the Arabic language he found not in the Quran, but in the language of the Arab Bedouins.

Arabic lexicography originated at the same time, initially in the form of brief word lists that were devoted to individual areas of the Arabic vocabulary. The ineradicable thesis persists that Arabic lexicography owes its existence to the endeavor to properly understand the Quranic text. But even a cursory glance over the titles of the earliest works of this discipline shows the opposite. Abū Khayrah (died around 150/767) compiles terms for crawlers; Abū ʿAmr Ibn al-ʿAlāʾ (Baṣrah, died 154/771) collects the ancient Arab heritage in all its breadth (proverbs, among other topics); Abū ʿAmr ash-Shaybānī (Kūfah, died 213/828) leaves behind, along with a roughly alphabetically arranged collection of ancient Arab Bedouin vocabulary,[8] monographic collections on the human body, the horse, and the date palm. From the pen of the Baṣrian Abū ʿUbaydah (died 213/828), we will mention only the treatises on horses, camels, the rein, and the bucket; of the work of his contemporary al-Aṣmaʿī (died 213/828), who worked in Baṣrah and Baghdad, we mention lexicographic treatises on the human body, wild animals, the horse, sheep and goats, plants, the game of chance with arrows (*maysir*), and so on.[9] All these treatises on crawlers, parts of the body, camels, horses, sheep, goats, and well fixtures, almost never contain a word that also figures in the Quran, and if such a word is mentioned, we find almost always a lexeme that is most common and least in need of a commentary. When the devout Aṣmaʿī treats in lexicographic detail the ancient Arab game with arrows that is forbidden by the Quran (n.b., without using any words requiring explanation), it becomes fully clear that Arabic lexicography initially did not serve religion, but helped to safeguard and understand the Arab secular heritage. In a time when much nonsense is being written about the allegedly "holy" Arabic language,[10] it cannot be strongly enough stated that the sensational and historically unique upsurge of the Arabic linguistic sciences *did not have any religious reasons*. It was not a "holy" language (which Arabic never was), or the endeavor to understand a holy text, that spurred the early scholars of Arabic to peak performances, but rather their interest in the Arabic language itself and in the secular heritage of Arabic poetry and folklore.

Those who wanted to interpret the Quran were ultimately confronted with the problems of those who wanted to explain ancient Arabic poetry, and thus, in parallel to the explanation of the old Arabic vocabulary of the Bedouins, evolved the explanation of the Quran text and the hadith.

At first these enterprises happened independently of each other, even if now and then, one and the same person (who would have been one of the experts in difficult texts) was tapping both the profane and the religious traditions. Not until one-and-a-half centuries later was a dictionary compiled that united the work of understanding old Arabic poetry and its world, and the work of understanding the Quran and the hadith.

This work is the *Tahdhīb al-lughah* (Sieving of the vocabulary) by al-Azharī (died 370/980), a dictionary that is still indispensable today. In its modern two-columned print, the dictionary comprises 15 volumes, with 7,600 pages in all. This achievement of Arabic lexicographers in their fourth century (our tenth century), which they would far surpass in the following centuries, was unmatched anywhere in the world.

Religions cannot originate and revelations cannot happen independently of the culture surrounding them. Just as Christianity cannot be conceived of without classical antiquity, and has developed in constant dispute with it, Islam cannot be understood without its secular-Arab roots, which evolved in their own manner and entered into a dynamic and constructive mutual interaction with the religion. The Western view of the Islamic world has studiously avoided looking at the secular roots of that world, as well as its achievements in the linguistic sciences. Even well-meaning accounts praising the accomplishments of Arab scholars in the fields of philosophy, mathematics, and the natural sciences concentrate precisely on those fields that are important for modern Western Europe. In Europe, linguistic sciences developed beyond the ancient level only at a late stage, and reached the level of reflection of the classical Arabic linguists only in the nineteenth and twentieth centuries, whereas Arab scholars had already gained many of the insights of modern linguistics centuries ago.

Another factor is that Western linguistics, in contrast to the fields of philosophy, mathematics, medicine, and the natural sciences, did not owe the Arabs any thanks. In the Middle Ages and early modern times, there was no linguistic science in Europe on a level that would have allowed for receptivity to Arabic theories. In the nineteenth and twentieth centuries, when such a reception would have been possible, the West was so convinced of its superiority over all other cultures that it could cast only an ethnological glance on Arabic linguistics; it did not take into account the possibility of learning something in a scientific area from another culture.

There is still another reason why the field of linguistic sciences so central to the understanding of Arab-Islamic culture is not addressed, even with a single word, in any Western survey of the history of the Arab or Islamic worlds known to us. The linguistic sciences never had that central position in the West—despite the linguistic boom of the sixties and seventies in the twentieth century—that the *truth generating* sciences occupied (of which, as we shall see from the linguistic skepticism of Fakhr ad-Dīn ar-Rāzī, the linguistic sciences were no part).

The Arab-Islamic world presents a totally different picture. The beginnings of conscious reflection on the capacities and limits of linguistic expression must date back to pre-Islamic times. This is indicated not only by the quick start performed by linguistic scholars after the consolidation of the Arab empire—a feat that is hardly explicable without a precursor—but also by ancient Arabic poetry itself.

A poet of the seventh century brags that the rare and recherché expressions in his poems will bring his transmitters (who, after all, will have to explain them) to tears.[11] Even the earliest poets known to us endeavor to borrow from a demanding, nonquotidian vocabulary. One of the most important stylistic devices of pre- and early Islamic poetry is the "proxy word," which means that a living being or a thing is referred to not by its common term but by an expression signifying a quality of the living being or thing. A poet would not have said, "I mounted a camel and took up a sword," but "I mounted a light brown one, a desert-traversing one, and grasped a cutting one, a bluish-glistening one." In choosing his proxy words through a dexterous combination of conventional and newly coined words, a poet could show his prowess.[12] It is said that Arabic knows several hundred words for the camel; to understand this, we have to think of such poetic proxy words, or of the technical terms of camel breeders, which were collected by the Arabic lexicographers with the same diligence they showed in gathering the literary expressions they encountered in the poems.

The works of early lexicographers who transmit and explain this vocabulary find practical uses in quite varied ways. Collections of technical terms of Arab cattle breeders and oasis farmers retain the memory of the *material* heritage of the ancient Arabs. This heritage was cultivated for reasons of antiquarian interest and out of pride for Arab traditions, but had lost its practical use. The commitment to the *literary* heritage, however, met with broader interest; for a long period, ancient Arabic poetry formed the core of the educational canon of intellectuals and administrative officers. For a time, it was cultivated less in the form of lexicographical works than in the form of commentaries on poems. Of immediate practical interest were those treatises that helped students acquire a better

Arabic, that is, books on how to avoid dialect forms, how to correctly apply expressions that are often wrongly used, how to put the right short vowels in problematic words, and so on. Instruction with the help of such treatises helped to establish norms for the Arabic written language and to standardize and stabilize its usage in the entire, newly conquered language area.

There are also quite a number of works that are conceived in the pattern of such didactic books but do not reveal any practical usefulness, other than a general enhancement of a linguistic consciousness. The driving force behind the composition of such treatises can only have been the fascination with language as such.

All in all, we may discern four motives that promoted the speedy development of Arabic lexicography during the eighth and ninth centuries:

(1) An *antiquarian* interest directed at the conservation of knowledge on the material culture of ancient Arabia;
(2) a *literary* interest that strives for the right understanding of ancient Arabic literature, first of all poetry;
(3) a *language-cultivating* interest that is concerned with the formation and implementation of a standardized, homogeneous, and efficient language of administration and scholarship;
(4) a *playful* interest fueled by a fascination with the structure of the lexicon, which leads to investigating the relations between words and meanings in ever new forms.

Especially revealing, for this last group, are books with the title *Kitāb al-Aḍdād*. *Aḍdād*, a plural form of *ḍidd*, means "antithesis, opposite," and also signifies a "contronym," or a "word with contradictory meanings"—that is, a word that signifies a fact and simultaneously its opposite. Such a word, for instance, would be the verb *shāma*, purportedly meaning "to put a sword into a sheath," but also "to draw a sword from a sheath." The first treatise devoted to this topic was written by a lexicographer and grammarian from Baṣrah. As a student, he used to turn up at his class with his venerated teacher Sībawayh at dusk in order to be there ahead of his fellow students. This earned him his nickname *Quṭrub al-layl*, "nocturnal werewolf," which eventually stuck to him. The bibliography of this Quṭrub (died 206/821) reflects all the various interests of the early Arabic linguistic sciences.[13] His best-known work helps to distinguish between words that differ only by a single short vowel, and to explain how to use them correctly. Then there are treatises on ancient Arabic terms for parts of the human body and weather phenomena, which open up the indigenous heritage. He is interested both in poetry—he writes poetry himself—and in the Quran, and he comments on both. But why does he collect in one treatise more than two hundred words that—allegedly—designate a fact and its opposite?

Quṭrub himself gives the answer. In the introduction to his collection, he writes that he has composed this monograph on the phenomenon of *aḍdād* because it is so rare and so charming (*li-qillatihī wa-ẓarāfatihī*).[14] That is, he found *aḍdād* nice, interesting, sophisticated, and fascinating. He does not claim any practical usefulness for his book.

Many of his contemporaries shared his fascination with the ambiguity of words. There is no other explanation for the fact that Quṭrub's most useless book, comparatively speaking, triggered a downright avalanche of imitators. With a speed remarkable for premodern conditions, there followed further *kutub al-aḍdād* by important lexicographers of the century. In the ninth century, al-Aṣmaʿī (died 213/828), at-Tawwāzī (died 230/845 or somewhat later), Ibn as-Sikkīt (died 243/857), and Abū Ḥātim as-Sijistānī (died 255/869) wrote on the same topic.

Then there was a longer pause, perhaps caused by general doubts about the viability of the *aḍdād* concept. The grammarian Ibn Durustawayh (258–347/872–958) had written a work (not extant) in which he denied the existence of words with contradictory meanings.[15]

Perhaps the background for this was an unexpressed discomfort with Arab hubris. A later author, in any case, defends the Arabs against allegations that their language lacks precision, as might be observed with the *aḍdād*. Words, he counters, always function in context—which, in the case of the *aḍdād*, ensures a disambiguation.[16] The writer of this defense is Ibn al-Anbārī (271–321/895–940), one of the best-known grammarians and lexicographers of his time, and the author of the most thorough *aḍdād*-work of the Arabs. He and Abū ṭ-Ṭayyib al-Lughawī (died 351/961) are responsible for bringing to an end the series of books on words with contradictory meanings (if one disregards a few latecomers).[17]

It seems there are three reasons for this. First, the subject, in the form of the two last-named comprehensive works, was pretty much exhausted. Second, the lexicographers of subsequent generations concentrated their efforts on the composition of comprehensive dictionaries. The old-style monograph on a selected topic was widely defunct. And thirdly, the *aḍdād* topic was absorbed into a more comprehensive discussion on homonyms. Such homonyms became topics of proper writings such as the books on *al-wujūh wa-n-naẓāʾir*, which we have already met in the chapter on the Quran.[18]

In the West, the problem of "words with opposite meanings" made quite a stir. Here, the early Arabic treatises were often regarded with condescension.[19] Fault was found with an insufficient analysis of single cases and a mixing of variant phenomena. To a certain degree, this critique is justified.

In fact, we meet with quite diverse cases. We are presented, for instance, with a verb *ʿafā,* whose primary meaning "to cover" expands to "sprouting densely" (said about growing plants), on the one hand, and to "laying waste" (namely by being covered by sand, said about a stretch of land) on the other. Here, we seem to be speaking of a word with opposite meanings. But less clear is the case with a word such as *jawn*, which means "intensely colored, monochrome," and is used by the ancient poets for totally black and totally white objects, but also for brown ones.[20] Another category is that of euphemisms, for instance when a blind person is called *baṣīr*, "clear-sighted," or of the ironic use of a word in verse. Still another category is that of different meanings of the same word in different dialects. For example, *wathaba*, "to jump up," means "to sit" in a south-Arabian dialect—a *ḍidd* which lends itself to anecdotes.

Many of these phenomena were well known to the Arab lexicographers, who mention them from time to time but do not make them the object of a systematic analysis. Beginning with Quṭrub, there are words in his work on *aḍdād* that he himself does not deem to be real *aḍdād*.[21] Ibn al-Anbārī presents around twice as many *aḍdād* as does Quṭrub, because he is primarily interested in the completeness of the tradition. However, Ibn al-Anbārī differentiates between *aḍdād* words and quasi-*aḍdād* words; it becomes clear that he does not share the assessment of his predecessors, even if he protests against their views only occasionally.[22]

It is clear that all Arabic authors were interested in unearthing as many words as possible that could pass in some manner as *aḍdād*. Their motivation to compose collections of *aḍdād* was pure fascination with the phenomenon of ambiguity. After all, the most extreme and least probable case of lexical ambiguity is a word with contradictory meanings. Quṭrub wrote during an era in which literature was feeling its way only gradually toward stylistic means *plus risquées* of ambiguity—when Quṭrub died, the eccentric scholar of metaphors Abū Tammām wrote his first youthful poems. There was not yet a developed theory of rhetoric. But in contrast to later periods, when one could rely on a range of competent and comprehensive dictionaries, in Abū Tammām's time, lexicography was a key science that had to do hard pioneering work for science, literature, religion, and the state. And so it is only natural that it was the first discipline to confront the phenomenon of ambiguity. The seven works on *aḍdād* of the ninth and tenth centuries present intriguing and curious testimony of the early fascination of Arabic scholarship with ambiguity.

Strangely, the not-insignificant number of nineteenth- and twentieth-century Western scholars who have looked into the *aḍdād* works have mostly failed to ask these questions of cultural history. In a collected volume with the promising (promising too much) title *L'ambivalence dans la culture arabe*,[23] the Arabic *aḍdād* works serve as a basis for discussion, but none of the essays asks the question why, after all, Arabic scholars had the idea of addressing the somewhat dubious category of words with contradictory meanings—of all lexicographical topics—in no fewer than half a dozen monographs.

Instead, the essays examine whether the phenomenon of words with contradictory meanings actually exists. There are explanations for the semantic conditions responsible for these (real or purported) contradictory meanings, and many words from the Arabic *aḍdād* works are debunked as not properly belonging to this category. The conclusions of this study (and others) are convincing: One can, in fact, state that Arabic has no more words with contradictory meanings than other languages have. The contrary impression is due to the lexicographers and their fascination with an ambiguity that seems to diametrically contradict the common mechanisms of language.

The thrust of the Arabic lexicographers and their modern Western successors, respectively, is the other way around. The Arabic authors are fascinated by the possible existence of words that can simultaneously denote "high" and "low," or "strong" and "weak," and try to collect as many of them as possible, including those they themselves count as dubious and those whose contradictory meanings are only rarely alleged.

Western scholars feel unsettled by the existence of such words, and attempt to validate as few of them as possible (and perhaps none). In reality, a single lexeme cannot be said to have contradictory semantic meanings; there are other semantic relations, such as the operation of mutuality, which means that in concrete usage, either one meaning or the other is actualized (compare in English "sanction" = "to permit by law" and "a penalty for disobeying the law").

If one has analyzed these relations, nothing remains for the category of *aḍdād*. The Arabic lexicographers presumably would not have been impressed by such an analysis, because in actual usage (the so-called surface structure) there are words that may be used in apparently contradictory meanings, even if the contradictoriness is only secondary or imaginary. To charge the Arabic lexicographers with the accusation that they did not classify and analyze the *aḍdād* thoroughly enough overlooks the fact that none of the *aḍdād* presents a practical problem. There are few cases in which the lexical meaning of a word with an (alleged) contradictory meaning would have been relevant for the interpretation of the Quran or a hadith text; in any case, these would not have been open to such an analysis.

Such problems of interpretation can be traced to contradictory statements of earlier philologists and commentators. A more precise knowledge of the mechanisms behind the *aḍdād* would not have helped here. In common usage, none of the *aḍdād* are used with contradictory meanings. There were no difficulties of mutual understanding caused by words with contradictory meanings. It was unnecessary to remove the ambiguity by analysis. Therefore, one conclusion remains: treatises on *aḍdād* were composed not in order to *eliminate* ambiguity, but to *play* with it. This also explains why *aḍdād* treatises originated in a series. Games assume a competitive character. Quṭrub had initiated the game, and the best philologists of the rival Basrian and Kūfan schools wanted to participate in it. This is further proof that "culture arises in the form of play, that it is played from the very beginning."[24]

This practically useless game with lexical ambiguity proved to become eminently useful for culture. Ultimately, the Arab-Islamic world owed its political achievements and intellectual flourishing not least to the existence of a well-structured and functional language of administration, literature, and scholarship. Such a language does not assert itself if no advanced linguistic conscience exists in wide sections of the population. The game of *aḍdād* was one of the training tools that contributed to the formation of such a linguistic conscience. The treatises on *aḍdād* may be only a facet of this broad linguistic formation, but they also may be a proof of the fact that the acceptance of ambiguity can well help to enhance efficiency.

The Western eagerness to debunk the phenomenon of the Arabic *aḍdād* shows up as arrogant, because it overlooks this *playful* aspect. In the end, however, the job of debunking became necessary, because in Europe, the thesis of the existence of words with contradictory meanings produced strange effects. In 1884, the German linguist Carl Abel devised a theory on the "contradictory meanings of the primeval words": he took the idea of words that denote both a thing and its opposite and developed it, in a typically European manner, toward a comprehensive theory on the progression of language (an idea that the Arabs, of course, would never have entertained). According to Abel, when men first began to develop language they did not yet have terms for "strong" and "weak," and similar semantic pairs, because they were able to experience and communicate the phenomenon of strength only in relation to its opposite, weakness. The primeval word for *strong/weak* "in reality denotes neither 'strong' nor 'weak' but only the relation between the two, and the difference between them which created both of them simultaneously."[25] Only later, Abel goes on, had men learned to conceive each side of the antithesis without consciously measuring against the counterterm. Words with contradictory meanings in modern languages are thus, according to Abel, remnants of archaic ways in which humans perceived the world. Among these remnants are the Arabic *aḍdād*, of which Abel gives a list taken from Ibn al-Anbārī.[26]

Abel could not convince his linguistic colleagues of his theory. But Sigmund Freud seized on it and used it for his theory of dream interpretation.[27] What a subtle revenge of the ambiguity of *aḍdād*—to let itself be expelled from linguistics and find asylum in psychology!

For Arabic linguists, engagement with conceivably the most extreme case of ambiguity must have constituted an important stimulant. It helped them to expedite lexicography as a means to domesticate the semantic variety of the world. Later on, they returned only sporadically to the concept of *aḍdād*. In the meantime, the fascination with ambiguity had found other and more interesting playgrounds.

REFINEMENT AND PIETY

The Psalter begins with the well-known saying: "Blessed is the one who does not walk in step with the wicked or stand in the way that sinners take or sit in the company of mockers" (Ps 1, 1). This verse is also mentioned in the Quran, where we read (4: 140): "He has sent down upon you in the Book: When you hear God's signs being disbelieved and made mock of, do not sit with them until they plunge into some other talk."[28]

Is it therefore permitted to mock this very verse, putting it into a totally different context? A poet in the Mamluk era had no compunctions about doing this when he composed a love epigram in which the favored topic of concealing one's love appears:[29] the lover wants to keep his love secret, but alters his outward appearance so visibly (for instance, by losing weight) that his fellows become attentive and urge him to admit that he has fallen in love. That is the theme of the epigram, in which a quotation from the Quranic verse quoted above forms the punch line. In freely adapted form, it runs as follows:

> My critics all pounce when tears flood my eyes:
> Tell us why, friend! What is the matter?
> But I keep our love secret; I give no replies
> "Till they pounce somewhere else with their chatter."[30]

It is a pretty epigram that derives its fun from the fact that the last half-verse constitutes a Quranic quotation known to every listener—which, however, is brought here into a totally different context, and thus gains a meaning quite different from its original one. But is this allowed? May one misuse a phrase of God by inserting it, in an explicitly frivolous manner, into a love poem, thereby giving it a meaning that the divine originator—even considering all the semantic diversity of Quranic speech—certainly did not intend? Probably not. It is not difficult to find Islamic texts that censure the stylistic device of willful misuse of a Quranic quotation (*iqtibās*) when it is not used for an edifying purpose.[31] Is one really not allowed to do this?

Yes, one is! Hundreds, indeed thousands of similar examples of *iqtibās* crowd the anthologies of Arabic poetry, and among the authors there are many writers who are not at all of dubious reputation, but are the most respectable and pious religious scholars of their time. The author of the epigram quoted above is none other than the most significant hadith scholar of postformative Islam, Ibn Ḥajar al-ʿAsqalānī, whom I have mentioned several times. No other official held the office of the Shāfiʿite supreme qadi in Cairo—the highest religious post the Mamluk empire had to offer—as long as he did.

But more was to come. Badr ad-Dīn al-Bulqīnī (821–890/1419–1486), a religious scholar of equal renown, particularly in the field of law, and for a short period the successor to Ibn Ḥajar in the office of the Shāfiʿite supreme qadi of the empire, utilized a Quranic verse that tells the happenings of the Judgment Day. On this day, when the dead who have turned to dust will be raised and given a body again, the unbelievers, in the face of the punishment they must await, will wish they had remained earth and dust: *Yā laytanī kuntu turāban* ("O would that I were dust!," Q 78: 40). Of course, this verse would have fit very well into an exhortative religious poem, but it must be admitted that a Quranic quotation within a religiously tuned text does not produce a real punch-line effect. This is achieved only if a contrast emerges between the sacred text and its profane usage. So we should not be astonished to encounter the Quranic passage in an epigram that can hardly pass as religious, although it had a religious occasion: as sometimes happened, one Mamluk sultan felt compelled to demonstrate his religious seriousness by ordering the pubs to be closed and their wine supplies spilled.[32] Badr ad-Dīn al-Bulqīnī witnessed this and rhymed:[33]

kassarū l-jarrata ʿamdan, saqawū l-arḍa sharābā
qultu wa-l-islāmu dīnī "laytanī kuntu turābā"

They broke the jug deliberately and soaked the earth with the wine,
I spoke—and Islam is my religion—"O would that I were dust!"

Despite its brevity, this epigram unites several layers of ambiguity. First of all, a stylistic device of ambiguity is used, namely the *iqtibās*, the Quranic quotation that obtains a different meaning in its new context, but as a literary measure is effective only because a contrast emerges between its original meaning and its present use.

A second element of ambiguity arises from the manifest discrepancy between the positive evaluation of wine drinking in the poem and the prohibition of wine in the Quran, from which the quotation of the last verse is taken. On this second level, we seem to be confronted with a phenomenon of norm and deviation: the Quran prohibits the drinking of wine, but the poem celebrates it as a good thing, thus contradicting the norm. But this alone does not create ambiguity. Ambiguity is attained by the violation of the norm only by presenting it, on a further, third level, as the *fulfillment of a norm.*

This is possible because in the life of religious scholars—similar to other fields—different norms are valid side by side, which cannot be harmonized without mutual contradiction. I have characterized the two most important guiding principles orienting the lives of classical period scholars as "refinement and piety."[34] The poet al-Mutanabbī formulated this double ideal in a poem praising a Mālikite qadi:[35]

tafakkuruhū ʿilmun wa-manṭiquhū ḥukmun
wa-bāṭinuhū dīnun wa-ẓāhiruhū ẓarfū

His thought is knowledge and his talking is wise judgment.
His inner side is religion, his outer side is refinement.

In al-Mutanabbī's time, the worlds of the secular elite—that is, the court and the administration—and of the religious elite were still rather clearly separated. But they were beginning to approach each other. Only a little later, the training to be a judge, often in a madrasah, began to be the usual first step for both a career as a civil servant in the administration, and a career as a religious scholar. The common course of training for both the secular and religious elite from Seljuqid times onward, however, did not result in a weakening of the secular side of culture. On the contrary, it became more and more important for religious scholars to distinguish themselves not only by piety and learnedness but also by worldly elegance and literary learning. Al-Mutanabbī's verse shows that this quite secular ideal of *ẓarf*, "refinement," was firmly rooted in the minds of religious scholars by the first half of the tenth century.

Soon thereafter, we meet ambitious religious scholars who are not content with just having a literary training, but who actively participate in the literary arena. Precisely by their linguistic brilliance, and their ability to compose letters and poems that were stylistically polished and aesthetically effective, they could demonstrate their *ẓarf*.[36] In this arena, they were obliged to prove themselves in the genres that were most popular—that is, primarily in amatory poetry. From then on, we have love poems (but also panegyric and nature poems, poetical riddles, and many other kinds of poems) in vast numbers from the pens of legal scholars, Quranic exegetes, and transmitters of hadith, a tradition that has partly held into the twentieth century.

Even a poem such as the following was composed by an established religious scholar:

> The creaking of the waterwheel in early morning and the sound of flute and chord
> And the places which, when they smile, bare teeth of white and many-colored flowers
> Have made me a neighbor of a wine press where I never wake up from my drunkenness.
> That is my way of life to which I shall stick as long as I am given life!

The author of this wine poem is a highly respected hadith scholar by the name of ʿĀṣim, who died in his eighty-seventh year in 483/1090.[37] There are no reports on his way of life being dissolute—quite the contrary. But that is not the point. It is not important to know whether real experiences are hiding behind the eroticism and the wine drinking of these poems. Rather, it is important to note that these poems reflect an ideal that peacefully coexisted with the ideal of a religious society. In all these love, wine, and nature poems, a worldly utopia finds expression that praises the good life in this world, a life full of eroticism and intoxication in an Arcadian landscape. This utopia exists side by side with the utopia of a society that wholly follows the laws of God.

The poems of the religious scholars address both utopias. We often encounter poems on renunciation from this world and asceticism (*zuhd*) next to erotic poems. Most beautifully, both aspects converge in poems that lament the passing of time and invite the reader to relish the moment. In this vein, the Ḥanafite legal scholar and preacher from Damascus Muḥammad b. Asʿad (died 567/1171–1172) wrote:

> You who heedlessly live from day to day and do not know when you will die and be buried:
> Do not be careless, for life is too short for that![38]

What lesson is to be learned from this epigram? Since the poet was a preacher, one might understand it as an appeal to lead a God-fearing life and to be prepared for death at any moment. In fact, there are a great number of sermons and poems that say exactly this. But many poems proceed in a different direction and request the listener instead to enjoy every moment of life with wine and love, before it is too late. Muḥammad ibn Asʿad's poem—like many such poems—leaves the end open. The text might go on to request the listener, in the light of the transience of life, to strive for the ultimate reward. But it could also advocate cherishing every moment with earthly pleasures. The poet does not make the decision for us. It is left to the listener what conclusions to draw from the realization that his existence is transitory.

Muḥammad ibn Asʿad's profession of preacher does not allow for deducing the lesson to be learned from the epigram. In fact, a continuation of the poem that would prompt the listener to enjoy worldly life would be quite conceivable. For Ibn Asʿad is also the author of the following poem:

> O my boon companion: Bring wine (*rāḥ*), because the evening (*rawāḥ*) has come,
> And pour it for me in the darkness of night, for the morning is already approaching!
> A wine which is mixed with tears is nothing sinful.

Note the touching final verse of this wine poem, in which the poet postulates the compatibility of the religious and the secular ideal, since it is true that the secular ideal, given its transitory nature, is never to be realized completely.[39]

The poems by religious scholars on love, wine, and nature show to what a large degree the ideal of a this-worldly, secular happiness was also accepted in religious circles. As authors of secular poems, they strive for an ideal of learning that consists in the refinement of *ẓarf*. In many respects, it resembles the Renaissance ideal of the *gentiluomo* and is not perceived as being in contradiction to the ideal of the *homo religiosus*. Rather, both ideals exist side by side (if not together) from the period of the "Sunni revival," at the latest, until the nineteenth century. In their coexistence, they furnish a considerable contribution to the humanism of classical Islam.

There were times and places in which the coexistence of an ideal of piety and learnedness and an ideal of refinement and elegance was not restricted to Islamic scholars. Exactly the same phenomenon may be observed with the rabbis in al-Andalus. Ross Brann has devoted an extensive study to the "court rabbis" of the so-called golden era (around 950–1150) in al-Andalus, in which he shows how the Jewish scholars of that period were deeply connected with their tradition and carefully observed their law, and at the same time absorbed Arabic culture and wrote poems on wine and love poems devoted to young men and women:[40] "The ideal man lived in both worlds and found the ambiguity highly attractive."[41]

This attractiveness of ambiguity, however, has its roots not in a courtly ideal, as Brann thinks, but in the ideal of Islamic scholarship, which cultivates exactly this ambiguity.

AMBIGUITY AS STIGMA

The psychologists S. Budner and A. P. MacDonald advance the hypothesis that people with a high degree of tolerance of ambiguity not only do not avoid ambiguity, but also search for it and enjoy it; when they are confronted with problems involving ambiguity, they solve such problems with particular skill.[42] If we apply this hypothesis to our topic of cultural ambiguity, we might expect that in cultures in which ambiguity was *tolerated* to a relatively strong degree, ambiguity was also *produced* with zeal and joy. For instance, many texts would have been created that were consciously ambiguous and confronted their readers with the opportunity to solve ambiguity and have fun with it.

It is hardly conceivable to find a better confirmation of the Budner–MacDonald hypothesis than in the literatures of the precolonial Near East. In fact, the tolerance of ambiguity that we find in a number of different fields corresponds with an incredible abundance of texts that consciously employ ambiguity, play with polysemy, and baffle, fascinate, and entertain their listeners and readers by their range of possible interpretations. It is probably not too risky a statement to say that among the literatures of mankind, the literatures of the Near East between the twelfth and nineteenth centuries offer the greatest wealth of ambiguity.

Perhaps one could write the history of the literatures in Arabic, Persian, and Turkish languages in the precolonial period as one of progressively complex ambiguity. However, Western literary historians and many of their indigenous postcolonial colleagues interpret this history differently. In their eyes, the history of the Near Eastern literatures was a history of decay. The "prevalence" of "linguistic wordplay" was seen as the most characteristic sign of this decay. In 1851, for instance, when Heinrich Leberecht Fleischer, a professor of Arabic in Leipzig, presented a work by the Lebanese Christian poet and scholar Nāṣīf al-Yāzijī (1214–1287/1800–1871) to a German audience, he did not fail to issue a warning against "sterile artistic play."[43] Shaykh Nāṣīf was one of the most important representatives of Arabic literature in his time. A Greek-Catholic Christian, he was very receptive to Western culture. But in his writing and scholarship he unwaveringly continued to follow his own classical tradition—much to the chagrin of Western authors like Fleischer, who basically valued al-Yāzijī but deemed his persistence in the tradition a grave mistake. For Fleischer, the most problematic point was precisely al-Yāzijī's delight in ambiguity—in Fleischer's own words, the "sterile artistic play"—that marks all of the author's works. For Fleischer, these "sterile artistic games" not only are a flaw of al-Yāzijī's works but also constitute a real danger to the entire Near East:

> The vain delight in this technique, and the incommensurate appreciation devoted to it, present all Oriental peoples affected by a stagnant education system with a heavy obstacle to the creation of a taste for fresh scientific realism and an elevation to serious intellectual labor. May the humane and reasonable men of the West who nourish and guide that new life of our Oriental friends devote the deserved attention to this object! It is part of an old, tenacious, intricate malady inflicting the Orient; it cannot be remedied overnight and in one stroke; but it must be remedied, if the Oriental spirit, now still captured in the fetters of barren scholasticism and self-pleasing rhetoric, wants to gain the power to embrace the scientific horizon of the West, to enter into its ideas, and to participate independently in its works.[44]

Fleischer's polemic against the shaykh Nāṣīf is a prime example not only of modern Western condemnation of ambiguity, but also of the Western bent for universalization. Arabic literature receives a right to exist at all only if it is Western, if the "Oriental spirit" dissolves in "the ideas of the West"—in other words, ceases to exist. In this same vein is the obituary of al-Yāzijī composed a few years later by the Austrian Arabist and diplomat Alfred von Kremer:

> True, it also becomes apparent . . . how misguided is the course that Arabic poetry has taken: everything rests on the vain pomp of rare and often unintelligible words, word play . . . , and inimitable poetic artificialities. . . . Among those who were active in this field, Nāṣīf deserved to be named in first place. However, he overdid things in attributing to purely linguistic studies an exaggerated importance, compared to realistic ones. For the modern Arab, it is indeed the latter studies that are necessary to extract him from the *circulus*

> *vitiosus* of old Arabic fake learning and introduce him into the halls of modern European civilization.
>
> All our newspapers call him a great poet, but according to European cultural standards, he was not that.[45]

Quotations from German Oriental studies such as this one could easily be multiplied simply by consulting French and English Oriental scholarship of the nineteenth and twentieth centuries. These quotations show that the Orient as a culture of ambiguity was a central topic of colonialist discourse. In the eyes of the West, the immaturity of Orientals and the stagnation of their culture are manifested precisely in their passion for ambiguity. Only when Orientals renounce this culture, leave ambiguity behind, and advance to the "fresh realism" of the West, can they enter "the halls of modern European civilization." In the nineteenth century, a tolerance of ambiguity was not appreciated. Further, the tolerance of, and love for, ambiguity of the Near Eastern people were taken to be an argument for cultural imperialism. "Reasonable men of the West" had the task of casting out ambiguity from the Oriental. As we know, the British and the French have not stopped at this merely cultural imperialism.

Western propaganda against ambiguity was successful. With the growing influence of the West, indigenous elites soon adopted foreign literary standards of value and distanced themselves more and more from their old enthusiasm for ambiguity—at least when they wanted to be regarded as "modern" authors and intellectuals, and to be acknowledged by the West. Soon the Western view prevailed, according to which Arabic literature, after a flowering up to the tenth century, suffered a steady process of decay. The numerous works saturated with ambiguity that originated during this period of "decay" were seen, and are often still seen, as the main characteristics of decadence. (Other works, often completely devoid of ambiguity, were simply ignored.) Every figurative device, every ornament, every pun, and every riddle is a charge against a literature that constantly offends the dogma of the antiambiguity modern era, which pronounces, as does the architect Adolf Loos (1870–1933), ornament and crime in one breath.[46] The "ornament," in the form of stylistic figures and linguistic play, becomes the stigma of a literature, indeed of a whole culture, that resists modernity and remains in utter stagnation.

This thesis of stagnation and decadence became nothing less than a dogma. Especially in nationalist discourse, all literature originating in a time when rulers were not purebred Arabs was regarded, and is still regarded, as decadent and worthless. Islamists as well regard this literature as decadent, although for moral reasons, not nationalist ones. In the Near East, it still requires courage to study the Arabic literature of the Mamluk and Ottoman eras. As late as in 2006, in a standard English-language work, authors of Arab origin deplore the decay of Arabic literature: its alleged "mannerism," the prevalence of "stylistic embellishments" and "word play," the lack of "unaffected" expression of "natural, true feelings," the lack of moral seriousness, and even a deficit of "virility."[47]

TRAINING IN AMBIGUITY

Around the turn of the twentieth century, the impact of the imperialist discourse of the West meant that the literary tradition of cultivating ambiguity—the beginnings of which date back to pre-Islamic times—came to an end. If one wanted to trace the history of ambiguity in Arabic literature (not to speak of Persian and Turkish literature), one would have to do nothing less than write a complete history of this literature. Even this would not be sufficient, since Arabic authors at an early stage had already begun to reflect on ambiguity and to compose literary-critical and theoretical works about it. Hence one would also have to write a history of Arabic rhetoric and literary theory. But even this would not suffice. For joining these texts, both *full of* and *about* ambiguity, are those that address the ambiguity of existence, reflecting again and again the idea that everything has two sides. We can offer here only a very incomplete outline of these, in note form, which nevertheless will show that a mature tolerance of ambiguity was constantly accompanied by training in ambiguity.

In *ancient Arabic poetry* (beginning around 500 AD), the most important stylistic devices are comparisons and the *substituting word* (proxy word) mentioned above. This gives pre- and early Islamic texts a certain amount of ambiguity (which, in the Quran, is enhanced by other devices). But another ancient Arabic institution is perhaps even more important for the development of the culture of ambiguity, namely the *muʿāraḍah*, the "contrapoem," or "emulative poem." This is a poem that answers another poem and is exactly identical in meter and rhyme. Just as Jacob Burckhardt views the spirit of contest as a central characteristic of the ancient Greeks, the Arab of the pre- and early Islamic era must also be described as an "agonal person" (in the sense of the Greek *agon*, referring to contest and competition).[48] Along with armed fights between clans and tribes, there were contests of hunting, racing, and shooting. Even more important were the contests among poets, who were often, at the same time, the speakers of their tribes. Contests between poets were staged in front of an audience and were occasions for the composition of "contrapoems" of the sort described.

The agonal character of poetry survived Islamization. In the Umayyad period, in fact, the tradition of the "contrapoem" reached the climax of its popularity, when the greatest poets of the time gathered at the caliphal court in Baghdad or on the Mirbad, the large plaza outside the gates of Basra, to insult each other in long poems. Such "contraorations" (*naqāʾiḍ*) are full of exaggerations and are not reluctant to use coarse obscenities. The best-known polemics were those between Jarīr (died 111/729) and al-Farazdaq (died 110/728), who entertained audiences with their *naqāʾiḍ* for almost forty years.[49] Above and beyond the entertainment value of the "contrapoems," it should be emphasized that they served to playfully recreate political and societal conflicts. The collapse of the traditional tribal order and the eruption of new tribal conflicts presented a serious challenge to Umayyad society, a challenge that found its outlet in the wild insults launched by star poets in their "contraorations." In the agonal culture of the Umayyad and the early Abbasid period, of which the *naqāʾiḍ* are only one feature among others, there was an intensifying awareness that all groups could present their own respective deeds of glory—and also their own respective infamies.[50]

The urban culture of the Abbasid period no longer viewed public insult contests as a suitable means to conduct and settle conflicts as a game. Instead, scholarship developed its own art of disputation, first in theology, and then in other disciplines, especially in the methodology of jurisprudence.[51] The agonal and playful element of contest enters into a synthesis with the quite serious quest for truth, respectively probable truth, and Johan Huizinga is certainly right when he states: "This mixture of rhetoric, warfare and play can also be found in the scholastic competitions of the Muslim theologians."[52]

Literary disputations also are to be found close to the very beginning of Arabic prose literature. The first genius of Arabic entertaining-edifying prose, al-Jāḥiẓ (died 255/869), demonstrates that he is wholly pervaded by the awareness of the relativity of human judgments and valuations. In many of his works, he collects arguments for praise or blame of objects and groups of people or professions, without having the ideology of his presentations "work out" cleanly. For example, he composes epistles in praise of the Turks and the Blacks that portray him as a partisan of peoples for whom the dominant status of the Arabs was like a thorn in their side. At the same time, he sings the praises of the Arabs, in a book which may be counted as the oldest Arabic book on rhetoric.[53] On some topics, al-Jāḥiẓ has written two straightforward treatises (on state secretaries, merchants, silence, and talking)—one in praise, the other in censure. Some works present a veritable literary debate, for instance the debate on whether love for young women is preferable to love for young men.[54]

This tradition, in which the literature of *rangstreit* (rank dispute) has its place, continued into modern times. Preferred topics were disputes between different plants and animals (e.g., rose and narcissus), seasons of the year (winter and summer), specific cities, different fields of scholarship, or, in modern times, between donkey and bicycle, streetcar and bus.[55] Of political significance is the popular dispute between pen and sword, which reflects the dualism between the civil and military elite. Ibn Nubātah's dispute between pen and sword, from the year 729/1329, is probably the most stylistically brilliant (and most elaborate) composition upon this topic.[56] It is small wonder that the dispute ends in a draw.

Works on *al-maḥāsin wa-l-masāwī* (the good and the bad sides of things) constitute another literary tradition to which al-Jāḥiẓ belongs.[57] The best-known author in this field is ath-Thaʿālibī (350–429/961–1038), who spent his life in the Iranian East, where he upheld the banner of Arabic literature. One of his numerous anthologizing works is titled *Taḥsīn al-qabīḥ wa-taqbīḥ al-ḥasan* (Making the ugly beautiful and the beautiful ugly).[58] In the first part of this book, ath-Thaʿālibī collects arguments that support things normally regarded as ugly. These include lying, insolence, poverty, being in jail, being fat, being stingy, the word "no," the farewell, old age, sickness, and death. In the second part, subjects that are vilified include intelligence, books, the office of vizier, gold and wealth, wisdom and courage, asceticism and frugality, the bath, youth, friendship, rain, roses and narcissi; even the moon is not spared this transvaluation. A student of ath-Thaʿālibī endeavored to complement this work with statements from the author's other books, which treat the good sides of good things and the bad sides of bad things. The result is a work (mostly ascribed to ath-Thaʿālibī himself) in which we may learn about all these things in succession what makes them loveable and what makes them hateful.[59] This book offers perhaps the finest introduction to the history of mentalities of the classical Arabic world.

The genre of "the good and the bad sides of things" was represented down into Mamluk times by the author al-Waṭwāṭ (632–718/1235–1318).[60] However, another literary form had attained even more vitality long before, a genre that also dealt with the relativity of human value judgments: the *apologetic epigram.* Its beginnings lay in the love poetry of the end of the second/eighth century, when poets such as Abū Nuwās were seeking excuses for their love of youths whose beards are beginning to sprout (about which more in greater detail later).[61] The panoply of topics expanded rapidly, and soon almost any contradiction of conventional value judgments could serve as a topic of such an epigram.

But the most frequent and most beautiful apologetic epigrams are to be found in love poetry, when a poet apologizes for a "defect" of the beloved person and proves, with the whole repertoire of stylistic devices containing ambiguity, that the defect is no defect at all. For instance, Ibn al-Wardī (691–749/1292–1349) makes use of the fact that a pretty person is often compared to the sun or the moon. In defense of his love for a girl with conspicuously short legs, he writes:[62]

> For a long time I am in love with a small one
> Who in her delicacy is like a gazelle.
> People malign her: "She has no legs at all,"
> To which I reply, "Neither do the moon and the sun."

Apologetic love epigrams frequently concern pockmarked people. Ibn Makānis (745–798/1344–1392), another poet of the Mamluk period, similarly finds the appropriate comparisons for this, which are then reinterpreted until the pockmarked appearance turns out to be the very cause for love:

> I love the one with pockmarks which now
> Adorn as stars the sky of my heart.
> No wonder that he catches all the hearts—
> With a net of pockmarks on his cheeks![63]

One may dismiss such epigrams as playing around, and in fact they were meant to amuse rather than to deal with actual everyday problems. But: "We must emphasize yet again that play does not exclude seriousness."[64] The apologetic epigram has taught whole generations to question ideals of beauty and conventional value judgments in all areas. For many, it has opened their eyes to the ambiguity of human existence and saved them from accepting their judgments or prejudices as certainties. The texts on *rangstreit*, the collections of the "good and bad aspects of things," and the apologetic epigrams could originate only in a culture that tolerates ambiguity. And all these texts are formed so attractively that they are bound to exert a great fascination on their listeners and readers, whose awareness of the multilayered nature of the world is thereby sharpened—which helps to perpetuate tolerance of ambiguity. This process functioned until the West, precisely in the era of its strongest intolerance of ambiguity, gained power over the Near East. The Near East was confronted with the economic and technological supremacy of the West exactly in the latter's "ornament is a crime" phase, in which the principle of play had reached the nadir of its appreciation. The Near East learned the lesson thoroughly. Even today, there are quite a few intellectuals in the Arab world who consider poems such as the ones quoted above to be regrettable errors.

As the play with images in the quoted epigrams shows, Arabic poetry gained considerably in stylistic refinement during the Abbasid era. In the second/eighth century, the ancient Arabic stylistic device of the proxy word went out of fashion. In its stead, the metaphor gained increasing importance, and it was used by the poet Abū Tammām (died around 231/845) to such an extent that a veritable poetic controversy ensued, dividing the entire cultural elite. The partisans of Abū Tammām were confronted by those of his disciple, al-Buḥturī (206–284/821–897), who avoided the stylistic excesses of his teacher and found the way to a more balanced style, which was regarded for a long time as classical. The controversy over Abū Tammām's poetry had an important side effect. The writer of poetry and Abbasid prince Ibn al-Muʿtazz (247–296/861–908), to whom Arabic literature owes several of its most beautiful similes, composed a small booklet in defense of the "new style" as it was represented most radically by Abū Tammām. This book on the "New Style,"[65] from the year 274/887, is commonly seen as the charter of Arabic stylistics; later on, it would come to be a pivotal element of the theory of rhetoric. In the sixth/twelfth century, theoreticians writing in Arabic—most prominently as-Sakkākī (555–626/1160–1229), from today's Uzbekistan—developed a theory of the indirect and figurative use of language that even today offers an analysis of the metaphor that is much more adequate than can be found in Western theories.

In poetic practice, the play with metaphors attains its climax not in Arabic but in Persian literature. Here, the so-called Indian style, beginning with the tenth/sixteenth century, displays unique fireworks of metaphor.[66] The West, which had learned from Hobbes that metaphors are "delusive lights" (*ignes fatui*),[67] could not but see this as a phenomenon of decadence.

Arabic poetry after the controversy over Abū Tammām is more reticent regarding experiments with metaphors. Instead, linguistic means of expression are developed that are based on the polysemous character of single words. The most important among these is the *tawriyah*, the stylistic device of ambiguity par excellence. The term roughly corresponds with the French double entendre. In European languages, it was used mostly for jokes or satirical sayings, as for the instance discussed earlier in the book when Karl Kraus gave his judgment on the press: "The bigger the boot, the bigger the heel." Here, the meanings intended in the first place ("boot" [Stiefel] in the sense of "idle prattle," and "heel" [Absatz] in the sense of "sold copies") are "hidden" behind the "shoe" meanings (hence *tawriyah*, "hiding") that one primarily associates with these words.

From the middle of the sixth/twelfth century onward, Arabic literature likes to make use of the *tawriyah* to end epigrams with a witty punch line. But it is also used more and more in serious literature, especially in the stylized letter. In poetry, Ibn Nubātah is regarded as its great master. Starting with his earliest poetry, he played with multiple layers of meaning in order to furnish the texts with a measure of semantic concentration and an abundance of mutual relations that had not been seen before.[68] In his later poems, he also makes frequent use of the *tawriyah*, through which he opens up yet another level of meaning. Needless to say, such poems ultimately defy translation.

Tawriyah has also been the object of theoretical investigation. Both aṣ-Ṣafadī (died 764/1363) and Ibn Ḥijjah al-Ḥamawī (died 837/1434) wrote treatises on this stylistic device and its various subspecies, which remain unsurpassed.[69]

Intellectuals of the Mamluk and Ottoman era were confronted with the accusation that their sophisticated play with words addressed only a small elite.[70] It may be correct to say that the stylistic device of ambiguity found great interest within the learned elite, which consisted largely of legal scholars. This is not astonishing, since legal scholars, as interpreters of normative texts, were charged with the task of domesticating the ambiguity of these texts. Their awareness of ambiguity kindled a delight in playfully creating ambiguity in texts of all sorts. Ambiguity is regarded here not as a defect, but as artistry.

However, it would be entirely wrong to think that this pleasure was confined to the elite. Quite the contrary: it is linguistic play that forms the common denominator between elite and popular literature, and indeed represents the bridge to the oral literature of the peasants and the Bedouins. In the eighth/fourteenth century, a popular poet who was by profession a stonemason and architect (al-Miʿmār) became so famous for his mastery of the *tawriyah* that his poems were collected and presented to a large literate audience.[71] The popular literature of the rural population was known for its great fondness for the *tawriyah* well into the twentieth century, and perhaps up to today. For this literature, linguistic play is no less than "the salt in the soup," and poems that do not contain dexterous linguistic play are disregarded.[72] It is only Western critics and members of the pro-Western indigenous elite who, since the beginning of the twentieth century, have considered Arabic linguistic games to be worthless.

This audience reacted with special condescension to all the varieties of Arabic literature that were particularly popular in Ottoman times.[73] Their most distinctive genres are: (1) the riddle, (2) the chronogram, and (3) the *badīʿiyyah*. *Riddles* were already present in ancient Arab times. In the Mamluk period, they became a popular game in which every participant could show his or her linguistic dexterity. The *chronogram* makes use of the fact that each letter of the Arabic alphabet has a numerical value. To commemorate a historical event in literary terms, the task was to figure out an epigraph that yields the date of the event if the numerical values of all the letters used are added up. Chronograms are also to be found in postmedieval Europe, but the Arabic chronogram is much trickier than the Latin one, and it attained a greater cultural significance, particularly in the nineteenth century. A Christian poet like al-Yāzijī, composing chronograms on the occasion of events that are equally important for Christians as for Muslims, takes into account the dates according to both the Christian and the Islamic calendar.[74]

The *badīʿiyyah*, finally, is a literary variety in which ambiguity itself assumes center stage. Its inventor was Ṣafī ad-Dīn al-Ḥillī (667–750/1278–1330). He had originally wanted to write a treatise on stylistic devices, but then he contracted a serious illness. During this illness, it seemed to him more appropriate to devote himself to a religious subject rather than pursue a scholarly one, so he composed a poem in praise of the prophet Muḥammad. This was a *muʿāraḍah*, a "counter-poem" to another praise of the prophet, the extraordinarily famous poem by al-Būṣīrī (died around 694/1294). Al-Būṣīrī himself had written his poem during an illness and had miraculously recovered afterwards. So Ṣafī ad-Dīn took this poem as a model, imitating its meter and rhyme, but introducing one decisive modification. Since he had already accumulated so much material on the stylistic devices of Arabic poetry, he wanted to incorporate this knowledge into his poem. So he did not merely compose a "counterpoem" to that of al-Būṣīrī, but took for each verse the opportunity to exemplify (at least) one stylistic device of the discipline (*ʿilm al-badīʿ*). He then wrote a commentary in which he explained all the stylistic devices that he had illustrated in the course of his poem.

Al-Būṣīrī's poem consists of two parts, an introductory love poem and a poem in praise of the Prophet. This structure is imitated by Ṣafī ad-Dīn, and most later *badīʿiyyah* poets follow him in this. Thus Ṣafī ad-Dīn al-Ḥillī's *badīʿiyyah* is both a love poem and a poem in praise of the Prophet; both a work of art that claims to be appreciated aesthetically and a prayer, a work both secular and religious; an aesthetic and a scientific text; and finally, a text that not only expresses ambiguity but also reflects it, since a large part of the exemplified stylistic devices represent those of ambiguity—thus offering a reflective ambiguity.

Al-Ḥillī's work was a great success and stimulated more than a hundred imitators during the following centuries. Some of them, however, found his poem much too simple still, and endeavored to also incorporate the technical term of the stylistic device illustrated into each respective verse (of course, with a different meaning). Eventually, other authors added commentaries to their *badīʿiyyah*, and some commentaries were augmented by a comprehensive anthology of verses and poems in which the respective stylistic device played a role. The first author who composed such a *badīʿiyyah* with a commentary and a comprehensive anthology was Ibn Ḥijjah al-Ḥamawī, mentioned before; the last one was probably the Damascene aṣ-Ṣalāḥī (died 1265/1849).

Each of these *badīʿiyyāt* has its own focus. The poetess ʿĀʾishah al-Bāʿūniyyah (died 922/1516), for instance, places greatest importance on the aesthetic features of the poem, and extends the amatory part of the poem by more than half. Other poets find it more important to discover stylistic devices that are not yet analyzed by older authors. The most artistic *badīʿiyyah*, however, is probably the work of al-Yāzijī, who not only is able to compose a palindrome over a whole verse, but also creates a truly ecumenical work by writing a *badīʿiyyah* that may be read both as a Christian and an Islamic text.[75]

Whatever the focus of a given *badīʿiyyah* may be, one point is common to all of them: they are, to use Huizinga's words, "played cultures."[76] However, it must be emphasized that by no means does the entire Arabic literature of the Mamluk and Ottoman eras fall under this category, as its adversaries have contended again and again. On the contrary, about a hundred *badīʿiyyāt*, several thousand chronograms (which amount to just one verse in the context of a longer poem), and several hundred extant poetic riddles stand in contrast to a multiple number of poems that display no exorbitant rhetorical design whatsoever, and are often astonishingly simple and direct in their stylistic expression.[77] The simple form was appreciated too, but it always was situated *alongside* the complex. All attempts to identify *periods* of classicism and mannerism in the history of Arabic literature are bound to fail, due to the fact that both styles, "classically" tempered on the one hand and highly stylized and mannered on the other, are always encountered alongside one another, often even by one and the same poet.[78]

The awareness of ambiguity achieved by the world of Arabic literature by the third/ninth century (at the latest) did not allow for a return to innocence. This awareness did not preclude pleasure in seemingly unambiguous simplicity, but always endeavored to cope creatively with a world full of ambiguity. There was a constant fascination with artistically enacting the ambiguity of the world, which may be domesticated but never eliminated.

The resulting works of art are the opposite of superficial baubles. Rather, they are "played culture," and they extend down into much deeper cultural levels than their modern critics, who are victims of the illusion that a world without ambiguity is possible, want to acknowledge. However, the culture of ambiguity could be "played" not only in the form of works of art; there were also written scientific works that display a more or less strong element of play. At the end of this chapter, I would like to present a work of "played science" which allows us to visually realize how seemingly definite scientific statements are grounded in ambiguous material.

The author is a Yemenite scholar and man of letters by the name of Ibn al-Muqri᾿ (754–837/1353–1433), also a writer of a *badīʿiyyah*, whose highest ambition was to attain the position of the supreme judge in the Rasūlid dynasty. In order to impress the ruler, he decided to write a book that in terms of artistic sophistication would surpass all its predecessors. This work is a collection of five short books,[79] each giving a succinct but instructive introduction to a scientific or literary discipline. One is a short but comprehensive presentation of Islamic law, according to the Shāfiʿite school; another is a conspectus on the history of the Rasūlids; there is also an introduction to Arabic grammar, an introduction to Arabic prosody, and an introduction to Arabic rhyme. So far, this is nothing exceptional. The extraordinary point of this work is that Ibn al-Muqri᾿ presents these five books not one after another, but *simultaneously*. And that is how it works: If the text is read in the usual direction—that is, horizontally, from right to left—it yields the presentation of Shāfiʿite law. If one reads the first letter or letters of each line vertically from up to down, the introduction into prosody emerges. This is followed in the next column to the left by the history of the Rasūlids, and in the next by the introduction into grammar, and at the end the theory of rhyme. The letters and words of all four books to be read vertically are also a part of the book on law. Letters and words that belong to two books have a different function and meaning according to the direction of reading, or to the context in which they are read. The illustration below shows a page from the work in which the horizontal columns are set against each other. This work, which Ibn al-Muqri᾿ completed in Muḥarram 804/August 1401 in Taʿizz, found several emulators. As for that supreme judge position, though . . . Ibn al-Muqri᾿ didn't get it.

In the precolonial Near East, ambiguity was not only tolerated, but also considered worth striving for. The exegete had the ambition of finding in a text as many meanings as possible. Collecting words with contradictory meanings became a sport for lexicographers. Men of letters continued to produce ambiguity with the greatest passion. They endeavored to create texts that encompass as many meanings as possible in the narrowest space possible.

Finally, this endeavor is transferred to scholarship, as Ibn al-Muqri᾿'s example shows. In a playful manner, a text is produced that breaks through linear dimensions. A work on law that at first glance looks no different from other books on

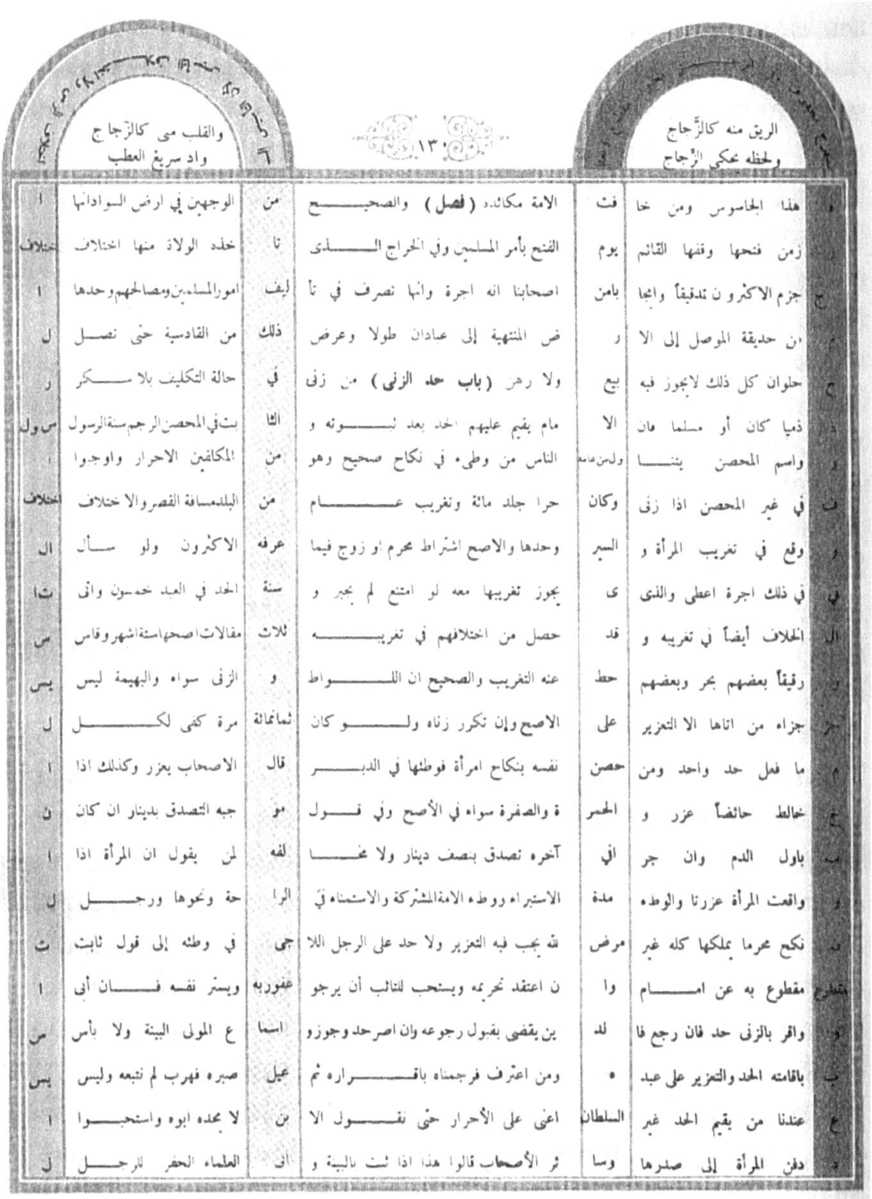

law actually contains within it four further books—books that become discernable, however, only in a quite specific, unalterable formal structure.

Often has the Western or Westernized view discounted the production of such texts that condense ambiguity, labeling them as scholastic nuisance, even as a symptom of decadence. But in fact these are highly complex forms of literary and scientific play that train the awareness of ambiguity. Due not least to this *training in ambiguity*, the people of the precolonial Near East were aware of the fact that ambiguity can never be eliminated, only domesticated. In this area, classical Islamic culture achieved a mastery that was never surpassed anywhere. The producers of literary and scholarly texts were able to domesticate the ambiguity with which they were confronted, as well as to produce ambiguity in a playful manner and in great abundance. Play with ambiguity was "played culture." People want to play what their culture achieves. Conversely, a culture can achieve only what is played in it.

7
The Ambiguity of Sexual Desire

In the universality of the Western ratio, *there is this demarcation line which marks the Orient: . . . the Orient that is offered to the colonizing reason of the West, but remains indefinitely inaccessible, for it always will mark the limit. . . . For the West, the Orient is everything that it is not, although it must search in the Orient what is its original truth.*

—Michel Foucault, *Folie et déraison*

AN IMPOSED—AND PARADIGMATIC—DISCOURSE

Whether in the context of Quranic readings and interpretations, of the plurality of scholarly opinions, or of linguistic play, we have encountered an identical pattern at every turn: the traditional discourses of the Islamic world, with their domesticated but not contested ambiguity, are challenged by Western discourses that are intolerant of ambiguity and advance the claim of universal validity. In reaction to the Western challenge, two discourses evolve in the Islamic world, an Islamist one and a Western-"liberal" one. At first sight they appear opposed to each other, but they have one and the same basis.

This identical basis is the order that the West assigns to things. In consequence of this structure of thought, that is, the Western episteme (to use Foucault's term), they turn away to the same, radical extent from traditional discourses that have become incomprehensible in the new order of knowledge.

Attempts by the West to strengthen the "liberal" discourses by no means weaken the Islamist positions. On the contrary, such attempts only make the foundations of both Islamist and liberal thought appear more plausible, and thus weaken the traditional discourses. So an Islamist discourse emerges as the actual, distinct answer of the Islamic world to the challenge of the Western discourses. On the one hand, it shares the principles of Western ways of thinking (otherwise, it would not be in a position to answer them); on the other, it offers a basis for positions that appear to be anti-Western and are perceived by the West as such. Of traditional discourses, it has no understanding. They are incompatible with those of the West, and are powerless in the face of the West's claim to cultural hegemony.

The belief in one truth, the intolerance of ambiguity, and the ambition of universalization on the part of the West, to which non-Western cultures more tolerant of ambiguity are forced to react without any prospect of resolving the contradictions they incur—this nexus of beliefs becomes nowhere more evident than in the field of sexuality.

With regard to one important point, however, the subject of this chapter is different from most of the other subjects of this book: the foregoing chapters have dealt with discourses originating in the Islamic world itself, from Quranic readings down to words with contradictory meanings that have become problematic in their confrontations with the modern West. But this chapter on love and sexuality, and the following section on foreignness, deal with subjects that were not imposed on us by the Islamic world. To review the Arabic literature of the millennium between 850 and 1850 is to be struck by the fact that while a multitude of discourses and texts on eroticism and sex existed, they lack entirely the excitement and obsessiveness that characterized analogous Western discourses for many centuries. Of its own accord, the classical Arab-Islamic world would never have made a discussion of the subject of "sexuality" necessary.

Considerably more spectacular, in contrast, were the reactions of the West to the sexuality of "the Orient," or to what the West fantasized about it. Needless to say, this Western interest was not matched by an interest in Western (or any other foreign) sexuality on the part of the Islamic world. But by the middle of the nineteenth century, the West had gained enough power to impose its own discourses on sexuality upon the rest of the world. From then on, the Orient not only presented to the West a cause for *arousal* (in every sense of the word) but also offered itself as an object of education. Beginning in this period, there ceased to exist in the Arab world (and not only there) any discourse on sexuality that was not a direct reaction to the West, or at least partially but substantially shaped by it. It is particularly in the area of sexuality that the hegemonic power of Western discourses manifests itself, since its influence reaches the most private areas of people's lives. If modern Arab discourses on sex prove to be reactions to Western ones, shouldn't discourses on Quranic readings and political concepts constitute such reactions all the more?

In all this, the power of Western discourses cannot be based in their conceptual superiority—if only for the reason that their contents perpetually changed. The Victorian sexual ethics preached during the nineteenth century is in many respects the exact opposite of the sexual revolution with which Western NGOs try to bless the world today. In spite of this obvious contradiction, the representatives of these discourses have never doubted that the knowledge organized in the discourses is *true* and *universally valid*, or that it is of great importance to move the rest of mankind toward accepting this knowledge. Until that goal is reached, their fight against the ambiguity of sex that has worried the West for many centuries will not be won.

WESTERN SEX AND ITS AMBIGUITIES

The history of Western sex is the history of a large-scale fight against ambiguity—which led, however, only to further ambivalences and ambiguities. The point of origin is the ambivalent position of late antique Christianity on the sexual act; on the one hand, it is indispensable for the continuation of mankind; on the other, its pleasurable practice was a damnable sin deserving of the most horrible eternal punishment.

In Catholic Europe, the convention of confession made it possible to disentangle the irresolvable ambiguity of the procreative act, which was legitimate, and at the same time sinful because of the pleasure that accompanied it. Every act had to be described exactly, and every accompanying emotion was expected to be particularized, in order to trace even the faintest intrusion of sinful lust. From the beginning of the second half of the sixteenth century onwards, even laymen were regularly obliged to deliver their auricular confession and had to face the probing questions of the priests. "The confession manuals taught priests to insistently question people, especially women, about the sexual positions they adopted, any possible attempts by the man to avoid leaving his semen inside the woman, and other uses of the body regarded as degrading."[1] In contrast to the Near East and other parts of the world, people learned to constantly analyze and morally evaluate their own sex lives. Every act was charged with an unsurpassable ambiguity; one must investigate whether one was merely fulfilling a marital duty or whether there was a secret lust hiding within the act; this would determine whether that act had to be placed on one or the other side of the thin line between duty and damnation.

The secularization of the West, which was probably due more to an urge to escape from the sexual morals of the church than to the philosophical ideas of a few Enlightenment thinkers, did not bring about relief. That is because post-Enlightenment society, too, "has pursued the task of producing true discourses concerning sex, and this by adapting . . . the ancient procedure of confession to the rules of scientific discourse. Paradoxically, the *scientia sexualis* . . . kept as its nucleus the singular ritual of obligatory and exhaustive confession, which in the Christian West was the first technique for producing the truth of sex."[2] The new paradigm is perhaps even more effective and more comprehensive than the old one, "in that it connects the ancient injunction of confession to clinical listening methods."[3] Sex in the West thus remained, and respectively became, "an object of great suspicion; the general and disquieting meaning that pervades our conduct and our existence, in spite of ourselves; the point of weakness where evil portents reach through to us; the fragment of darkness that we each carry within us: a general signification, a universal secret, an omnipresent cause, a fear that never ends."[4] A "terror of their own body"[5] has plagued the people of the West for centuries. We have seen that ambivalent feelings may trigger a fear of ambiguity, leading to a strong intolerance of ambiguity. Ambivalence with respect to one's own body, the fear of "the fragment of darkness that everybody carries in oneself," must be a principal cause for the Western fear of ambiguity.

In order to make the ambiguity of sex accessible to science (which was, however, doomed to fail in coping with it, just as religion had failed before), a wholly new concept had to be developed, that of *sexuality*. Today it seems self-evident that this term denotes something that really exists; it is scarcely conceivable that we could do without it and its underlying concept. In fact, however, it is not at all self-evident to regard all acts and emotions directly and indirectly connected to the sexual organs as a distinct area of the human personality, an area in which the various components are causally connected to each other. No one would think of regarding grief, joy, operatic emotion, and pollen allergy as phenomena of a single, neatly definable area of human nature, simply because they are all apt to trigger the activity of the lachrymal glands. In the case of sexuality, however, it is taken for granted that a tender hug and wartime rape[6] are assigned to one and the same area of human nature.

In fact, "sexuality" is a modern Western concept that arose only in the nineteenth century.[7] Before that, human beings had sex, but no sexuality, and they could talk about sex very well without believing that a certain group of emotions, desires and acts might be singled out and subsumed under a distinct phenomenon by the name of "sexuality." Thanks to the new concept of sexuality, all the quite-diverse sins committed through thinking, talking, and acting came to be distinguished as one discrete component of the human personality, and to be grouped together as a unit differentiated from other areas of a person's emotions and actions.

This seemed to signify a further important victory over the ambiguity of sex. After learning to investigate and classify sexual acts, people were now in a position to cope with this sharply defined area with new means and methods precisely fitted for it. Since the nineteenth century, these means have been governed by medicine, which took over from religion the exclusive authorization to interpret sexuality. Warnings against sin were secularized and translated into rules for a "healthy" sexual life, and the horrors of eternal punishment were replaced by fears of perversion, illness, and death.[8]

The project of establishing a sphere of "sexuality" distinct from all other areas of human experience has given the West the chance (ultimately hopeless, but in the meantime quite successful) to disambiguate acts that seem to be connected in some way with sexual life. All widely spoken languages have developed a word meant to match the Western term "sexuality"; in addition, in most cases, a discourse has been established that attempts to adjust the indigenous "sexuality" to Western standards. It is self-evident that this attempt to disambiguate sexual desire and erotic emotions is doomed to fail—as are all other attempts at the annihilation of ambiguity. The detailed lists of sins devised by priests were substituted by the even more detailed classifications of innumerable perversions accumulated by physicians. A differentiated variety of sexual identities is available on today's market of identities, but an end to the ambiguity of sex keeps receding into the far distance.

The procedure of curbing ambiguity by differentiation claims its victims. One early such victim is *friendship*. For men of the Near East, amicable relations with other men have always been, and are to this day, perhaps the most emotionally important social relations in adult life. Western travelers are frequently irritated by friendly affection shared between men, and often react to it with incomprehension, if not with malice.[9] However, a culture of male friendship was common not so long ago in the West as well. Here, too, men walked hand in hand and exchanged friendly kisses and embraces. Without such a culture of friendship—definitely underpinned by eroticism—classical and early romantic German culture is hardly conceivable. The question of *how much* eroticism went into a friendly relationship of this kind was not asked in those times, because a "sexuality" that was always at work, openly or hidden, did not yet exist. Hence there was no dictate of unambiguity, no compulsion to differentiate between friendship and love. Today we regard Western categories not only as universal but also as timelessly valid, and we ask whether the intimate relation between Schubert and Mayrhofer was a close friendship or a love relation, assuming that the latter would mean that Schubert and Mayrhofer were "homosexual." Neither of them, however, would have begun to comprehend this question, because the categories through which the West would disambiguate desire would not have made sense to them.

Schubert and Mayrhofer lived in a time, it is true, when the constraint to render relations between men unambiguous had started to make itself felt—if not in continental Europe, then in England, where capitalist kinds of economy and mentality asserted themselves earlier. Capitalist competitive attitudes and empathetic friendship are hardly compatible. Educating young men into becoming future competitors meant that by the end of the eighteenth century in England, the unambiguously unerotic handshake had replaced the kiss and embrace that were still accepted on the Continent as an expression of friendship.[10] In a parallel to this, "the sphere of privacy constituted itself as a product of dissociation";[11] in other words, marriage was now the exclusive place for legitimate sex as well as for tender, empathetic friendship.

Still, there remained too much disorderly sex in the world, which troubled the division between the spheres of sexuality and nonsexuality. In order to produce unambiguity, it was not enough to stay on the level of acts, as had been the case in the premodern assessment of sexual acts as sins. After all, each person is a sinner, and each person is expected to commit all kinds of sins. If everything is possible at all times, unambiguity cannot be established. It is a different thing if sex is considered as an expression of *personality*. This change of perspective took place toward the middle of the nineteenth century. "Disorderly" sex was now regarded not as a surplus of desire and lack of self-control, but as a symptom of a pathologically changed personality. Within this new perspective, the world of sex appeared much more orderly, and at the same time, the respectable bourgeoisie could absolve itself from any "disorderly" desire—a bourgeoisie that now started an eager "hunt for peripheral sexualities," as Foucault calls it, a hunt in which the most important prey is the discovery of the homosexual.

> This new persecution of the peripheral sexualities entailed an *incorporation of perversions* and a new *specification of individuals*. As defined by the ancient civil or canonical codes, sodomy was a category of forbidden acts; their perpetrator was nothing more than the juridical subject of them. The nineteenth-century homosexual became a personage, a past, a case history, and a childhood, in

> addition to being a type of life, a life form, and a morphology, with an indiscreet anatomy and possibly a mysterious physiology. Nothing that went into his total composition was unaffected by his sexuality. It was everywhere present in him: at the root of all his actions because it was their insidious and indefinitely active principle.[12]

This newly "discovered" binarity of "hetero" and "homo"[13] inflicted, upon the minority who did not want to abandon desire between man and man, a pain that superseded everything the persecution of sodomites had brought about in earlier historical periods. But it seemed, for the time being at least, to introduce a better order into the dark realm of sexuality.

However, there still remained one piece of evidence that clouded the picture. The nineteenth century saw the triumph not only of capitalism and psychoanalysis but also of colonialism. And there exists solid evidence of the fact that "historically, the European construction of sexuality coincides with the epoch of imperialism and the two interconnect."[14] The power of the West now also grabbed at those faraway, "disorderly" exotic shores, where a kind of sex flourished that was dangerously apt to topple the Western systems of sex.

These Western systems could be true only if they were universal, and it is this universality that the reports of travelers, colonial officers, and ethnologists apparently brought into question. In the process, sex in the Near East caught the increased interest of the European West, which had already developed its own ideas about this exotic sex and now, in the nineteenth century, derived from those ideas its rationale and justification for intervention.

But let us first take a look at the Near Eastern discourses on sex, directing our special attention to the aspect that has provoked particular outrage but also fascination among Westerners—namely, the attitude regarding love and sex between men.

THE NEAR EASTERN PLURALITY OF DISCOURSES

In all cultures, sex is regulated by social norms, and everywhere there are transgressions against these norms. Apparently, sex without ambiguity does not exist. Sex was full of ambiguity in classical Islamic cultures as well. However, this ambiguity did not seriously challenge the tolerance of ambiguity that was prevalent in these cultures. There was no discernibly deep or permanent suffering due to the ambiguity of sex. Presumably, this was because the principal ambiguity that marked the beginning of the history of Western sex—the elimination of which ambiguity the West would be toiling away at for the following centuries—was not felt in Islamic cultures. In the Near East, there simply did not exist an ambiguity arising from the belief that sex brings about simultaneously pleasure *and* ruin.

The Islamic sexual ethic, as formulated by al-Ghazālī in his *Iḥyāʾ ʿulūm ad-dīn* (Revivification of the religious sciences), for instance, regards sex as something unrestrictedly positive. Sexual intercourse, he writes, serves first to give man and woman a foretaste of Paradise, and second to ensure the continuity of humankind—note the order of things![15] Of course, the legitimacy of the relation between the partners is an important condition. Other sexual acts, it is true, are counted as sinful in Islam, but even these do not have a privileged position in the treatises on the "grave sins."[16] Another factor is that in early Sunni Islam, the conviction gained prevalence that a Muslim believer, even if he was a grave sinner, did not have to roast in Hell forever.[17] This position was formulated against the school of the Muʿtazilites, which insisted on the concept of eternal punishment in Hell. This school, however, did not prevail—much to the regret of modern "reform" Muslims and Western observers of Islam, who deem the suppression of the (allegedly rationalist, but most of all rigorous) Muʿtazilah in the ninth century a calamity, and who expect a more "liberal" Islam from a revival of Muʿtazilite ideas.[18] But since the idea of eternal punishment did not prevail, a powerful disciplining instrument was taken away from the religious personnel in Islam.

In the Near East, sex is fundamentally not something scary, somber, dangerous, and potentially bringing ruin, no "piece of night that everyone carries around with him." By contrast, love is much more dangerous, because it contains the risk of losing oneself within another person and of becoming an antisocial being through a fixation upon this other.[19] Thus, while love does contain a dangerous dimension of ambiguity, Near Eastern sex lacks such a dimension to a large degree. Its ambiguities are secondary, and manageable by the usual methods of domesticating ambiguity.

Here, as elsewhere, the most important cause for ambiguity is the plurality of discourses. Different pertinent discourses stand side by side, and none of them may lay a claim to exclusive validity. Even if this may result in manifest contradictions, there is no notable ambition to dissolve them once and for all. Here too, love and sex are not different from other areas of life. And as in other areas, Western observers have almost totally failed to realize this plurality of discourses, let alone to appreciate it. Anyone who consults the *Encyclopaedia of Islam* on this topic is inevitably fobbed off with Islamic law. There is, however, an entry on *bāh* (coitus) that deals exclusively with juridical aspects—as if the author had assumed that people "in Islam," even while having sex, are unable to think of anything other than religion and religious law! There are also numerous secular sex manuals whose titles often contain the word *bāh*. But that encyclopedia entry on *bāh* does not mention them at all. Instead, the reader is informed in detail about which kinds of intercourse are permitted and which ones interdicted according to legal opinions.[20]

Since this encyclopedic entry appeared in 1960, the Western fixation upon the juridical discourse has become more intense. Originally, this was caused by cases of execution after adultery or sexual intercourse between men in the Afghanistan of the Taliban or in the Islamic provinces of Nigeria that were striving for more independence from the central government.

In any case, there is a tendency in the Western world to consider Islamic law as the "essential" Islamic discourse, the one in which the "essence" of Islam manifests itself most clearly. This tendency has led to understanding the stoning of adulterers as another expression of the "essence" of Islam, and from here it has been only a small step to portray *the* Islam as clearly unenlightened, archaic, cruel, and hostile to sexuality. Such conclusions played into the hands of those who handed out the punishments. For behind the application of these *ḥadd* sentences, which had next to no historical models, stood a political agenda opposed not so much to the entire West as to the indigenous elites who cooperated with the West and obtained power and influence from it. What could more conveniently demonstrate opposition to the elites' value system than to apply punishments that provoked the greatest disapproval of the West, and at the same time could be interpreted as a symbol of one's own "severe" morality as against the "decadence" of the West?

As happens so often, a fundamentalist Islamic position and a Western one coincide here in their common rejection of ambiguity. The classical legal regulation is an exemplary case of ambiguity. On the one hand, Islamic law decrees the most severe sentences for vaginal intercourse between a man and a woman who have no marriage or concubinage contract (*zinā*), and furthermore for anal intercourse between man and man (*liwāṭ*) (also the latter between man and woman, albeit attenuated in some legal schools).[21] On the other hand, the law itself renders the execution of these sentences almost impossible. Four witnesses are necessary who have observed the sexual act in all its details and who, should any among them provoke doubts about his testimony, must expect a public flogging because of false statement—not to mention that the witnesses would have trouble justifying their unseemly curiosity.

Most legal schools even have ways not to admit the birth of an illegitimate child as proof for *zinā*: the woman, they say, might have conceived the child while sleeping. In the Mālikite sphere, for instance in Tunisia and Northern Nigeria, where this argument is not accepted, the concept of the dormant pregnancy is common. This is based on the idea that embryos are apt to "sleep" for a longer period, sometimes for years, in the uterus, without developing. If it happens that the unborn is "awakened," it is born. In these ways, extramarital pregnancies are legitimized.[22]

No wonder, then, that it is difficult to find mention of a single execution on the grounds of *zinā* or *liwāṭ*, even in chronicles that otherwise meticulously record every case of violence and crime. In my reading of all kinds of sources, I have never come across an execution, or even an indictment, for sex between consenting males in the period before the twentieth century. The only case of stoning because of *zinā* known to me took place in Constantinople in 1680 and was politically motivated. The judge was a supporter of the rigorist and fundamentalist Kadizadeli movement, and with his sentence triggered a scandal. His name was Sinān ad-Dīn al-Bayāḍī (died 1098/1687), and toward the end of his career he held the not insignificant office of the kadiaskar of Rumelia. That made him important enough to be listed among the 1290 people whom the writer and linguist al-Muḥibbī (1061–1111/1651–1699) has collected in his encyclopedia of famous personalities of the eleventh/seventeenth century. In the twenty lines that al-Muḥibbī devotes to Sinān ad-Dīn, he describes Sinān ad-Dīn's career as a judge and lists his most important writings; this routine is not different from the other entries. But then he reports a legal case on which the qadi had to decide during his time in office, and this report is in striking contrast to the other biographies.

Sinān ad-Dīn's spectacular ruling concerns a death sentence on a woman whose *zinā* was considered proven by four witnesses, whereupon the sentence of stoning was issued and executed according to the proper regulations. The chronicler describes these regulations in great detail, either because he does not suppose the details to be known to the general reader or because he considers it outrageous that they can be in fact applied. His horror of the act—not that of the woman, but that of the judge, who had perhaps complied with a sentiment about lynching among the village population rather than acting on his own initiative—finally culminates in the exclamation: "And such a case has never happened since the early days of Islam!" Subsequently, this judge was discharged from his post (although it is not completely clear whether his deposition was the direct result of his judgment) and spent the rest of his life as a private man without ever attaining another office.[23]

Both in al-Muḥibbī's understanding (and certainly that of most of his contemporaries), and in the eyes of today's Western observers of Islam, the stoning of an adulteress (we do not learn what happened to the adulterer; he would have had to face the same sentence) is something inconceivable, something that never should have been allowed to happen. But the views differ in one regard. Western self-appointed reformers of Islam take offense primarily at the norm, that is, the existence of drastic threats of punishment in Islamic law (which in the case of stoning cannot be traced back to the Quran, contrary to common prejudice). They see enforcement as a necessary consequence of these norms. The stoning is thus only the symptom of a graver evil, which is ultimately to be found in the "essence" of Islam. Al-Muḥibbī, in contrast, takes offense not at the existence of the drastic regulations, but at their execution. For him, it is not hard to conceive of norms and laws that at the same time are and are not valid. The stoning of adulterers is accepted as a norm, and may even have been enforced under particular circumstances in "the early times of Islam," but by virtue of the obstacles put up by the law itself, it is inapplicable and therefore, in a practical sense, invalid. Such an acceptance of ambiguity is not compatible with a modern understanding of norms, and thus a position such as that of the classical Arab-Islamic world is simply incomprehensible. It is characteristic that the Islamic fundamentalists of today share the mentalities of their Western critics, for they, too, are convinced that laws are there to be enforced, even if other regulations that appear to be of secondary rank must be bypassed.

As a matter of fact, however, we have already spent too much time on the discourse on sexuality in law; its importance for the classical period is heavily overrated today. As we have seen, the few pertinent regulations have very little practical relevance; all the other areas of sex, with the exception of regulations for ritual purity or the marriage contract, are not dealt with by legal scholars. Even the sections on *zinā* and *liwāṭ* are treated, as a rule, "without passion," and briefly, and their commentaries only rarely record controversies. Averroes, in his four-volume work on comparative law, does not devote a single word to *liwāṭ*, a "shortcoming" that is corrected by its modern editor in a long footnote.[24] On many subjects that have substantially codetermined the Western discourse on sexuality, classical legal scholars remain silent. The subject of masturbation, for instance, attained top priority in the societal discourse of nineteenth-century Europe. "Masturbation obsessed the doctors of the nineteenth century. This resulted in the artificial construction of an obsessional pathology comparable to the collective witchcraft fantasy which had been responsible for so many deaths in the sixteenth and seventeenth centuries."[25] Islamic legal scholars, who had something to say about virtually everything, did not come up with any ideas on this particular topic. The late scholar al-Juzayrī (1882–1941), in his widely distributed survey of "the law according to the four schools," does not mention masturbation; this "gap," however, is filled by commentators in the new edition (1998) of the work.[26]

To resume: The most significant discourse on sexuality in the Islamic world is by no means the law, even with respect to *religion*. As mentioned above, sexual ethics, as formulated by al-Ghazālī and others, was probably of greater practical importance for everyday life.

But again, we must free ourselves from the idea that in "Islam," religious discourses are principally more important than secular ones. In the areas of love and sex, secular texts were composed in far greater number than religious ones, and these are distributed over several different discourses. This plurality of discourses is supported by the fact that the idea of a homogeneous area of "sexuality" simply did not exist.

As a first discourse, we will consider the literature of advice, which, in almost a direct continuation of the literature of antiquity, started at an early stage and continued throughout the centuries. When Michel Foucault subsumed Islam within the category of cultures that had at its disposal an *ars erotica*,[27] it may have been these texts of which he was thinking. However, Foucault awakens expectations that are very much informed by Western ideas, and are not quite satisfied by the Arabic texts, which discuss anything but sensuous seraglio fantasies. Most works are rather thoroughly sober guides to sexual hygiene; they do not offer unheard-of pathways to sexual climax, instead giving advice on such banal topics as the best times of day for intercourse and the relation between diet and sex. When the West discovered these treatises in the nineteenth century—Guy de Maupassant acted as a "pioneer"—they caused a sensation, oddly, as pornographic works.[28] This stark misunderstanding can only be understood by bearing in mind that since the end of pagan antiquity, Christian Europe had not known any texts that displayed such a sober and unforced attitude toward sex as did the Arabic guides on sexual hygiene.

A similar misapprehension concerned the literary genre of *mujūn*, often translated as "jocular and scurrilous poetry." These poems sometimes talk about sexuality quite openly, but it would be a great misunderstanding to view them as a parallel to the modern phenomenon of pornography. First of all, not all poems under the heading of *mujūn* deal with sexual topics; secondly, the allusions to sexual matters in common *mujūn* poems hardly serve as a means of sexual titillation. A large number of them deal with accounts of sexual mishaps in the form of epigrams, as in "impotence poems," in which the poet complains about how his penis always stirs at the wrong time, but not when it is supposed to. Other *mujūn* poets, such as the "classics" of the Abbasid period, Ibn al-Ḥajjāj and Ibn as-Sukkarah, commit calculated breaches of taboo.[29] The way these poems should be appreciated has been expressed by Ibn Nubātah, the important writer of the Mamluk period, in the title of his selection of poems by Ibn al-Ḥajjāj. He called his book *Talṭīf al-mizāj min shiʿr Ibn al-Ḥajjāj* (Harmonization of the mixture [of the bodily juices] by the poetry of Ibn al-Ḥajjāj), and indicated clearly that the purpose of this literary genre was to serve as a compensation for a "civilization and its discontent," a refuge of relaxation, and a relief from the compulsive dignity a publicly active scholar is permanently obliged to maintain.

It seems to me a not inconsiderable cultural achievement to be able to cross this border of propriety in a subtle literary manner. Ibn Nubātah was the most sophisticated stylist of his time, a pious man who spent his whole life building his reputation as a respected intellectual. Precisely for this reason, it seemed to him meritorious to cultivate those areas at the margin of culture; in this, he felt at home in an old tradition—which today has become incomprehensible.

Much more important than *mujūn* poetry is love poetry, the *ghazal*, which inarguably represents the most prominent discourse on desire between human beings from the eighth to the nineteenth century.[30] There is hardly any significant poet who did not devote a prominent part of his work to *ghazal* poetry; there are poets who never wrote anything else; and there are a host of amateur poets who pleased their contemporaries and posterity with their love poems, many of which are extant to this day. The thousands—if not hundreds of thousands—of *ghazal* poems composed over more than a millennium in Arabic, Persian, Turkish, Urdu, and other languages, and transmitted all the way to the present, represent a secular heritage of the "Islamic" world that deserves to be taken no less seriously than the (equally overwhelming) body of religious literature.

However, the classical *ghazal* written in Arabic, Persian, Turkish, or Urdu confronted the Western reader of the nineteenth century with a seemingly intractable problem: the fact that a great number of the poems, written by male authors from the ninth century on, are addressed not to women but to young men. And since the modern elites of the Near East have adopted Western perceptions of love and sex, this primarily Western problem has become a Near Eastern problem as well. Attempts at solving this problem are sometimes ludicrous, sometimes tragic, and always absurd. One relatively harmless attempt is to "heteroeroticize" homoerotic poems in translation; that is, to replace the male beloved person by a female one—an attempt that is always doomed to fail if the beloved appears to the poet particularly attractive because of his peach fuzz.

Less harmless are theories attributing pathological traits to the entire "Islamic" culture.

The problem does not lie in the texts; it lies in the eyes of the beholder. It must be noted that the *ghazal* is a discourse not on "sexuality" but on *love*, and as such is not congruent with the discourse of Islamic law on permitted and prohibited sexual acts. In other words, the Islamic doctrine of legal duties considers it a sin to have sexual intercourse with other men, but it is not prohibited to fall in love with other men. For this reason, men who wanted to be regarded as law-abiding Muslims (and often, no doubt, were rightly considered as such) could compose poems about handsome young men. To many Muslims today, it appears hardly tolerable that the greatest hadith scholar of the postformative period, Ibn Ḥajar al-ʿAsqalānī, composed homoerotic verse. Ibn Ḥajar himself would have been at a total loss to comprehend such a rejection of his amatory poetry. For him—as for the precolonial Near East in general—it was self-evident that handsome young men are desirable, and that men may fall in love with them as well as with young women. Therefore, it seemed to him a good idea to begin a poem that is (unusually) a deeply felt love poem for his own lawfully wedded spouse with a few homoerotic verses.[31] For a modern observer who has gone through the mad fire of disambiguation, this is somewhat disconcerting, since Ibn Ḥajar does not comply with the hetero/homo binarity. And what is true for Ibn Ḥajar may be applied, more or less, to all men of the precolonial, pre-twentieth century Near East whose pertinent testimonies are extant. The central Near Eastern discourse on love may be understood only if one dismisses the universal claim of the Western discourse.[32]

This does not mean that the Near Eastern discourse is not aware of its own limits, namely at that point where—as in antiquity—a basic acceptance of desire between men collides with a patriarchal notion of manliness. On the one hand, it is considered normal that men fall in love with men. On the other, it is expected that a man takes the active (i.e., penetrating) role in the sexual act, the actual sex of his partner being irrelevant. This restricts the possibility of sexual relations between men, as accepted by society, because in a relation between coeval men it is not clear who is the "true," that is active, man, and who assumes the passive role. At this point arises an absolutely archetypal situation of ambiguity, and it is significant that this highly ambiguous situation is not suppressed or fought against, but is passionately celebrated in its own literary genre.

I call this genre, which existed in the Mediterranean region and the Near East long before the Arabic expansion, the "apologetic epigram on the beard's growth." The point of origin of these epigrams is a typical ambiguity crisis: the beloved youth begins to grow a beard. This means that the love relationship should be ended, since it is no longer discernible who is the lover and who the beloved. But since such relations are fraught with deep emotions, this is easier said than done. The ambivalence is now shaped in an epigram in which the poet justifies the continuation of a love relationship that is regarded as problematic by public moral concepts. Most of these epigrams consist of two parts. A first verse depicts the situation or mentions the reproach of the censors, and a second verse offers an argument of justification, which as a rule leads to a punch line.

One of the most ancient "apologetic epigrams on the beard's growth" known to me is to be found in the "Greek Anthology." It was written by the poet Straton, who lived in the second century AD, and it shows how vigorously the ideas of antiquity lived on in the Near East: "Even though the invading down and the delicate auburn curls of thy temples have leapt upon thee, that does not make me shun my beloved, but his beauty is mine, even if there be a beard and hairs."[33]

After the Christianization of the empire (and certainly as its result), the epigrams on the beard's growth fell silent, but soon after the Arab conquest they came to life again. Abū Nuwās and Abū Tammām are among the first of those whose epigrams are recorded. Their argumentation is quite in line with that of Straton. First, the young man may already show a sprouting beard, but he is still as ravishing as before. Then the figure of speech "yes—but" is replaced by another figure of argument. Using the quasi-logic inherent in poetry, the beard's growth is depicted as something wholly positive, for instance in this three-stanza epigram by al-Ḥarīrī, mainly known as an author of *maqāmah*s (446–516/1054–1122)[34]:

> They said, when they saw whom I love:
> Doesn't it irritate you that he grows a beard?
>
> But they are blind! If they really looked at the matter
> How soon they would let go of their censure!
>
> Because he who is at home in a bare landscape,
> Will not go elsewhere when the spring flowers start to blossom.[35]

Such apologetic epigrams on the beard's growth are poetic feats of ambiguity. Not only is an ambiguous situation their object, but a stylistic means of ambiguity shapes the final line, in this case a quasi-logical argumentation: the beard is identified with the growth of plants ("spring flowers"), and so the false syllogism comes about—the beard matches the flowers; flowers are considered to be good; hence the beard, too, is good.

The beard's growth epigram attained a popularity matched by few other forms and subjects of poetry. Thousands of such epigrams were composed between 800 and 1800. An-Nawājī (788–859/1386–1455), a writer and hadith scholar famous for his popular anthologies and poems in praise of the Prophet, compiled an entire book of these epigrams.[36] When authors of the Ottoman era started to cultivate the literary genre of the chronogram, there appeared epigrams marking the beginning of a beard's growth; if the literature of that period were more accessible to us, we would be able to date the end of this tradition—due to Christian moral concepts imported from Europe—to the exact year, probably in the 1840s or 1850s. Thus comes to an end a tradition spanning a thousand years—and probably almost two thousand, since it is hardly conceivable that the Arabic apologetic epigram on the beard's growth does not continue a tradition of its ancient forerunners. This makes it all the more problematic to cling to the West's claim to the universality of its idea of sexuality, especially since the West seeks to present itself—contrary to all evidence—as the direct and sole heir to ancient culture. The ancient concepts of love, sex, and family lived on not in the West, but in the Near East, where they found their expression in literature until they were silenced in the middle of the nineteenth century due to Western influence.[37]

Let us conclude this chapter with an attempt to summarize the main features of ancient Islamic concepts of love and sexuality. A Eurocentric perspective is inevitable, since we need to address precisely those points—and only those—that appear particularly significant in the light of the ideas of the modern West. It seems that (1) both young women and young men appear to be attractive to men. It seems natural for men to fall in love both with pretty women and with handsome youths, and it is moreover (2) not prohibited to compose love poems about young men (except in the eyes of very severe scholars, who scent in this an incentive to illicit action). It is felt (3) to be entirely proper behavior to exchange displays of affection with friends. In contrast, (4) anal intercourse is forbidden by Islamic law. But it cannot be punished, as long as it is performed by mutual consent and privately. (5) An adult man should take the role of the active lover. The ambiguity that arises in love relations with youths who are already growing beards should be avoided . . . and yet, this is one of the most beloved topics of literature, and could continue to be so beloved for such a long time, only because it reflected a real, everyday problem.

SEX AND THE CLAIM TO UNIVERSALITY

The story could come to an end here, since such ideas, or similar ones, are to be found not only in almost the entire premodern Islamic world, but also in Greek, Roman, and Persian antiquity; during the Italian Renaissance; and far beyond Southern Europe, North Africa, and the Near East in Japan, where quite similar conditions can be observed.[38] But these ideas clash with what the West thought, and thinks, it knows about sexuality. So the story goes on.

Actually, the universal scope of notions about sex that contradict those of the West should be enough to unsettle one of the most important arguments in the Western discourse on sexuality, the argument of *nature*. The discourses of the Islamic world spoke of nature in the context of guides to sexual hygiene, but this is only with regard to the nature of the body and the equilibrium of its humors. Moral principles are not derived from nature. And it should be easily evident that moral arguments generally cannot be deduced from nature, because there can be no certainty about whether something that is *natural* is therefore, a priori, good or bad (and vice versa, whether something is necessarily good or bad because it is *not* natural). In spite of this, ever since the Middle Ages, nature has been abused as "the whore of morality,"[39] and the Christian churches' discourses on sexuality continue to do so today.

The primary arguments of the West have always been that: (1) sexuality has to be explained; (2) it must be explained on the grounds of nature, with the natural and the morally desirable ideally matching each other; and (3) the Western notions of "normal" sexuality always coincide both with nature and with the moral world order, and hence may claim to have universal validity. Proponents of these arguments were not fazed by the fact that notions of "natural" sexuality were subject to change over time, in Western culture more than elsewhere, and that therefore they cannot *always* have been in agreement with a nature conceived as essential. Such proponents were equally unfazed by the fact that a large part of humankind—in fact, the greater part of it—felt, and still feels, another kind of sex as more self-evident, and unfazed still less by the fact that the decidedly questionable axioms (1) and (2) may be accepted much more easily if one gives up axiom (3).

Consider the following scenario: Assume that sexuality is indeed in need of an explanation, and must be explained by the fact that it conforms, or does not conform, to the natural foundations of human existence. There now arises an irresolvable contradiction between, on the one hand, Western ideas of sexuality as something natural, and on the other hand, the most important modern discourse on nature, namely the theory of evolution. For if homosexual desire is understood as a hereditary anomaly, there is no way to explain why it has not become extinct; after all, homosexual men are survived by distinctly fewer progeny than are heterosexual men.

However, if we assumed the ancient-Islamic variety to be a "natural" form of human sexuality, the problem would not arise. The capacity to feel homoerotic attraction would be accepted as a condition important for social cohesion, and would hence be explicable by its evolutionary function. The existence of a predominantly homosexual-feeling minority and of a predominantly heterosexual-feeling minority would constitute a fact that would need no further explanation, because they would simply present specific cases of the capacity to enter into relations with both sexes. This biological fact could be seamlessly connected with patterns of explanations of cultural phenomena. Since, for two millennia in the West, erotic relations between men have been condemned and (contrary to the practice of the Islamic world) punished thousands of times by torture and death, a cultural explanation of the "heteronormalization"[40] of the Western world is quite plausible. Not for nothing is homophobia, as a result of suppressed desire between men, a common phenomenon in the West and in all parts of the world where Western heteronormalization spreads.[41] In the premodern Islamic world (and in the ancient world, etc.), however, such a phenomenon was unknown.

Vice versa, the largely tolerant and relaxed handling of sexuality between men in non-Western cultures cannot be explained culturally. Such attempts lead to inextricable contradictions, if they are not absurd from the very beginning. There have been two competing theories for the omnipresence of homoeroticism in the Arab world. The first was advocated mainly by Western Orientalists, and ascribed the "homosexuality" (quite an inept term here) common in the Islamic world to the *shortage* of women. This view was espoused as recently as 2009 in an article of the *Encyclopedia of Jews in the Islamic World*, in which the author wants to explain the prevalence of eroticism between men among Jews living in the Islamic world: Jews, who do not have the Islamic division of the sexes, have adopted it from the Muslims, among whom it has spread due to that shortage of women.[42]

However, in the premodern Islamic world, women were by no means as inaccessible as this hypothesis claims. Some men could afford to marry more than one woman, and, if they were affluent enough, could have concubines. Furthermore, the existence of prostitutes is well attested for many cities and historical periods.

In view of these facts, other scholars, primarily Arab, who were more familiar with the social contexts, have come up with the inverse theory: it is not the *shortage* of women, but the *abundance* of them, that furthers "homosexuality." It was exactly the easy accessibility of women of all races and peoples, they say, that caused such ennui in men that, seeking ever more novel sensual thrills, they took up with young men.[43] Thus both *too few* and *too many* women must serve as an explanation of the existence of homoerotic feelings—and each of these approaches is supposed to be valid for both the ninth-century caliph al-Maʾmūn who entertains a harem, and the poor Cairene artisan al-Miʿmār in the fourteenth century, let alone Athenian, Florentine, and Ottoman men of the most diverse eras.

As a result of our proposed scenario, let us note the following: The attempt to explain Western sex as something *natural* is doomed to fail, just as the attempt to explain ancient and Islamic sex as something *cultural* is doomed to fail. It would be simpler to argue the other way round. But while attempts to explain the widespread homoerotic desire in other cultures obviously fail, the "conditions of the emergence of an exclusively heterosexual way of life . . . have scarcely been the object of research until today."[44]

The reason for this is not only the fact that Western culture considered everything it thought and did as natural and universal, and hence also regarded its view of sex as the only "true" one. Even more important is the fact that it always did this *in dissociation* from other cultures. In the Near East, sex was probably regarded as equally self-evident there as in the West, but this was not done in dissociation from the ideas of other societies. Sex in other parts of the world was, at most, interesting enough to embellish a travel account with some curious details—which did not carry more weight, however, than did remarks on food, clothes, or lodging. In no way was sexuality conceived as a characteristic of cultural distinction, of higher or lower value. Never was sex in their own culture seen in contrast to that of other cultures, and never does it serve as an instrument of construction of a cultural difference.

The situation in the West is quite different, where since the so-called Middle Ages the discourses of sexuality and otherness have been closely interwoven. Perhaps it is not too much to say that Western sexuality has evolved, to a not insignificant degree, in contrast to an "alien" sexuality, and this "alien" sexuality was, in the first place, that of antiquity and of the Islamic world.

THE CULTURAL HEGEMONY OF WESTERN DISCOURSE

For centuries, the sexual fantasies of the West were kindled by "the Orient," which for some represented the abyss of all sinful excess, for others the dreamed-of paradise of forbidden erotic pleasures. The peoples of the Near East did not have to be concerned as long as they were left in peace. But this came to an end in the nineteenth century. By force of capitalism and industrialization, the West had grown so strong economically and militarily that it was able to carry its colonialist foray against the Islamic world directly into the Near Eastern core countries.

Such an enterprise is in need of an ideological underpinning. This purpose was served by the claim that the West had to fulfill a civilizing mission toward the rest of the world. The Near East, however, already possessed nearly everything that, according to the opinion of the colonial powers, constituted a Western-type civilization. They lived in stable houses, had a "real" religion (namely monotheistic and theologically examined), clad themselves properly, and had regular baths; there existed literature, historiography, and scholarship, and even "real" states with an established legal system. To exploit the Near East colonially was clearly more difficult to justify, even according to Western standards, than was possible in regions classified as primitive.

The solution to this problem came through the model of *rise and decline,* in which the complex of sex played an important role. Following a Hegelian concept, world history was conceived as a history of permanent progress to which the civilizations of the ancient world, one after the other, made their contributions. When one culture had delivered its contribution, the summit of progress was transferred to the next one, which handed over its contribution to another culture in turn, before being superseded by the latter.[45] According to this system, the contribution of the Islamic culture consisted in providing the West, during its "dark Middle Ages," with the knowledge of antiquity. From that era on, Europe alone is seen as the stronghold of progress. All other cultures—the Islamic culture included—have now lost their right to existence, because progress has left them behind. Their fate is to remain in an ahistorical sphere until the West brings them progress again.

It remains only to furnish proof for the assumption that donating cultures are strong enough to give something to other cultures, but then too weak to develop in the direction of the respectively "more progressive." In order to explain this, the concept of progress must be joined by its complement, that is, the concept of decline. In the case of the Near East, this concept of *decadence* was the most effective instrument for implementing the hegemonic episteme of the West. According to this construction, there was a "Golden Era" of Islam in the eighth and ninth century, when the texts of the Greek sciences and philosophy were translated into Arabic (from which the West could subsequently derive profit) and when the rational school of theologians, called the Muʿtazilah, was the authoritative doctrine of the state. Then, however (according to the Hegelian concept of history), sinister religious scholars took over and made sure that free thought was stifled under the heel of "orthodoxy." At this time, a period of decadence began—a truly impressive decadence, lasting a whole millennium!—during which scholarship degenerated into a mindless repetition of old texts, the sciences were forbidden and died away, literature deteriorated into senseless wordplay, and emperors were cruel tyrants who brutally and sadistically tortured and exploited a submissive crowd of subjects. That, roughly, is the conventional image of the decline of the Islamic world believed to be true not only by many Western intellectuals but also by intellectuals in the Near East.

The preceding pages have demonstrated the incoherence of this concept in many aspects, but one important component of this concept of decadence is still missing, namely the *decadence of sex*.

In the middle of the nineteenth century, the French psychiatrist Bénédict Augustin Morel published his "theory of degeneration," which synthesized his religious convictions with the most recent scientific theories of Lamarck.[46] To achieve this synthesis, the deeply orthodox Catholic Morel translated the Biblical story of the Fall of Man into the sphere of reasoning of nineteenth-century medicine, theorizing that man, originally created as a perfect human being, succumbs to the influences of noxious environments, which contribute to his moral and bodily deterioration. His progeny inherit the deterioration, which makes the already impaired environment still worse; deterioration thus intensifies from generation to generation.[47]

This theory quickly became ascendant. It was widely embraced by the English middle class of the 1880s and '90s as a reaction to its fears of the "juggernaut" metropolis, social decline, a rebellious proletariat, and immigration, in a time of advancing industrialization.[48] In addition, the theory of degeneration, originally a reaction to conditions of the urban lower classes in the beginning era of industrialization, lent itself to an explanation of "deviant" sexual behavior, defining such behavior—in good Christian and Darwinist form—as anything that does not serve procreation. In Germany, Richard von Krafft-Ebing, in his famous *Psychopathia sexualis*—the work that established the modern science of sex—described all such behavior as "functional degeneration."[49]

The theory of degeneration prevailed so swiftly not because it offered an explanation of the "deformation" of individuals, but because, from the start, it was aimed at collectives. The problem it addressed was not the "degeneracy" of the single individual but that of whole population groups. Its interior logic implied that, without massive intervention against the degeneration of parts of the population, the people as a whole would fall victim to a process of degeneration. This theory made it not only possible, but indeed imperative, for physicians to step in to combat and prevent crime, alcoholism, prostitution, etc., which constituted an important step toward the medicalization of the Western world.[50] Where the Church had been responsible, the physicians took over; public health services not only took care of ill people but also declared poverty, depravity, crime, and sexuality to be medical problems.[51] Sex between men had changed from being a sin to being first an illness and then a phenomenon of inherited degeneration—and thus a problem that concerned the whole of society.

The theory of degeneration had further advantages. For one, it could easily be linked to social-Darwinist and racist theories; for another, it offered both an explanation for the "backwardness" of non-European peoples and a justification for launching interventions for the sake of "civilization." Napoleon had already legitimized his attack of Egypt in 1798 with the argument that it was necessary to "liberate" the country from "the Turks," who had led it into decadence and barbarianism.[52] Thanks to medical progress, it was soon possible to put the anti-decadence offensive on a stricter, more "scientific" basis. Science thus became the basis of an "educational process," which has continued to the present day, and part of which strives to correct the sexuality of the Near East. The colonial powers sent not only soldiers and administrative officers but also physicians and psychiatrists, who ministered to the "deformed" psyches of the natives.[53]

Still more important was the fact that indigenous elites soon reacted to Western charges of decadence by adopting Western values, largely unchanged, and striving to implement them in their own countries. In the second half of the nineteenth century, therefore, the Near East witnessed a moral buildup in which Western interventionist aspirations and indigenous assimilative endeavors strengthened one another. In the end, this process has altered sex in the Near East more strongly than has been the case in any previous historical era, including Islamization in the seventh century. As for the West, it is largely unaware of this development. Western observers of Islam refuse to believe that Near Eastern discourses and practices in the areas of love, sex, marriage, and family have their own history—a history, moreover, that has been substantially coauthored by the West.[54] Instead of acknowledging this fact, such observers reduce every idea, statement, or practice found in the Near East to Islam. This includes phenomena that may be traditional in some regions but have little or nothing to do with the religion of Islam (for instance, female genital mutilation and so-called honor killings) and even phenomena that are nothing but reflexes of Western values and ideas. Ultimately, they believe, the Islamic world is thoroughly "pervaded by Islam," whose "essence" expresses itself everywhere—even in areas of the Near East where people subscribe to civil values of the sort that the West itself cleaved to relentlessly until as late as the 1970s.

Nearly every edition of a German daily newspaper contains instances of such a misunderstanding. One characteristic example is the marital crisis of the Egyptian opposition politician Ayman Nour, which was—astonishingly—fairly extensively covered. The *Süddeutsche Zeitung* had the headline "Privater Krach, politische Folgen. Eine überraschende Ehescheidung schwächt die Opposition in Ägypten" ("Private row, political consequences. An unexpected divorce weakens the political opposition in Egypt").[55] The story, the journalist writes, sounds like "an Oriental soap opera." What happened, supposedly, is the following: Ayman Nour is a well-known liberal opposition politician who was in jail for several years. During this time, his wife agitated vehemently on his behalf, and thereby gained a great deal of publicity. Shortly after his release from prison, she apparently left him, whereupon he tried to downplay his marital crisis and to stop press reports about it.

That is the whole story. And what is "Oriental" about it? Didn't we have the "affairs" Waigel and Seehofer in the German Bavarian party CSU not too long ago? Didn't a President of the United States nearly have to resign because of a sexual affair? And isn't it true that Ireland did not introduce divorce until 1997? So why this attempt to paint an obviously banal marital drama in exotic colors?

It is because, in the "Islamic world," absolutely nothing can happen without Islam being responsible for it: "The moral concepts as shaped by Islam are severe. Transgressions are held under cover. For an Egyptian politician, divorce is a stigma. A Gerhard Schröder with his three failed marriages is hardly conceivable in this country [Egypt]." Might we point out that Egypt, from the seventh-century beginnings of the Islamic conquest to the twentieth century, never had a ruler who lived in lifelong monogamy? In Islamic law, divorces are straightforward affairs, and by no means defamatory. Marriage is not a sacrament and is not contracted for life. Speaking of "failed marriages," therefore, is senseless. Saddam Hussein was married three times, and King Hussein of Jordan four times (and divorced twice). Also divorced were Libya's Qaddafi, the Sultan of Oman, the Malaysian Prime Minister, and the deposed Tunisian head of state. So where in the "Nour affair" do "Islamic moral concepts" manifest themselves?

The answer is: in reality, Western bourgeois value concepts, not Islamic morals, are what manifest themselves in the "Nour affair." It is not for nothing that the fuss concerns not a conservative or even an Islamist politician but the figurehead of the Western-liberal "Party of the Future." Ayman Nour, the party leader, owed his popularity not least to the fact that he and his wife played the role of a middle-class dream couple, embodying the wholehearted yearning for Western bourgeoisie that drives large parts of the Egyptian upper middle class even today.

Thus it is understandable that Nour wanted to do everything possible to prevent the publicizing of his marital problems. It was because he was emulating the Western way of life that these problems became a scandal, when in former times they would not have been (and would not have been even today in Islamist circles). Conversely, in almost all European countries, a divorce meant the end of a politician's career only a few decades ago, and only recently have divorced politicians become a common phenomenon.

The asynchronicity that becomes apparent here is characteristic of this whole process of adaptation of Western values. As a rule, the process begins with the nontraditional indigenous upper-middle class, who adapt Western ideas because they do not want to be "decadent" and because to be "Western" promises a gain in prestige and frequently also power. To enjoy esteem in the West means to be able to participate in Western strategies of power and influence. This adaptation strategy, then, provides them with a decisive advantage over the traditional elite and groups who reject following the example of the West. If the strategy is successful, and social advancement is achieved, the lower middle class will join them in adapting Western values—which they do not acknowledge as such, however, but as values of the indigenous elite. It takes some time before the Western ideas originally adopted by a small elite are accepted by a greater part of the population as their own values.

We must recall, though, that in the nineteenth and twentieth centuries, value systems in the West did not tend to last for long periods of time. So again and again, a paradoxical situation arises: Western values are internalized by large parts of the populations of non-Western countries, but this development happens at a moment when these values have totally lost their validity in the West, and are substituted by other value systems. Thus a discrepancy of values marks both the beginning and the end of the process; but in both cases, Western observers consider the current constellation of values in the Near East as the *typically Islamic* one, even if these are merely reflections of values of Western provenance. At the same time, Western observers consider the values they champion at the moment as superior, and the values held in the Near East as backward and in want of revision.

A typical example of this process is the Western charge that Islam is prudish and hostile toward sex. "Until today, Islam has not found its way out of prudery and narrow-mindedness":[56] this is a common verdict. As a matter of fact, "Islamic" prudery can be dated easily—namely, to the beginning of the last decades of the nineteenth century.

In the years 1879–1883, the divan (the collected poems) of Ṣafī ad-Dīn al-Ḥillī was printed in Damascus. This poet, who lived from 677/1275 to 750/1349–1350, was regarded, along with Ibn Nubātah, as the most important man of letters of his time. Like many of his colleagues before and after, he also composed frivolous *mujūn* poems. In his divan, and also in a collection of his epigrams, these have their own, relatively brief, chapter. When the divan was printed for the first time, around 1880 in Damascus, this chapter was included—not, however, in its original place, but at the end of the volume, to allow readers who took offense with it to remove it. Thus poems that for five hundred years had provoked no offense at all were suddenly felt to be problematic.

But this was only the beginning of the alleged "Islamic prudery." When Ṣafī ad-Dīn's divan was printed again a few years later in Beirut, where Western influence was still stronger than in Damascus, the whole chapter containing *mujūn* poems was removed. Unsurprisingly, the reprints (Najaf 1956 and Beirut 1961) do not contain it either. When a collection of epigrams by Ṣafī ad-Dīn was edited in Damascus in 1998, the chapter on *mujūn* was eliminated once again.[57] In 2000, Ṣafī ad-Dīn al-Ḥillī's divan appeared in a critical edition for the first time, but the editor, Muḥammad Ḥuwwar, did not dare to include the chapter on *mujūn*. In the foreword to his edition, he writes that their artistic value is not high enough to outweigh moral objections.[58]

It would be easy to continue the list of examples.[59] While Western media always burst into outrage when the works of some Western authors are banished or censured, those same media largely ignore the fact that in the Near East, censure and self-censorship of its own traditions run riot at least as vehemently. Numerous classical works—to mention one example among many, the oeuvre of the bestselling author an-Nawājī from the Mamluk era—are preserved in manuscripts from all centuries in the libraries of the East and the West, but do not find editors, because for Near Eastern scholars of Arabic, they are too "immoral," and for their Western colleagues, in their craze for the early periods, they are too recent. Opposition to the liberality of these works is not a problem of *Islam* but a problem of the modern era, and it originated, as did modernity, in the West. "Islamic" prudery is nothing but a reaction to the Western image of a *decadent* and *sexually rampant* Islam that prevailed during and after the so-called Middle Ages. Arab intellectuals—among them many Arab Christians—quickly appropriated this Western perspective, with which they were able to make advances to the powerful West, on the one hand, and on the other, to oust the traditional Islamic scholarly elite. Since their strategy was successful, and they were soon able to occupy all influential positions, from minister to university president, Western prudery finally asserted itself as the ruling ideology, and was eventually regarded both by the West and by Islamist Muslims as the truly Islamic position. In reality, however, this position only masks the sexual morality of the

Victorian era—which, through the mechanism of asynchronicity, is still alive in the Near East, while in Northern and Central Europe it is no longer understood and recognized as part of European history. Thus the prudery of the Near East is not *Islamic*. Rather, it has its origins in the West, and is entirely *modern*, because it reflects the early capitalist asceticism of work and the disdain for the human body central to the Victorian Age.

The same pattern is followed—although with far more drastic consequences—in the field of desire between men. Here, too, the initiative was taken by the West, which discovered this area as a battlefield against Oriental decadence—a battlefield on which it believed it was capable of proving its moral superiority. The beginning is marked by Western indignation:

> The unnatural passion . . . constitutes the delight, or, more properly speaking, the infamy of the Egyptians. . . . Such depravity, which, to the shame of polished nations, is not unknown to them, is universally spread in Egypt. The contagion has seized the poor as well as the rich."[60]

Thus does the French natural historian Sonnini formulate his disdain in 1798, thereby anticipating the central theses of the theoreticians of decadence. But while Sonnini leaves his sentiments at simple disdain, later representatives of the theory of decadence call for an immediate and thorough intervention. The explorer and Orientalist Richard Burton, in the concluding essay to his translation of the *Arabian Nights* in 1885/86, extensively deals with this subject, which "is one of absolute obscenity utterly repugnant to English readers, even the least prudish."[61] He justifies his addressing this subject "in order to combat a great and growing evil deadly to the birthrate—the mainstay of national prosperity."[62]

The European discourse on the Orient as something stagnant, retarded, and decadent, a discourse meant not least to justify its own imperialist agenda, was finally heard and accepted in the Near East. As early as 1859, the Christian Lebanese intellectual Buṭrus al-Bustānī takes up the Western concept of decadence, for the moment without setting up a connection between decadence and sex.[63] A change in ways of thinking and behaving had already become noticeable, at least in the circles that had the most intensive contact with Europeans. Richard Burton himself stated that "in the present age extensive intercourse with Europeans has produced not a reformation but a certain reticence amongst the upper classes."[64] Burton's observation was confirmed by the interior view of the Ottoman jurist and statesman Ahmed Cevdet Pasha (1822–1895), who noted that "ever since then the well-known love for and relationships with the young men of Istanbul was transferred to young women as the natural order of things," and he is well aware of the fact that this change of behavior is caused by the confrontation "with the disapproval of foreigners."[65]

The break caused by confrontation with the Western discourse on sexuality was nowhere so visible as in love poetry. For a whole millennium, the *ghazal* had been one of the most important genres of Arabic literature. The poems address themselves to both young women and young men, and the latter address is the one preferred by most poets at most times. Around the middle of the nineteenth century, this tradition came to an abrupt end; from then on, no love poems to young men were written. In the history of Arabic literature, this is the greatest rupture recorded by poetry since the advent of the "new" poetry toward the end of the second/eighth century. During that period, the poetry of the urban centers of the Abbasid era became more individualistic, and in this context, homoerotic poems were written—written again, that is, if we consider the ancient tradition—and formed a significant constituent of the literary canon. All this came to an end around 1850, and since then, Arab intellectuals have faced a great problem with their literary heritage. It was the "progressive" intellectuals who faced the greatest problem, those who were nationalist minded and oriented themselves most strongly to Western standards. These intellectuals, who had adopted the Western critique of decadence with the greatest zeal, were convinced that "decline" was mostly due to the foreign rule of "the Turks." The task now was to overcome this decadence by a return to the "golden era." However, in exactly that era, a period regarded by the West as the "golden era" of Islam, the leading men of letters had composed poems that appeared to the West to be decadent!

But it was not only the sex of the "golden era" that caused discomfort. The whole *culture of ambiguity* came into question, a culture incompatible with the Western standards that had become increasingly dominant. Thus, those thinkers who are particularly considered reformers, and who today enjoy a special reputation in the West, have issued the most severe and narrow-minded judgments on their culture. Ṭāhā Ḥusayn, for instance, denounced the Abbasid era as a period of immorality and atheism, a time of decline in ethics, religion, and family values.[66] For his compatriot Aḥmad Amīn (1886–1954), this time exhibits a general "degeneration" that manifests itself particularly in sexual escapades.[67] All these judgments are understandable only by paying attention to the intrusion of the Western perspective. In the Arab world as well as the Western, Arab history was evaluated by incorporating Western concepts of history and civilization and thus "the gaze of Arab historians was squarely fixed on European judgment of their *civilization*."[68] Finally, the Western concept of "naturalness" was introduced into the discourse. Thus the Lebanese literary historian ʿUmar Farrūkh, writing in 1932, psychologized about Abū Nuwās, basing his critique on Western psychology and uncritically regarding the current Western version of sex as the "natural" one[69]—and, in using the criterion *pro natura / contra naturam*, employed a category that up to his time had not been applied to sex in the Arab world.

Based on the authority of Western authors, Near Eastern writers were now beginning to classify sex in order to exorcize its ambiguity. The paradox is only that sex in the Near East never possessed a problematic ambiguity that would have called for elimination by classification. Quite to the contrary, such an ambiguity is created only by the application of Western criteria. For only if sex is an expression of a person's identity, as in the modern Western model of identity-oriented sex, can the danger arise in personality and sex being divergent. Thus, one can have "wrong" sex (one that does not match one's personality), which at the same time may be "right" sex (if it matches the social and religious norms)—or vice versa, or in any conceivable combination. In this way, the connection between sex and truth, characteristic of the West, arrived in the Near East.

The Western obsession with truth was eventually transferred to the entire field of emotional life. Some Arab historians of literature finally knew of no other criterion in judging their classical literature except the question of whether a work expresses "true feelings." It must be said, however, that before the twentieth century, no Near Eastern writer would have had an urge to express "true feelings." Arabic poets of all eras did not want to *express* feelings; they aimed at *evoking* feelings in their audience (which, since they arise only when the poem is heard and do not originate in the listener, consequently cannot be called "true"). Thus the adaptation of the episteme of the modern West has thoroughly obstructed the view of Arabic readers and scholars on whole periods of their literary history.[70]

But the whole impact of the Western phobia regarding ambiguity hit the Near East in the form of the hetero–homo binarity. Again, the West has presupposed, and still presupposes, that its view on sexuality is universally valid, and that a "heterosexual" majority and a "homosexual" minority exist everywhere in the world.

In the Near East, however, these terms made no sense at all at first. Occasionally, people wondered about a fellow citizen who never got married and nowhere signaled an interest in women. But such peculiarities met with little more interest than might have been displayed for someone's culinary preferences. No one would have thought of placing a person in a special category with specific properties and a distinct identity just because of his sexual inclination. Especially in regions where there had been no particular stir about sexuality between men, it must have been hardly expected at first of a man who experienced desire for men to understand that he belonged to a different category of men, and to understand that one can have this desire only if one belonged to this other category—a category, to boot, that was viewed as pathological by the Western physicians and psychiatrists from whom he had learned about it.

In this way, along with the appropriation of Western ideas about the "right" sexuality, the belief was accepted that desire between men is an expression of a personality disorder by the name of homosexuality, while "normal," healthy men do not know such desire. The consequences were severe. Desire between men was concealed more and more (and even retroactively deleted from literary history), and the discrepancy between sex as experienced, on the one hand, and sex deemed as the right kind, on the other, led to exactly the same kind of ambivalence that had long characterized the Western attitude toward one's own body. The increasing suppression, in the Near East, of the "wrong" kind of desire finally resulted in the emergence of homophobia, that inevitable concomitant of the hetero–homo binarity. Thus, over the course of the twentieth century, the Near East has acquired homophobia as a Western export.

As in many other cases, however, we see here the phenomenon of asynchronicity, because in the meantime, Western ideas about sex have changed. Whereas from the nineteenth until the middle of the twentieth century, the West fought against the decadent, promiscuous, and perverse Islam, today it fights against the prudish and repressive Islam—without being aware of the fact that it was the West that has changed, not so much "the Islam," and without realizing for a second its own contradictoriness.

The current discussion of the West on sex between men in "Islam" has recently been the subject of three thorough studies. In an extensive study, Joseph Massad has described the Arab world's reactions to the hegemonic discourses on sexuality of the West in the twentieth century, and has analyzed the effects of campaigns of Western gay movements in the Near East.[71] Georg Klauda has also pursued the problem of the emergence of "Islamic" homophobia, and has questioned the hypothesis that homophobic violence in Germany is particularly present in the circles of migrants.[72] Both authors state that the Western commitment to gay rights presupposes the transfer of the hetero–homo binarity to the conditions of the Near East, and therefore frequently proves to be more destructive than useful. The most recent and particularly noteworthy contribution to the subject is Khaled El-Rouayheb's Before Homosexuality.[73]

As Klauda puts it,

> The transformation of erotic relations among men from the system of friendship towards that of homosexuality changes their own world in a threatening way. It marks the panicky start of a sorting of human beings according to their sexual orientation. This is linked to the compulsion to exercise, on oneself and one's sexual acts, an "hermeneutics of desire" (M. Foucault), and if need be, to confess: "I am different." Guilt and defense, dissociation and projection are the terms by which the terrorist climate of suspicion and draconian punishment can be explained.[74]

The authors Massad and Klauda both have their doubts on whether the commitment to gay rights in the Near East will have the desired effects—or will in fact have the converse result, that is, a "heteronormalization of the Islamic world."[75] "By inciting discourse about homosexuals where none existed before, the Gay International is in fact *heterosexualizing* a world that is being forced to be fixed by a Western binary. . . . Its missionary achievement, however, will not be the creation of a *queer* planet . . . but rather a *straight* one."[76]

Much of what applies to the Western discourse on the "liberation" of gay people in "Islam" is probably also valid for the discourse on the "liberation of the suppressed Muslim woman." At the least, the law of asynchronicity pertains here, too. After all, as Klauda points out, most women travelers to the Near East in the nineteenth century stated that women in the Islamic world were freer and had more rights than European women.[77] Today, at any rate, the talk of the suppressed Muslim woman has become the single most important hegemonic discourse of the West vis-à-vis the Islamic world. Testimonials of suppressed Muslim women today form a distinct, well-assorted genre with which the West can satisfy its voyeuristic appetite with as much pleasure as it once got from the bombastic harem paintings in the style of *Orientalisme*. In any case, the voyeuristic pleasure in (real or imaginary) Oriental sex is accompanied by a claim to superiority, which finally justifies actions of military intervention. The colonial powers justified their conquest of the Near (and Far) East by a *mission civilisatrice*, which was supposed to return the decadent and sexually degenerate Orient to the family of civilized peoples. Similarly, in our day, enterprises like the invasion in Afghanistan are justified as a measure to fight the suppression of women and gay people in that country.[78]

The bizarre history of Western sex and of Western ideas on love and family, however, should warn us against maintaining our present attitudes as universal and universally enforceable. The fact is that, ultimately, there is no known culture whose ideas on love, sex, and family have been subject to stronger and more abrupt changes than the Western one. If there is any common characteristic of these contradictory Western ideas, it is—as shown by the example of the hetero–homo binarity—the sometimes smaller, sometimes greater, but always present fear of ambiguity that burdened Western sexuality from the beginning.

To summarize: The hetero–homo binarity, and more generally, the Western zeal to classify sex, are results of the Western *fear of ambiguity*. It is not enough that sex is unambiguous; it must also be *true*, that is, a person's sexuality must match his *identity*. For this reason, he must become *known* as such. The duty to come out is a consequence of the Western *obsession with truth*. Ultimately, all possibilities of doubting one's ideas about oneself must be eclipsed by the measure of regarding them as *universal*, and striving to induce all of mankind to accept these ideas.

The topic of sex makes particularly conspicuous the Western nexus of *fear of ambiguity*, *obsession with truth*, and the *ambition of universalization*. But that nexus constitutes an essential factor to be taken into consideration in all other topics discussed in this book. It is even possible that in this triad lies the core of the conflict between Western modernity and the rest of the world.

8

The Serene Look at the World

There is only *a perspectival seeing,* only *a perspectival "knowing"; the* more *affects we are able to put into words about a thing, the* more *eyes, various eyes we are able to use for the same thing, the more complete will be our "concept" of the thing, our "objectivity."*

—Friedrich Nietzsche, *On the Genealogy of Morals*

THE PERSPECTIVALITY OF VALUES

In 1882, the British army under General Garnet J. Wolseley attacked Egypt, and, with only 57 British losses crushed the Egyptian army, which lost more than two thousand soldiers. The general received the title of Baron Wolseley of Cairo (apparently such a title was not yet regarded as ridiculous), and the British occupation of Egypt, which would last for forty years, began a new stage in the Western colonization of the Islamic world and hence the universalization of Western values and concepts of the world. In the same year, Friedrich Nietzsche published his book *The Gay Science*, in which he diagnosed the inevitability of a perspectival view of the world:

> How far the perspectival character of existence extends, or indeed whether it has any other character; whether an existence without interpretation, without "sense," doesn't become "non-sense"; whether, on the other hand, all existence isn't essentially an *interpreting* existence—that cannot, as would be fair, be

> decided even by the most industrious and extremely conscientious analysis and self-examination of the intellect; for in the course of this analysis, the human intellect cannot avoid seeing itself under its perspectival forms, and *solely* in these.... But I think that today we are at least far away from the ridiculous immodesty of decreeing from our angle that perspectives are *permitted* only from this angle. Rather, the world has once again become infinite to us: insofar as we cannot reject the possibility *that it includes infinite interpretations.*[1]

Nietzsche's diagnosis of the perspectivality of the world was conceived at a pinnacle of the "universalizing ambitions"[2] that seized the Western world again and again with all its might, and it is evident that this universalizing craze was bound to deny the perspectivality of the human view of the world. But Nietzsche's idea, once conceived, could no longer be disposed of, and so the Western part of the world (and, for that matter, the rest of it) has found itself confronted ever since with an unresolved tension between a universalizing drive and a consciousness of perspectivality. Indeed, this tension could be one of the fundamental motors of the culture of the present age.

The precolonial Islamic world, during the greater part of its history, was not aware of a universalizing drive comparable to that of the West. This is all the more remarkable since the dominating religion of this sphere, Islam, is a monotheistic religion with a claim to universal truth, quite as much as is Christianity. Contrary to what Jan Assmann maintains, however, a theological claim to truth as such is not bound to lead to religiously motivated violence.[3] Cultures are more complex than are the theologies pursued within their frameworks. Therefore it is not fruitful merely to examine theological ideas; rather, it is more important to ask what rank is accorded to a theological claim to universality in a given culture. In a culture as tolerant of ambiguity as was classical Islam, a "tradition of readiness to use violence due to a theology of revelation"[4] can hardly be discerned. The "distinction between truth and falsehood that characterizes monotheistic religion, and only it"[5] manifests itself in classical Islam as generating violence to a far lesser degree than elsewhere, because it was understood that the one truth of the one God is in itself perspectival, and because the culture was ready to tolerate, if not even to appreciate as a source of cultural power, the ambiguities that originate from the plurality of perspectives.

The inhabitants of the Islamic cultural space in classical times had a high degree of tolerance for ambiguity that allowed them a *serene view of the world.* No greater contrast to this attitude is conceivable than in the religious fervor of the Taliban. And yet both are grounded on the same theological fundaments.

Thus it cannot be the fault of the theology if, in one and the same culture, religiously motivated violence is limited for centuries to rare and locally confined outbreaks, while at another time and place it becomes an everyday phenomenon. The outbreak of religiously motivated violence must instead be seen in connection with a loss of tolerance for ambiguity, resulting in an inability to bear the idea of the perspectivality of one's own truth and to tolerate the existence of other claims to truth. A singular truth, perceived from one perspective only, thus raises the claim to universality both internally and externally. It is this claim to universality that produces a readiness for violence—not simply the belief in a single truth.

So it is necessary to examine more closely the universalizing drive that shaped large parts of the Christian world for relatively long periods, and that was largely absent from the precolonial Near East. In particular, we want to analyze two aspects of this drive. First, we will examine the claim to universality directed at the inside, urging the expansion of "the right" norms over all areas of life, without exception and modification. Using the example of the concepts of the state and political rule, it will be shown that in the classical Islamic world, norms and values were seen as perspectival and could not lay claim to universal validity. Second, we will examine the universalizing drive directed at the outside with regard to the stranger in his otherness. The attitude toward foreignness and the stranger will be dealt with in the following section.

POLITICS WITH AND WITHOUT RELIGION

ʿAlī ibn Muḥammad al-Māwardī, one of the protagonists of the so-called *Sunni revival,* has already been cited for his rich Quran commentary and his great and small compendia of Shāfiʿite religious law. But it is not these books for which al-Māwardī is famous today. Nowadays, it is his book *al-Aḥkām as-sulṭāniyyah* that is being studied and translated everywhere and that counts as the most important source for the Islamic concept of the state and political rule.[6] But does this book really constitute, as one translator claims, a "theory of the state"?[7] And does it indeed contain *the* Islamic conception of state and political rule?

The title itself shows that this is the case only to a limited degree. It should be translated as "The legal judgments of the matters concerned with the exercise of power." Thus the book presents itself as what it ultimately is: a treatise on Islamic law. As such, it has been assessed quite differently by different readers. Carl Brockelmann criticized it as being "a purely ideal presentation of Islamic state law, without consideration of reality."[8] Other scholars see in it an attempt at conciliating the anything-but-ideal political situation with Islamic notions of the ideal state at a time when the caliphate had reached a nadir of its power.[9] According to some authors, al-Māwardī failed in this attempt, too, for, as G. E. von Grunebaum writes, "in the eleventh century, the discrepancy between reality and ideal had become so flagrant that it could no longer be overlooked by the body of the believers."[10] The saying of a Syrian legal scholar of the eighth/fourteenth century, according to which a bad ruler is still better than anarchy, expresses, says von Grunebaum, "the utter hopelessness and resignation that marks the political life of the later period." He concludes with the bitter verdict: "The *civitas Dei* had failed, and the Muslim community had accepted its failure."[11]

It is strange to notice that, in 1962, when the revised edition of von Grunebaum's book was published, political Islamism was still a virtually irrelevant phenomenon. And yet this enlightened Western scholar of Islamic studies uses exactly the same arguments that an Islamist would use today. For both, it is self-evident that an Islamic "theocracy" (*civitas Dei*) is the only legitimate form of political rule in the Islamic world. Any other form of political rule must be perceived as "a grievous problem." This is so certain a diagnosis for von Grunebaum that he can dispense with the need for any sources in which to discern "utter hopelessness and resignation." For him, it suffices to have found in a book such as al-Māwardī's an Islamic norm that allows viewing any deviation from it as a violation of an Islamic order—something that everyone, by necessity, feels is problematic. For both von Grunebaum and an Islamist of today, it is beyond dispute that in the Islamic world (1) there can exist only one set of political norms; (2) this can only be an Islamic one; and that (3) this can be only one single system. Furthermore, both see it as self-evident that this has always been the case, and that all Muslims fell into deep despair when the reality was different. It is true there are no extant statements that justify this analysis; but what other reaction should be expected, according to these authors, if norm and reality are seen to diverge?

This diagnosis, however, is as wrong today as it has been wrong in history. In the Islamic world there were always—and there still are today—different discourses on politics, the state, and political rule. And there have been, and still are, more religiously informed discourses and discourses that are secularly informed. Since this was already the situation in al-Māwardī's time, his *al-Aḥkām as-sulṭāniyyah* cannot be adequately classified without an awareness of this plurality of discourses; it is even highly probable that al-Māwardī's treatise is a deliberate answer to this plurality of discourses.

This can be explained by the fact that, in the early history of Islam, religious disputes were accompanied by political controversies on the leadership of the young Islamic community. This power struggle not only resulted in a split of Muslims between Sunnis, Shiites and Kharijites, but also entailed controversies on divine predestination and free will, the status of the sinner, and other such problems. The positions taken by the different parties to these conflicts were laid down in works of *ʿilm al-kalām* (speculative theology). This is why the topic of leadership over the community is treated in these works. Even today, handbooks on doctrinal theology contain a chapter on *al-imāmah*, the "Imamate," that is, "leadership over the community."

This theological discourse is the oldest genuinely religious Islamic discourse on political rule, but it is by no means the oldest political discourse in the Islamic world. That distinction is held by Arabic poetry, a body of literature that is older than Islam, and that dealt, even in pre-Islamic times, with the qualifications of political leaders and the right practice of political rule. The tradition of the panegyric for the ruler (*madīḥ*), initially used to address tribal chiefs and Lakhmid and Ghassānid princes, was continued into Islamic times without a break. Here, the *madīḥ* came to be the most important political discourse *par excellence*. For the entire higher and lower political elite, poetry became the central means of representation; for intellectuals, it became the most important medium for issuing comments on political topics. In this context, thousands and thousands of poems were written, some of which are among the most significant literary products of the Arabic language. Many of the most creative Arabic poets—Abū Tammām, al-Buḥturī, and al-Mutanabbī, to name only a few—have devoted their whole energy to the panegyric poem, attending only marginally to other genres. They have received fame and honor over the centuries, and, until the present day, have had their place in primers and anthologies. For the authors of studies on "political thought in Islam," however, they do not seem to exist. A thorough saturation of Eurocentricism is required, it seems, for a study on "six centuries of medieval Islamic political thought,"[12] almost 500 pages strong, to ignore this panegyric discourse—to name not a single poet and to quote not a single line from a poem, although it was poetry that acted as the most important and most reliable source for the image the rulers in the Islamic world had of themselves.

The panegyric poems may not depict the rulers as they actually were, but as they wanted to be seen. Western historians probably find it hard to imagine that in a given culture, significant social discourses are conducted in the form of poetry. And perhaps the Islamic panegyric is not Islamic enough for them, since in fact, in this poetical genre, neither the ruler's religious legitimacy nor his religious actions are at the center. The doctrine of virtues relevant for him still largely remains the pre-Islamic one. Martial courage toward outsiders and social engagement within the society are his principal virtues. Even in the poems on caliphs, religion plays only a small role, and often none at all—and this is the case even for elegies on deceased princes. Thus, the panegyric discourse on politics is semisecular, and in some periods and some regions—an example will be presented later—even purely secular.

But the panegyric discourse is not the only example of this phenomenon. Another pre-Islamic tradition, that of Greek antiquity, was taken up by the Islamic world, initially by al-Fārābī (died 339/950), who, in his "Model State" referred to Plato's *Republic*.[13] Still more important than this philosophical discourse is the "advice to the ruler," which drew its inspiration from yet another pre-Islamic tradition, in this case an ancient Iranian one.[14] This is perhaps the most variegated discourse of all. The texts range from morally exhortative mirrors for princes to purely Machiavellian treatises like that of Ibn Nubātah—upon which more later. Finally, one may include the discourse of the historians, who also have to contribute to the topics of politics and political rule.

We see that in the time of al-Māwardī, therefore, there were at least four political discourses that viewed our subject from quite different perspectives. Only the legal scholars had not contributed anything substantial to it, at least not in the form of a monograph. But it was this group whose discourse, during the period of the *Sunni revival*, surpassed in importance that of the representatives of speculative theology. Here al-Māwardī steps in. It is his aim to say everything that can be said from the perspective of jurisprudence (*fiqh*) on the state and political rule. Indeed, a great part of his book addresses practical problems. Sections on taxation and trade control, for instance, can be read as direct instructions for a civil servant with a training in law. However, in the sections on the Imamate and the Sultanate, which today are denounced as unrealistic, al-Māwardī has been able to show that the legal scholars (*fuqahāʾ*) are prepared to present a consistent and complete discourse on the state and political rule, and that the theologians have ceased to possess the sole prerogative of interpretation of religious discourse on politics. It is highly questionable to assume that al-Māwardī and the other *fuqahāʾ* really thought that every state must always exactly obey these rules, and that they fell into "utter hopelessness and resignation" if the reality was different. For it is quite rare for a representative of one of the discourses mentioned to ever doubt the legitimacy of another discourse. No *faqīh* has accused the panegyric poets of subscribing to wrong opinions on the practice of political rule or on supporting dubious moral qualities, and no theologian has lambasted books containing advice to the ruler that do not bother with theological doctrines.

The immediate impact of al-Māwardī's book was in fact different from what those authors believe who see in it the formulation of *the* theory of the Islamic state. Al-Māwardī, as he himself writes, had done nothing but outline the *madhāhib al-fuqahāʾ*, the "schools of thought of the legal scholars" on this subject.[15] Thus he had merely added a further perspective to the existing perspectives on political rule and politics, or, more precisely, had sharpened an already existing perspective by condensing the relevant material scattered over the whole body of *fiqh*. By doing this, he became the actual originator of the political discourse of the *fuqahāʾ*—without denying the other, still-existing discourses their authority.

Not only did the other discourses continue to exist unchallenged, but they also developed, in the long run, far greater dynamism than the legal discourse. It is probable that al-Māwardī influenced the theological discourse—if my impression is right, later treatises on Islamic faith formulate the doctrine of the Imamate with a stronger emphasis on religious law than do the earlier ones—but as a constituent of the doctrine of Islamic faith, politics remained largely insignificant for a long time, until, in the context of the theologization of modern Islam, it was resuscitated with great force. In the realm of *fiqh*, al-Māwardī had several successors, first of all Abū Yaʿlā (380–458/990–1066) and Ibn Taymiyyah (661–728/1263–1328), who in a sense gave the Ḥanbalite answer to the Shāfiʿite al-Māwardī. But over the following centuries, the legal discourse on politics did not produce more than a handful of books. By no means can it be taken for granted that before the Ottoman era, the *fuqahāʾ* composed more books on the subject of the state than did the philosophers, especially if we also take into account the allegorical-philosophical works of Ibn Sīnā (370–428/980–1037), Ibn Ṭufayl (died 581/1185), Ibn an-Nafīs (died 687/1288), and others.[16]

And yet, the author already mentioned can maintain that a historian of "mainstream Islam" may simply pass over the philosophers, because their opinions were viewed as heretical by the Islamic religious scholars who shaped "mainstream Islam."[17] It is not incorrect to say that the religious scholars were the ones who shaped "mainstream Islam." But this statement does not even marginally contribute to the question of the respective significance of the different discourses in different segments of Islamic culture. Although the philosophical discourse never really became central, it has maintained its vitality for many centuries and produced innovative works that were studied and copied. It may have been marginal, but it was not excluded—a finding we shall meet again in the reflection on the stranger in the Islamic world.

Let us jump over three centuries from al-Māwardī to take a look at the actual central discourses at work. In the Mamluk era, as in al-Māwardī's times, there were several clearly different discourses on politics and political rule:

(1) The *theological* discourse continued to exist, but gradually decreased in significance, as compared with
(2) the *legal* discourse of the *fuqahā'*, which received new fuel primarily from Ibn Taymiyyah, an authority who was highly appreciated by everyone and who also, with his self-importance, got on everyone's nerves.
(3) The *panegyric* discourse of the poets, in the meantime, wholly secularized, still remained one of the most significant public discourses on politics, although many rulers were of Turkish descent and preferred to be represented through architecture rather than poetry, while the bourgeoisie, for their part, had discovered the panegyric as a medium of middle-class self-representation.
(4) The highly flourishing *historiography* also provides much cultural knowledge on politics and political rule, which is taken up as well in
(5) the equally flourishing genre of *mirrors for princes*, utilized for empirical verification of abstract virtues. Finally,
(6) the *philosophical* discourse, in all its marginality, has survived in authors such as Ibn an-Nafīs, and adds its own facet to intellectual discourse.

It is evident that, today, these discourses meet with quite diverse degrees of attention. In the context of the "Islamization of Islam," there is a conviction that the authentic expression of "political thought in Islam" can only be captured in discourses (1) and (2). But this is a trap of circular reasoning: the false assumption that the designation of the culture is simply "Islam" leads to the belief that it is necessary to consult Islamic religious scholars to find out what political thought in Islam looks like. Since, in the modern Western way of thinking, there can be only one sole norm at a time, scholars are convinced that in the combined theological and legal discourse on politics in the Islamic world, they have found the *only* political norm and discourse of *the* Islamic faith. Simply because a religious discourse on political rule exists, they believe that religion and political rule (in modern times, respectively, religion and state) cannot be separated "in Islam." If in fact history has produced different constellations of the two—and even though almost no political ruler ever enjoyed religious authority, let alone had an influence on the system of religious norms—these things are seen, as we have observed in von Grunebaum's analysis, as deviations from the norm. In reality, we have here a *coexistence* of different, apparently irreconcilable discourses. Today, however, only those discourses are perceived that are in harmony with the prejudice that politics and religion are inseparable in Islam.

In our own times, the alleged impossibility of "separating religion and politics" has gained the highest political relevance. This impossibility is widely regarded as an indication of the incompatibility of Islam and democracy, and a major obstacle to the modernization of the Islamic world. The German political scientist and consultant Wolfgang Merkel summarizes this widespread view in the following words:

> The central problem of the incompatibility of democracy and Islam is the fact that until today, Islam has not experienced a real age of enlightenment. There have been repeated attempts. . . . They failed, however, in one cardinal question: the (extensive) separation of state and religion. . . . There was neither a Renaissance in which Machiavelli had already influentially revised the concept of the divine order in favor of human autocracy, nor the modern European tradition of the theory of constitutional treaty. . . . Regarding the legitimacy of the forms of political rule, the theocentric worldview was not, or not sufficiently, replaced by an anthropocentric one. The latter, however, is a necessary . . . prerequisite for sovereignty of the people and democracy.[18]

Even in the debate on Turkey joining the European Union, the question of whether there was ever an Islamic Machiavelli and an Islamic Renaissance plays a role. For Helmut Schmidt, the former German chancellor (1918–2015), it is precisely the alleged nonexistence of a phenomenon comparable to the European Renaissance that serves as a principal argument against the admission of Turkey to the EU. In an article with the telling title "Sind die Türken Europäer? Nein, sie passen nicht dazu" ("Are the Turks Europeans? No, they do not fit"), Schmidt argues: "In Islam, the developments that are decisive for European culture are missing: the Renaissance, the Enlightenment, and the separation between religious and political authority. It is also for this reason that Islam . . . has been unable to establish itself in Europe."[19]

Now it may be an easy task to demonstrate that, Helmut Schmidt's opinion notwithstanding, there was a very clear "separation between religious and political authority" for virtually the entire history of Islam. Almost never did rulers let religious scholars interfere with their affairs; if they were able to talk a mufti into issuing an accommodating opinion, this did not at all mean that the other legal scholars accepted the fatwa. The rulers had no influence on Islamic dogma, and the religious scholars mostly took care to keep as far away from politics as possible.

But in order to decide whether we have here a case of norm and deviation, and whether, as von Grunebaum assumes, people would have fallen into deep despair because of this discrepancy, it is necessary to examine original documents of "concerned authors." For this purpose I am choosing texts not from discourses (1) and (2), but from discourses that were doubtless more representative than those, because they were situated much closer to the authorities, and have produced a far greater number of texts. I mean discourses (3) and (5), that is, the panegyric poetry in which rulers had their portraits painted the way they wanted to be perceived, and the works containing mirrors for princes in which the authors were able to talk about political power, its premises, and its exercise, without any religious or ideological constraints.

Luckily, one of the leading intellectuals of the eighth/fourteenth century offered contributions to both discourses. No less a figure than Ibn Nubātah al-Miṣrī (686–768/1287–1366), the most famous poet and prose stylist of his time, composed both a work containing advice for the ruler and panegyric poems on rulers. Chance also has it that the sultan al-Afḍal of Ḥamāh (reigned 732–742/1332–1341), one of the rulers to whom Ibn Nubātah addressed his works, became more and more pious after taking office, a development which downright forced the poet to address the subject of religion in his poems. Thus the case of Ibn Nubātah/al-Afḍal is an ideal example that allows us to examine the norms and values to which the political elite in a center of the Islamic world of the eighth/fourteenth century oriented themselves, and the role religion played in this process.

Ibn Nubātah, the son of a hadith scholar and historian, was born in Cairo, but chose Damascus as the stage of his literary debut in 716/1316,[20] since the greater part of the intellectual elite of his time resided in the Syrian part of the Mamluk empire. Very soon, Ibn Nubātah established his reputation as one of the leading authors of poetry and prose. His readership was composed not only of men of letters and civil servants in the chanceries, but also of judges and other religious scholars, to whom he addressed numerous poems. It was this quasi-bourgeois milieu of the Syrian cities that formed the focus of Ibn Nubātah's works. The great exception was the court of Ḥamāh, where Ibn Nubātah advanced to become the "personal poet" of the prince. This ruler, Abū l-Fidāʾ, who was an intellectual in his own right, belonged to the Ayyubid dynasty and was the author of one of the most important geographical works of his time.[21] The Mamluk sultan an-Nāṣir Muḥammad had installed him in 710/1311 as governor of the town and the province of Ḥamāh, and invested him with all the dignities and titles of a sultan, even though his real capacities did not exceed those of the other provincial governors.

Ibn Nubātah was a regular guest in the citadel of Ḥamāh; he composed around forty long poems and numerous epigrams in praise of Abū l-Fidāʾ, wrote a prose *maqāmah* on a contest between pen and sword, and dedicated to him several prose writings of general literary interest. Abū l-Fidāʾ died in 732/1332 and was succeeded on the throne by his son, who bore the title al-Malik al-Afḍal, "the most excellent prince." The relation between Ibn Nubātah and the court of Ḥamāh continued to flourish for a while, but then al-Afḍal retreated more and more from worldly life and finally lost all interest in literature. Since with all his praying and fasting he began to neglect his political duties, and grew to accept the fact that the Bedouins were seizing ever greater parts of the fertile regions, he was finally deposed in 742/1341 and transferred to Damascus, where he died the same year. Even though Ibn Nubātah was not as close to al-Afḍal as he had been to al-Afḍal's father, he still composed for the young prince of Ḥamāh seventeen long panegyric poems, the longest hunting poem known, several strophic poems in which he combined wine poetry and the panegyric, and the above-mentioned advice to the ruler.

Let us first consider the picture the panegyric draws of the ruler. The principal virtues for which the prince is praised in this poetic genre have remained the same since pre-Islamic times. They are munificence and courage. In a poem that was to become famous, composed by Ibn Nubātah on the occasion of al-Afḍal's inauguration and brilliantly combining the poet's condolence for the deceased father and felicitation for the son's enthronement, he formulates these themes in verses such as these (which sound magnificent in Arabic, but, alas, not so in the English translation):[22]

> All the dew of his gifts he distributes among us, and arrows he sends to the enemies as a gift in the terror of the battle.
> Your pen, in the times of peace, lets stream a continuous rain; your sword, in war, strives to quench its thirst for blood.

Neither the virtue of munificence nor the virtue of courage is part of a system of religious norms. Indeed, we have here not ethically founded virtues, but qualities a ruler must possess in order to govern *efficiently*, as other verses express it even more clearly:

> It is the aim of his firm decisions (*ʿazamāt*) to lead the weak with the favor of his munificence and to dominate the strong.

His pens and his swords share the task to show mercy and to crush
the rebels.

Thus munificence serves to motivate people to voluntarily follow the ruler; courage, to force those to follow him who do not do so voluntarily. The two qualities do not, as such, constitute moral values. A reader who deems this too Machiavellian may be referred to Ibn Nubātah's advice to the ruler, whose ninth maxim reads: "The competent prince fosters the popularity of the heir to the throne among the subjects and the military by granting them benefits through the latter, and lets him take care of their just treatment and avert injustice from them."

Nota bene, the heir to the throne is not supposed to *be* beneficent and just, but to *appear* beneficent and just to his subjects, and therefore the reigning prince should offer him opportunities for presenting himself in such a way. This strongly reminds us of that maxim of the *Principe* which has most strongly contributed to the defaming argument that Machiavelli was an immoral author: "Thus it is not necessary for a prince to actually have all of the above written qualities, but it is very necessary to seem to have them."[23]

In panegyric poetry—not only that of Ibn Nubātah for al-Afḍal—the ideal ruler does not figure as a virtuous authority who looks after his own spiritual welfare and that of his subjects (in fact, this idea is nowhere to be observed), but as a powerful and efficient agency who is capable of winning over adherents and crushing enemies in order to enforce his own will. The key terms in poetry that express this combined quality of the ideal ruler are *ʿazm* (resolve, firm will), *himmah* (zeal, fervor, striving), *ṭumūḥ* (ambition, high aspirations), *suʾdad* (leadership), and finally *ḥazm* (competence, resoluteness). The principal virtue of the prince, according to Ibn Nubātah, is "capability, energy, resoluteness"—and these are exactly those words with which Bernhard H. F. Taureck translates the term *virtù*, the pivotal virtue of the Machiavellian *principe*.[24]

The quality of *virtù* is also decisive for the third principal theme of panegyric poetry, the praise of the ruler's ancestry. This too is a very old theme, already evidenced in pre-Islamic times and still retaining its attractiveness in a society that had no hereditary nobility and did not require a specific lineage—except for the office of the caliph—but that nevertheless utilized that distinction—in poems about princes who could produce a reasonably presentable lineage. Such was the case with al-Afḍal, the last sultan in a glorious series of Ayyūbid rulers and a direct descendant of a brother of Saladin. Thus Ibn Nubātah writes:

He is replete with ambitious Shādhawite zeal that, once wakened,
strives for the highest position.

This means that the prince has inherited not an abstract right to the throne, but the qualities that allow him to attain and practice power. It is ash-Shādhī, the half-legendary father of Ayyūb, from whom he has inherited the "Shādhawite zeal"; it is only thanks to the fact that this *virtù* is handed down in the family, from generation to generation, that the family receives its legitimation as a dynasty.

But where is religion? It is to be found, first of all, in several everyday phrases ("May God bless," "May God protect") that do not, however, testify to the religiosity of the text. In this context, God never appears as a protector of the dynasty or the princedom, but always only as a protector of the individual person of al-Afḍal. He, in turn, owes his rule not at all to God or to divine providence, but first to his own power and second to the capability of his forebears. "Yours is the princedom by heritage and acquisition," says verse 33 of the poem, praising al-Afḍal's enthronement quite clearly, and it is the new ruler's "noble qualities," not divine predestination, that allow a new star of the dynasty to rise. Only the virtues of the prince and his ancestors legitimize his rule, virtues that overcome fate itself (verse 12: *ad-dahr*)—a notion with which readers of Arabic panegyric poetry are well acquainted, but which is difficult to justify theologically; after all, *ad-dahr* is a fundamentally pagan concept. Islamic theology has transformed *ad-dahr*, the pagan "fate," to a synonym for divine providence, supported by a hadith that says: "Do not revile fate (*ad-dahr*), for God *is* the fate."[25] In the light of this theologoumenon, the poems in praise of Islamic rulers, composed over centuries, read as pure blasphemy—after all, it is always the ruler who vanquishes *ad-dahr* and crushes it into dust.

In the panegyric discourse, religion does not play a role, not even in the legitimation of the ruler. For instance, when al-Afḍal celebrated his enthronement in Cairo, he was awarded three turbans, two yellow ones from the sultan, and a black one from the Abbasid caliph.[26] A Sunni ruler could not ask for a better legitimation than to be acknowledged by the caliph from the family of the Prophet. Yet Ibn Nubātah, in all his Afḍaliyyāt, does not say a single word about this fact; it must have been quite irrelevant to him, to the prince, and to the public.

Furthermore, the vision of the prince's rule depicted by the poem lacks a religious dimension. The prince is supposed to provide prosperity, safety, and order for his country. There is no mention anywhere of the realization of an Islamic state or the enforcement of Islamic law, and there is no religious, let alone theocratic, concept of rule.

Nothing changes in this regard even when al-Afḍal starts to grow more and more pious and devout. But Ibn Nubātah is bound to react in some manner to al-Afḍal's status as a born-again Muslim. As a matter of fact, he does react, but solely in a literary manner. He mentions a religious virtue, namely piety (*taqwā*). But this term—which is rather weak, and might be rendered as "decency"—is the only one he names. And so writes Ibn Nubātah about the sanctimonious al-Afḍal:

> Piously he rules his principality. So God has clad him with the garments of one who instills fear and hope,
> Who spreads justice and disperses gifts so that he becomes a pure incorporation of reward and deterrence.

Read closely: There is no change in the original concept of political rule, even if it sounds more religious now. God may be the one who has equipped the prince at birth with the qualities he needs for his rule; however, they are still not religious qualities, but simply that *virtù* which helps to instill "fear and hope." Even "justice" serves only to arouse "reward and deterrence." The fact that this pair of terms, *at-targhīb wa-t-tarhīb*, also figures in the ascetic discourse of religion (namely as inciting hope for God's reward and instilling fear of His punishment) is a deft move on Ibn Nubātah's part, because in this manner he is able to formulate a purely mundane concept in religious language—an ingenious stylistic device of this poet, who was celebrated as the greatest master of the double entendre.

In the same manner, the theme of praiseworthy ancestors is being reformulated. Here we read:

> In Ayyūb's family, noble qualities are hereditary, quite as prophethood was hereditary among the descendants of Jacob.

Again, nothing factual is changed. The Ayyūbids acquire their right to political rule through the "noble qualities" passed on from generation to generation. The fact that Ibn Nubātah, speaking of "hereditary qualities," hits on a comparison from the sphere of religion does not make the matter more religious.

This passage and many others show that, even after al-Afḍal's reformation, no genuinely religious motif comes to Ibn Nubātah's mind. For him, politics and religion simply do not have anything to do with each other. So he tries to soothe the pious soul of his prince with literary devices.

What about the legitimation of the prince, which was in any case unassailable on religious-constitutional bases? Not even here do we see the slightest sign of a religious legitimation—let alone any doctrine of divine right, which in

Europe was still being invoked in the twentieth century. Quite the contrary. About al-Afḍal—the reformed believer, of all people—Ibn Nubātah writes:

> He is a prince whose rule is based on one source, on merit and on fortune: How noble are [his] ancestor, eagerness, good fortune (*al-jaddu wa-l-jiddu wa-l-juddu*)!

As in the poems cited above, it is descent from energetic ancestors as well as proper qualities and merits that grant the prince his legitimacy. The only additional element is good fortune, exactly the pagan *fortuna* that functions as an antagonist of *virtù*, quite as with Machiavelli.[27] Thus panegyric poetry, the most important medium of representation of sovereign power in the Islamic world of this period, presents politics as a wholly secular domain that does not draw on religion for its legitimacy or its norms, tasks, and aims.

This thoroughly secular approach to politics and governance—contrary to all modern prejudices—is also to be found in the advice to the ruler presented by Ibn Nubātah to the young al-Afḍal, probably on the occasion of his enthronement. This disproves the notion that poetry's secular view on politics may be explained as a literary convention. In the case of works of advice to the ruler, such conventions are difficult to discern. Some "mirrors for princes" do betray religious motivations, but others have a very secular style. An advice to the ruler written much earlier by the Sicilian author Ibn Ẓafar (born 497/1104, died 565/1172 or three years later) has invited some readers to compare it to Machiavelli's *Il principe*.[28] But in terms of Machiavellianism, Ibn Nubātah's advice to the ruler by far exceeds Ibn Ẓafar's work.

When Ibn Nubātah presented al-Afḍal with this text on the occasion of his inauguration, it did not yet have an established title. Later, he published it under the title of *Sulūk duwal al-mulūk*, which, in an ambiguous double entendre typical for the author, may mean both "The ways that the states of princes take" and "The ways of the ups and downs of princes."

The most striking feature of the book is its consistently empirical approach. It is the aim of the author to deduce from history how a ruler who wants to be successful should act. This approach results in around fifty maxims, most of which are introduced with the phrase *al-malik al-ḥāzim* (the competent prince [does this or that]). Every maxim is then justified in the form of examples from history. Many of the examples are taken, certainly not by chance, from the history of the Ayyubids; but there are also examples from the times of the early Abbasids, the Būyids, and other dynasties. On the other hand, the book lacks didactic fables, stories of the ancient Persians and Greeks, and in general wise sayings of all peoples. It is still more striking that the person who is the model *par excellence* for all Muslims, the Prophet Muḥammad, is nowhere named. At no time are historical examples from the time of the Prophet or his companions mentioned—and this is certainly intentional, since the conduct of the Prophet may yield religious norms but offers no empirical data for promising action. The acts of the Prophet and his companions constitute not only a history of events but also a history of salvation. Therefore, the Prophet's life and example were not interesting for Ibn Nubātah's purposes. For an empiricist, there was nothing to be gained here. To be sure, Ibn Nubātah was a pious devotee of the Prophet. He composed panegyric poems about Muḥammad and transmitted Ibn Isḥāq's biography of him, in the version of Ibn Hishām, with a particularly brief *isnād*, as recorded by contemporary dictionaries of the biographies of hadith transmitters.[29] But as a political author, Ibn Nubātah deemed this information irrelevant.

Not only are fables and prophets missing in his text, but it also lacks, in general, any reference to normative texts. Nowhere is a maxim for a prince's action derived from the Quran or the sunna; nowhere does one meet a maxim taken from the corpus of Islamic law. Nowhere is religion a giver of norms. On the contrary, religion only occurs as an object of policy. If maxim 41 says that the competent prince should not violate a good legal custom and should not annul a sentence that results from an established doctrine of one of the legal schools,[30] this does not mean that the prince is bound by Islamic law, but simply offers a utilitarian justification. As the examples cited show, a prince taking such a step would hardly be likely to win the resulting power struggle against the judges and legal scholars. The same principle appears in maxim 38: "The competent prince does not allow two sermonizers to preach in one town at the same time, for there will arise dissent between them, and each one of them will attract followers who support his opinion and follow his views."[31]

Again, we notice the limits of a ruler's influence on religion. He is by no means required to prescribe to the sermonizers the content of their sermons. Such an attempt would be doomed to fail. However, by restricting the number of sermonizers he nominates, he is able to ensure peace and order.

In Ibn Nubātah's book, as in his poems, politics and religion are two separate spheres. Religion does not provide norms for the execution of politics, nor does religious advancement appear as an aim of political action. Religion is merely the object of a kind of politics that uses religion as a means to contribute to the success of the ruler and the welfare of his subjects. It appears that for this purpose the domestication of religion rather than its advancement is indicated.

It is no wonder, then, that several maxims impinge on Islamic law. This corpus contains a martial law that makes initiating warfare dependent on a number of conditions, and ties an armistice to certain requirements. The author of our "advice to the ruler" does not care about all this. The example of history indicates that "the competent prince concludes peace when it is advantageous" (maxim 50). And "when the competent prince is resolved to march against his enemy and wage war with him, he must send out a reliable scout in order to find out whether his own army or that of his enemy has more combat strength and willingness to die" (maxim 49). Again, Ibn Nubātah does not acknowledge any normative or moral reasons. Nothing counts but success, and history alone teaches us how to attain it. It is quite irrelevant which side serves as an example. In substantiating maxim 49, Ibn Nubātah draws on the conquest of Washqa (Huesca) by Pedro I of Aragon, who took the town in 489/1096 because he acted precisely as the maxim prescribes.[32] Ibn Nubātah does not hesitate to put up a Christian ruler like the Aragon as a model for Islamic princes—as long as one can learn from him!

But what does it mean to assume that one may learn from history? First of all, this is a quite *nonmedieval* concept, as indicated by Wolfgang Kersting in his book on Machiavelli:

> As long as history is a context woven from the divine working of salvation and the commitment of sins . . . and is consistently oriented, according to divine providence, towards the goal of salvation, one cannot learn from [such a] history [one that is informed by theology]. Medieval theology of history has ended the concept of history as a teacher (*historia magistra vitae*) valid for the entire ancient world. Its finalism, following divine providence, stands crossways to its epistemic premises. . . . History can only be the teacher of political acting if people in their history are among themselves.[33]

This applies precisely to Ibn Nubātah's concept of history. Here (and even with some of his predecessors), history no longer furnishes *ʿibar*, *exempla*, warning examples, from which people may derive moral teachings. His examples are completely disengaged from the perspective of a history of salvation; they give empirical material for successful or unsuccessful acting, beyond any moral criteria. The evaluation of a given act is not established from the beginning because it is not performed according to moral, legal, or religious criteria. Rather, an act is assessed subsequently, according to its success or failure. Only its suitability for success determines whether it will be recommended for imitation or rejected. Kersting's characterization of Machiavelli's concept of history, and that of the Renaissance, may be equally and unrestrictedly applied to Ibn Nubātah: "The historical thought of the Renaissance is secularized; it liberates history from divine guidance and disengages the course of human affairs from the divine plan of salvation. History for him [Machiavelli] is the pure work of man, which is shaped by the deeds of great individuals."[34]

Ibn Nubātah's secular approach to history presents itself not only in the way he deals with his historical models, but also in the theoretical foundation he formulates in the beginning of his book. In Ibn Nubātah's view, there are three basic human powers that move history: the intellectual faculty (*al-quwwah al-mumayyizah*); the aggressive faculty (*al-quwwah al-ghaḍabiyyah*), which manifests itself either positively as courage and fortitude or negatively as destructive assault; and the faculty of desire (*al-quwwah ash-shahwiyyah*), which occurs positively as the urge for acquisition and negatively as greed. These three powers clearly reflect the Platonic tripartition of the human soul: the rational, the combative, and the concupiscent. There are also parallels to Plato's *Republic*, insofar as the institutions of government are identified with these powers (respectively "parts of the soul"). In this system, the army and the police are the organs of the princely aggressive faculty, and the tax collector that of his faculty of desire. This shows that philosophical discourse has left more traces upon Ibn Nubātah's book on politics than has theology or religious law, even if his sources cannot yet be identified (perhaps they include Ibn Rushd's commentary on Plato's *Politeia*).[35] Plato's thought, adapted and developed by Ibn Nubātah for a new political environment, serves to describe his own view of history. For him, the human passions drive history forward. It is the task of the ruler to become the master of these passions. First, he must become the master of his own passions, in order to use them for the acquisition and maintenance of his power. Then he must learn to steer his family, the ruling elite, and the common folk; finally, he must learn to repel enemies. This is the only way for him to maintain his power, transmit it to his offspring, and direct a prospering commonwealth. Any other religious or moral purpose of political rule is not part of Ibn Nubātah's reasoning.

With this theory of history, Ibn Nubātah was in no way anachronistic. The historian Ibn Khaldūn (732–808/1332–1406), for one, developed a similar secular view of history; in his *Muqaddimah*, the "preface" to a multivolume historiography, he devises a cyclical theory of history. For Ibn Khaldūn, it is the *ʿaṣabiyyah* that drives history forward. The term originally denotes "communal spirit, feeling of solidarity"; ultimately, this is simply an attempt to convert Ibn Nubātah's elements of *virtù*—"zeal, endeavor, capability"—into something collective. Social groups that possess *ʿaṣabiyyah* (Bedouins, for example) are able to use this quality to conquer a region, only to lose it again in the course of a few generations because they succumb to the decadent influence of the luxurious, urban way of life.[36]

We do not know whether Ibn Nubātah and Ibn Khaldūn ever met, or whether Ibn Khaldūn was aware of Ibn Nubātah's book on politics. But this question is peripheral. The important point is that a secular concept of history had established itself in the Islamic world, long before the eighth/fourteenth century, and long before it became possible in Christian Europe. Ibn Nubātah's *Sulūk* appeared in 732/1332—that is, exactly two hundred years before the (posthumous) publication of the *Principe*. Ibn Nubātah was not the only author who regarded history as the result of human passions and activities.

Hence the Islamic world did not at all lack a "Renaissance in which Machiavelli had decisively reversed the concept of a divine order in favor of human autocracy," and it is wholly wrong to maintain that in the Islamic world, the "theocentric worldview . . . , with regard to the legitimacy of forms of political rule, was not, or not sufficiently, replaced by an anthropocentric one."[37] Exactly the opposite view is correct. As early as the fourteenth century, not only were there political rulers in the Islamic world who did not see themselves as religious leaders, and who oriented themselves in their offices toward purely secular criteria, but there was also a theoretical formulation of secular concepts of politics and political rule.

In this century, the fourteenth, it is an anthropocentric conception of history, in which "people in history are among themselves" (Kersting), which is at the basis of works such as those by Ibn Nubātah and Ibn Khaldūn. These authors are not marginal to their societies, but work in their centers. In their works, they do not address a readership at the fringes; they are an active part of the central political and literary discourse of their times. Ibn Nubātah and Ibn Khaldūn were widely known, well-established intellectuals who held eminent posts, were consulted by sultans, and were in contact with important *ʿulamāʾ* of their times. Their works were widely copied and read, and their biographies received the longest entries in the collections on famous personalities of their eras. And their nonreligious works on history and politics did not cause a public outcry. No one protested the idea of a history that proceeds cyclically or is driven forward by the passions of people, and no one took offense at an "advice to the ruler" that is no less secular than the "Machiavellism" of the *Principe*.

Furthermore, it is not accurate to say that Ibn Nubātah's and Ibn Khaldūn's works were not actually noticed in their own culture and had to await their rediscovery by Western readers—as has been maintained, in particular, about the latter's *Muqaddimah*. The *Muqaddimah* was even translated into Ottoman-Turkish,[38] and Ibn Nubātah's advice to the ruler is known by now in three manuscripts. It is true that this makes the work one of the least known among the oeuvre of an author who, up to the end of the nineteenth century, was celebrated as one of the greatest Arabic poets. However, regarding "mirrors for princes," which have often survived only in one single manuscript (frequently the one dedicated to the prince), three copies are not so few—especially if one takes into account that, as a rule, for every extant manuscript from the Mamluk era, several hundred copies of the same text have been lost. Indeed, Ibn Nubātah has been forgotten only in the twentieth century. To this day, a satisfactory edition of his *Sulūk duwal al-mulūk* does not exist.[39]

In their own times, Ibn Nubātah and Ibn Khaldūn—and this list could easily be extended if one were to do more research—were neither disregarded nor ignored, let alone prohibited, as secular thinkers on the history and politics of their time. It is thus wrong to assume that secular approaches were marginalized. But it is right that they did not produce a public *outcry*. Machiavelli's *Principe*, on the other hand, caused a mighty anti-Machiavellian movement; the *Principe* was put on the *Index*, and a Machiavelli effigy was publicly burned in Ingolstadt as late as 1635.[40] "Anti-Machiavellianism, soon flourishing in the climate of the Counter-Reformation, condemned in particular Machiavelli's doctrine of the autonomy of politics, and vigorously stressed the supremacy of Church over State."[41]

Ibn Nubātah's book, too, depicts politics as an autonomous sphere that derives none of its norms of action from religion. But no religious scholar is known to have protested. Ibn Nubātah and Ibn Khaldūn were read with interest, but did not provoke strong feelings in any reader. The reason for this equanimity is, again, nothing other than the *tolerance of ambiguity* of the contemporary society, a tolerance that afforded people a *perspectival* view of central areas of human life. This must also have been the case with the authors themselves. As historians and writers on the theories of society and politics, both Ibn Nubātah and Ibn Khaldūn were convinced of the fact that history—excluding, it is true, the work of the Prophet Muḥammad—is the work of humans, and that it can be adequately represented only from this perspective. However, both authors were incontestably religious Muslims. Ibn Nubātah wrote deeply felt poems in praise of the Prophet and, into his old age, held sessions devoted to the transmission of hadiths. Ibn Khaldūn always presented himself as a quite serious and pious—sometimes even overpious—Mālikite legal scholar. As Muslims, both are likely never to have doubted the Islamic doctrine of predestination. And yet the two spheres—divine predestination on the one hand and the course of history, which obeys its own autonomous laws, on the other—cannot have appeared to them as mutually exclusive.

For them, the difference arises only because of the diverging perspectives through which one looks at the world. The criterion of truth was tied to the kind of discourse engaged in. What is right and true within political discourse can be gathered in an exemplary manner from the study of history. What is right and true within the discourse of *fiqh* may be deduced, with some probability, from a careful interpretation of the normative texts and their exegetical tradition. Nothing and nobody demands that both discourses must lead to *the same truth*. So two or more discourses that offer two or more perspectives on the world may continue to coexist, not without competition and attempts to replace each other, but accepting the mostly tacit premise that it takes several perspectives in combination, in all their contrariness, to offer an adequate picture of the truth—which can never be grasped, in fact, under one single perspective.

For many centuries, the different perspectives coexisted side by side, mostly in an unspectacular fashion, sometimes pollinating each other, sometimes rivaling and even fighting against each other, but always reined in by the knowledge that one single perspective can never claim the whole truth for itself. The situation changed abruptly when suddenly an opponent appeared who claimed exactly this—namely, to be in possession of a truth that was the only truth and did not allow for another truth to exist at its side. As proof for his truth, and obsessed with the endeavor to propagate this truth worldwide, this opponent could proffer his military and economic supremacy. His truth did not allow for being viewed perspectivally, but was regarded by him as absolute and universal; it did not admit other truths. The old serene view of the world was destroyed, and the search for an absolute truth of one's own, that could be set against the truth of the other contestants, began.

One of the first victims turned out to be the perspectival view on the state and politics. Until this point, the Ottoman sultans had employed for the inscriptions on their coins three titles, in suitably ambiguous fashion, which were derived from three different languages and evoked quite diverse ideas of political power: the Arabic title *sulṭān*, the old Turkish title *khān* or *khāqān*, and the Persian title *shāh*. In this new context, through a fairly wild act of usurpation, they produced the title of caliph, which for centuries had not played a role; concentrated more and more elements of religious competence at their court; and attempted, more intensely than had been the case since the early times of Islam, to unite political and religious authority in one ruler. The First World War did away with all these efforts and consigned the Near East to being a battleground of ideologies. But since, at the same time, the Near East constituted the object of sacrifice for Western colonialism, the attempt by the Islamic world to ideologize its own tradition turned out to be less than successful. Initially, then, instead of Pan-Islamic currents, there emerged the ideology of nationalism, imported from the West, which blended with the allegedly anti-imperialist ideology of socialism. However, the realization of "Unity, Freedom, Socialism" (the motto of the Syrian and Iraqi Baʿth party) failed, as did all those halfhearted attempts at imitating the Western capitalist success story, due to the incomplete decolonization of a region too rich in natural resources and too strategically important to make a lasting escape from Western and Eastern interference.

Against this background, it is no wonder that there was a second attempt made by the Islamic world toward the ideologization of its own tradition. This process, which started in the 1970s, is denoted, not quite correctly, as "re-Islamization." It is rather a project to create from piecemeal elements of tradition an ideology that, in a manner no worse than Western ideologies, meets the criterion of self-consistency and may lay a comprehensive claim to truth and validity. The slogan that Islam is *dīn wa-dawlah* (religion and state), is not a classical Islamic principle and not an essential part of Islam. In fact, it is found for the first time in the Islamic anti-colonial movement from the end of the nineteenth century.[42] With the intellectual pioneers of "political Islam," like Abū l-Aʿlā al-Mawdūdī and Sayyid Quṭb, it occupies a central place and ultimately becomes the leading maxim of modern political Islam. For the first time, the claim is raised that all aspects of public life, from culture to politics and economy, are to be governed from a homogeneous Islamic perspective. It is evident that the old tolerance of ambiguity has no place here.

Regrettable as this development may be, it also offers new opportunities. The deideologization of the world has left its traces in the dogmatic Islamism of the twentieth century, and everywhere that Islamist movements are integrated into politics, one may also observe a "normalization of Islamist parties."[43] If one observes the historical background, it becomes clear that precisely in the integration of Islamist movements, a not-insignificant potential of democratization may be tapped. The borders between the religious and the political sphere in the Islamic world were different from those of the West. For a long time, the Western bourgeoisie was confronted by an alliance of "throne and altar." Its emancipation was by necessity accompanied by emancipation from religious authorities.

The situation in the Islamic world was quite different. Here, the religious experts were part of the bourgeoisie, and the state authorities were never lastingly successful in converting the religious system into an obedient tool. On the contrary, it was the religious scholars who, again and again, came to the defense of the people against the claims of the rulers and the military. It was in the realm of scholarship, where the most important power base was the *de facto* autonomous sphere of the law that the classically educated bourgeoisie could freely develop and allow to flourish over centuries. This bourgeois space, in which religion had a pronouncedly emancipatory function, was confronted by the power sphere of the rulers and the military. In the course of history, colonial officers and military dictators replaced the sultans, but there was no great change in the traditional constellation. The alliance between the ruler, the military, and the upper class (the latter, in the twentieth century, mostly Western-oriented and secular) has shaped the power structure of almost all Near Eastern states up to the present day. This alliance is faced by a politically near-powerless middle class that, not accidentally, often sees itself better represented by Islamist parties than by secular ones, which are regarded as corrupt because of their alliance with the military and the upper class.[44] Ibn Nubātah's secular, "Machiavellian" concept may be appealing because it is secular, but *democratic* it is not. It shows that a secular conception of political rule did exist in the Islamic world, contrary to what is mostly maintained today. But it also shows that, for the time being, a more vigorous secularization is not necessarily the most important condition for more democracy in the Near East.

THE AMBIGUITY OF THE STRANGER

The Arabic language has not only a singular and a plural form, but also a dual form—that is, a special grammatical form for "two," which is always employed if one addresses or speaks of two persons or objects. If there are two eyes, two friends, or two pieces of cake, Arabic uses the dual form. Some words occur in the dual frequently, especially paired organs; friends and pieces of cake, not so often. It is quite difficult, however, to conceive of a context in which the dual of *foreignness* is used. And yet Ibn Khaldūn employed precisely this expression in order to describe his situation to the Mongol ruler Timur.

This is what happened: in the year 803/1400, the theologian, historian, and "first sociologist" Ibn Khaldūn accompanied the Mamluk sultan on his campaign against Timur (Tamerlane), who had laid siege to Damascus. When Ibn Khaldūn was admitted to Timur for an audience and asked what he, Timur, could do for Ibn Khaldūn, Ibn Khaldūn replied: "In this country, I am a foreigner with regard to two foreignnesses (*gharībun bi-hādhihī l-bilādi ghurbatayn*), one of them concerning the Maghreb, where I was born and grew up, and the other concerning Cairo, where the people of my environment (*ahl jīlī*) live. Now I have entered the sphere of your shadow and beseech you to advise me as to what lets me attain familiarity in this foreignness of mine (*fīmā yu'nisunī fī ghurbatī*)." Timur replied: "Tell me what you wish and I shall do it for you." Upon which Ibn Khaldūn said: "The situation of foreignness (*ḥāl al-ghurbah*) has made me forget what I wish. But perhaps you—may God give you strength—can tell me what I want."[45]

What Timur wants Ibn Khaldūn to want is not relevant in this context. Rather, it is important to examine the concept of foreignness articulated in this passage. The first striking observation is the fact that foreignness is perceived exclusively with reference to the point of origin. Ibn Khaldūn is a foreigner not because he is in Damascus, but because he is *not* in Tunis or in Cairo. Hence he does not talk of *foreignness to Damascus*, but of *foreignness from Tunis and Cairo*. That is why he uses the dual form. If foreignness were conceived of in relation to the place where one is rather than the place where one is from, the word "foreignness" would hardly ever occur in the dual form, because one can always be located only in one place. It is a different matter if one conceives of foreignness in relation to the place of origin, that is, the place or places in which one is not a foreigner. In Ibn Khaldūn's case, as he himself explains, the place of origin is actually two places. There is first his homeland—more precisely, the town of Tunis, in which he was born and grew up, in which he pursued his studies, in which his family lived, in which he spent the first twenty years of his life, and to which he was drawn back later. In this place he was not a foreigner. He left Tunis against his will in 784/1382 and spent the rest of his life in Cairo. When he stood before Timur, he had lived in Cairo almost as long as he had lived in Tunis. In Cairo, too, he had been a stranger initially; his style of clothing always remained that of a Maghribī, a "Westerner." But gradually he became at home in Cairo. He had an income there; he occupied the post of a Mālikite judge; he had gained students and friends and survived quite a few altercations. Thus the foreign place became a home for him. In a way, Ibn Khaldūn now had two "homes," or, as one would express it in classical Arabic, which conceives of foreignness from the point of view of the homeless, two places in which he was not foreign.

This experience of foreignness has been addressed in Arabic literature innumerable times.[46] "The foreigner is like a seedling," much-quoted wisdom has it, "that is separated from its ground and has nothing to drink. Now it is wilted, blossomless, wispy and fruitless." Another piece of wisdom: "The foreigner is like an orphan. No mother caresses it, no father takes pity on it."[47] In his treatise on "the good aspects of bad things and the bad aspects of good things," ath-Thaʿālibī has obvious difficulties finding good aspects of "foreignness." The passages quoted by him tell us little more than that it is sometimes inevitable to betake oneself to foreign places, and that it is certainly better to be lonely in a foreign place than to starve at home:

> Never will he achieve greatness, I say,
> Who stays in his country, at rest—
> Just as the falcon will catch no prey
> By spending his life in his nest.[48]

With these words, ath-Thaʿālibī quotes the poet Abū Firās (320–357 /932–968)—who knew what he was talking about, since he had spent many years in a foreign place, that is, in Byzantine captivity.

It was a very clever move of Ibn Khaldūn to begin his talk with Timur by discussing the subject of foreignness; quite apart from how he may have been feeling himself, he could latch onto a well-known discourse. Ibn Khaldūn even argues that his foreignness has strained him so much that he no longer knows what he wants. Such hyperbole is comprehensible only if viewed against the background of the cultural knowledge of his time, according to which being a foreigner was one of the worst hardships a person could confront. And Timur goes along with the game. He asks Ibn Khaldūn what he can do to restore the state of "familiarity," and promises the fulfillment of all his wishes. Here we encounter the term *uns* (familiarity, sociability), the antonym of *ghurbah.* This shows that the Arabic term for foreignness is not primarily a geographical one. The concept of *uns* is encountered in all places that offer respect, appreciation, love, sympathy, and care. An anecdote in the account of the arch-traveler Ibn Baṭṭūṭah illustrates how important such qualities were, particularly in foreign lands. It is a vignette that seems so insignificant to a Western reader that one can hardly understand why Ibn Baṭṭūṭah dictated it to his secretary. Still more amazing is the fact that this secretary appended an elaborate commentary to it.

The passage figures in the very first pages of the travel report. In the year 725/1325, Ibn Baṭṭūṭah has left his hometown, Tangier, with a group of Mecca pilgrims, and goes ashore in Tunis—the first stop of a journey that would take him all the way to the Far East. But in Tunis, where the language is the same as the one spoken at home and the customs are more or less the same, Ibn Baṭṭūṭah is already overwhelmed by a feeling of foreignness when he disembarks and nobody runs toward him to welcome him: "Everybody now approached each other to exchange salutations; only I was saluted by nobody because nobody knew me. This had me feel a pain in my heart that made it impossible for me to withhold my tears, and I wept bitterly. But one of the pilgrims noticed how I was feeling and turned to me with a salutation and comforted me by his company."[49]

Inspired by Ibn Baṭṭūṭah's account, his secretary then relates a similar incident that happened to another scholar. This man, he wrote, drew the attention of an empathetic fellow human being—"may God well recompense him"—because nobody greeted him. Thereupon that empathetic person hurried toward him, greeted him, kept company with him, and said: "When I noticed how you stood apart from people and nobody greeted you I realized that you are a foreigner (*gharīb*) and I wanted to console you through my company (*īnās*)."[50] Here, too, the foreignness of the foreigner (*gharīb*) is overcome, or at least mitigated, by the (re)creation of familiarity (*īnās*: the creation of *uns*).

As perceived by the members of classical Arab civilization, foreignness is thus not a characteristic of origin, lineage, race, or language,[51] but an emotional deficit in an individual who feels himself to be foreign. Therefore it is not a permanent characteristic, but a status that is, in principle, alterable. Most importantly, foreignness is always conceived from the point of view of the person who feels foreign. In fact, in the whole body of classical Arabic literature, the word *gharīb* is never used with a meaning different from the usage of Ibn Khaldūn and Ibn Baṭṭūṭah; in hundreds of references containing the word *gharīb*, I have not come across a single instance in which an outside spectator ascribes foreignness to a person. Nowhere is the foreigner foreign because he comes from outside and, because he is different, is felt to be out of place. And there is no other word that would denote a foreignness predicated by another person. The only possibility for this kind of foreignness would be the word *ajnabī*, which in fact denotes someone from outside. In classical Arabic, however, it is used only for someone outside the family. An *ajnabī* is a person who does not belong to the inner circle of a family and therefore is not entitled to inherit and is restricted in his access to the women of the family. The word is occasionally used metaphorically, for instance when a scholar dabbles in a discipline that is actually alien to him: "He also wrote legal treatises, although he was a stranger (*ajnabī*) in law," we read sometimes. Today, *ajnabī* means foreigner in the political sense; but in the sense of foreigner designated as such from outside it does not occur prior to the nineteenth century.

How, then, were foreigners seen from this exterior perspective referred to in classical times? The simple answer is: not at all. The plural of *gharīb* is *ghurabāʾ*, but *al-ghurabāʾ* would denote not "the foreigners" from an exterior perspective, but only those who *feel themselves to be foreign* in a place. There is every indication that an expression like "the foreigners in our town" cannot be immediately translated into classical Arabic. One could of course paraphrase it by saying "all people who were not born in our town" or "all people who have not lived here for many years"; one might also specify "all Iranians, Turks, merchants, travelers, etc. in our town." But neither language nor perception offered an obvious opportunity to speak of *the foreigners* as collectively opposed to *the natives*. Therefore, it was impossible to perceive foreigners as a collective threat. Not least, this affected everyday dealings, of which one may state, "that, happily, xenophobia is not a word that comes to mind when considering the situation and treatment of strangers in daily life."[52]

This does not mean, of course, that no prejudices existed at all. People from Marw were regarded as misers, and black skin was perceived as ugly. But since foreignness and otherness were not perceived as threats to the identity of the indigenous, such prejudices could not consolidate and lead to discrimination and violence, let alone systematic persecution.

The perception of foreignness in Arab-Islamic culture is therefore different from perceptions in many other cultures that show a close relation, even in their languages, between "foreigner" and "enemy"—as for instance the Latin *hostis* and the Middle High German *gast*.[53] The etymology of *gharīb* is not quite established; the basic meaning might be "someone who has gone away," which would tally with the findings of the history of mentalities.[54] But even independent of linguistic expression, it is noteworthy that in the construction of identity, a dissociation from foreigners hardly played a role, and that the perception of foreigners as a group of people who come from outside, and are in contrast to the group of indigenous people, was far more moderate than in most other cultures.

This fact evidently correlates with the tolerance of ambiguity we have diagnosed in the precolonial Near East. The foreigner becomes a phenomenon of ambiguity through the fact that he belongs neither to the category of the enemies nor to that of friends, but forms a third category: "There are friends and enemies. And there are *strangers*."[55] The sociologist Zygmunt Bauman has extensively discussed the role of the foreigner and its meaning when it comes to the mentality of modernity. In the fact that foreigners do not lend themselves to be assigned to the category friend or enemy—that is to say, in their *ambiguity*—he sees the decisive feature: "The stranger is one (perhaps the main one, the archetypal one) member of the family of *undecidables*."[56] By occupying exactly this position, the foreigner constitutes a threat, "more horrifying than that which one can fear from the enemy," because he challenges the opposition between friend and enemy. "As that opposition is the foundation on which rest all social life and all differences which patch it up and hold together, the stranger saps social life itself."[57] Those "undecidables" (whose most significant representatives, for Bauman, are foreigners), "put paid to the ordering power of the opposition, and so to the ordering power of the narrators of the opposition. . . . Undecidables brutally expose the artifice, the fragility, the sham of the most vital of separations. They bring the outside into the inside, and poison the comfort of order with suspicion of chaos. This is exactly what the strangers do."[58]

For Bauman, "the stranger is a person afflicted with incurable sickness of *multiple incongruity*. The stranger is, for this reason, the bane of modernity."[59] Bauman has extensively dealt with the forms and effects of the "fight against indeterminacy"[60] that modern times have conducted. He shows how the modern nation-states promote *uniformity*,[61] how the stigmatization of foreigners serves as "a convenient weapon in the defence against the unwelcome ambiguity of the stranger";[62] the essence of assimilation, he says, is "a declaration of war on semantic ambiguity";[63] and the will to annihilate all ambiguity has ultimately resulted in the Holocaust, for the Jews "were the only element that belonged everywhere and nowhere, were at home everywhere and nowhere. That made them a focus of all modern disturbances: they represented the uncertainty, the ambivalence"[64] (where the term "ambiguity" would have been more appropriate).

Howsoever one reacts to Bauman's arguments in detail, it becomes clear at any rate that in the apperception of foreignness, no greater contrast is conceivable than that between the classical Arab-Islamic culture and the modern West. A culture that derives its guiding principles from the "horror of ambiguity"[65] is confronted with a culture based to a far lesser degree on the regulatory power of opposite forces, one that leaves a wide space for ambiguity. In this culture, essentially tolerant of ambiguity, the category of the foreigner finds no place. As long as the foreigner does not appear as the enemy, he is not perceived as belonging to a distinct category. For the native population, foreigners do not exist as a group, but only as individuals, and they can be treated as such—negatively, by taking advantage of their ignorance of local conditions, and cheating them, or positively, by empathizing with their foreignness and trying to establish *uns*, "familiarity."

In the precolonial Near East, foreigners were not perceived as a collective group that could be put in opposition to the indigenous collective group. Also, the single groups of foreigners who definitely constituted a potential object of perception and designation hardly lent themselves to the establishment of an identity. In the cultivation of prejudices—in the form of jokes and anecdotes—this culture never surpassed the level of slander practiced by, say, the people of New York against those of New Jersey (and vice versa). In Arabic literature, it is the genre of love poetry that most frequently refers to ethnic groups, since from the eleventh century onward it became fashionable to write love epigrams about beloved ones from all regions of the Islamic world. So we read epigrams about handsome young men and pretty young women from Cairo, Kairouan, and Baghdad; epigrams about Arabs, Turks, and Persians; epigrams about beautiful Blacks, Berbers, gypsies and Kurds, Christians, and Jews—but never is the punch line at the expense of the "object." Members of the marginalized groups are as loveable as members of the established core society. The poets are impelled not by prejudice but by the fun of diversity, which rouses the ambition to compose a catalog of all loveable persons as completely as possible. Many of these texts—among them, the comprehensive anthology, extremely popular through the centuries, called *Marātiʿ al-ghizlān* (Pastures of the gazelles) by an-Nawājī—are extant in numerous manuscripts but still await publication.

The group of "interior foreigners" who may be considered the most foreign in the classical Arabic world were the Bedouins.[66] On the one hand, they were regarded as the ancestors of Arab culture, experts in the Arabic language and powerfully eloquent masters of ancient poetry. On the other hand, they occupied the pole opposite to the cultured urbanity of the townspeople. This could be viewed as positive or negative. They were the unspoiled outdoorsmen who withstood the decadent dissipations of civilization, but they were also the uncivilized boors of the desert who did not understand culture, religion, hygiene, good food, and refined eroticism. If there was ever a social group in Arab-Islamic premodern times whose image was shaped by ambiguity, it was that of the Bedouins.

They were, however, not really *foreign*. There was constant contact with them, mostly in peaceful commerce, although the sedentary population in the arable regions of the Fertile Crescent was frequently forced to make a stand against the Bedouins who were pressing forward. The eleventh century, a period of crisis, is above all a time of the Bedouinization of Iraq and Syria.[67] So behind the ambiguity of the figure of the Bedouin there hides a situation of real conflict, and this is probably the reason that, in classical Arabic literature, the Bedouins appear as the most foreign of the foreigners. It is quite wrong, however, to talk of exclusion of the Bedouins, or of the Bedouin as an enemy image. For right next to anecdotes and poems showing the Bedouins in all their dangerousness and lack of civilization, we hear of anecdotes and poems—often written or transmitted by the very same authors—in which Bedouins appear as bearers of wisdom and models of a simple, natural way of life.

The Bedouins are allowed to play this ambivalent role only because they are not really foreigners, and because, as heirs to the pillars of the ancient Arab culture, they are indeed part of the indigenous culture. Even Christians and Jews, for whom one would allow a claim to the status of "interior foreigners," do not represent such ambivalence. They are not foreign enough because they are thoroughly integrated into the urban culture of the Islamic world. This makes them unfit as objects for jokes. Among the great collections of jokes and anecdotes of classical times, the *Nathr ad-durr* (Scattering of pearls) by al-Ābī (died 421/1030) devotes two chapters to the Bedouins. One chapter collects Bedouin sayings of wisdom; the other entertains the reader with Bedouin jokes. In contrast, Christians and Jews, like the ancient Greeks and Indians, are fit only for wise sayings. A number of the sayings of Jesus or his disciples, or of a Jewish prophet, find their way into collections of wise sayings and anecdotes, but these works do not contain a single joke about a Jew or a Christian. It is true that a Jew or a Christian could become the target of a joke—anything else would be an indication of marginalization. Jokes on physicians, for instance, are very popular, and we also encounter jokes on Christian doctors. A physician by the name of Jesus is made fun of with the line that his eminent namesake could bring the dead back to life, whereas he, the doctor, brings the living into the grave. Similar fun is poked at Muslim doctors.[68] But nowhere do we find jokes that deride Jews, Christians, or Zoroastrians because of their religion, or because of an allegedly typical Jewish, Christian, or Zoroastrian property.

This corresponds with the status of non-Muslims in the precolonial Islamic world, a society that could not define itself otherwise than as an *umma*, that is, an Islamic community, and that assigned to non-Muslims a lower rank—but without excluding them, and providing them with legal autonomy and largely integrating them into urban and rural life. All professions were accessible to Jews and Christians in the Islamic world. The only exception was the military, which, however, from Mamluk times onwards had scarcely any recruits from the ranks of Arab Muslims. The presence of Jewish and Christian communities in the villages and towns of the Islamic world was a matter of course until modern times. Until the end of World War I—that is, after the first eruption of the Western ideology of nationalism in the Near East, in the form of the persecution of Armenians—around one fourth of the population of the territory of contemporary Turkey was not Muslim. If today this figure has been reduced to less than one percent, it is due not to Islamic intolerance but to the zeal of enforced conformity found in the modern nation-state. A similar picture emerges everywhere for Near Eastern Jewry. Until 1948, about 75,000 Jews lived in Egypt. Today they amount to less than a hundred. Again, it was not Islam that expelled them but Nasser's nationalism and the conflict with Israel.[69]

Mark R. Cohen, probably the best current expert on Jews in the classical Arab-Islamic world, describes the traditional situation of the Jews as marginalized and integrated at the same time. Unlike in the Christian world, where Jews were equally marginalized and relative integration gradually devolved to exclusion and ultimately to persecution, the situation of the Jews in the Islamic world remained stable, and rested on a safe legal basis: "Islamic society allowed Jews and Christians the benefits of living in a marginal situation within its hierarchical social order, but the marginal situation had greater staying power there. And, it did not degenerate into exclusion via expulsion."[70] The few cases of persecution on record do not admit of a comparison with the situation of the Jews in Christian Europe.[71] They are the exceptions that prove that, in the precolonial Islamic world, Christians and Jews occupied in all places and at all times a legally safeguarded position—a position that perhaps marginalized them in some ways but, on the other hand, secured them safety as well as a considerable amount of autonomy.

Even in the Mamluk era, the situation had not principally changed, although under Mamluk rule, Jews and Christians had to suffer sharper restrictions than under their predecessors and their successors. From this period, we have a letter written by a learned Italian rabbi who in 1487 had emigrated, via Egypt, to Mamluk Palestine, and who wrote to his people at home, a year later, about his community in Jerusalem: "In truth, the Jews do not experience *galut* from the Arabs at all in this place. I have traveled the entire country . . . and no one says a negative word. Rather, they are very kind to the foreigner, especially to one who does not know the language. When they see many Jews together, they do not express any envy."[72]

As Cohen writes, the term *galut*, here and in other letters of the fifteenth and sixteenth century, carries not only a geographical dimension in the sense of "exile," but also a psychological one:

> I believe, rather, that *galut* in the letters comes close to meaning *exclusion*. Three Jews from Christian Europe—where, by the end of the Middle Ages—the Jews were substantially excluded from majority society—observed with considerable surprise that the indigenous Jews of Islam were not similarly excluded from the social order of their surroundings. Each sensed that Jews "here," in their relationship to gentiles, were less relegated to the "outside" than were Jews in Christian lands. . . .
>
> If this lexical interpretation [of *galut*] is correct, what we have expressed here is one of the most important differences between Christian–Jewish and Islamic–Jewish relations in the Middle Ages. In the West, Jews came to be

> excluded from the organic hierarchy of society: assaulted as aliens, persecuted collectively for alleged crimes against Christians and Christianity, increasingly isolated in their Jewish quarters, soon to be confined to legal ghettos, and all too often expelled from lands where they and their ancestors had lived for hundreds of years.
>
> For all their marginality, Jews in the Orient remained, *marginal*, at least during the classical period; but they were not "excluded." . . . Seen from the perspective presented in this book, the embeddedness of the Jews of Islam, the product of intertwining religious, legal, economic, and social factors, constitutes the most important reason for their relative freedom from violent persecution, and hence for a collective historical memory that was fundamentally different from that of the Jews of Christendom.[73]

As a psychological term of exile and the experience of homelessness (compare the German term *elend*, "miserable," which can be traced back to Middle High German *ellende*, "in a foreign country"), *galut* corresponds with the Arabic word *ghurbah*. The fact that the Jews did not feel themselves to be foreigners is in line with the observation, gleaned from Arab-Islamic texts, that they did not appear as foreigners. This corroborates our thesis that the category of the foreign—both in the sense of "foreigner coming from outside" and in the sense of "foreigner inside"—had an extremely low profile in the precolonial Islamic world.

Today, the situation of Jews and Christians in the classical Islamic world is often characterized as one of discrimination. But the situation is more complex; after all, every community, in order to form its identity, requires some sort of differentiation between the interior and the exterior. In the Islamic world, political rule and important social institutions were legitimized by the religion of Islam. Furthermore, Islam offered the only spiritual bracket that served as a common denominator for the different peoples in their regions beyond the level of tribes. The members of other religions were part of Islamic society because they were an integral part of urban and rural life; on the other hand, they remained outside because they did not share the religious basis of the commonwealth. This created a situation of ambiguity that threatened to blur the inside–outside differentiation. But this case of ambiguity was not treated differently than the other ambiguities this book has so far discussed: as in other cases, there was an attempt to *domesticate* the ambiguity, not to eliminate it. This domestication of ambiguity was achieved by granting the non-Islamic communities a legal status that on the one hand made them part of the effective legal order and thus a legitimate part of society, and on the other hand separated them from the

Islamic core society through restrictions, but also through privileges such as their own jurisdiction. The ambiguity of belonging and not belonging was dissolved in a way that *integrated ambiguity itself.* The not-belonging became part of the belonging. Delimitation prevented exclusion. For a thousand years, this model appears to have been one of the most successful ones for regulating the integration of population groups that did not share the core characteristic by which a society defined itself.

What a cultural achievement this practice represents can be shown by a comparison with parallel phenomena in modern Western societies. Here, religious affiliations no longer play a significant role. The modern state does not define itself by religion; therefore, the equal treatment of citizens of different religious affiliations is a matter of course, or at least it should be. For a modern nation-state, there is instead another criterion that is decisive: nationality. The role of non-Muslims in the premodern Islamic world thus corresponds, in the modern nation-state, with that of the foreigner. They live in the country, it is true; they often speak the language, go to work, and send their children to school; but they do not share the quality by which the political community defines itself, namely, belonging to the constitutive people. To change one's nationality is more difficult than to change one's religion. A person who cannot establish belonging to a nation by nationality, or does not have a residence permit, experiences the most radical form of exclusion, expulsion. In order to enforce this procedure, many people who have not committed any crime other than simply being present are dealt a punishment equal to the most severe one that Western constitutional democracies can issue, that is, a prison sentence: a detention pending deportation. "According to the files of the German federal police, 30,000 people per year on average were deported since 1998. Together with Austria, Germany is the sole country in Europe that imposes detentions pending deportation on children and adolescents. In Hamburg alone, in the year 2003, around 125 minors were held in detention for longer than three months."[74]

We do not intend to discuss here whether such a procedure is legitimate or makes sense. It should only be pointed out that the inside–outside differentiation necessary for the shaping of the identity of a community may assume quite diverse forms, and that these forms are not necessarily more moderate or more humane than they were in certain premodern times. In the West, the law functions not to integrate ambiguity but to draw a sharp line between belonging and not belonging to the community. The foreigner without a right of residence no longer possesses any ambiguity. Free of ambiguity, he simply does not belong, as only an enemy does not belong. So he is treated like one.

In modern societies, the ambiguity of the foreigner begins only where the law establishes his non-foreignness, free of any ambiguity. By attaining citizenship, the foreigner is by law not a foreigner anymore; but in society he remains one. Here he finds himself in a state of ambiguity that he feels to be highly problematic and that has to be resolved by the process of *integration*. The foreigner, if he is lucky, now becomes the object of a bustling integration industry that tries to expel the bad elements of his foreignness and to feed the good elements, through "diversity management," into the economy. If he is not so lucky, he finds himself confronted by a society that understands *integration* exclusively as *assimilation*. The language used is revealing. In older usage, *to assimilate* was understood only as a reflexive verb and *to integrate* as a transitive verb. One could say "to assimilate *oneself*," but exclusively "to integrate *something* or *someone*." Nowadays, "to integrate" is also used as a reflexive verb: "The immigrants have to integrate *themselves*." A Minister of State for Migration, Refugees, and Integration may launch a campaign for "Diversity as a Chance,"[75] but the common understanding of the term integration is certainly represented with greater accuracy in this list, from an Internet dictionary, of synonyms for "to integrate oneself": "to acclimatize oneself, to fit oneself into, to familiarize oneself, to fall into line, to follow someone/something, to assimilate oneself, to settle, to take to something/someone, to adapt oneself, to accustom oneself, to conform to, to get used to."[76] Here it may be observed how the Arabic *īnās*, "bringing about familiarity," which residents offer to the person who feels foreign, is transformed into the foreigner "familiarizing themselves" as an additional responsibility, which is obviously attained by obeying the pressure of conformity exerted by the surrounding society, through assimilation, adjustment, and blending in.

The legal disambiguation of the foreigner, by granting him citizenship, does not remove his ambiguity. Indeed, in several respects, citizenship may produce ambiguity, since supposedly a new citizen should no longer be foreign, but he is felt to be foreign precisely because he persists in being different. In this way, despite the political wisdom of many conceptions of integrating diversity, a massive pressure to assimilate is felt on the part of the non-autochthonous population of the community, as well as a marked expectation that the foreigner assimilate is felt by the indigenous population. It is anything but certain that assimilation leads to a decrease in the ambiguity of the foreigner. The contrary effect manifested itself in the example of European Jewry, where initially it was the assimilated Jews who were the targets of anti-Semites.[77]

Zygmunt Bauman has extensively dealt with the question of what modern conceptions of foreignness and assimilation meant for the Jews of the nineteenth and twentieth centuries. He shows how it was in fact the legal equality of the Jews in the nineteenth century that occasioned an enormous pressure to assimilate:

> Equality before the law meant, after all, the sapping of communal autonomy, discreditation of communal authority, undermining the centrifugal influences of communal and corporate elites. . . .
>
> Abolition of legal privileges and discriminations was but one aspect of the modern thrust toward uniformity. Modernization was also a *cultural* crusade; a powerful and relentless drive to extirpate differences in values and life-styles, customs and speech, beliefs and public demeanour. It was, first and foremost, a drive to redefine all cultural values and styles except those endorsed by the modernizing elite (and particularly the values and styles that resisted the *Gleichschaltung* process) as inferior.[78]

In the Islamic world prior to the First World War, such a "modern drive for uniformity" never existed. The preconditions for this evidence in the history of mentalities lie in the fact that the specific perception of foreigners and foreignness was diametrically contrary to that of the modern West.

Foreignness was always conceived from the perspective of the one who felt foreign. A person was foreign when he had lost his social ties, and he remained foreign until he had established new ties and had overcome the status of foreignness by gaining new "familiarity." Foreignness was a problem of individual psychology, not collective psychology. Being different, as such, did not generate foreignness. Foreigners coming from abroad, or local groups of people who looked different or lived differently, were not perceived as a collective of foreigners. Again, the most important precondition for this was the high level of social tolerance of ambiguity. In the Islamic world, the ambiguity of the foreigner who is neither friend nor foe, and who simultaneously belongs and does not belong, simply was not perceived as a problem. This went hand in hand with a relaxed way of dealing with people who had a different religion, color, language, or set of customs, both in one's own country and in foreign countries.

This relaxed attitude had positive effects for a coexistence with minorities of all sorts, fairly free from disruptions, but it also had historical consequences for dealings with countries and peoples outside the *Dār al-Islām*. The relaxed attitude toward countries and peoples that were different manifested itself not least in a widespread lack of interest in them. People outside one's own circles hardly played a role in establishing one's own identity. Their being different was not felt as a threat, but also not as a potential source of enrichment. Within the ambiguity-tolerant attitude of "live and let live," one left others to their otherness.

The Arabic geographical literature has clear examples of this basic attitude. Arab geographers not only inherited the scholarship of the Greeks, Persians, and Indians, but also superseded it rapidly, and for centuries commanded the most comprehensive and detailed geographical knowledge in the world. Without the fundamental data made available by Arab cartographers, the expeditions of discovery led by the Portuguese and the Spaniards would not have been possible.[79] Arab writers were also well informed about the cultures of different parts of the world. Nevertheless, their writings merely served practical purposes and satisfied a basic curiosity about the world and its inhabitants. This curiosity did not move people toward organizing systematic expeditions in order to explore foreign countries. Among the numerous travel accounts in classical Arabic literature, there are only a few authors whose travels have gone beyond the borders of the *Dār al-Islām*. And only rarely were those travels undertaken voluntarily.

One of the most well-known writers, Ibn Faḍlān, traveled in 309/921 on a diplomatic mission to the king of the Volga Bulgars, and described his encounter with the Rūs, who probably represented either Vikings or a population of Norse origin in the process of acculturation with the Slavic environment.[80] Since Ibn Faḍlān's travel account is one of the very few sources on the peoples of the Volga region of this time, it has aroused much attention among historians, not least because of its factual and completely unemotional style of presentation. Recently, Ibn Faḍlān has even become a film star. The bestselling author Michael Crichton was inspired by Ibn Faḍlān's account to write a novel, *Eaters of the Dead* (1976), which in 1999 was made into a film, *The 13th Warrier*, directed by John McTiernan and starring Antonio Banderas. The film retained only two scenes from Ibn Faḍlān's report, but they are distinctive. The first scene shows the morning wash of the Rūs, which features a water bowl being passed around, from which every man takes his washing water, spitting and blowing his nose into the bowl. Ibn Faḍlān shows clearly that he is disgusted.[81] The second scene shows the cremation of the body of a chieftain of the Rūs, which is depicted, as in the travel account, in great detail. In fact, Ibn Faḍlān made a detour for the sole reason of witnessing the funeral. So it was pure curiosity that prompted him to make this side trip. In the course of the funerary ceremony, which he describes in all its detail without exhibiting any emotional involvement, the body of the deceased prince is carried to a boat along with numerous sacrificial offerings, among them a female slave. There is then a ritual killing of the slave, and the boat with all its freight is burned.[82] For the Muslim believer Ibn Faḍlān, such a ceremony, which included human sacrifice, was bound to constitute the worst possible embodiment of paganism and idolatry. And yet he depicts the procedure with a downright ethnographic objectivity, and without the slightest sign of outrage, after having dwelt at length upon the "disgusting filthiness," as he perceives it, of this country.

In about the same period as Ibn Faḍlān, another writer named al-Masʿūdī (died 345/956), himself a well-traveled man, reports on the cremation of Rūs women living in the area of the Khazar princes:

> The infidels who live in the city of the king of the Khazars belong to different groups. Among them there are Slavs and Rūs who live in one part of the city. They have the custom of cremating their deceased ones together with their riding animals, their arms, and their jewels. When a man dies, they even cremate his living wife with him; however, when a woman dies, her husband is not cremated along with her. If someone dies as a bachelor, he is married after his death. The women themselves wish for their cremation, because they believe that they will thereupon enter paradise. Cremation of the wives is a custom also followed in India; the difference, however, is that a woman is cremated only if it is her own wish.[83]

We hear again the same sober tone, the same impersonal attitude of taking for granted the fact that women are cremated together with their deceased men but not the other way around. At the end of the passage, there is even an attempt to offer a rational explanation for the outrageous custom: the women themselves would allegedly wish for the observance of the custom. In contrast with Indian practice, however, these widows cannot choose whether or not they are cremated. This lack of voluntariness is the only point of criticism one can discern in the passage.

It is beyond dispute that both Ibn Faḍlān and al-Masʿūdī, along with all the other travelers not mentioned here, strongly disapprove of this custom. Ibn Faḍlān's equanimity is instantly gone when he talks about tribes already converted to Islam trespassing against religious prescriptions, and he is not afraid of entering into an open quarrel with the prince of the Bulgarians, in whose town the call for prayer is practiced in a way that the author thinks wrong.[84]

He and other travelers may show a measure of curiosity about that gruesome custom of the foreigners, but they are obviously not personally concerned in the sense of feeling compelled to explain and confirm their own system of values. They believe they do not have to argue against customs they are convinced are wrong. They are not outraged or scandalized, and they do not call for or design measures to abolish pagan atrocities. At no point does Ibn Faḍlān plan to convert the Vikings to Islam, or at least to dissuade them from their human sacrifices. He is challenged only when he witnesses Muslims who practice Islam wrongly, and when he sees his individual integrity endangered. The lack of cleanliness, which he feels is not only basically unpleasant but also violates religious ideas of purity—this is experienced as a danger, and awakens in him the wish for a change in the situation.

What applies to al-Masʿūdī and Ibn Faḍlān may be readily generalized: people in the Arab-Islamic world (and probably in the whole Islamic world) experienced the otherness of the people outside their world not as a threat or a challenge. They did not feel their identity troubled by the otherness of the foreigners outside their own space, and they did not have a problem with leaving the other in his otherness. The precondition for this is a personality tolerant of ambiguity; a personality without tolerance of ambiguity can perceive the other as a danger even when it is outside. If one entertains ambivalence toward one's own personality, then the sole fact that some people have fundamentally different convictions and ways of life becomes a threat to one's own identity. It is not by chance that many of the important missionaries of the Christian West feature a conversion experience in their biographies. A complete turnaround in life, such as a conversion or a "born-again" experience, always leads to a position of ambiguity toward one's own person, which is divided into two parts, a bad old one and a good new one. In order to assure oneself of the good new part, and to confirm the rightness of the fight against the bad old part (which is, after all, a part of one's biography), the conversion experience has to be staged again and again. Since this experience cannot be repeated in one's own person, others have to be converted, who by their conversion confirm the truth of one's own insight—which is jeopardized as long as there are people who do not share it. This is the incessant fuel for missionary zeal. Since an ambivalent attitude toward one's own personality leads to a general intolerance of ambiguity, one may surmise that people with a missionary zeal, both "born-again" Christians and "born-again" Muslims, are not imbued with a high degree of tolerance of ambiguity.[85]

The reverse side of the coin is the fact that classical Islam exhibited a very low degree of missionary zeal. This is true even for the early campaigns of conquest, whose aim was the expansion of Islamic territory but not the imposition of a way of life—not even the religion of Islam—upon others. Although Islam is a world religion with a universal claim to truth, it lacks "(t)he universalizing ambitions of emerging nation-states, that later became a ubiquitous, and arguably the most salient, trait of all modernization."[86]

Where Islam established itself over the centuries, it entered into a strong symbiosis with the existing cultures. In sub-Saharan Africa and in Indonesia, to name only two geographical corners, extremely diverse Islamic cultures developed that incorporated many elements of non-Islamic regional cultures. Today, these indigenous varieties of Islam have been forced into a defensive position vis-à-vis Wahhabi and Salafi Islam, which tries, with much missionary zeal, to enforce worldwide its claim to absolute authority in the interpretation of Islam.

In fact, it was precisely the lack of a *universalizing ambition* that contributed to the Arab-Islamic world's tendency to lag behind in its race with the West for the conquest of the world, for without this ambition, it lacked a significant driving force of global conquest and colonization.

In classical times, the scientific and technological preconditions of the Islamic world were clearly superior to those of contemporary Europe. For centuries, the Indian Ocean was well known to Arab seafarers, who utilized the compass and Jacob's staff, operated with numerous kinds of navigation charts, and commanded the best sea maps worldwide, which apparently enabled them to determine the lines of longitude while at sea, arriving at "a more or less modern representation of the entire Indian Ocean. The standard reached at that time was the result of continuous and hard work carried out in the Islamic world from the 3rd/9th century until toward the end of the 10th/16th century."[87] Partly through a series of detours, these Arab sea maps came into the possession of the Portuguese and other European nations, who were thus able to acquire overnight a knowledge that had been "the fruit of work that was done in the course of several centuries" on the part of the Arabs.[88]

The Arabs did not utilize this knowledge in an attempt to establish a monopoly position in trade across the Indian Ocean; instead, they shared it with the Indians and the Chinese. In view of this competitive situation, and of the enormous profits yielded by this trade, it is all the more remarkable "that it was conducted largely without resort to force of arms. African dhows (traditional boats), Chinese junks, and Indian and Arab merchant ships all sailed without naval convoys from their native lands. None of the great ports of trade—Aden, Hormuz, Calicut, Puri, Aceh, or Melaka—were walled and fortified. The assumption in this wide-ranging trade seems to have been that force of arms was not needed to protect shipping or to enforce deals."[89]

All this changed when the Portuguese arrived. Álvares Cabral and Vasco da Gama—perhaps one of the most savage mass murderers of world history—"had introduced armed trading into the Indian Ocean and . . . abruptly ended the system of peaceful oceanic navigation that was such a marked feature of the region."[90]

The Atlantic Ocean, too, was not such a *mare ignotum* to the Muslim seafarers as the Eurocentric historiography of "the discovery of the world" would have it. Early on, al-Masʿūdī relates that among the many who dared sail the "sea of the darknesses," some of them returning safe and sound while some were lost, there was a band of foolhardy young men under a certain Khashkhāsh who returned after a long voyage with rich booty and became the talk of the day in al-Andalus.[91] Such voyages across the Atlantic Ocean had lost their sensational appeal in the fifteenth century. We have some evidence that Arab seafarers had started to survey the South American coast even before Columbus. They must have known about the existence of the Strait of Magellan in the beginning of that century.[92] Its "discoverer," Ferdinand Magellan, was most probably in possession of a map based on Arab maps that already included his "discovery."[93] And Columbus had started out on his first journey with a map that "contained quite a number of Meso-American islands."[94]

But it remains difficult to furnish irrefutable proof for a pre-Columbian "discovery" of America by Muslim seafarers. The only extant map drawn by a contemporary Muslim author is that of Pīrī Reʾīs, from the year 917/1513. Other maps have to be reconstructed from their afterlife in European cartography. One crucial point is that Muslim seafarers did not leave permanent traces in the countries through which they traveled. The Spaniards and the Portuguese took possession of the countries they arrived in, on behalf of their respective royal empires, and fought, subjugated, forcibly converted, or massacred the indigenous population, securing their new possessions by strongpoints and colonies. The Muslim seafarers did nothing of the sort. They did not even bother to publicize their achievements as discoverers. For Portuguese, Spanish, Dutch, and English discoverers and conquerors, there was no more important task than to let the whole world know that they were the first to discover and take possession of this or that country. The Arab seafarers could not have cared less. They "discovered" countries and drew maps of their coastlines in the interest of practical use for traders, with nothing but the pride of craftsmen polishing their technique. None of them had the idea that he might become famous only because he was the first to sail up the Río de la Plata ("discovered" by Juan Díaz de Solís in 1516, but already mapped by Pīrī Reʾīs in 1513)[95]—well, except that there would have been a poet to compose an extravagant piece in praise of that feat . . . The rulers of the Islamic world, too, were not particularly interested in geographical discoveries. An unusual eruption of expeditionary zeal shown by the sultan of Mali (which he did not survive) is the exception that proves the rule.[96] On what benefit, in any case, were rulers supposed to count? They were, and they remained, the masters of the most lucrative trade routes.

As for the people of the "New World"—they were assuredly pagan peoples with strange customs; but enough was already known of such people in sub-Saharan Africa and in the Far East. Why, then, discover new ones? If they did not have enough missionary zeal to lead these long-known heathens to the true religion, why should they get up and start a search for new heathens?

This way of thinking canceled most of the motives that made the search for new countries so important for the European powers. Arab merchants and seafarers did not consider their job as something spectacular—this is not a promising precondition for a history of discoveries without a gap! If today the achievements of Arab seafarers are ignored by Western historiography in a way that amounts to a distortion of history, there are, according to Fuat Sezgin, two primary reasons for this. The first is "that the 800-year period of creative scholarship in the Arab-Islamic cultural sphere has not been taken cognizance of, let alone understood, by the modern history of sciences." The second reason is the fact that "Arab geographers and cartographers report the important achievements in their own cultural sphere only incidentally and sparsely. Therefore, many significant discoveries and innovations have been reported in contemporary historiography only belatedly or not at all. Apparently, the Arab-Islamic navigators and cartographers were not aware of the world-historical significance of the progress they had achieved."[97]

Apart from the material motives mentioned above, it was above all the *mental* motives that drove the Europeans to "discover" and conquer the world, thus propelling it into the era of modernity and globalization. Social historians and historians of economy will be able to explain the phenomenon of modern times only to a certain degree: they may define factors without which the pathway to globalized modernity would not have been possible, but they overlook the factor that first initiated the development, that is the *universalizing ambition* that is apparently unique to Western culture and must be ascribed to an uncommon *intolerance of ambiguity*. Up to the present day, this is manifested in a phenomenon that seems to be almost totally missing from the Islamic world (and probably all the rest of the world), and that may explain the Western urge to conquer the world more adequately than do most political, economic, and religious-sociological theories. We might call it, borrowing from Schikaneder's and Mozart's *Magic Flute*, the "Papageno syndrome." In this opera, the human bird Papageno lives happily and untroubled in his identity as such until he encounters the prince Tamino, by whom he is confronted with the fact that outside his own world, there exists another much larger world, and that his world is only a small part of that larger world: "Are you trying to tell me that beyond those mountains there are other lands and people?"[98] The fact that there are other countries and people, and most of all that there are *other*, that is *different*, people, destroys Papageno's reliance on the naturalness of his existence as a human bird. But he insists all the more on the universality of his being what he is, and when asked a question about what he lives on, he answers like this: "On eating and drinking, like *all* human beings."[99]

The Papageno question is the trauma of the Western world. No other culture has gazed so spellbound at "the others"; no other culture has dealt so insistently with other countries and people as has Western culture. As Tzvetan Todorov has shown, no other culture has learned so thoroughly to understand the other—which turned out to become the precondition for the elimination of the otherness of the other.[100] Curiosity about the other was not based on open-mindedness; it may be traced primarily to the fact that no other culture was so easily put into question by the otherness of the other.

Every time truth—*the* truth—had been laboriously arrived at, from Christianity in the Middle Ages down to the nineteenth-century ideologies explaining all of world history, there were always those other countries and people who, by their sheer existence, called that hard-won certainty into question. If the Westerner had arrived finally and felicitously, and after a long struggle, at the eternal, exclusive, and sole truth, how could other people maintain and live a different truth?

Beyond the level of ideology, the simple fact that there were people who look, think, act, and feel different could be experienced as a threat to the Westerner's own personality. His own life lost its ability to be taken for granted because of the existence of the other. If there existed so many other, and different, people, didn't this mean: *It all could be otherwise*? This question can only be answered in the affirmative by someone who has a sufficient measure of tolerance of ambiguity, that is, a "willingness to accept a state of affairs capable of alternate interpretations, or of alternate outcomes: for instance, feeling comfortable (or at least not feeling uncomfortable) when faced by a complex social issue in which opposed principles are intermingled."[101] The collective consciousness of the West, however, did not provide for the possibility that there may exist two truths on an equal footing. There could only be truth or falsehood. Either it was one's own thinking, feeling, acting that was wrong, or it was the thoughts and feelings and actions of the others. In Western culture, the former view was frequently taken by artists or adventurers fleeing civilization; but they remained a minority. The majority insisted on the universal validity of its own properties and strove to eliminate the threat of ambiguity in the world by doing away with otherness. From the time the Europeans succeeded in dominating the oceans (not least on account of the nautical knowledge of the Arabs), this project has been conducted with great effectiveness. "Since the period of the conquest, for almost three hundred and fifty years, Western Europe has tried to assimilate the other, to do away with an exterior alterity, and has in great part succeeded. Its way of life and its values have spread around the world; as Columbus wished, the colonized peoples have adopted their customs and put on clothes."[102]

Todorov names the price to be paid for this victory: "But this victory from which we all derive, Europeans and Americans both, delivers as well a terrible blow to our capacity to feel in harmony with the world, to belong to a preestablished order.... By winning on one side, the Europeans lost on the other; by imposing their superiority upon the entire country, they destroyed their own capacity to integrate themselves into the world."[103]

Furthermore, the struggle against foreignness, against "the other" on the outside, is very far from settled. The ambivalence human beings feel toward their own egos remains, and the fear of ambiguity arising from it is not cured. The foreigner inside and outside remains a problem, and globalization is labeled "successful" only where its result achieves the greatest possible identity with the Western model.

But even the total coordination of the world would not eliminate the fear of ambiguity and fear of foreignness, since the obsession with foreigners is not in need of actual foreigners. If need be, it invents its own. Today, the invented foreigner who holds innumerable people in his spell is the alien. Again, it is the West that stares spellbound at this enigmatic foreigner, while in the Islamic world no one seems particularly interested in aliens. Perhaps this is the reason that unidentified flying objects steer clear of Islamic countries. In the West, seekers of extraterrestrial life have no doubt that the existence of such beings is of prime importance for our worldview, our thinking, and feeling. In the manifesto of the "German Initiative for Exo-politics," for instance, we read: "The fact that we are not alone in the universe is of the greatest significance *for all areas of human life*. It is high time that humanity acknowledges this fact and adopts a position in the universe it shares with many other races."[104] The organization therefore requests "a scientifically-based analysis of the imminent paradigm shift on our planet, taking into account the philosophical implications of quantum physics as well as the socio-cultural challenges that accompany this significant planetary change."[105]

The search for extraterrestrial beings is not confined to cranks; neither is it confined to nongovernmental circles. Since the 1970s, government institutions like NASA and renowned academic institutions like the Ohio State University and the University of California at Berkeley have taken part in multimillion dollar radio-astronomic programs called SETI (Search for Extraterrestrial Intelligence).[106] NASA, a governmental organization of the most powerful Western country, resorted to an even more direct means of communication with aliens:

the space probes Voyager 1 and Voyager 2, sent into orbit in 1977, were equipped with disks containing messages to extraterrestrials. One of them carries greetings in 55 languages (at least one of them, supposedly, understandable to any extraterrestrial being) and music from Bach, Mozart, and Chuck Berry, which technologically well-versed intelligent beings from outer space will undoubtedly be able to listen to on their record players.[107]

As if to replay the triumph of the conquest of America, in which "Western civilization has conquered, among other reasons, because of its superiority in human communication,"[108] the extraterrestrials are stocked with records and radio signals, while radio telescopes listen for extraterrestrial messages, since it cannot but be true that extraterrestrial intelligent beings, should they exist, possess the same interests, passions, and complexes as the members of Western civilization.

"There is also hope that extraterrestrial civilizations have already discovered the Earth as an inhabited planet and are intentionally sending signals in the direction of the Earth."[109] How should one be able to understand the relaxed attitude of the Islamic peoples toward the world, and, as Todorov puts it, their "capacity to feel in harmony with the world," if one cannot even imagine extraterrestrials who are *not* interested in foreign countries and peoples, and are not troubled and perturbed by the existence of foreign, unknown worlds?

Under these conditions, the Islamic discovery of the world is bound to remain incomprehensible to Western culture, although it is doubtless an early phenomenon of *globalization*. Large parts of the Old World—from Senegal to Indonesia, from the Comoros to the Aral Sea, from Bosnia to Zanzibar—were components of a network of communicative, commercial, and cultural exchange. It was not an ideal world without fights about power and hegemony, but it was a world characterized by "an acceptance of ineradicable plurality of the world; plurality which is not a temporary station on the road to the not-yet attained perfection . . . a station sooner or later to be left behind—but the constitutive quality of existence."[110] With these words, admittedly, Zygmunt Bauman describes not the Islamic premodern period but his vision of the *postmodern era*. For him, this era is characterized by the acceptance of plurality, mentioned above, and by "a resolute emancipation from the characteristically modern urge to overcome ambivalence and promote the monosemic clarity of the sameness."[111]

Bauman's concept of the postmodern era is a hope for the future. But the premodern Islamic world, tolerant of ambiguity, was a reality. Its failure in the face of the West's *universalizing ambition* is not an unconditional result of the emergence of Western modernity, just as Western intolerance of ambiguity is not restricted to the modern era. It may also be observed that within the modern West, especially in literature and art, there are significant refuges of the culture of ambiguity. However, a survey of cultural attitudes toward the foreigner shows that a strong intolerance of ambiguity and a pull toward equalizing differentness are longstanding premodern features in many regions of Europe. As early as the sixteenth century, a great amount of cultural diversity had fallen victim to this furor, and because of this, Islamic globalization, with its acceptance of diversity, plurality, and contradictoriness, failed in the nineteenth century. Still, the very different concept of foreignness alive in the people of the Islamic world is apt to inform the conditions of a world that is tolerant of ambiguity and encourages plurality. Such a situation does not have to be conceived of as a historical era of postmodernity but is, as the example of the Islamic world shows, in principle possible at all times. However, history also shows that the apperception of foreignness and the attitude toward the foreign(er) is an essential—perhaps *the* essential—factor in the success or failure of a "modernity reconciled to its own impossibility—and determined, for better or worse, to live with it."[112]

9
In Quest of Certainty

Tolerating the resulting plurality, ambiguity,
or the lack of certainty is no error, let alone a sin.
Honest reflection shows that it is part of the price
that we inevitably pay for being human beings, and no gods.

—Stephen Toulmin, *Cosmopolis*

THE ERA OF ISLAMIC SKEPTICISM

It seems that Western observers of the Near East—and, in addition, a large percentage of the intellectuals of the Islamic world—can hardly imagine a society in which a struggle for truth does not continuously rage. But such a society seems to have been the case in large parts of the Islamic world of the postformative era. To Western eyes, this situation is not normal. Accordingly, it has been viewed as something pathological: a stagnation or even a decline; a morbid development. Scapegoats were soon at hand. It was said that "orthodoxy" had stifled any free spirit; that religious scholars, with their antireason "fiqh doctrine," had oppressed people, battled rationalism, and done away with philosophy. But such shady characters are the products of the horror chamber of European anticlericalism.[1] They have little to do with the reality of the classical Islamic world, in which there existed no organized clergy (not even among the Shiites), no suppression of philosophy and the natural sciences, and next to no trials of heretics. In fact, in the greater part of the Islamic world of the postformative era, a relative peace reigned—as compared, at any rate, to Europe's more dynamic development (to put it euphemistically). After the civil wars of the first century of Islam, religious wars comparable to those in Europe were a thing of the past. Battles about power were fought in no small number, but only rarely did they have a religious background, even if a religious legitimation was utilized from time to time (all in all, in only a few cases).

This "lack" of religious wars and of executions of heretics was not the result of clerical oppression or forced standardization of religion by rulers. It was the result of a suspension of all claims to an exclusive truth—a suspension that was largely successful due to an intensive training in ambiguity. To put it even more pointedly: The Western way was to *eliminate* ambiguity. This necessarily led to competing claims to the one and only definite truth. The only way out from the inevitable consequence of violence was the attempt to domesticate these competing *claims* (for instance, by democratic procedures, which also accomplished a sort of suspension of truth). In contrast to this, the way of classical Islam was to begin one step ahead—to have already domesticated *ambiguity*. If ambiguity can be domesticated only, not eliminated, one can avoid struggles over the truth.

But this can only succeed if the leading intellectual class possesses a thorough measure of skepticism regarding all radical claims to truth, and if society is also capable of tolerating this skepticism in a lasting way. This was achieved in large parts of the Islamic world for an amazingly long time.

The preceding chapters have shown how radically this skepticism was sustained within different areas of the Islamic disciplines, even by the mainstream of the "orthodoxy." It has become clear that, contrary to Jan Assmann's well-known hypothesis, the phenomenon of monotheism alone does not lead to an intolerance toward all competing claims to truth. For the *one* God may reveal His *one* message in *numerous* variants and furnish them with an *endless wealth* of possible interpretations. He can judge the acts of human beings, but He may either appropriate the different judgments that human beings derive from His revelation (the proponents of this position would not formulate it this way, but that is what it boils down to), or at least tolerate those who arrive at a dissenting opinion. The problem lies not in the number of gods—that is, on the transcendental side, that of the ultimate truth—but on the side of the human beings who realize or do not realize the truth, and whose scope of action is ultimately at stake.

This is exactly the side on which the Islamic scholars of the postformative period focus, for most of them are legal scholars interested in the scope of human action and knowledge, and not theologians interested in the one truth. (To be fair, the theologians of this time were also frequently interested in other things.)[2] The scholars of this time were unafraid to question even the certainties that were most apparently solid; just how little they felt that fear is clear in the discussion of the problem of whether certainty of knowledge is ever possible, since, after all, it is always mediated through *language*.

The Islamic disciplines of the postformative period have already passed one "linguistic turn." Fakhr ad-Dīn ar-Rāzī, for instance, states drily that linguistic signs (1) are arbitrary, and (2) refer not to objects of reality but to the concepts of objects in human brains. What is basic linguistic knowledge for ar-Rāzī, a scholar of the twelfth century, is for his modern editor, who gives a somewhat clueless commentary, a provocation.[3]

It is fairly well established that before Wittgenstein, no one had pondered the question of the conditions for the possibility of knowledge mediated by language as thoroughly as did the linguists, legal scholars, and philosophers writing in Arabic between the eleventh and fifteenth centuries. We have an early example of the meticulousness with which the linguistic limits of human knowledge were measured in the work *Sirr al-faṣāḥah* (The secret of eloquence) by the Syrian diplomat, poet, and rhetorician Ibn Sinān al-Khafājī (422–466/1031–1074), who was poisoned by order of the ruler of Aleppo because he had planned to establish an independent princedom. Indeed, his book on rhetoric shows that he was not content with doing things by halves. In order to fathom the preconditions imposed by language on man, he decided to start with a chapter on the physical nature of sound, based on the minor Aristotelian treatises on the natural sciences as mediated by Avicenna. More important for us is the fact that al-Khafājī endeavored—perhaps for the first time in intellectual history—to design a scientific "theory of linguistic ununderstanding." As he shows, the reason for such ununderstanding or misunderstanding (see table below) is either (1) an un- or misunderstanding of a single term (a given word is difficult to understand, or ambiguous); (2) the composition of the single terms (the author expresses himself too briefly or too circuitously); or (3) to be found in the contents. Here al-Khafājī focuses on reasons related to the perspective of the listener, who either is not sufficiently interested in the topic or has too little knowledge of it. We may remember the communications model of Ibn Juzayy, which formed the basis of his entire legal theory.[4]

Ibn Sinān's personal sufferings are expressed in the examples with which he illustrates the different causes for misunderstandings. For the urbane diplomat, the Arabic translations of Greek theories of rhetoric were important, and he applied himself with great commitment, although they apparently were quite

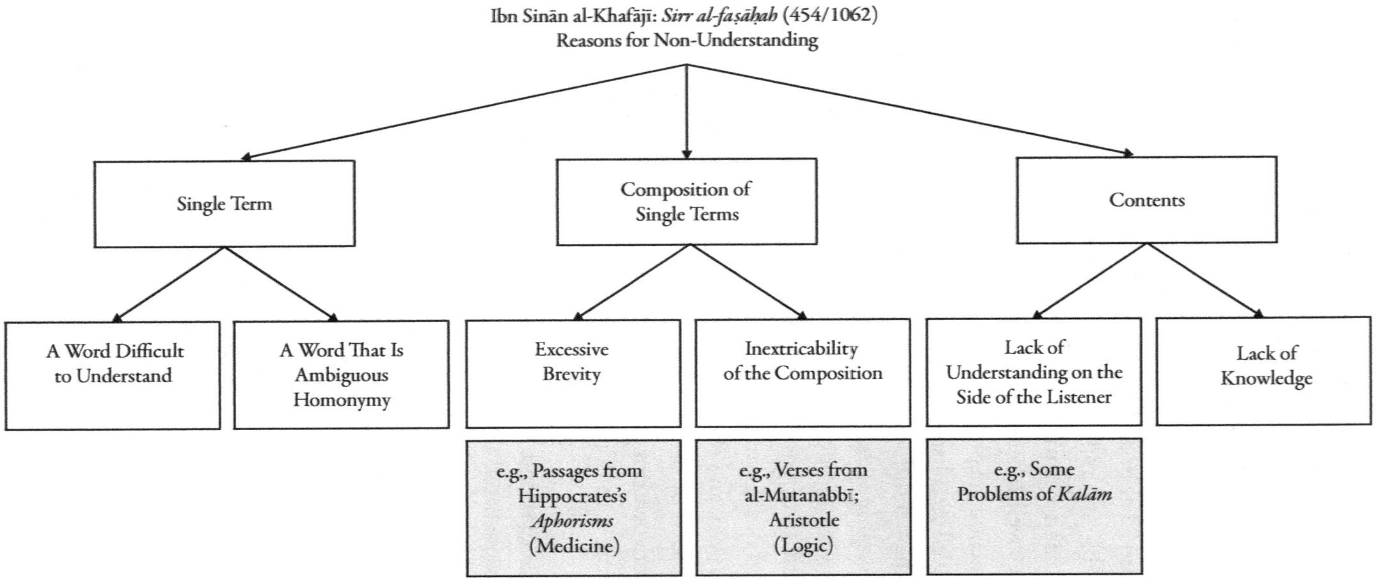
Ibn Sinān al-Khafājī: *Sirr al-faṣāḥah* (454/1062)
Reasons for Non-Understanding
Single Term
Composition of Single Terms
Contents
A Word Difficult to Understand
A Word That Is Ambiguous Homonymy
Excessive Brevity
Inextricability of the Composition
Lack of Understanding on the Side of the Listener
Lack of Knowledge
e.g., Passages from Hippocrates's *Aphorisms* (Medicine)
e.g., Verses from al-Mutanabbī; Aristotle (Logic)
e.g., Some Problems of *Kalām*

demanding. And he was irked—as were many of his contemporaries—by the linguistic provocations of the poet-genius al-Mutanabbī.

As an example of unintelligibility induced by a lack of interest on the side of the listener, he chooses (a little maliciously) the issues of "philosophical theology" (*ʿilm al-kalām*). It is mere lack of interest that is the reason why we do not understand these! But apart from personal prejudices and the intellectual fashions of his time, Ibn Sinān's considerations show, above all, how high was the degree of awareness of the limitations of knowledge mediated by language—and all knowledge is mediated by language.

Ibn Sinān was a theoretician of rhetoric who, incited by his great model Qudāmah ibn Jaʿfar, was suffused with a scientific optimism that encouraged him to grasp the fundamental situation of human communication, namely ununderstanding, through a scientific theory. Lest anyone think that Islamic religious scholars would not appropriate such linguistic skepticism, the evidence conclusively proves otherwise. One prominent example is the great compendium of the methodology of religious law, the *uṣūl al-fiqh*, by Fakhr ad-Dīn ar-Rāzī, which may claim a unique position simply by virtue of its immense influence on all following generations. Moreover, ar-Rāzī—a legal scholar, linguist, theologian, and philosopher, all at the same time—was one of the most outstanding and influential intellectuals of postformative Islam.

In his *al-Maḥṣūl* (Result) regarding the methodology of religious law, ar-Rāzī poses the question whether, in light of the fact that all knowledge of the divine order is mediated by language, certainty can be attained at all. Problems like these are presented in his book (and not only in his) in the form of a disputation between two opponents who present propositions and arguments—again, an indication of how close the science of *uṣūl* is to the discipline of rhetoric. Writing on the question of whether or not, in the process of acquiring evidence (*dalāʾil*) from written texts, one can arrive at certain results, ar-Rāzī starts out with the presentation of one position, that of someone who answers the question in the negative. One might think that the opposite position would be that of answering the question in the affirmative. In fact, such a position has been maintained, namely by the rationalist school of theology, the Muʿtazilah. But this is addressed only by ar-Rāzī's commentator. The author himself does not think this position deserves discussion. Instead, he confines himself to presenting the arguments of skeptics—and making them his own.

The position of the skeptics starts from the fact that every endeavor to gain knowledge from texts is based on premises characterized by probability, and therefore can only lead to a probabilistic judgment. The first of these premises is the correct understanding of the words and their composition. If a proof is based on a passage from the Quran or the hadith, it has to be first ensured that we know the meaning of the employed words and the grammatical rules according to which they are composed. Our knowledge of classical Arabic vocabulary is due to the lexicographers, who were by no means infallible. The rules of classical Arabic grammar (that is, of the language of the Quran and the hadith) are essentially derived from ancient Arabic poetry. If one uses the same standard for the transmission of poetry as for that of the hadith, one must conclude that Arabic poetry does not meet the requirements of the criteria one would use for an impeccable hadith, not least because the first links of the transmission (of a poem) are quite unknown. It must be kept in mind that certain knowledge cannot be attained even through a flawless hadith, but can be attained only through a hadith transmitted so widely that it excludes any error (the term is, as has been mentioned before, *mutawātir*). But this can hardly be maintained for poetry. In addition, there is the fact that the poets themselves are certainly not beyond doubt; time and again, the grammarians have demonstrated their errors, which ar-Rāzī parades with relish over many pages.[5]

After ar-Rāzī has thoroughly demolished our trust in our knowledge of the Arabic lexicon and Arabic syntax and morphology, there follows a volley of further conditions for the attainability of certain knowledge from texts. The precondition of (1) knowledge of the lexicon and grammar is followed by the premise (2) that there is no case of polysemy, that is, that a word is not meant in another way than one would suppose. Premise (3) excludes the possibility that a term is meant metaphorically, (4) that its meaning is according to technical terminology and not common usage, (5) that anything is omitted ("Forbidden to you is carrion," meaning "*to eat* carrion"?), (6) that there is a specified, not a generally accepted, meaning, (7) that there is an abrogation, (8) that there is a syntactical switch, and (9) that the statement contradicts reason, since transmission cannot contradict reason, reason being the precondition of transmission.[6]

None of these premises, however, exists without a trace of doubt. In the final analysis, we may say only that "we have done our best" (*ijtahadnā*) without discovering any of these sources of error. In such a final judgment, however, there is no absolute certitude. The final conclusion must be: arguing about transmission, which inevitably is based on language, always results only in hypothetical knowledge.[7]

This is an established fact for ar-Rāzī (*thabata*). But where is the opposite standpoint? It is represented by ar-Rāzī himself—but his opposite standpoint accepts the arguments of the first standpoint without reservations. His sole objection is: If there exists a context that is based on the testimony of an eyewitness or that meets the criterion of overwhelming frequency of transmission (*mutawātir*), then certainty is possible. In order to admit this much, no more than one brief sentence is enough for ar-Rāzī; it is the end of a long chapter in which he makes every endeavor to destroy the basis of belief in the possibility of attaining certainty. It is only too obvious that, according to ar-Rāzī, the line between the two standpoints is defined as a line between radical skepticism and reasonable skepticism, both of which expose as a delusion the possibility of attaining certain knowledge.

To summarize: The world of postformative Islam was not one of certainties but one of probabilities. This is, to say the least, a reason for the fact that the socially leading group was that of the legal scholars, not that of the theologians. The certainties of belief demanded by the theologians were few, and they were largely uncontested. The legal scholars seldom demanded certainties, but confined themselves mostly to domesticating and making habitable the world of ambiguities. And quite as jurisprudence, which strove for probability (rather than theology, which strove for certainty), had established itself as the most important religious science, so the discipline of rhetoric, whose domain is probability, had established itself as the epistemologically leading discipline (rather than philosophy, with its pursuit of truth). The proximity between jurisprudence and rhetoric is obvious. Ibn Khaldūn treats the discipline of the methodology of jurisprudence together with the art of disputation (*ʿilm al-jadal*),[8] and, in fact, works on disputation deal primarily with problems that are objects of the methodology of jurisprudence.[9] The compendium of the theory of rhetoric that attracted the most commentaries in the Islamic world was the *Talkhīṣ* of al-Qazwīnī; it was read in virtually every madrasah from Mauretania to Central Asia. One of its most astute commentators, Bahāʾ ad-Dīn as-Subkī, justly declared that the greatest part of the methodology of jurisprudence consists in nothing other than *ʿilm al-maʿānī* (science of meanings), a subdiscipline of the classical Arabic theory of rhetoric, comparable to the modern discipline of pragmatics.[10]

This era of skepticism, in which jurisprudence and rhetoric were the leading sciences, began, at the latest, with the so-called *Sunni revival* in the tenth and eleventh century, and ended during the time of European colonialism in the nineteenth century. It was this colonialism that confronted the Islamic world not only with its military and economic supremacy, but also with its claims to truth, formulated according to theological and philosophical patterns that could be dealt with only by following the argumentative patterns of theology and philosophy. This was the beginning of the phase of the *theologization* of Islam, which continues to the present day. Not accidentally, it is Ḥanbalism, the form of Islam that from the outset was theologically rather than jurisprudentially motivated, that lent itself most easily to modernization. The old theological school called Muʿtazilah also finds its supporters today, most of all among liberal reform Muslims who, by their rationalist approach, promise themselves a chance at the modernization of Islam.[11] In the West, it has become a veritable stereotype to lament the decline (no talk about suppression) of Muʿtazilite thought, and even to declare this decline responsible for the plight of contemporary Islam. The clear-sighted pioneer of modern Islamic studies, Ignaz Goldziher, had already realized that the Muʿtazilite fanaticism for truth represents the most radical and intolerant manifestation of classical Islam. Today we have grown so used to viewing the Muʿtazilah as something positive (whereas in fact it comes closer than any other Islamic movement to the Western approach to religion) that Goldziher's 1910 account seems to be forgotten. The following extensive quotation from his *Introduction to Islamic Theology and Law* is therefore appropriate:

> All that we have learned so far about the nature of the Muʿtazilite movement confers on these religious philosophers the right to lay claim to the name of rationalists. . . . But is that enough for calling them liberal? That title we must certainly refuse them. They are in fact, with the formulas they directed against orthodox conceptions, the very founders of theological dogmatism in Islam. . . . With their definitions, it is true, they meant to bring reason and religion into harmony. But to a conservative traditionalism unencumbered with definitions they opposed rigid and narrow formulas, and engaged in endless disputations to maintain them. Moreover, they were intolerant in the extreme. A tendency to intolerance lies in the nature of the endeavor to frame religious belief in dogma. During the reign of three ʿAbbāsid caliphs, when the Muʿtazilites were fortunate enough to have their doctrines recognized as state dogma, those doctrines were urged by means of inquisition, imprisonment, and terror until, before long, a counterreformation once again allowed those Muslims to breathe freely for whom religion was the sum of pious traditions, and not the result of dubious ratiocination.[12]

It will not escape the attention of readers of this passage that the roots of Western modernity are, in fact, struggles about monopolies of truth, in the manner in which the Muʿtazilites represented such monopolies. But in Islam, their dogmatism did not ultimately prevail. In the centuries to come, the "old, pious believers" would utilize ever more refined intellectual strategies to fathom the foundations of their belief. Their zeal in the linguistic disciplines, in rhetoric, and in textual exegesis was no less rationalist than the zeal of the Muʿtazilites, but it was not directed at establishing a dogmatism, since it was precisely their scientific activity that brought them to realize the limits of the human capacity for knowledge.

When traditional Islam was first confronted with Western modernity's claim to universal truth, Islam's approach to religion, incapable of dogmatism as it was, turned out to be largely incompatible with that of the West. In this confrontation, however, the power structure was the other way around: The "Muʿtazilites" of the West possessed all the power, against which the "old believers" could only set their knowledge and culture—and these, under the new conditions, were no longer worth anything.

Inevitably, a new orientation developed, which meant the transformation of Islam according to the Western (and also the erstwhile Muʿtazilite) episteme. The result—a dogmatic Islam that announces simple and comprehensive claims to truth—has proved compatible with modernity. If, for many people today, this Islam appears to be "medieval," this is a result of the law of asynchronicity, according to which non-Western societies that emulate the West begin to fulfill the standards of the West at the precise moment when those standards are not valid anymore.

It is an established view in modern Islamic studies that the *Islamism* of our day is not a restorative movement, let alone a traditionalist one. Rather, Islamism is a phenomenon of the *modernization* of an Islam that cannot (and does not wish to) base its epistemological foundations on classical Islam (which, the Islamists maintain, was a distorted, decadent Islam), but adopts the epistemological foundations of the Enlightenment and modernity. This becomes apparent in the terminology of the Islamists, who consider Islam the truest system (*niẓām*) and the truest method (*manhaj*)—that is, it is subsumed under the terminology of the Cartesian worldview.

No classical author would have been able to make sense of terms like *niẓām islāmī* and *manhaj islāmī*. The classical Islamic sciences present a pluralistic approach to Islam. Theology, jurisprudence, and Sufism differ in their methods and in their epistemological foundations; they pose different questions, and by no means give identical answers to identical questions. Modern Islamism, by contrast, strives for a uniform and universally valid approach that comprehends all areas with one single method and according to one single principle. This Islamist project is, in the words of Ahmad S. Moussalli, "simultaneously the scientification of epistemological Islamism and the Islamisation of science. It systematizes all the basic doctrines of Islamism—*tawhid*, *hakimiyyah*, *jahiliyyah*, science, textual authority, human thought and jurisprudence—into a body of coherent epistemology that can absorb all disciplines of knowledge. It uses Western concepts in Islamic garments and tries to overcome the theoretical difficulties by combining Islamic thought and Western thought."[13]

Here, too, the representatives of a "modern" reformist Islam and Islamists show themselves to be twins, for, as Moussalli writes, "both modernist thinkers and Islamist projects develop substantively a modern Islamic theory of knowledge that Islamises basic modern epistemological issues like phenomenology, historicism and relativism, as well as concepts like democracy and state."[14]

Today, Islam is enacting a transition that Europe carried out around the year 1600. It is this transition that is primarily responsible for the separate European route (*sonderweg*) and is the reason that the premodern and modern history of the Islamic world and Europe have followed such different paths. In order to understand this part of Islamic history, we have to understand that transition in European history.

SONDERWEGE

The problem of what triggered Western modernity, and what ultimately caused the separate route of the West, has been discussed innumerable times and in the most controversial constellations. Most authors, who admittedly think that Western modernity is a good thing, begin their analysis with the assumption that the roots of this modernity must be searched for in some phenomenon through which the West distinguished itself from all other cultures in a positive way. But as soon as these theories go beyond very sweeping or not very meaningful formulations, they all call upon phenomena that also exist outside of Europe—not exactly in the same form, but in a similar manner. This is true for the free market economy, individualism, the division of labor, secularism, and the differentiation between social subsystems. All these phenomena are also to be found in certain times in the classical Islamic world or in classical China; most of them can be found in both cultures. In fact, it can be demonstrated that "virtually every factor that its proponents have identified with the 'European miracle' can be found in other parts of the world."[15]

A stronger analytical power is contained in approaches that start out with the assumption that the roots of modernity are not to be found in a positive phenomenon; after all, modernity also has its dark side, which manifested itself only too obviously in the totalitarian systems of the twentieth century. Thus it is not at all inconceivable that Western modernity must also be interpreted as an attempt to cope with a fundamental cultural deficit, and may constitute a reaction to problems that other, happier cultures did not have. On the other hand, it stands to reason that Western modernity did not have a single root (which, if it existed, should be identifiable with some certainty), but had several roots.

All these theoretical flaws are avoided by the Canadian historian of science Stephen Toulmin, who, in his perspicacious book *Cosmopolis*, gives an account of the prehistory of modernity that is convincing, not least in view of the history of the Islamic world.[16] Toulmin's central thesis is that Western modernity originally grows from two roots that are in no way causally connected to each other, even though one follows the other chronologically. The first is the humanism of the Renaissance, which is characterized by skepticism—in the sense of openness to different approaches to truth—and tolerance. It is represented by names like Montaigne, Erasmus, and Machiavelli. The second is the rationalism of Descartes, with his attempt to put the central kinds of human knowledge on clear, distinct, and reliable foundations:

> The key features of the modern age were products not of a single intellectual origin, but of two distinct beginnings. The first was embodied in the Renaissance humanists, from Erasmus on, who lived in times of relative prosperity, and built up a culture of "reasonableness" and religious toleration. The second beginning was embodied in the 17th-century rationalists, starting with Descartes, who reacted to times of economic crisis—when toleration seemed a failure and religion took to the sword—by giving up the modest skepticism of the humanists, and looking for "rational" proofs to underpin our beliefs with a certainty neutral as between all religious positions.[17]

A decisive historical date, writes Toulmin, is the assassination of the French king Henry IV in 1610. This marks the end of an age of tolerance (a tolerance, *nota bene*, in regard to different interpretations of Christianity, not in regard to non-Christian religions). It must be kept in mind that Catholicism and Protestantism were much more similar to each other than were, for instance, Islam in its Ḥanbalite school in the interpretation of Ibn Taymiyyah, on the one hand, and a Sufism inspired by Ibn al-ʿArabī's concept of the "unity of all being" on the other. Nevertheless, this difference did not lead to wars, and in spite of all the polemics on both sides, a slogan such as that of the Catholic league—"*Un roi, une loi, une foi*"—would have met with incomprehension in the Islamic world, in which the right to exist, even for Jews, Christians, and Zoroastrians, was never challenged.

"In practical terms, Henry's murder carried to people in France and Europe the simple message, that 'a policy of religious toleration was tried, and failed.' For the next forty years, in all the major powers of Europe, the tide flowed the other way."[18] It is certainly not by chance that, according to Robert Muchembled, a decisive intensification of sexual surveillance and repression can be observed exactly at this time in Europe, an intensification manifested in stricter marital jurisdiction following the council of Trent (1545–1563), and closer surveillance of marital sex:

> The end of the optimistic humanist dreams, finally buried at the Council of Trient in 1563, on which Catholics and Protestants each scattered purificatory salt, was enough to destabilize the intellectuals. Thinking on the margins became increasingly suspect and dangerous.... The Self bent before the storm.[19]
>
> Protestants and Catholics vied with each other in zeal by claiming to assure Christian salvation more effectively than their enemies. Marriage increasingly attracted their attention.... The intellectuals of this generation often rejected the irenicism of the Erasmians, that is, the optimistic conception of relations between the Creator and humankind. This way of thinking had dominated the humanism of the 1520s, in the wake of Erasmus himself, of Thomas More in England, of Rabelais in France.... Their heirs of the 1560s saw things very differently, as they observed the religious chaos then turning into terrible and cruel wars of religion, in France, England and the Low Countries.[20]

The longer the Thirty Years' War raged and the more brutal it became, "the more firmly convinced the proponents of each religious system were that their doctrines *must be* proved correct, and that their opponents were stupid, malicious, or both."[21]

And Toulmin continues:

> By 1620, people in positions of political power and theological authority in Europe no longer saw Montaigne's pluralism as a viable intellectual option, any more than Henry's tolerance was for them a practical option. The humanists' readiness to live with uncertainty, ambiguity, and differences of opinion had done nothing (in their view) to prevent religious conflict from getting out of hand: *ergo* (they inferred) it had helped *cause* the worsening state of affairs. If skepticism let one down, certainty was more urgent. It might not be obvious what one was supposed to be certain about, but *un*certainty had become *un*acceptable.... If uncertainty, ambiguity, and the acceptance of pluralism

> led, in practice, only to an intensification of the religious war, the time had come to discover some *rational method* for demonstrating the essential correctness or incorrectness of philosophical, scientific, or theological doctrines. . . . If Europeans were to avoid falling into a skeptical morass, they had, it seemed, to find *something* to be "certain" about.[22]

Here we come to the second root of modernity, the "quest for certainty"[23] that would shape Western history in the centuries to come and would become a pillar of Western modernity. Based on Descartes, who "set out to place the central areas of human knowledge on 'foundations' that are 'clear, distinct, and certain,' "[24] the rational program "outshone the modest, skeptical lights of the Renaissance humanists."[25]

> The Cartesian program for philosophy swept aside the "reasonable" uncertainties and hesitations of 16th-century skeptics, in favor of new, mathematical kinds of "rational" certainty and proof. In this, it may . . . lead philosophy into a dead end. But, for the time being, that change of attitude—the devaluation of the oral, the particular, the local, the timely, and the concrete—appeared a small price to pay for a formally "rational" theory grounded on abstract, universal, timeless concepts. In a world governed by these intellectual goals, rhetoric was of course subordinate to logic: the validity and truth of "rational" arguments is independent of *who* presents them, *to whom*, or *in what context*—such rhetorical questions can contribute nothing to the impartial establishment of human knowledge. For the first time since Aristotle, logical analysis was separated from, and elevated far above, the study of rhetoric, discourse and argumentation.[26]

The Islamic world had thoroughly adopted ancient Logic and Dialectics and integrated them with philosophy, theology, and jurisprudence, where they were to have a permanent place. But while logic and dialectic have prime importance for philosophy and theology, in jurisprudence that prime position is occupied only by rhetoric. If jurisprudence becomes the leading discipline, rhetoric accompanies it; it is significant that in as-Sakkākī's *Key to the Sciences*, the most influential standard work on the classical Arabic theory of rhetoric, "Dialectics," turns up as an appendix to "Rhetoric."

This privileged position of rhetoric also characterizes the subsequent Islamic centuries. Only the curricula designed by colonial powers would eliminate it from the syllabus of the Islamic countries.[27] Religious pluralism, regarding both the inner-Islamic spectrum and the non-Muslim communities, was a characteristic of the Ottoman Empire. Law, philosophy, and Sufism offered quite diverse interpretations of Islam, even within their respective disciplines. Literature indulged in the enjoyment of ambiguity and developed, in the form of the chronogram, a new and enthusiastically received device to express equivocation. In the Islamic world, "toleration of diversity, ambiguity and uncertainty—the hallmarks of Renaissance culture and rhetoric"[28] continues to exist, while in Europe it ends for a time.

The decisive break between European and Islamic history must be set at exactly this point: "In choosing as the goals of Modernity an intellectual and practical agenda that set aside the tolerant, skeptical attitude of the 16th-century humanists and focused on the 17th-century pursuit of mathematical exactitude and logical rigor, intellectual certainty and moral purity, Europe set itself on a cultural and political road that has led both to its most striking technical successes and to its deepest human failures."[29]

This development applies to *all* spheres of human life. For instance, the pursuit of "moral purity" expresses itself in a new wave of intensified sexual repression, which now begins to focus on masturbation. "If there is one area in which sexual repression was particularly apparent in the Enlightenment, it is that of the sin of Onan, in other words, masturbation,"[30] writes Robert Muchembled. Stronger than before, the policing of sex extends to the individual's way of thinking and feeling:

> Things changed, gradually but radically, between the middle of the sixteenth and the end of the seventeenth century. Expressed in laws and moral regulations, a vigorous and spectacular sexual repression was put in place with the support of the churches and states now seeking to impose their will by controlling bodies as closely as souls.[31] . . . The seventeenth century certainly saw a powerful de-sexualization, which even affected the legally constituted couple, who were now enjoined to perform their conjugal duties without seeking sensual enjoyment.[32]

As a matter of fact, the histories of the West and the Islamic world went separate ways twice. The first separation took place when the ancient urban culture in the Western Roman Empire collapsed, while it continued to exist in the East and was carried on by the Islamic empire of the Abbasids at a highly complex level, partly on Roman and partly on Persian foundations. The break between Antiquity and the "Middle Ages" that characterizes the history of Western Europe is absent from the East of the Mediterranean world. Therefore, it makes no sense to talk of the "Islamic Middle Ages."[33]

From the twelfth century onwards, Europe gradually reached a level—partly with the help of Islamic culture—that corresponded to that of the Islamic world. In their living conditions, their mentality, their feelings and passions, the Near East and Europe were probably never as close, since Antiquity, as they were in the fifteenth and sixteenth centuries. But then it was once again Europe that went its separate way (*sonderweg*) with its project of the search for certainty.

Toulmin is certainly right when he recognizes the decisive catalysts of this *sonderweg* in the bloody religious conflicts and religious wars of the sixteenth and seventeenth centuries. Since its very first centuries, the Islamic Near East had not witnessed religious conflicts on such a scale. The reason for this, I believe, is that well into the nineteenth century, the people of the Islamic world were able to preserve a high degree of tolerance of ambiguity, which was at risk only rarely and only in few geographical regions. But why did Western and Middle Europe not experience a comparable tolerance of ambiguity in the Early Modern Age?

With all caution, a quite tentative hypothesis may be proffered here. It suggests that Late Antiquity and the so-called Middle Ages saw developments that resulted in a feeling of *ambivalence* experienced by individuals with regard to themselves. The experience of ambivalence tends to lead to *intolerance of ambiguity*. In the Near East, these developments either did not occur, or, within the strengthened formation of Islamic culture, were reversed. In Europe, however, they led to an extended period of strong intolerance of ambiguity, ultimately resulting in what constitutes—in both its good and bad senses—the "European *sonderweg*."

I consider the following three factors to be particularly important: (1) In postformative Islam, the conviction had gained general acceptance that even a serious sinner is not doomed to eternal punishment as long as he professes Islam. And there was no church that could make people compliant by threatening the torments of hell. In Western Christianity, the concept of *sin* was much more central than it was in Islam, which in fact does not know the idea of original sin. Someone who has learned to see himself as a damned creature of sin is more apt to develop an ambivalent relation to himself than is someone who meets God, first and foremost, as the Merciful.

This mechanism is enhanced by a second factor, namely (2) Western Christianity's hostility, the most radical one in world history, to the body and sex—an animosity that for centuries condemned as a cardinal sin even the sensual consummation of the marital act and the mere thought of sexual joy, and conveyed to all a very ambivalent relation to their bodies.

Finally, the fact must be mentioned that (3) Europe's societies were characterized for most of their history by a *class concept* of origin, in the sense that persons of different estates were, in principle, different kinds of human beings. The struggle against this concept imbued the course of European history with a dynamic that extended into modern times via the French Revolution. In contrast, the Near East never entertained such a concept. Here, social mobility was downright boundless, and there are abundant examples of lower-class children who were able to become acclaimed poets or leading scholars or holders of the highest public offices. For a long time, the United States has cultivated the (mostly illusory) idea of "dishwasher to millionaire"; this has contributed to a vast identification with the prevailing social system. In the Near East, one could, in fact, be a slave and become a ruler. Although this opportunity was granted to few, the experience of being doomed to a subordinate position simply because of one's origin was alien to the people of the Near East. This counts as another important reason for the lack of an ambivalent view of the self.

This catalog may not be complete, but there is good reason to assume that in some periods of postancient Europe, these three factors caused a very strong ambivalence with regard to one's own personhood, which in turn resulted in a low level of tolerance of ambiguity. This development, it seems, culminated in the religious wars of the Early Modern Age and in the project of founding societies upon indubitable certainties. Ultimately, it has led to the movements described above.

If we follow Toulmin's argument, we may interpret the European history of the subsequent centuries as an attempt to come to grips with the rationalist project of the seventeenth century. Frequently, a move away from rationalism was followed by a countermovement that made even more vehement claims to the sole truth. Even the totalitarianisms of the twentieth century are a part of this development: "The Second World War, then, represented the culmination of social and historical processes that began in the 1650s, with the creation of the Modern era—the 'modern' world, the 'modern' state, and 'modern' thought. As such, it was the last time when the people of Europe could endorse, and act out, the ideals and ambitions of Modernity in a quite *unselfconscious* manner."[34]

Since its European colonization, the Near East has inadvertently become a part of this controversy. It has been handed the conflicts staged in Europe since the seventeenth century as a kind of belated and unwanted heritage, and it can hardly be blamed for the fact that in coping with this heritage, it has not attained the status Europe has achieved.

The accomplishments that we in Western democracies enjoy in the beginning of the twenty-first century are by no means a direct gift of the Enlightenment.

But this is exactly what is suggested by texts that reduce all deficiencies in the Islamic world to the observation that Islam has never seen an age of Enlightenment. However, the tolerant attitudes of which today's West is so rightly proud—from religious pluralism to the rejection of racism and the rights of women and gay people—are not the direct result of the Enlightenment. They are the consequence of a long and bloody strife against its mortgage. To quote Toulmin again:

> The culture and society of 17th-century Europe were transformed by changes that set aside the tolerance of late Renaissance humanism for more rigorous theories and demanding practices: these changes culminated in the new cosmopolis built around the formal structure of mathematical physics. After 1750, that change was undone, bit by bit. The history of science and philosophy from 1650 to 1950 was not simply a triumphal procession of geniuses building on the work of their predecessors: rather, it had both light and shade, both an up and a down side. As the experience of humanity was collected and digested, the fundamental picture of nature went through major changes, the presuppositions of the new cosmopolis were discredited, and by the mid-20th century the demolition was complete. At that point, thought and practice were free to return to the vision of the Renaissance.[35]

If there is some stage of Western history that has bypassed the Islamic world, it is the "re-renaissance" that Toulmin places in the decade 1965–1975. In contrast, developments in the Near East ran in the opposite direction. Confronted with the universalizing claim of the West, the Islamic world in the era of imperialism launched a new search for axiomatic truth and suppressed its old tolerance of ambiguity and its plurality. Decolonization did not bring about an easing of tension. The British and French powers cut up the Arab world with senseless borders, creating new states ruled by dictators who, for better or for worse, committed themselves to Western powers (the Soviet Union, too, was a Western power) in order to retain their rule.

Their favored ideology was nationalism, modeled after the Western example and largely oriented toward secularism. However, it was not only the ideologies of the West that were exported, but also its problems and conflicts. For example, as a reaction to *Western* anti-Semitism, a new colonial state emerged in the middle of the *Arab* world. During the wars that subsequently ravaged the Near East, its world divided itself along the ideological borders delineated by the Cold War. The hopes for social advancement that the educated middle class had anticipated by subscribing to the nationalist-secular ideology were fulfilled only for a minority. The discontented population whose voice was silenced by the ruling elite was controlled by massive repressions. No civil society could develop under these conditions. For the bourgeoisie, religion was the only forum that was outside the ideological and police-controlled reach of the ruling oligarchies. It was therefore inevitable that after the collapse of Western ideologies, primarily nationalism, a new ideological orientation in the Near East could only happen within the framework of religion.

In a way, this situation resembled the conditions in the classical period, when religious discourses—in particular, the law—frequently constituted a bulwark of the middle and lower bourgeoisie against the claim to power of the military elite. And yet, ultimately, the modern situation was completely different. The modern state demands substantially more kinds of interventions than do traditional forms of political rule, and it also has the power to usurp these modes of intervention. A juridical self-empowerment of the bourgeoisie, as had been the practice of traditional Islamic law, could no longer be tolerated. In addition, the traditional religious elite had largely lost its influence in the course of the Westernization of the Near East; during the century between 1850 and 1950, it had to cede almost all its competences to the modern state and finally even lost sovereignty over religious discourses. Initially, the new religious discourses were dominated primarily by people who were not professional experts on religion but had received a Western-secular education. Even now, the percentage of physicians and engineers in political Islamism is high. On the contrary, a traditional religious education is quite scarce in this milieu.

This is one among several reasons that the new religious discourses are frequently oriented toward Western ideologies. Perhaps an even more important reason is that political and social development in the Near East of the second half of the twentieth century was not exactly conducive to the advancement of a new tolerance of ambiguity. While in the West a "re-renaissance," as Toulmin calls it, blossomed, challenging the belief in a sole truth and bringing about a social liberalization (not least in the field of sex), repression continued to increase in the dictatorships of the Near East. In 1966, when in Germany the "nonparliamentary opposition" (APO) took shape, Sayyid Quṭb in Egypt was executed and became the most important martyr of political Islamism. It can hardly be denied that the events subsumed under the term "the '68 movement"—even taking that movement's ambivalence into account—have ultimately contributed to a consolidation of democracy and the plurality of opinions in the West. The Near East, plagued with wars, dictatorships, and ideological struggles (in which the West was not uninvolved) lacks precisely this development. To put it in a too-pointed way: it was not the accomplishments of the Enlightenment that never made it to the Near East; it was the '68 movement. Or, to put it a little less boldly: doubting the claim to ideological truth and about the possibility of explaining the world by one sole comprehensive theory (in the sense of Toulmin's "re-renaissance") is, in the contemporary Islamic world, the less attractive option. Also, "in the bloody theological deadlock of the Thirty Years' War, philosophical skepticism became *less*, and certainty *more*, attractive."[36]

This insight should have consequences for how the West deals with the Islamic world, because that Western attitude contributes to the aggravation of ideological tensions in the Near East. The example of modern Iran is instructive. In 1979, this Islamic country freed itself through its own efforts from one of the worst Near Eastern dictatorships—and promptly became the archenemy of the West, which brought about sanctions and armed the still worse Iraqi dictator, inciting him to a war against Iran that led to millions of victims. Particularly strange afterwards was the West's amazement that in Iran, the liberal forces had still failed to prevail!

Even today, the situation has not fundamentally changed. Several Islamic states are occupied by Western troops; the occupation and colonization of Palestine by Israel is almost unquestioningly tolerated by the West; almost all countries between the Atlantic Ocean and India make military bases available to the United States and other Western countries[37] and those that do not comply are (or were, until only recently) assigned to an "axis of evil." Every Near Eastern politician who merely uses the word "Islam" is considered to be an Islamist and hence an enemy of the West. Free elections in the Near East are not wanted by the West, which fears the danger of a victory of Islamist parties. In every Near Eastern region where the tender plant of democracy was seen to sprout a little too much, leading to strong showings by Islam-oriented parties, there followed either sanctions and boycotts or military interventions. This is not a good soil for a skeptical worldview of multiple perspectives.

There is much evidence that the West today, as so often in its history, receives a part of its identity from the enemy stereotype of Islam. The distorted image of an essentially violent, antidemocratic, intractable Islam, and finally the monstrous bugbear of Islamism threatening Western freedoms, are what ultimately motivate the political actions of Western protagonists dealing with the Islamic world. However, they thereby impede the reduction of ideological conflicts in the Near East. Contrary to what is frequently assumed in the West, radical Islamism is far from the political position favored by people in the Islamic world. On the other hand, in the foreseeable future, no political movement that does *not* base itself on Islam, in one or another manner, will be able to gain a wide base. Today, the currents of political Islam are manifold, and the political aims of their representatives are highly diverse. The broad public debate that could start from this point often breaks down due to censure by political interdictions. Instead of allowing such a debate, some regimes seek their refuge in Islamization from above. Often, governments that are close allies of the West champion a narrow-minded, dogmatic Islam because they hope to take the wind out of the sails of the Islamic political forces that want to gain influence by democratic means. These governments can frequently count on Western consent. But such tactics impede the inevitable process of democratization in the Near East, which simply cannot happen without including Islamist movements.

In the area of ambiguity, European culture cannot boast of many achievements, apart from visual arts and music—these constituting, in many circumstances, the refuge where ambiguity, socially outlawed, could thrive. Polyphonic music and "the impossible work of art,"[38] the opera, are without doubt achievements that contribute to the eternal glory of the Western world in the area of ambiguity-oriented culture. In the social sphere, it is certainly democracy that constitutes the greatest Western achievement in the matter of ambiguity. Its way, however, is lined by hecatombs of victims. It took half a millennium and some of the most terrible wars of humanity before the inability to sustain different truths side by side was replaced by the process of suspension of truth that is democracy.

The process of democracy, however, has prevailed in the West only because, for a long time, the West did not command sufficient tolerance of ambiguity to warrant peaceful coexistence among people. In the Near East, where for centuries this kind of obsession with truth and intolerance of ambiguity did not exist, the pressure to introduce the democratic process was not strong enough. Today things are different, and it is in the interest of all to give in to this pressure. The West should be conscious of the fact that the introduction of the truth-suspending process of democracy must be accompanied by the mental termination of an ambiguity-intolerant claim to truth. Quite to the contrary, I consider the sinister Western alliance of *fear of ambiguity*, *obsession with truth*, and *universalizing ambition* to be very much alive today, especially in dealing with Islam and with the people of the Near East, but also in the debate about integration at home.

All surveys show that the overwhelming majority of Muslims worldwide endorse democracy.[39] But a large percentage of these Muslims live in a region regarded by the West as one of its prime spheres of interest. In a globalized world such as we have, the democratization of the Islamic world cannot succeed if the Western powers do not cooperate. This cooperation must begin with a decision to give up, in dealings with the Islamic world, the triad of fear of ambiguity, obsession with truth, and universalizing ambition, and to follow the process of democratization favorably, even if it takes courses that do not seem to be in the interests of the West.

The "other" will never adopt one's own truths. But this is threatening only if it is believed that there are no truths apart from one's own. One can tolerate the fact that there are other truths besides one's own beliefs only if the act of acknowledging other truths does not lead to inevitably giving up or relativizing one's own truths.

This presupposes that one accepts the polysemous character of the world, which in turn presupposes a high degree of tolerance of ambiguity. Such tolerance of ambiguity can only prosper if human beings do not have a feeling of unease with themselves; this is possible only if they are met with respect. In the interaction between the West and the Near East, the Western universalizing ambition continues to present a great obstacle. It would be appropriate to have greater trust in the ability of the people of the Islamic world to find, through controversial debates, their own way to democracy. All attempts to control such a process through Western intervention are bound to fail. A better way would be to do less and allow for more.

After innumerable struggles that claimed countless victims, the thinkers of the Western world have finally brought themselves to accept a skeptical approach to dogmatic claims to truth. But in the mentality of many of the people of the Western world, this new approach is by no means firmly rooted. Up until now, the Western world cannot be characterized as explicitly tolerant of ambiguity. It is time that the West, in its relation to the Islamic world, recognizes the ideas of its own intellectuals, ideas that would make it possible for the people of the Near East to find their way back to their old tolerance of ambiguity. There are intellectuals like Max Born, the Nobel laureate of Physics, who said:

> I am convinced that concepts such as absolute rightness, absolute accuracy, conclusive truth, etc., are phantoms which should not be admitted in any science. . . . This loosening of thought appears to me to be the greatest blessing which today's science has brought us. After all, the belief in one sole truth and the imagination to be its exclusive owner is the deepest root of all evil in the world.[40]

Notes

FOREWORD

1. Shahab Ahmed, *What Is Islam? The Importance of Being Islamic* (Princeton, NJ, 2015); Frank Griffel, "Contradictions and Lots of Ambiguity: Two New Perspectives on Premodern (and Postclassical) Islamic Societies," *Bustan: The Middle East Book Review* 8, no. 1 (2017): 1–21.
2. Frank Griffel, *Den Islam Denken: Versuch, eine Religion zu verstehen* (Stuttgart, 2018).
3. Thomas Bauer, *Die Vereindeutigung der Welt: Über den Verlust an Mehrdeutigkeit und Vielfalt* (Stuttgart, 2018).

INTRODUCTION

1. Karl Kraus, *Magie der Sprache: Ein Lesebuch*, 3rd ed. (Frankfurt, 1979), 43.
2. Thomas Bauer, *Liebe und Liebesdichtung in der arabischen Welt des 9. und 10. Jahrhunderts: Eine literatur- und mentalitätsgeschichtliche Studie des arabischen Ghazal* (Wiesbaden, 1998); Syrinx von Hees, "Historische Anthropologie in der Islamwissenschaft," in *Islamwissenschaft als Kulturwissenschaft*, ed. Stephan Conermann and Syrinx von Hees, vol. 1, *Historische Anthropologie: Ansätze und Möglichkeiten* (Bonn, 2007), 21–35.
3. Maxime Rodinson, *Europe and the Mystique of Islam*, trans. Roger Veinus (London, 2002).
4. Adam Mez, *The Renaissance of Islam*, trans. Salahuddin Khuda Bukhsh and David Samuel Margoliouth (London, 1937); Joel L. Kraemer, *Humanism in the Renaissance of Islam: The Cultural Revival During the Buyid Age* (Leiden, 1992).
5. Wael B. Hallaq, "Was ash-Shafiʿi the Master Architect of Islamic Jurisprudence?," in *International Journal of Middle East Studies* 25 (1993), 587–605.

1. CULTURAL AMBIGUITY

1. Jürgen Gerhards, *Die Moderne und ihre Vornamen* (Wiesbaden, 2003), 58.
2. Gerhards, *Die Moderne und ihre Vornamen*, 59.

3. "Toleranz," Wikipedia.de, accessed November 7, 2006, http://de.wikipedia.org/wiki/Toleranz.
4. Hadumod Bußmann, *Lexikon der Sprachwissenschaft* (Stuttgart, 1990), 75; see also Norbert Fries, *Ambiguität und Vagheit: Einführung und kommentierte Bibliographie* (Tübingen, 1980).
5. Kraus, *Magie der Sprache*, 85.
6. Aristotle uses this term in his *Poetics*, 1461a25; see Roland Bernecker and Thomas Steinfeld, "Amphibolie, Ambiguität," in *Historisches Wörterbuch der Rhetorik*, ed. Gert Ueding (Tübingen, 1992), 1:438.
7. Wolfgang Ullrich, "Grundrisse einer philosophischen Begriffsgeschichte von Ambiguität," *Archiv für Begriffsgeschichte* 32 (1989): 125.
8. Ullrich, *Philosophische Begriffsgeschichte*, 125.
9. Ullrich, *Philosophische Begriffsgeschichte*, 125.
10. For this aspect, see Irène Rosier, ed., *L'ambiguité: Cinq études historiques* (Lille, 1988).
11. Ullrich, *Philosophische Begriffsgeschichte*, 141.
12. Marie Jean Antoine Nicolas Caritat de Condorcet, *Esquisse d'un Tableau historique des progrès de l'esprit humain*, ed. Jean-Pierre Schandeler and Pierre Crépel (Paris, 2004), 456. "elle servirait à porter sur tous les objets qu'embrasse l'intelligence humaine une rigueur, une précision qui rendrait la connaissance de la vérité facile et l'erreur presque impossible. Alors la marche de chaque science aurait la sûreté de celle des mathématiques, et les propositions qui en forment le système toute la certitude géométrique, c'est à dire toute celle que permettent la nature de leur objet et de leur méthode." Translated in English as *Outlines of an Historical View of the Progress of the Human Mind* (Philadelphia, 1796), 288. See also Donald N. Levine, *The Flight from Ambiguity: Essays in Social and Cultural Theory* (Chicago, 1985), 6.
13. Gert Ueding, *Moderne Rhetorik: Von der Aufklärung bis zur Gegenwart* (Munich, 2000), 56–59.
14. Ullrich, *Philosophische Begriffsgeschichte*, 154–55.
15. Quoted from Ullrich, *Philosophische Begriffsgeschichte*, 157: "l'équivoque est essentielle à l'existence humaine, et tout ce que nous vivons ou pensons a toujours plusieur sens."
16. John D. Caputo, "In Praise of Ambiguity," in *Ambiguity in the Western Mind*, ed. Craig J. N. de Paulo, Patrick A. Messina, and Marc Stier (New York, 2005), 15.
17. Caputo, "In Praise of Ambiguity," 23.
18. Caputo, "In Praise of Ambiguity," 20.
19. William Empson, *Seven Types of Ambiguity* (London, 1953), 1.
20. Empson, *Seven Types of Ambiguity*, 1.
21. Umberto Eco, *The Open Work*, trans. Anna Cancogni (Cambridge, MA, 1989); Christoph Bode, *Ästhetik der Ambiguität: Zu Funktion und Bedeutung von Mehrdeutigkeit in der Literatur der Moderne* (Tübingen, 1988).
22. Ernst H. Gombrich, *Art and Illusion: A Study in the Psychology of Pictorial Representation* (London, 1962).
23. See Craig Paulo et al., eds., *Ambiguity in the Western Mind* (New York, 2005), to name only this most recent work.
24. Caputo, "In Praise of Ambiguity," 23.
25. Else Frenkel-Brunswik, "Intolerance of Ambiguity as an Emotional and Perceptual Personality Variable," *Journal of Personality* 18 (1949): 113; see also Jack Reis, *Ambiguitätstoleranz: Beiträge zur Entwicklung eines Persönlichkeitskonstrukts* (Heidelberg, 1997); Torben Kloss et al., *Ambiguitätstoleranz und Stereotypie*, Bericht der Fernuniversität Hagen, 2005, http://psychologie.fernuni-hagen.de/Sem03282/Bericht_Ambiguitaet.pdf.
26. Frenkel-Brunswik, "Intolerance of Ambiguity," 115.
27. Frenkel-Brunswik, "Intolerance of Ambiguity," 119–41.
28. Theodor W. Adorno et al., eds., *The Authoritarian Personality* (New York, 1950), especially 461–64; see also John Levi Martin, "The Authoritarian Personality, 50 Years Later: What Lessons Are There for Political Psychology?," *Political Psychology* 22 (2001): 1–26.
29. For a summary of the problem, see Reis, *Ambiguitätstoleranz*, 109–31.

30. Reis, *Ambiguitätstoleranz*, 112; see also Gülçimen Yurtsever, "Ethical Beliefs and Tolerance of Ambiguity," *Social Behaviour and Personality* 28 (2000): 141–48.
31. Stanley Budner, "Intolerance of Ambiguity as a Personality Variable," *Journal of Personality* 30 (1962): 40–41.
32. R. W. Norton, "Measurement of Ambiguity Tolerance," *Journal of Personality Assessment* 39 (1975): 608.
33. A. P. MacDonald Jr., "Revised Scale for Ambiguity Tolerance: Reliability and Validity," *Psychological Reports* 26 (1970): 791; see also Budner, "Intolerance of Ambiguity."
34. Budner, "Intolerance of Ambiguity," 29.
35. Budner, "Intolerance of Ambiguity," 30.
36. Bauman, *Modernity and Ambivalence*, 1.
37. See, for instance, Ross Brann, *The Compunctious Poet: Cultural Ambiguity and Hebrew Poetry in Muslim Spain* (Baltimore, 1991), 39: "In a society comprising six distinct ethnic-religious communities (Jews, Arabs, Berbers, *muwalladūn* [native Iberian converts to Islam and their descendants], *mustaʿribūn* [Arabized Andalusian Christians] and *ṣaqāliba* [European slave soldiers], the apprehension, if not reality, of cultural ambiguity was understandably widespread."
38. Brann, *Compunctious Poet*, 43.
39. Levine, *Flight from Ambiguity*, 21.
40. Levine, *Flight from Ambiguity*, 24.
41. Levine, *Flight from Ambiguity*, 25–28; see also Donald N. Levine, *Wax and Gold: Tradition and Innovation in Ethiopian Culture* (Chicago, 1972).
42. Levine, *Flight from Ambiguity*, 28.
43. Levine, *Flight from Ambiguity*, 29, 37.
44. Levine, *Flight from Ambiguity*, 37.
45. Levine, *Flight from Ambiguity*, 37: "self-protection through opaqueness."
46. Levine, *Flight from Ambiguity*, 35–37: "bonding through diffuseness."
47. Levine, *Flight from Ambiguity*, 43.
48. See, for instance, von Hees, "Historische Anthropologie"; Richard van Dülmen, *Historische Anthropologie: Entwicklung, Probleme, Aufgaben* (Cologne, 2000).
49. See Thomas Bauer, "Raffinement und Frömmigkeit: Säkulare Poesie islamischer Religionsgelehrter der späten Abbasidenzeit," *Asiatische Studien* 50 (1996): 275–95.
50. Muḥammad an-Nawājī, "Dīwān," edited by Ḥasan M. ʿAbd al-Hādī as a PhD diss. (Cairo, 1400/1980); Muḥammad an-Nawājī, *al-Maṭāliʿ ash-shamsiyyah fī l-madāʾiḥ an-nabawiyyah*, ed. Ḥasan M. ʿAbd al-Hādī (Amman, 1999).
51. Muḥammad an-Nawājī, *Muqaddima fī ṣināʿat an-naẓm wa-n-nathr*, ed. Muḥammad ibn ʿAbd al-Karīm (Beirut, n.d.), 67–70.
52. Frederick William Hasluk, *Christianity and Islam Under the Sultans*, 2 vols. (New York, 1929).
53. Georg Stauth, *Ägyptische heilige Orte*, vol. 2, *Zwischen den Steinen des Pharao und islamischer Moderne* (Bielefeld, 2008), 75.
54. Stauth, *Ägyptische heilige Orte*, 15.
55. Angelika Neuwirth, "Das islamische Dogma der 'Unnachahmlichkeit des Korans' in literaturwissenschaftlicher Sicht," *Der Islam* 60 (1983): 166–83.
56. ʿAbd al-Qāhir al-Jurjānī, *Die Geheimnisse der Wortkunst des ʿAbdalqāhir al-Curcānī*, trans. Hellmut Ritter (Wiesbaden, 1959).
57. Rudolf Sellheim, *Materialien zur arabischen Literaturgeschichte* (Wiesbaden, 1976–1987), 1:301–2.
58. For instance, see Elias John Wilkinson Gibb, *A History of Ottoman Poetry* (London, 1900), 1:124.
59. Seeger A. Bonebakker, *Some Early Definitions of the Tawriya and Ṣafadī's* Faḍḍ al-Xitām ʿan at-Tawriya wa 'l-Istixdām (The Hague, 1966).
60. Jalāl ad-Dīn ʿAbd ar-Raḥmān as-Suyūṭī, *Rashf az-zulāl min as-siḥr al-ḥalāl* (Beirut, n.d.).

61. Ḥusāmzādeh ar-Rūmī, *Risāla fī qalb Kāfūriyyāt al-Mutanabbī min al-madīḥ ilā l-hijāʾ*, ed. Muḥammad Yūsuf Najm (Beirut, 1392/1972).
62. See Thomas Bauer, "Vom Sinn der Zeit: Aus der Geschichte des arabischen Chronogramms," *Arabica* 50 (2003): 501–31; Thomas Bauer, "Die badīʿiyya des Nāṣīf al-Yāziǧī und das Problem der spätosmanischen arabischen Literatur," in *Reflections on Reflections: Near Eastern Writers Reading Literature*, ed. Andreas Christian Islebe and Angelika Neuwirth (Wiesbaden, 2006), 49–118.
63. See the articles by Salma Khadra Jayyusi, "Arabic Poetry," and Muhammad Lutfi al-Yousfi, "Poetic Creativity," in *Arabic Literature in the Post-Classical Period*, ed. Roger Allen and D. S. Richards (Cambridge, 2006), 25–73. See also my response: Thomas Bauer, "In Search of 'Post-Classical Literature': A Review Article," *Mamlūk Studies Review* 11 (2007): 137–67.
64. Samir Kassir, *Considérations sur le malheur arabe* (Paris, 2004).
65. See Bauer, "Badīʿiyya."

2. DOES GOD SPEAK IN TEXTUAL VARIANTS?

1. Descartes, *Meditationes* III, AT, 7:35: "videor pro regulâ generali posse statuere, illud omne esse verum, quòd valde clare & distincte percipio." English translation: René Descartes, *Meditations on First Philosophy*, in *The Philosophical Works of Descartes*, trans. Elizabeth S. Haldane and G. R. T. Ross (Cambridge, 1911), 1:131–99.
2. Gottfried Gabriel, "Klar und deutlich," in *Historisches Wörterbuch der Philosophie* (Basel, 1976), 4:846–47.
3. Descartes, *Meditationes* IV, AT, 7:59–61.
4. Siegfried J. Schmidt, *Grundriss der Empirischen Literaturwissenschaft* (Frankfurt, 1991), 197–215.
5. Levine, *Flight from Ambiguity*, 21.
6. Navid Kermani, *God Is Beautiful: The Aesthetic Experience of the Quran*, trans. Toby Crawford (Cambridge, 2015), 142.
7. Kermani, *God Is Beautiful*, 182.
8. See also Theodor Nöldeke, *Geschichte des Qorāns* (Leipzig, 1938), part 3, 116–18 on Ibn al-Jazarī. Aḥmad ʿAlī al-Imam, *Variant Readings of the Qurʾān: A Critical Study of their Historical and Linguistic Origins* (Herndon, VA, 1418/1998) presents a contemporary Quran scholar's exposition of the traditional concept of the variant readings.
9. Shams ad-Dīn Muḥammad Ibn al-Jazarī, *An-Nashr fī l-qirāʾāt al-ʿashr*, ed. ʿAlī Muḥammad aḍ-Ḍabbāʿ (Beirut, n.d. [ca. 1980]), 1:58–98.
10. Ibn al-Jazarī, *Nashr*, 1:2.
11. Ibn al-Jazarī, *Nashr*, 1:4.
12. Nöldeke, *Geschichte des Qorāns*, part 2, 13–14.
13. Similarly, see Hartmut Bobzin, *Der Koran: Eine Einführung* (Munich, 1999), 100–1; William Montgomery Watt and Alford T. Welch, *Islam* (Stuttgart, 1980), 1:176.
14. Ibn al-Jazarī, *Nashr*, 1:6.
15. Similarly, Nöldeke, *Geschichte des Qorāns*, part 2, 19.
16. Ibn al-Jazarī, *Nashr*, 1:7.
17. Nöldeke, *Geschichte des Qorāns*, part 2, 62.
18. Nöldeke, *Geschichte des Qorāns*, part 2, 50–54.
19. "*ḥattā qtatala l-ghilmānu wa-l-mutaʿallimūn.*" Jalāl ad-Dīn ʿAbd ar-Raḥmān as-Suyūṭī, *al-Itqān fī ʿulūm al-Qurʾān*, ed. Maḥmūd al-Qaysiyyah and Muḥammad al-Atāsī (Abu Dhabi, 1424/2003), 2:280.
20. Under www.al-eman.com, www.ibnothaimeen.com, and www.tafsir.org. The chapter on "kitābat al-Qurʾān wa-jamʿuhū" comprises around five pages. Since the division of the text varies according to its printed versions, I do not give exact page numbers.

21. Ibn al-Jazarī, *Nashr*, 1:6.
22. See also Nöldeke, *Geschichte des Qorāns*, part 2, 49, and al Imam, *Variant Readings*, 354, where also the year 30 after the hijra is given as the most probable date.
23. Nöldeke, *Geschichte des Qorāns*, part 2, 27–49; part 3, 57–97; and al Imam, *Variant Readings*, 79–86.
24. For this, see Nöldeke, *Geschichte des Qorāns*, part 2, 115–19.
25. Ibn ʿUthaymīn, *al-Uṣūl fī t-tafsīr* (Ad Dammām, 1423/2002–2003), 26–27.
26. Ibn ʿUthaymīn, *Uṣūl fī t-tafsīr*, 26–27.
27. Ibn al-Jazarī, *Nashr*, 1:7–8, 33.
28. Beatrice Gruendler, *The Development of the Arabic Scripts: From the Nabatean Era to the First Islamic Century According to Dated Texts* (Atlanta, 1993), 22.
29. Ibn al-Jazarī, *Nashr*, 1:7: "wa-jurridat hādhihī l-maṣāḥif jamīʿan min an-nuqaṭ wa-sh-shakl . . ." Incidentally, Ibn Taymiyyah takes the same position. See al Imam, *Variant Readings*, 67, 117.
30. Ibn al-Jazarī, *Nashr*, 1:33.
31. See, for e.g., Bobzin, *Koran*, 104.
32. Ibn al-Jazarī, *Nashr*, 1:9.
33. Ibn al-Jazarī, *Nashr*, 1:8.
34. Ibn al-Jazarī, *Nashr*, 1:32.
35. Bobzin, *Koran*, 104.
36. "al-Ḳurʾān," in *Encyclopedia of Islam*, 2nd ed., ed. P. J. Bearman et al. (Leiden: 1986), 5:408b.
37. Similarly, also see Christopher Melchert, "Ibn Mujāhid and the Establishment of Seven Qurʾānic Readings," *Studia Islamica* 91 (2000): 18.
38. Melchert, "Ibn Mujāhid," 18.
39. Melchert, "Ibn Mujāhid," 19; al Imam, *Variant Readings*, 128–31.
40. Shams ad-Dīn Muḥammad Ibn al-Jazarī, *Munjid al-muqriʾīn wa-murshid aṭ-ṭālibīn* (Cairo, 1996), 181.
41. Ibn al-Jazarī, *Nashr*, 1:33.
42. Ibn al-Jazarī is not quite certain; he most probably refers to a work by Ibn Qutaybah which is not extant.
43. Ibn al-Jazarī, *Nashr*, 1:35; see also Shams ad-Dīn Muḥammad adh-Dhahabī, *Tārīkh al-Islām*, ed. ʿUmar ʿAbd as-Salām Tadmurī (Beirut, [1987–2000]), 30:513–14.
44. Ibn al-Jazarī, *Nashr*, 1:35.
45. Ibn al-Jazarī, *Nashr*, 1:36.
46. Ibn al-Jazarī, *Nashr*, 1:37.
47. Ibn al-Jazarī, *Nashr*, 1:47–49.
48. Ibn al-Jazarī, *Nashr*, 1:9. The three criteria are attested to already in Makkī b. Abī Ṭālib's writings, see Ibn al-Jazarī, *Nashr*, 1:13–14. (for Makkī, see Angelika Neuwirth, "Makkī Abū Muḥammad," in *The Encyclopaedia of Islam*, 2nd ed., ed. P. J. Bearman et al. (Leiden, 1991), 6:188f.
49. See "the gate of *taṣḥīḥ*" (see p. 100 with note 6).
50. Ibn al-Jazarī, *Nashr*, 1:13.
51. Ibn al-Jazarī, *Nashr*, 1:10–11.
52. Ibn al-Jazarī, *Nashr*, 1:19.
53. Ibn al-Jazarī, *Nashr*, 1:20.
54. See Ibn al-Jazarī, *Munjid*, 57–58.
55. The following passage according to Ibn al-Jazarī, *Nashr*, 1:24–28.
56. Ibn al-Jazarī, *Nashr*, 1:26. In his position he follows ideas similar to those of Ibn Qutaybah; see al Imam, *Variant Readings*, 15–16.
57. al-Aṣmaʿī on the authority of Abū ʿAmr; see Ibn al-Jazarī, *Nashr*, 1:49.
58. A case from the accepted readings (Q 2:132: *waṣṣā* versus *awṣā*) is mentioned by Ibn al-Jazarī and discussed in Adrian Brockett, "The Value of the Ḥafṣ and Warsh Transmissions for the Textual History of the Qurʾān," in *Approaches to the History of the Interpretation of the Qurʾān*, ed. Andrew Rippin (Oxford, 1988), 35.
59. Ibn al-Jazarī, *Nashr*, 1:49.

60. Ibn al-Jazarī, *Nashr*, 1:50.
61. Ibn al-Jazarī, *Nashr*, 1:52–54.
62. Ibn al-Jazarī, *Nashr*, 1:53.
63. Ibn al-Jazarī, *Nashr*, 1:53.
64. Werner Bergengruen, *Dichtergehäuse* (Zürich, 1966), 172.
65. Brockett, *Value of Ḥafṣ and Warsh Transmissions*, 43.
66. Ibn al-Jazarī, *Nashr*, 1:52.
67. See, e.g., in the Islamic University Medina Website, accessed August 7, 2019, http://enweb.iu.edu.sa.
68. See, e.g., *Khaymat al-qirāʾāt al-Qurʾāniyya*, Khayma, accessed August 7, 2019, http://bawaba.khayma.com/البوابة.
69. See Islamweb.net, accessed August 7, 2019, http://audio.islamweb.net/audio/index.php?page=rewayat. A project that registers the Qurʾān in all its readings on a record was already started in 1960; see Labib as-Said, *The Recited Koran: A History of the First Recorded Version* (Princeton, NJ, 1975).
70. Nöldeke, *Geschichte des Qorāns*, part 3, 274.
71. Mohamed Al-Nowaihi, "Towards the Reappraisal of Classical Arabic Literature and History: Some Aspects of Ṭāhā Ḥusayn's Use of Modern Western Criteria," *International Journal of Middle East Studies* 11 (1980): 192.
72. Al-Nowaihi, "Towards the Reappraisal," 189.
73. Al-Nowaihi, "Towards the Reappraisal," 191; Ṭāhā Ḥusayn, *Fī l-adab al-jāhilī* (Cairo 1927), 67–70.
74. Ḥusayn, *Fī l-adab al-jāhilī*, 94–95.; see also as-Said, *The Recited Koran*, 97–99.
75. Sayyid Abū l-Aʿlā al-Mawdūdī, *Tafhīm al-Qurʾān*, 6 vols. (Lahore, 1949–1972). Translated into English by Abdul Aziz Kamal as *The Meaning of the Qurʾān*, 5 vols. (Delhi, 1992), http://www.bdislam.com/quran/menu.html, accessed April 1, 2007. See also Charles J. Adams, *Abū ʾl-Aʿlā al-Mawdūdī's Tafhīm al-Qurʾān*, in *Approaches to the History of Interpretation of the Qurʾān*, ed. Andrew Rippin (Oxford, 1988), 307–23.
76. English version, among others, to be found in BDIslam, http://www.bdislam.com/quran/intro.htm, or Quran, http://www.quran.net/quran/introductionToQuranMaudoodi.asp, both accessed April 1, 2007. Arabic translation *Mabādiʾ asāsiyya fī fahm al-Qurʾān*, Tawhed, accessed April 1, 2007, www.tawhed.ws/a?i=74.
77. BDIslam, http://www.bdislam.com/quran/intro.htm, 12. In the Urdu original: Sayyid Abū l-Aʿlā al-Mawdūdī, *Tafhīm al-Qurʾān* (Lahore, 1949), 1:28.—For the problem, see al Imam, *Variant Readings*, 23–24.
78. Supplemented from the Arabic version.
79. See BDIslam, http://www.bdislam.com/quran/intro.htm, 14 (30–31 in the Urdu original, 21 in the Arabic translation).
80. "An Introduction to the Study of the Qurʾan," Muslim Canada, accessed April 1, 2007, http://muslim-canada.org/introstudy.pdf, 9.
81. Samuel Green, "The Different Arabic Versions of the Qurʾān," Answering Islam, accessed August 8, 2019, https://www.answering-islam.org/Green/seven.htm.
82. Saifullah et al., "Reply to Samuel Green's 'The Seven Readings of the Qurʾan,'" Islamic Awareness, accessed April 1, 2007, http://www.islamic-awareness.org/Quran/Text/Qiraat/green.html.
83. See Answering Islam, accessed August 7, 2019, https://www.answering-islam.org.uk/Campbell/s3c3c.html.
84. See John Gilchrist, "Sources of the Quran," Truthnet, accessed August 7, 2019, https://truthnet.org/islam/Qurangil5.html.
85. M. S. M. Saifullah, "Versions of the Qurʾan?," Islamic Awareness, accessed August 7, 2019, http://www.islamic-awareness.org/Quran/Text/Qiraat/hafs.html.
86. See Al Mawrid, accessed August 7, 2019, http://www.al-mawrid.org.
87. See Shehzad Saleem, Renaissance, accessed April 1, 2007, http://www.renaissance.com.pk/febqur20.htm, 1.

88. Saleem, Renaissance, 4.
89. Saleem, Renaissance, 4.
90. Saleem, Renaissance, 8.
91. Saleem, Renaissance, 9.
92. Saleem, Renaissance, 13.
93. Ibn al-Jazarī, *Nashr*, 1:47.
94. Ibn al-Jazarī, *Nashr*, 1:47
95. Ibn al-Jazarī, *Nashr*, 1:48.

3. DOES GOD SPEAK AMBIGUOUSLY?

Epigraph. Erasmus of Rotterdam, *De libero arbitrio* I a 7: "Sunt enim in divinis literis adyta quaedam, in quae deus noluit nos altius penetrare, et si penetrare conemur, quo fuerimus altius ingressi, hoc magis ac magis caligamus, quo vel sic agnosceremus et divinae sapientiae maiestatem impervestigabilem et humanae mentis imbecillitatem." English translation from E. Gordon Rupp and Philip S. Watson, eds., *Luther and Erasmus: Free Will and Salvation*, 38.

1. Ibn al-Jazarī, *Nashr*, 1:5: Fa-inna ʿulamāʾa hādhihī l-ummati lam tazal mina ṣ-ṣadri l-awwali wa-ilā ākhiri waqtin yastanbiṭūna minhu mina l-adillati wa-l-ḥujaji wa-l-barāhīni wa-l-ḥikami wa-ghayrihā mā lam yaṭṭaliʿ ʿalayhi mutaqaddimun wa-lā yanḥaṣir li-mutaʾakhkhirin bal huwa l-baḥru l-ʿaẓīmu lladhī lā qarāra lahū yuntahā ilayhi wa-lā ghāyata li-ākhirihī yūqafu ʿalayhi wa-min thamma lam yaḥtaj hādhihī l-ummatu ilā nabiyyin baʿda nabiyyihā.
2. Christian J. Troll, Interview, *Die Welt*, November 10, 2006, accessed June 1, 2007, http://www.sankt-georgen.de/leseraum/troll30.pdf.
3. al-Suyūṭī, *Itqān*, 2:189.
4. Nöldeke, *Geschichte des Qorāns*, part 1, 104.
5. Gerald Hawting, "Oaths," in *The Encyclopaedia of the Qurʾān*, ed. Jane Dammen McAuliffe (Leiden, 2003), 3:561–66; Angelika Neuwirth, "Der Horizont der Offenbarung: Zur Relevanz der einleitenden Schwurserien für die Suren der frühmekkanischen Zeit," in *Gottes ist der Orient, Gottes ist der Okzident: Festschrift für A. Falaturi zum 65. Geburtstag*, ed. Udo Tworuschka (Cologne, 1991), 3–39.
6. See Thomas Bauer, *Altarabische Dichtkunst: Eine Untersuchung ihrer Struktur und Entwicklung am Beispiel der Onagerepisode* (Wiesbaden, 1992), 1:172–80.
7. Maḥmūd ibn ʿUmar az-Zamakhsharī, *al-Kashshāf ʿan ḥaqāʾiq ghawāmiḍ at-tanzīl wa-ʿuyūn al-aqāwīl fī wujūh at-taʾwīl* (Beirut, n.d.), 4:692–700.
8. Khalīl ibn Aybak aṣ-Ṣafadī, *al-Ghayth al-musajjam fī sharḥ Lāmiyyat al-ʿajam* (Beirut, 1395/1975), 1:24.
9. Ibn ʿUthaymīn, "Tafsīr Juzʾ ʿAmma, http://ibnothaimeen.com/all/books/printer_17863.shtml and https://web.archive.org/web/20140312001104/http://ibnothaimeen.com/all/books/printer_17863.shtml, both accessed November 2014.
10. See, e.g., aṭ-Ṭabarī; Jalāl ad-Dīn ʿAbd ar-Raḥmān as-Suyūṭī, *ad-Durr al-manthūr fī t-tafsīr bi-l-manthūr*, 5 vols. (Beirut, 1983).
11. Abū l-Faraj ʿAbd ar-Raḥmān Ibn al-Jawzī, *Zād al-masīr fī ʿilm at-tafsīr* (Beirut, 2002), 1511, commenting on Sūrat an-Nāziʿāt, verse 4.
12. For this issue see the extensive discussion in Robert Pfaller, *Die Illusion der anderen: Über das Lustprinzip in der Kultur* (Frankfurt, 2002).
13. See Khalid Zaheer, "Qasr: Shortening of Prayers," Khalid Zaheer Official Website, Accessed on May 30, 2007, http://www.khalidzaheer.com/qa/253.
14. The following passage refers to as-Suyūṭī, *Itqān*.
15. Ibn al-Jazarī, *Nashr*, 1:15 (italics by T. B.).
16. See p. 57.

17. For instance, see Manfred Kropp, "Den Koran neu lesen: Über Versuche einer Vereinbarung des koranischen mit dem modernen Weltbild," in *Religion und Weltbild*, ed. Dieter Zeller (Münster, 2002), 159.
18. Christine Schirrmacher, *Der Koran—die heilige Schrift des Islam*, accessed August 14, 2019, https://www.islaminstitut.de/wp-content/uploads/2005/07/2005_IfI_Der_Koran.pdf, 1.
19. al-Jurjānī, *Asrār al-balāgha* [The secrets of eloquence]; Jurjānī's *Dalāʾil al-iʿjāz* has not been translated, but the pertinent arguments in as-Sakkākī's adaptation can be studied in Udo Simon, *Mittelalterliche arabische Sprachbetrachtung zwischen Grammatik und Rhetorik: ʿIlm al-maʿānī bei as-Sakkākī* (Heidelberg, 1993).
20. See the detailed discussion in Kermani, *God Is Beautiful.*
21. See az-Zamakhsharī, *al-Kashshāf, ad* Q 14:4.
22. See also Bobzin, "Translations of the Qurʾān."
23. Hans-Georg Gadamer, *Truth and Method*, 2nd ed., trans. and rev. Joel Weinsheimer and Donald G. Marshall (London, 1989), 388; see also Caputo, *In Praise of Ambiguity*, 26.
24. Gadamer, *Truth and Method*, 386.
25. See Bobzin, "Translations of the Qurʾān."
26. Bauman, *Modernity and Ambivalence*, 180.

4. THE BLESSING OF DISSENT

1. Gerhard Böwering, "Prayer," in *The Encyclopaedia of the Qurʾān*, ed. Jane Dammen McAuliffe (Leiden, 2006), 4:215–31.
2. Ibn Ḥajar al-ʿAsqalānī, *an-Nukat ʿalā kitāb Ibn aṣ-Ṣalāḥ*, ed. Rabīʿ ibn Hādī ʿUmayr (Riyadh, 1417/1996–1997), 1:299–300.
3. James Robson, "al-Bukhārī," in *The Encyclopaedia of Islam*, 2nd ed., ed. P. J. Bearman et al. (Leiden, 1960), 1:1296–97.
4. For a survey, see Muḥyī d-Dīn Yaḥyā ibn Sharaf an-Nawawī, *Das Buch der Vierzig Hadithe: Kitāb al-Arbaʿīn, mit dem Kommentar von Ibn Daqīq al-ʿĪd*, trans. and ed. Marco Schöller (Frankfurt, 2007), 303.
5. Ibn Ḥajar al-ʿAsqalānī, *Sharḥ sharḥ Nukhbat al-fikar*, ed. Muḥammad and Haytham Nizār Tamīm, commentary by Mullā ʿAlī al-Qāriʾ (Beirut, n.d. [ca. 1994]), 243–44.
6. Ibn Ḥajar, *Nukat.*
7. Ibn Ḥajar, *Sharḥ sharḥ Nukhbat al-fikar*, 256.
8. Ibn Ḥajar al-ʿAsqalānī, *Tahdhīb at-Tahdhīb* (Hyderabad, 1325–1327/1907–1910), 2:341–42, no. 606.
9. Ibn Ḥajar, *Sharḥ sharḥ Nukhbat al-fikar*, 161–63.
10. Ibn Ḥajar, *Sharḥ sharḥ Nukhbat al-fikar*, 186–89.
11. an-Nawawī, *Das Buch der Vierzig Hadithe*, 289.
12. Frenkel-Brunswick, "Intolerance of Ambiguity," 130.
13. Ḥājjī Khalīfah [Kātib Čelebī], *Kashf aẓ-ẓunūn ʿan asāmī l-kutub wa-l-funūn* (Beirut, 1994), 2:261–62.
14. See for instance Fakhr ad-Dīn ar-Rāzī, *al-Maḥṣūl fī ʿilm uṣūl al-fiqh*, ed. ʿĀdil Aḥmad ʿAbd al-Mawjūd et al. (Beirut, 1419/1998), 1:89.
15. Thus writes Ibn Taymiyyah; see G. Ch. Anawati, "Fakhr al-Dīn al-Rāzī," in *Encyclopaedia of Islam*, 2nd ed., ed. P. J. Bearman et al. (Leiden, 1965), 2:754.
16. See in particular Hallaq, "Master Architect."
17. Naṣr Ḥāmid Abū Zayd, *al-Imām al-Shāfiʿī wa-taʾsīs al-īdīyūlūjiyyah al-wasaṭiyyah* (Casablanca, 2007).
18. Abū l-Qasim Muḥammad Ibn Juzayy, *Taqrīb al-wuṣūl ilā ʿilm al-uṣūl*, ed. Muḥammad ʿAlī Farkūs (Algiers, 1990), 72.
19. Fakhr ad-Dīn ar-Rāzī, *al-Kāshif ʿan al-Maḥṣūl fī ʿilm al-uṣūl*, ed. ʿĀdil Aḥmad ʿAbd al-Mawjūd et al. (Beirut 1419/1998), 5:51–52.

20. See Yūsuf ibn ʿAbdallāh Ibn ʿAbd al-Barr, *al-Istidhkār al-jāmiʿ li-madhāhib fuqahāʾ al-amṣār wa-ʿulamāʾ al-aqṭār*, ed. Sālim Muḥammad ʿAṭā and Muḥammad ʿAlī Muʿawwaḍ (Beirut, 2000), 5:299, where a reference to the place of the hadith in the sources is given in a note.
21. Ibn ʿAbd al-Barr, *al-Istidhkār*, 5:301–2.
22. ʿAlī ibn Muḥammad ibn Ḥabīb al-Māwardī, *al-Ḥāwī al-kabīr fī fiqh madhhab al-Imām ash-Shāfiʿī*, ed. ʿAlī Muḥammad Muʿawwaḍ and ʿĀdil Aḥmad ʿAbd al-Mawjūd (Beirut, 1999), 1:59; Ibn ʿAbd al-Barr, *al-Istidhkār*, 5:304.
23. Ibn ʿAbd al-Barr, *al-Istidhkār*, 5:305.
24. al-Māwardī, *al-Ḥāwī*, 1:56–57.
25. al-Māwardī, *al-Ḥāwī*, 1:58–59.
26. al-Māwardī, *al-Ḥāwī*, 1:61; Ibn ʿAbd al-Barr, *al-Istidhkār*, 5:303–4.
27. Ibn ʿAbd al-Barr, *al-Istidhkār*, 5:300–1.
28. Ibn ʿAbd al-Barr, *al-Istidhkār*, 5:301.
29. Ibn ʿUthaymīn, "Fatwa," Islamway, accessed August 14, 2019, https://ar.islamway.net/fatawa.
30. Jalāl ad-Dīn ʿAbd ar-Raḥmān as-Suyūṭī, *Jazīl al-mawāhib fī ikhtilāf al-madhāhib*, ed. Ibrāhīm Bājis ʿAbd al-Majīd (Beirut, 1412/1992), 29.
31. There are chapters on the "meeting" of the *mujtahid* in nearly all *uṣūl* works, e.g., Ibn Juzayy, *Taqrīb*, 146–47.; most elaborately in ar-Rāzī, *Maḥṣūl*, 6:29–65.
32. al-Māwardī, *al-Ḥāwī*, 56–76.
33. Abū Isḥāq ash-Shīrāzī, *al-Muhadhdhab fī fiqh al-Imām ash-Shāfiʿī*, ed. Muḥammad az-Zuḥaylī, Part 1 (Damascus, 1996), 57.
34. ash-Shīrāzī, *al-Muhadhdhab*, 59–60.
35. ʿAlī ibn Muḥammad ibn Ḥabīb al-Māwardī, *al-Iqnāʿ fī l-fiqh ash-Shāfiʿī*, ed. Khiḍr Muḥammad Khiḍr (Kuwait City, 1402/1982), 32–33.
36. Wael B. Hallaq, "Was the Gate of Ijtihad Closed?," in *Law and Legal Theory in Classical and Medieval Islam*, ed. Wael B. Hallaq (Ashgate, 1994).
37. See Khayr ad-Dīn Sayyib, *al-Qirāʾāt al-qurʾāniyyah wa-atharuhā fī ikhtilāf al-aḥkām al-fiqhiyyah* (Algiers, 1428/2007). He treats 31 such cases.
38. Ibn ʿAbd al-Barr, *al-Istidhkār*, 5:299.
39. All *uṣūl* works contain a chapter on *tarjīḥ*. See, e.g., Ibn Juzayy, *Taqrīb*, 152–57.
40. as-Suyūṭī, *Jazīl al-mawāhib*, 17.
41. See, e.g., Imaam Muhammad Naasir-ud-Deen al-Albaanee, "The Weakness of The Ahaadeeth Endorsing Ikhtilaaf," Islamic Board, November 4, 2005, http://www.islamicboard.com/miscellaneous/35589-weakness-ahaadeeth-endorsing-ikhtilaaf.html.
42. as-Suyūṭī, *Jazīl al-mawāhib*, 21.
43. as-Suyūṭī, *Jazīl al-mawāhib*, 20.
44. as-Suyūṭī, *Jazīl al-mawāhib*, 22–24.
45. as-Suyūṭī, *Jazīl al-mawāhib*, 24.
46. Ibn ʿUthaymīn, *al-Khilāf bayn al-ʿulamāʾ: Asbābuhū wa-mawqifunā minhu* (n.p., n.d.), accessed February 2010, http://www.ibnothaimeen.com/all/books/article_16910.shtml.
47. Ibn ʿUthaymīn, *al-Khilāf*, 6.
48. On this topic and the following, see Ibn Juzayy, *Taqrīb*, 157–62.
49. Ibn ʿUthaymīn, *al-Khilāf*, 2.
50. Ibn ʿUthaymīn, *al-Khilāf*, 6.
51. See, e.g., twice on the same page: Ibn ʿUthaymīn, *al-Khilāf*, 5.
52. Muḥammad Saʿīd Ramaḍān al-Būṭī, *al-Lāmadhhabiyyah akhṭar bidʿah tuhaddid ash-sharīʿah al-islāmiyyah* (Beirut, 1958). Translated in English by M. Merza et al. as *al-Lā Madhhabiyya: Abandoning the Madhhabs Is the Most Dangerous Bidʿah Threatenting the Islamic Sharīʿa* (Damascus, 2007). See Stefan Wild, "Muslim und Madhab: Ein Brief von Tokio nach Mekka und seine Folgen in Damaskus,"

in Ulrich Haarmann and Peter Bachmann eds., *Die islamische Welt zwischen Mittelalter und Neuzeit: Festschrift für Hans Robert Roemer* (Beirut 1979), 674–89.

5. THE ISLAMIZATION OF ISLAM

1. Gustav Edmund von Grunebaum, *Medieval Islam: A Study in Cultural Orientation* (Chicago, 1946), 12, https://oi.chicago.edu/sites/oi.uchicago.edu/files/uploads/shared/docs/medieval_islam.pdf.
2. Almut Höfert, "Europa und der Nahe Osten: Der transkulturelle Vergleich in der Vormoderne und die Meistererzählungen über den Islam," in *Historische Zeitschrift* 287 (2008): 577.
3. The title of this chapter is taken from Aziz Al-Azmeh, *Islams and Modernities* (London, 1993). See also Thomas Bauer, "The Islamization of Islam," in *Perspectives in Literatures and Cultures*, 1–15, vol. 1 of *Ideological Battlegrounds—Constructions of Us and Them Before and After 9/11*, ed. Joanna Witkowska and Uwe Zagratzki (Newcastle upon Tyne, 2014).
4. Höfert, "Europa und der Nahe Osten," 577–82.
5. Claus-Peter Haase, ed., *Sammlerglück: Islamische Kunst aus der Sammlung Edmund de Unger; Katalogbuch zur Ausstellung in Berlin, 27.11.2007–17.2.2008*, Museum für Islamische Kunst (Munich, 2007) 106, 122–24, 128.
6. Emilie Savage-Smith, "Ṭibb," in *The Encyclopaedia of Islam*, 2nd ed., ed. P. J. Bearman et al. (Leiden, 2000), 10:452–60.
7. A well-documented example is given by Sabine Dorpmüller, *Religiöse Magie im "Buch der probaten Mittel": Analyse, kritische Edition und Übersetzung des Kitāb al-Muǧarrabāt von Muḥammad ibn Yūsuf as-Sanūsī (gest. um 845/1490)* (Wiesbaden, 2005).
8. Martin Plessner, "The Natural Sciences and Medicine," in Joseph Schacht and Clifford Edmund Bosworth, eds., *The Legacy of Islam* (Oxford, 1974), 2:427–28.
9. Johann Christoph Bürgel, *Allmacht und Mächtigkeit: Religion und Welt im Islam* (Munich, 1991), 191.
10. Bürgel, *Allmacht und Mächtigkeit*, 192.
11. Maya Shatzmiller, *Labour in the Medieval Islamic World* (Leiden, 1994), 75.
12. Ibn Bassām, *Nihāyat ar-rutbah fī ṭalab al-ḥisbah*. In *K. as-Siyāsah* [...] *wa-yalīhi an-Nahj al-maslūk* [...], ed. Muḥammad Ḥasan Ismāʿīl and Aḥmad Farīd al-Mazīdī (Beirut, 1424/2003), 340.
13. See Gotthard Strohmaier, "La longévité de Galien et les deux places de son tombeau," in *La science médicale antique: Nouveaux regards; Études réunies en l'honneur de Jacques Jouanna*, ed. Véronique Boudon-Millot, Alessia Guardasole, and Caroline Magdelaine (Paris, 2007).
14. See, e.g., Shatzmiller, *Labour*.
15. Von Grunebaum, *Medieval Islam*, 108.
16. Friedrich Nietzsche, *The Antichrist*, trans. H. L. Mencken (New York, 1927), 175.
17. See Thomas Bauer, "Ibn Ḥajar and the Arabic Ghazal of the Mamluk Age," in *Ghazal as World Literature*, ed. Thomas Bauer and Angelika Neuwirth (Beirut, 2005), 1:35–55.
18. See "Ibn Ḥajar al-ʿAsqalānī," in *Encyclopedia of Arabic Literature*, ed. Julie Scott Meisami and Paul Starkey (London, 1998), 1:327–28.
19. See, with critical commentary, Mariam Popal, *Die Scharia, das religiöse Recht—ein Konstrukt? Überlegungen zur Analyse des islamischen Rechts anhand rechtsvergleichender Methoden und aus Sicht postkolonialer Kritik* (Frankfurt, 2006), 23 and elsewhere.
20. Najm ad-Dīn an-Nasafī, *Ṭilbat aṭ-ṭalaba*, ed. Khālid ʿAbd ar-Raḥmān al-ʿAkk (Beirut, 1416/1995). For Islamic law as a legal system, see also Popal, *Scharia*, 51–54.
21. See Popal, *Scharia*, 39, with an apposite critique of Joseph Schacht.
22. Irene Schneider, *Das Bild des Richters in der "Adab al-Qāḍī" Literatur* (Frankfurt, 1990), 246.
23. Schneider, *Das Bild des Richters*, 245.

24. Schneider, *Das Bild des Richters*, 245.
25. ʿAlāʾ ad-Dīn Ibn al-ʿAṭṭār, *Adab al-khaṭīb*, ed. Muḥammad as-Sulaymānī (Beirut, 1996), 87–89.
26. Muḥyī d-Dīn Yaḥyā ibn Sharaf an-Nawawī, *at-Tibyān fī ādāb ḥamalat al-Qurʾān*, ed. Muḥammad Riḍwān ʿArqasūsī (Beirut, 1422/2002), 39.
27. Schneider, *Das Bild des Richters*, 59.
28. See Mez, *The Renaissance of Islam*, 218–20.
29. See for instance, the biographies of the judges of the postformative period in as-Subkī's collection of biographies of Shāfiʿite scholars: Tāj ad-Dīn ʿAbd al-Wahhāb as-Subkī, *Ṭabaqāt ash-Shāfiʿiyyah al-kubrā*, ed. Muṣṭafā ʿAbd al-Qādir Aḥmad ʿAṭā, 6 vols. (Beirut, 1999).
30. A particularly substantial collection of this kind is Aḥmad ibn Yaḥyā al-Wansharīsī, *al-Miʿyār al-muʿrib*, 13 vols. (Rabat, 1981–1983). The reader is especially referred to the chapter on "Damages," 8:435–87, and 9:5–74.
31. See Popal, *Scharia*, 39.
32. Plessner, "The Natural Sciences and Medicine," in Schacht and Bosworth, eds., *Legacy of Islam*, 2:428.
33. Max Meyerhof and Joseph Schacht, eds., *The Theologus Autodidactus of Ibn al-Nafīs* (Oxford, 1968), 6.
34. Meyerhof and Schacht, *Theologus Autodidactus*, 7.
35. Meyerhof and Schacht, *Theologus Autodidactus*, 7. See also, among other references, Khalīl ibn Aybak aṣ-Ṣafadī, *al-Wāfī bi-l-wafayāt*, ed. Hellmut Ritter et al. (Wiesbaden, [1962–2010]), 12:247–51.
36. Ignaz Goldziher, *Stellung der alten islamischen Orthodoxie zu den antiken Wissenschaften* (Berlin, 1916).
37. Goldziher, *Orthodoxie*, 25.
38. Goldziher, *Orthodoxie*, 26.
39. Goldziher, *Orthodoxie*, 39.
40. Fakhr ad-Dīn ar-Rāzī, *al-Maḥṣūl fī ʿilm uṣūl al-fiqh*, ed. ʿĀdil Aḥmad ʿAbd al-Mawjūd et al. (Beirut, 1419/1998), vol. 5.
41. Goldziher, *Orthodoxie*, 6.
42. Muḥammad ibn ʿAlī ash-Shawkānī, *Adab aṭ-ṭalab wa-muntahā l-arab*, ed. ʿAbdallāh Yaḥyā as-Surayḥī (Beirut, 1419/1998), 195.
43. Goldziher, *Orthodoxie*, 41.
44. Goldziher, *Orthodoxie*, 42 (italics in the original).
45. Jürgen Todenhöfer, *Warum tötest du, Zaid?* (Munich, 2008), 94.
46. Todenhöfer, *Warum tötest du, Zaid?*, 104.
47. Todenhöfer, *Warum tötest du, Zaid?*, 104.
48. Haim Blanc, *Communal Dialects in Baghdad* (Cambridge, MA, 1964).
49. Todenhöfer, *Warum tötest du, Zaid?*, 85–86.
50. Todenhöfer, *Warum tötest du, Zaid?*, 95.

6. LANGUAGE

1. Michael Zwettler, "Imraʾalqays, Son of ʿAmr: King of . . . ?," in *Literary Heritage of Classical Islam: Arabic and Islamic Studies in Honor of James A. Bellamy*, ed. Mustansir Mir (Princeton, NJ, 1993), 3–37.
2. Abū ʿAbdallāh al-Ḥusayn ibn Aḥmad az-Zawzanī, *Sharḥ al-Muʿallaqāt as-Sabʿ* (Beirut, n.d.), 224; see also Theodor Nöldeke, *Fünf Moʿallaqāt übersetzt und erklärt*, vol. 1, *Die Moʿallaqa des ʿAmr und des Ḥārith* (Vienna, 1899), 49. According to Nöldeke, by the "sea," the river Euphrates is meant.
3. See also Robert Hillenbrand, "For God, Empire and Mammon: Some Art-Historical Aspects of the Reformed Dīnārs of ʿAbd al-Malik," in *al-Andalus und Europa*, ed. Martina Müller-Wiener, Christiane Kothe, Karl-Heinz Golzio, and Joachim Gierlichs (Petersberg, Germany, 2004), 20–38.

4. The next paragraph follows Mechthild Reh, "Sprache und Gesellschaft," in *Die Sprachen Afrikas*, ed. Bernd Heine, Ekkehard Wolff, and Thilo C. Schadeberg (Hamburg, 1981), 546–48.
5. See Wolfdietrich Fischer, "Die Perioden des Klassischen Arabisch," *Abr Nahrain* 12 (1972): 15–18.
6. Reh, *Sprache und Gesellschaft*, 546.
7. Bauer, *Altarabische Dichtkunst*.
8. Werner Diem, "Das Kitāb al-Ǧīm des Abū ʿAmr aš-Šaibānī: Ein Beitrag zur arabischen Lexikographie," PhD diss. (Munich, 1968), 60–61. The *Kitāb al-Jīm* contains two Qurʾanic quotations, and one hadith citation, but around 4300 verses.
9. See Fuat Sezgin, *Geschichte des arabischen Schrifttums*, vol. 8: *Lexikographie*, 28 (on Abū Khayrah), 50–51 (on Abū ʿAmr), 67–76 (on Abū ʿUbaydah and al-Aṣmaʿī).
10. Particularly clueless is Dan Diner, *Versiegelte Zeit: Über den Stillstand in der islamischen Welt*, 2nd ed. (Berlin, 2005).
11. Bauer, *Altarabische Dichtkunst*, 1:237.
12. Bauer, *Altarabische Dichtkunst*, 1:172–89.
13. For the following, see *Geschichte des arabischen Schrifttums*, vol. 8, *Lexikographie*, 61–67.
14. Hans Kofler, "Das Kitāb al-Aḍdād von Abū ʿAlī Muḥammad Quṭrub ibn al-Mustanīr," *Islamica* 5 (1931–1932): 244. For instance, *shāma*, 270, 518–19.
15. ʿAbdallāh al-Jubūrī, *al-Aḍdād wa-mawqif Ibn Durustawayh minhā*, *al-Mawrid* 2/3 (1973): 42–48.
16. Ibn al-Anbārī, *Kitāb al-Aḍdād*, ed. Abū l-Faḍl Ibrāhīm (Kuwait City, 1960), 2.
17. Ibn ad-Dahhān (died 569/1174) and aṣ-Ṣaghānī (died 640/1252).
18. See p. 77.
19. See, e.g., Gotthold Weil, "Aḍdād," in Encyclopaedia of Islam, 2nd ed., ed. P. J. Bearman et al. (Leiden, 1960), 1:137–39.
20. Wolfdietrich Fischer, *Farb- und Formbezeichnungen in der Sprache der altarabischen Dichtung* (Wiesbaden, 1965), 27–36.
21. See, e.g., Kofler, *Kitāb al-Aḍdād*, 504.
22. See Kofler, *Kitāb al-Aḍdād*, 389.
23. Jacques Berque and Jean-Paul Charnay, eds., *L'ambivalence dans la culture arabe* (Paris, 1967).
24. Johan Huizinga, *Homo ludens: A Study of the Play-Element in Culture* (London, 1949), 46.
25. Carl Abel, *Über den Gegensinn der Urworte* (Leipzig, 1884), 15.
26. Abel, *Gegensinn der Urworte*, 46–65.
27. See Freud's account of Abel from the year 1910: Sigmund Freud, "Über den Gegensinn der Urworte"; English translation as "The Antithetical Sense of Primal Words," in Sigmund Freud, *Collected Papers* (London, 1949), 4:184–91.
28. Arberry's translation, 93.
29. See Bauer, *Liebe und Liebesdichtung*, 387–89.
30. Ibn Ḥajar, quoted in Taqī ad-Dīn Abū Bakr Ibn Ḥijja al-Ḥamawī, *Khizānat al-adab wa-ghāyat al-arab*, ed. Kawkab Diyāb (Beirut, 2001), 4:364.
31. See Geert Jan van Gelder, "Iqtibās," in *Encyclopedia of Arabic Literature*, ed. Julie Scott Meisami and Paul Starkey (London, 1998), 1:396–97; Abū Manṣūr ath-Thaʿālibī, *al-Iqtibās min al-Qurʾān al-karīm*, ed. Ibtisām Marhūn aṣ-Ṣaffār, 2 vols. (Al-Mansurah, 1412/1992).
32. My source does not explicitly say that there was such a cause, but in view of several similar literary texts originating from such incidents, this is quite probable. See, e.g., Thomas Bauer, "Ibrāhīm al-Miʿmār: Ein dichtender Handwerker aus Ägyptens Mamlukenzeit," *Zeitschrift der Deutschen Morgenländischen Gesellschaft* 152 (2002): 77, with note 48; Li Guo, "Paradise Lost: Ibn Dāniyāl's Response to Baybars' Campaign against Vice in Cairo," *Journal of the American Oriental Society* 121 (2001): 219–35.
33. Uways al-Ḥamawī, *Sukkardān al-ʿushshāq*, Manuscript, n.d., Berlin no. 8407, fol. 158a; the verses appear also (erroneously attributed and with a variant reading) in Bahāʾ ad-Dīn Abū l-Fatḥ Muḥammad al-Ibshīhī, *al-Mustaṭraf fī kull fann mustaẓraf*, ed. Ibrāhīm Ṣāliḥ (Beirut, 1999), 3:137 (meter *ramal*).

34. See Bauer, "Raffinement und Frömmigkeit."
35. Abū l-ʿAlāʾ al-Maʿarrī, *Sharḥ Dīwān Abī ṭ-Ṭayyib al-Mutanabbī (Muʿjiz Aḥmad)*, ed. ʿAbd al-Majīd Diyāb, 2nd. ed. (Cairo, 1413/1992), 2:21 (no. 61/23).
36. Cf. Bauer, "Raffinement und Frömmigkeit"; Emil T. Homerin, "Preaching Poetry: The Forgotten Verse of Ibn al-Shahrazūrī," *Arabica* 38 (1991): 87–101.
37. Bauer, "Raffinement und Frömmigkeit," 276, with note 2.
38. Bauer, "Raffinement und Frömmigkeit," 287.
39. Bauer, "Raffinement und Frömmigkeit," 288–89.
40. Brann, *Compunctious Poet*, 9.
41. Brann, *Compunctious Poet*, 11; see also Raymond Scheindlin, *Wine, Women, and Death: Medieval Poems on the Good Life* (Philadelphia, 1986).
42. See MacDonald, *Revised Scale*, 791; Budner, "Intolerance of Ambiguity."
43. Heinrich Leberecht Fleischer, "Literarisches aus Beirut," *Zeitschrift der Deutschen Morgenländischen Gesellschaft* 5 (1851): 97; Bauer, "Badīʿiyya," 86.
44. Fleischer, *Literarisches aus Beirut*, 98.
45. Alfred von Kremer, "Nâṣîf aljâziǧî," *Zeitschrift der Deutschen Morgenländischen Gesellschaft* 25 (1871): 244–45.
46. Adolf Loos, "Ornament und Verbrechen," in *Trotzdem: Gesammelte Schriften 1900–1930*, ed. Adolf Opel (Vienna, 1982), 78–88. Trans. by Michael Bullock as *Programs and Manifestoes on 20th-Century Architecture*, ed. Ulrich Conrads (London, 1970).
47. See Jayyusi, "Arabic Poetry," and al-Yousfi, "Poetic Creativity," in *The Cambridge History of Arabic Literature: Arabic Literature in the Post-Classical Period* (Cambridge, 1990), 25–73; See also Bauer's comments, "In Search of 'Post-Classical Literature.'"
48. Burckhardt, *Griechische Kulturgeschichte*, quoted in Christopher Ulf, "Ancient Greek Competition—A Modern Construct?," in *Competition in the Ancient World*, ed. N. Fisher and H. van Wees (Swansea, 2011), 85–111.
49. Geert Jan van Gelder, "Naḳāʾiḍ," in *Encyclopaedia of Islam*, 2nd ed., 7:920; and Geert Jan van Gelder, "Naqāʾiḍ," in *Encyclopedia of Arabic Literature*, 2:578; Arthur Schaade and Helmut Gätje, "Djarīr," in *Encyclopaedia of Islam*, 2nd ed., 2:479–50; Régis Blachère, "al-Farazdaḳ," in *Encyclopaedia of Islam*, 2nd ed., 2:788–89.
50. Charles Pellat, "Mathālib," in *Encyclopaedia of Islam*, 2nd ed., 6:828–29.
51. Ewald Wagner, "Munāẓara," in *Encyclopedia of Islam*, 2nd ed., 7:565–68.
52. Huizinga, *Homo ludens*, 155.
53. Abū ʿUthmān ʿAmr b. Baḥr al-Jāḥiẓ, *Kitāb al-Bayān wa-t-tabyīn*, ed. ʿAbd as-Salām Muḥammad Hārūn, 4 vols. (Cairo, 1960–1961); Susanne Enderwitz, *Gesellschaftlicher Rang und ethnische Legitimation: Der arabische Schriftsteller Abū ʿUṯmān al-Ǧāḥiẓ (gest. 868) über die Afrikaner, Perser und Araber in der islamischen Gesellschaft* (Berlin, 1979).
54. Abū ʿUthmān ʿAmr b. Baḥr al-Jāḥiẓ, *Kitāb Mufākharat al-Jawārī wa-l-ghilmān*, ed. Charles Pellat (Beirut, 1957).
55. See Wagner, "Munāẓara"; Ewald Wagner, "Rangstreit," in *Enzyklopädie des Märchens*, ed. Hermann Bausinger, Doris Boden, Rolf Wilhelm Brednich, and Kurt Ranke (Berlin, 2003), 11:194–99; Geert Jan van Gelder, "Debate Literature," in *Encylopedia of Arabic Literature*, 1:186.
56. Autograph manuscript in Esc. 548, foll. 34b–53b; see also Geert Jan van Gelder, "The Conceit of Pen and Sword: On an Arabic Literary Debate," *Journal of Semitic Studies* 32 (1987): 329–60.
57. Ibrahim Geries, *Un genre littéraire arabe: Al-Maḥāsin wa-l-masāwī* (Paris, 1977).
58. Abū Manṣūr ath-Thaʿālibī, *Taḥsīn al-qabīḥ wa-taqbīḥ al-ḥasan*, ed. Shākir ʿĀshūr (Damascus, 2006).
59. Abū Naṣr al-Maqdisī (erroneously published under the name of ath-Thaʿālibī), *al-Laṭāʾif wa-ẓ-ẓarāʾif min ṭabaqāt al-fuḍalāʾ* (Beirut, 1412/1992).
60. al-Waṭwāṭ, *Ghurar al-khaṣāʾiṣ al-wāḍiḥah wa-ʿurar an-naqāʾiṣ al-fāḍiḥah* (Beirut, n.d.).

61. See pp. 196–98.
62. Shihāb ad-Dīn al-Ḥijāzī, *Rawḍ al-ādāb*, Document no. 400, fol. 100b, Manuscript, n.d. Nationalbibliothek Wien.
63. al-Ḥijāzī, *Rawḍ al-ādāb*, fol. 95a.
64. Huizinga, *Homo ludens*, 180.
65. Ibn al-Muʿtazz, *Kitāb al-badīʿ*, ed. Ignatius Kratchkovsky (London, 1935).
66. Wilhelm Heinz, *Der indische Stil in der persischen Literatur* (Wiesbaden, 1973); for the same style in Ottoman-Turkish poetry, see Michael Glünz, "Betrachtungen zum 'indischen Stil' in der osmanischen Dichtung," in *Ghazal as World Literature*, ed. Angelika Neuwirth and Thomas Bauer (Beirut, 2005), 2:175–84.
67. Hobbes, *Leviathan*, chapter 5.
68. See Thomas Bauer, "Communication and Emotion: The Case of Ibn Nubātah's 'Kindertotenlieder,'" *Mamlūk Studies Review* 7 (2003): 49–95; Thomas Bauer, "Der Fürst ist tot, es lebe der Fürst! Ibn Nubātas Gedicht zur Inthronisation al-Afḍals von Ḥamāh (732/1332)," in *Orientalistische Studien zu Sprache und Literatur: Festgabe zum 65. Geburtstag von Werner Diem*, ed. Monika Gronke and Ulrich Marzolph (Wiesbaden, 2011), 285–315.
69. Bonebakker, *Some Early Definitions of the Tawriya*.
70. Sasson Somekh, "The Neo-Classical Arabic Poets," in *Modern Arabic Literature*, ed. Muhammad Mustafa Badawi (Cambridge, 1992), 36; see also Bauer, "Badīʿiyya," 81–83.
71. See Ibrāhīm al-Miʿmār, *Dīwān*, published with German title as *Der Dīwān des Ibrāhīm al-Miʿmār (gest. 749/1348–49): Edition und Kommentar*, ed. Thomas Bauer, Anke Osigus, and Hakan Özkan (Baden-Baden, 2018).
72. Frédéric Lagrange, *al-Tarab: Die Musik Ägyptens* (Heidelberg, 2000), 34; see also Pierre Pierre Cachia, "The Egyptian Mawwāl," *Journal of Arabic Literature* 8 (1977): 77–103.
73. Veronika Marschall, *Das Chronogramm: Eine Studie zu Formen und Funktionen einer literarischen Kunstform* (Frankfurt, 1997).
74. Bauer, *Chronogramm*.
75. Bauer, "Badīʿiyya."
76. Huizinga, *Homo ludens*, 46.
77. See also the analysis of a hunting poem from Mamluk times in Thomas Bauer, "The Dawādār's Hunting Party: A Mamluk Muzdawija Ṭardiyya, Probably by Shihāb al-Dīn Ibn Faḍl Allāh," in *O Ye Gentlemen: Arabic Studies on Science and Literary Culture in Honour of Remke Kruk*, ed. Jan P. Hogendijk and Arnoud Vrolijk (Leiden, 2007), 291–312.
78. Bauer, *Liebe und Liebesdichtung*, 106–49.
79. Ismāʿīl Ibn Abī Bakr Ibn al-Muqriʾ, *ʿUnwān ash-sharaf al-wāfī fī ʿilm al-fiqh wa taʾrīkh wa-n-nahw wa-l-ʿarūḍ wa-l-qawāfī*, ed. ʿAbdallāh Ibrāhīm al-Anṣārī (Beirut, 1417/1996).

7. THE AMBIGUITY OF SEXUAL DESIRE

Epigraph. Foucault, *Folie et déraison*. This passage from the preface does not figure in the original edition, nor in the English translation, but only in the reedition indicated in the bibliography, 161–62.

1. Robert Muchembled, *Orgasm and the West: A History of Pleasure from the Sixteenth Century to the Present*, trans. Jean Birrell (Cambridge, 2008), 83.
2. Michel Foucault, *The Will to Knowledge*, vol. 1 of *The History of Sexuality*, trans. Robert Hurley (New York, 1978–1988), 67–68.
3. Foucault, *The Will to Knowledge*, 68.

4. Foucault, *The Will to Knowledge*, 69.
5. Muchembled, *Orgasm and the West*, 30.
6. Carsten Bagge Laustsen and Bülent Diken, "Becoming Abject: Rape as a Weapon of War," *Body and Society* 11 (2005): 111–28.
7. Guido Sprenger, *Ethnologie der Sexualität: Eine Einführung*, in *Sex and the Body: Ethnologische Perspektiven zu Sexualität, Körper und Geschlecht*, ed. Gabriele Alex and Sabine Klocke-Daffa (Bielefeld, 2005), 11–20.
8. Muchembled, *Orgasm and the West*, 159.
9. See, e.g., Georg Klauda, *Die Vertreibung aus dem Serail* (Hamburg, 2008), 23.
10. David Greenberg, *The Construction of Homosexuality* (Chicago, 1988), 359; see also Klauda, *Vertreibung aus dem Serail*, 94–98.
11. Klauda, *Vertreibung aus dem Serail*, 95.
12. Foucault, *The Will to Knowledge*, 42–43.
13. The terms "homosexuality" (first attestation in 1869) and "heterosexuality" (1880) trace back to Karl Maria Kertbeny (1824–1882). See Rüdiger Lautmann, ed., *Homosexualität: Handbuch der Theorie- und Forschungsgeschichte* (Frankfurt, 1993), 46.
14. Kobene Mercer, quoted in Joseph A. Massad, *Desiring Arabs* (Chicago, 2007), 7.
15. Abū Ḥāmid al-Ghazālī, *Iḥyāʾ ʿulūm ad-dīn*, ed. ʿAbdallāh al-Khālidī (Beirut, 1998), 3:122.
16. See, e.g., Shams ad-Dīn Muḥammad adh-Dhahabī, *Kitāb al-Kabāʾir*, ed. Abū Ḥusayn al-Makkī (Mecca, 2004).
17. See various contributions to the collection of essays *Locating Hell in Islamic Traditions*, ed. Christian Lange (Leiden, 2016).
18. For this, see the study by Thomas Hildebrandt, *Neo-Muʿtazilismus: Intention und Kontext im modernen arabischen Umgang mit dem rationalistischen Erbe des Islam* (Leiden, 2007).
19. Bauer, *Liebe und Liebesdichtung*, 344–50.
20. Georges Henri Bousquet, "Bāh," in *Encyclopaedia of Islam*, 2nd ed., ed. P. J. Bearman et al. (Leiden, 1960), 1:910–11.
21. See Sara Omar, "From Semantics to Normative Law: Perceptions of Liwāṭ (Sodomy) and Siḥāq (Tribadism) in Islamic Jurisprudence," in *Islamic Law and Society* 19 (Leiden, 2012), 222–56; and Scott Siraj al-Haqq Kugle, *Homosexuality in Islam* (Oxford, 2010), 128–86.
22. Anke Bossaller, *"Schlafende Schwangerschaft" in islamischen Gesellschaften. Entstehung und soziale Implikationen einer weiblichen Fiktion* (Würzburg, 2004).
23. Muḥammad al-Muḥibbī, *Khulāṣat al-athar fī aʿyān al-qarn al-ḥādī ʿashar* (Beirut, n.d.), 1:181–82. For this incident, see also Madeline C. Zilfi, *Women and Slavery in the Late Ottoman Empire* (Cambridge, 2010), 71–72.
24. Ibn Rushd, *Bidāyat al-mujtahid wa-nihāyat al-muqtaṣid*, ed. Mājid al-Ḥamawī (Beirut, 1416/1995), 4:1729n3.
25. Muchembled, *Orgasm and the West*, 170.
26. ʿAbd ar-Raḥmān al-Juzayrī, *Kitāb al-Fiqh ʿalā l-madhāhib al-arbaʿa*, 5 vols. (Beirut, 1998), 5:222–23.
27. Foucault, *The Will to Knowledge*, 58.
28. Abū ʿAbdallāh Muḥammad an-Nafzāwī, *Der duftende Garten: Ein arabisches Liebeshandbuch*, trans. Ulrich Marzolph (Munich, 2002).
29. On *mujūn*, see Zoltan Szombathy, *Mujūn: Libertinism in Medieval Muslim Society and Literature* (Cambridge, 2013); Adam Talib, Marlé Hammond, and Arie Schippers, eds., *The Rude, the Bad and the Bawdy: Essays in Honour of Geert Jan van Gelder* (Cambridge, 2014).
30. For this and what follows, see Bauer, *Liebe und Liebesdichtung*, and Bauer and Neuwirth (eds.), *Ghazal as World Literature*, vol. 1: *Transformation*; Neuwirth et al. (eds.), *Ghazal as World Literature*, vol. 2: *Great Tradition*.
31. Bauer, *Ibn Ḥajar*.

32. See Khaled El-Rouayheb, *Before Homosexuality in the Arabic-Islamic World, 1500–1800* (Chicago, 2005); Thomas Bauer, "Male-Male Love in Classical Arabic Poetry," in *The Cambridge History of Gay and Lesbian Literature*, ed. E. L. McCallum and Mikko Tuhkanen (Cambridge, 2014), 107–24.
33. *Anthologia Graeca* XII 10, quoted from *The Greek Anthology*, ed. and trans. W. R. Patton (London, 1918), 4:287.
34. Friedrich Rückert, *Die Verwandlungen des Abu Seid von Serug oder die Makamen des Hariri* (Stuttgart, 1878); F[rancis] Steingass, *The Assemblies of al-Ḥarîrî* (London, 1898).
35. al-Ḥarīrī in an-Nawājī, *Marātiʿ al-ghizlān*, Manuscript, Document No. 722, Topkapı Saray, fol. 66b.
36. Ḥasan Muḥammad ʿAbd al-Hādī, *Muʾallafāt Shams ad-Dīn an-Nawājī* (Amman, 2001), 78–80, with indication of eleven manuscripts. His *Khalʿ al-ʿidhār fī waṣf al-ʿidhār* was edited by Ḥusayn ʿAbdalʿāl al-Lahībī (Damascus, 2017).
37. See the entry on "Homoerotik" in Thomas Bauer, *Warum es kein islamisches Mittelalter gab: Das Erbe der Antike und der Orient* (Munich, 2018), 45–47.
38. Gary Leupp, *Male Colors: The Construction of Homosexuality in Tokugawa Japan* (Los Angeles, 1995); Gregory M. Pflugfelder, *Cartographies of Desire: Male-Male Sexuality in Japanese Discourse, 1600–1950* (Berkeley, 1999).
39. According to Volker Sommer, *Wider die Natur? Homosexualität und Evolution* (Munich, 1990), 160, with instructive examples.
40. The term is Klauda's, in his *Vertreibung aus dem Serail.*
41. Henry E. Adams, Lester W. Wright, Jr., and Bethany A. Lohr, "Is Homophobia Associated with Homosexual Arousal?" *Journal of Abnormal Psychology* 105 (1996): 440–45.
42. Yaron Ben Naeh, "Homosexuality in Jewish Society," in *Encyclopedia of Jews in the Islamic World*, ed. Norman A. Stillman (Leiden, 2010), 2:431–33.
43. See, e.g., Massad, *Desiring Arabs*, 86, 106.
44. Dieter Haller, *dtv-Atlas Ethnologie* (Munich, 2005), 105.
45. See, e.g., Elmar Holenstein, *Philosophie-Atlas: Orte und Wege des Denkens* (Zurich, 2004), 48–49.
46. Bénédict Augustin Morel, *Traité des dégénérescences physiques, intellectuelles et morales de l'espèce humaine et des causes qui produises ces variétés maladives* (Paris, 1857).
47. Greenberg, *Construction of Homosexuality*, 49.
48. Greenberg, *Construction of Homosexuality*, 412–13.
49. Lautmann, *Homosexualität*, 49.
50. Greenberg, *Construction of Homosexuality*, 412.
51. The literature since Foucault's *Birth of the Clinic* is vast and does not need documentation here.
52. Massad, *Desiring Arabs*, 3.
53. See, e.g., Albert Diefenbacher, *Psychiatrie und Kolonialismus: Zur 'Irrenfürsorge' in der Kolonie Deutsch-Ostafrika* (Frankfurt, 1985); Jean-Michel Bégué, "French Psychiatry in Algeria (1830–1962): From Colonial to Transcultural," *History of Psychiatry* 7 (1996): 533–48.
54. Wilson Chacko Jacob, *Working Out Egypt: Effendi Masculinity and Subject Formation in Colonial Modernity, 1870–1940* (Durham, NC, 2011).
55. Tomas Avenarius, "Privater Krach, politische Folgen: Eine überraschende Ehescheidung schwächt die Opposition in Ägypten," *Süddeutsche Zeitung*, April 9/10, 2009, 9.
56. From a review of Mosbahi Heller, *Hinter den Schleiern*, May 5, 2009, Amazon.de. http://www.amazon.de/Hinter-Schleiern-Sexualit%C3%A4t-arabischen-Kultur/dp/3423047127.
57. Ṣafī ad-Dīn al-Ḥillī, *Dīwān al-mathālith wa-l-mathānī*, ed. Muḥammad Ṭāhir al-Ḥimṣī (Damascus, 1419/1998).
58. Ṣafī ad-Dīn al-Ḥillī, *Dīwān*, ed. Muḥammad Ḥuwwar (Beirut, 2000), 1:14–15.
59. See, e.g., Massad, *Desiring Arabs*, 73.
60. Sonnini de Manoncourt, *Voyage dans la Haute et Basse Égypte* (Paris, 1798), 1:227–28. Translated by Henry Hunter as *Travels in Upper and Lower Egypt* (London, 1799), 1:163.

61. Richard Burton, "Terminal Essay," in *The Book of the Thousand Nights and a Night* (London, 1886), 10:177.
62. Burton, "Terminal Essay," 10:177.
63. Massad, *Desiring Arabs*, 8, with note 17.
64. Burton, "Terminal Essay," 10:195.
65. Dror Ze'evi, *Producing Desire: Changing Sexual Discourse in the Ottoman Middle East, 1500–1900* (Berkeley, 2006), 164.
66. Massad, *Desiring Arabs*, 70.
67. Massad, *Desiring Arabs*, 75–76.
68. Massad, *Desiring Arabs*, 55.
69. Massad, *Desiring Arabs*, 79.
70. Thomas Bauer, "Review of Majd al-Afandī's *al-Ghazal fī l-ʿAṣr al-Mamlūkī al-Awwal* (Damascus, 1994)," *Mamlūk Studies Review* 3 (1999): 214–19.
71. Massad, *Desiring Arabs*.
72. Klauda, *Vertreibung aus dem Serail*.
73. See above, note 33.
74. El-Rouayheb, *Before Homosexuality*, 22.
75. This is the subtitle of Klauda's book.
76. Massad, *Desiring Arabs*, 188, 190.
77. Klauda, *Vertreibung aus dem Serail*, 100–3.
78. Klauda, *Vertreibung aus dem Serail*, 15.

8. THE SERENE LOOK AT THE WORLD

1. Friedrich Nietzsche, *Gay Science*, trans. Walter Kaufmann (New York, 1974), 239.
2. This term is borrowed from Bauman, *Modernity and Ambivalence*, 110.
3. The literature on the controversy over the impact of monotheism on religious communities has become boundless; I am naming here only Jürgen Manemann, *Monotheismus* (Münster, 2005).
4. Jan Assmann, "Monotheismus," in Manemann, *Monotheismus*, 132.
5. Jan Assmann, "Monotheismus," 132.
6. ʿAlī ibn Muḥammad ibn Ḥabīb al-Māwardī, *Kitāb al-Aḥkām as-sulṭāniyyah wa-l-wilāyāt ad-dīniyyah*, ed. Aḥmad Mubārak al-Baghdādī (Kuwait City, 1409/1989). Translated into English by Qamar ud-Din Khan as *al-Māwardī's Theory of the State* (Lahore, 1983) and by Wafaa H. Wahba as *The Ordinances of Government* (Reading, 1996).
7. Khan (trans.), *al-Māwardī's Theory of the State*.
8. *Geschichte der arabischen Litteratur*, ed. Carl Brockelmann (Leiden, 1943), 1:386.
9. See, e.g., Patricia Crone, *God's Rule: Government and Islam* (New York, 2003), 232–33.
10. von Grunebaum, *Medieval Islam*, 168. Von Grunebaum's German translation (*Der Islam im Mittelalter* (Zürich, 1963), 216) has, instead of "it could no longer be overlooked by the body of the believers," "that it posed for all believers a grievous problem."
11. von Grunebaum, *Medieval Islam*, 169.
12. That is the subtitle of Patricia Crone's book.
13. Edition, English translation and commentary: Richard Walzer, *Al-Farabi on the Perfect State* (Oxford, 1985).
14. Stefan Leder, "Aspekte arabischer und persischer Fürstenspiegel: Legitimation, Fürstenethik, politische Vernunft," in *Specula principum*, ed. Angela De Benedictis (Frankfurt, 1999), 21–50; Louise Marlow, "Advice and Advice Literature," in *The Encyclopaedia of Islam*, 3rd ed., ed. Marc Gaborieau et al. (Leiden, 2007), 1:34–58.

15. al-Māwardī, *al-Aḥkām as-sulṭāniyyah*, 1.
16. Muhsin Mahdi, "Philosophical Literature," in *Religion, Learning and Science in the ʿAbbāsid Period*, ed. M. J. L. Young, John Derek Latham, and Robert Bertram Serjeant (Cambridge, 1990), 87–105.
17. Crone, *God's Rule*, 167.
18. Wolfgang Merkel, "Religion, Fundamentalismus und Demokratie," in *Fundamentalismus, Terrorismus, Krieg*, ed. Wolfgang Schluchter (Weilerswist, 2003), 78.
19. Helmut Schmidt, "Sind die Türken Europäer? Nein, sie passen nicht dazu," in *Die Türkei und Europa: Die Positionen*, ed. Klaus Leggewie (Frankfurt, 2004), 162.
20. For Ibn Nubātah, see Thomas Bauer, "Ibn Nubātah al-Miṣrī (686–768/1287–1366): Life and Work, Part I; The Life of Ibn Nubātah," *Mamlūk Studies Review* 12 (2008): 1–35.
21. Fuat Sezgin, ed., *Geschichte des arabischen Schrifttums*, vol. 13 (Frankfurt, 2007).
22. For the following, see Bauer, "Der Fürst ist tot, es lebe der Fürst!"
23. Niccolò Machiavelli, *Il Principe*, in *Opere, a cura di Mario Bonfantini*, 3rd. ed. (Milan, 1986), ch. 18, p. 57: A uno principe . . . non è necessario avere in fatto tutte le soprascritte qualità ma è bene necessario parere di averle.
24. Bernhard H. F. Taureck, *Machiavelli—ABC* (Leipzig, 2002), 228.
25. Muslim ibn al-Ḥajjāj, *al-Jāmiʿ aṣ-Ṣaḥīḥ*, ed. M. F. ʿAbd al-Bāqī, 5 vols., Cairo 1955, no. 5827: *lā tasubbū d-dahra fa-inna llāha huwa d-dahru*, frequently used with this wording, or close to this wording.
26. Taqī ad-Dīn al-Maqrīzī, *Kitāb as-Sulūk fī maʿrifat duwal al-mulūk*, ed. Saʿīd ʿAbd al-Fattāḥ ʿĀshūr and Muḥammad Muṣṭafā Ziyādah (Cairo, [1934–1973]), 2:part 2, 345.
27. See the entry "Glück und Verdienst, fortuna/virtù" in Taureck, *Machiavelli—ABC*, 107–9.
28. Richard Hrair Dekmejian and Abel Fathy Thabit, "Machiavelli's Arab Precursor: Ibn Ẓafar al-Ṣiqillī," *British Journal of Middle Eastern Studies* 27 (2000): 125–37.
29. Bauer, "Ibn Nubātah: Life and Works," 6–7, with notes 17–18.
30. Ibn Nubātah, *Kitāb sulūk duwal al-mulūk*, Manuscript, Bodleian Library, Oxford, Seld. Superius no. 29, Folio nos. 84b–85a.
31. Ibn Nubātah, *Sulūk*, fol. 81a–b.
32. Ibn Nubātah, *Sulūk*, fol. 81a–b, 98b–99b; for the historical context, see Brian A. Catlos, "Washḳa," in *Encyclopaedia of Islam*, 2nd ed., ed. P. J. Bearman et al. (Leiden, 2002), 11:159.
33. Wolfgang Kersting, *Niccolò Machiavelli*, 3rd. ed. (Munich, 2006), 59ff.
34. Kersting, *Niccolò Machiavelli*, 59.
35. Erwin I. J. Rosenthal, *Averroes' Commentary on Plato's Republic* (Cambridge, 1969), 161; Ralph Lerner, *Averroes on Plato's* Republic (Ithaca, NY, 1974), 54.
36. Aziz Al-Azmeh, *Ibn Khaldūn: An Essay in Reinterpretation* (London, 1992); see also Francesco Gabrieli, "ʿAṣabiyya," in *Encyclopaedia of Islam*, 2nd ed., ed. P. J. Bearman et al. (Leiden, 1960), 1:681.
37. Merkel, "Religion, Fundamentalismus und Demokratie," 78.
38. *Mukaddime: Osmanlı Tercümesi*, trans. Pirizade Mehmed Sahib and Ahmed Cevdet Paşa (Istanbul, 2008).
39. Both publications under the title *al-Mukhtār min Kitāb Tadbīr ad-duwal* by ʿAbd Ṣāʾil al-Fahdāwī (Baghdad, 1431/2010) and Salmā Qandīl (Beirut, 1433/2012) suffer from incomplete referencing of the available manuscripts.
40. Kersting, *Machiavelli*, 164.
41. Kersting, *Machiavelli*, 164.
42. Reinhard Schulze, "Die Politisierung des Islam im 19. Jahrhundert," *Welt des Islams* 22 (1982): 115–19; Reinhard Schulze, "Islam und Herrschaft: Zur politischen Instrumentalisierung einer Religion" in *Der Islam im Aufbruch? Perspektiven der arabischen Welt*, ed. Michael Lüders, 2nd. ed. (Munich, 1993),

94–129; Gudrun Krämer, *Gottes Staat als Republik: Reflexionen zeitgenössischer Muslime zu Islam, Menschenrechten und Demokratie* (Baden-Baden, 1999), 43.

43. Olivier Roy, "Reislamisierung und Radikalisierung," *Internationale Politik* 2–3 (1999): 49; Olivier Roy, *L'Islam mondialisé* (Paris, 2002), 65. Translated as *Globalized Islam: The Search for a New Ummah* (New York, 2004).

44. For Egypt, see Ivesa Lübben, "Die Muslimbruderschaft und der Widerstand gegen eine dynastische Erbfolge in Ägypten," *Giga Focus Nahost* 5 (2009): 1–7.

45. ʿAbd ar-Raḥmān Ibn Khaldūn, *at-Taʿrīf bi-bn Khaldūn wa-riḥlatihī gharban wa-sharqan*, ed. Muḥammad ibn Tāwīt aṭ-Ṭanjī (Cairo, 2003), 377–78.

46. See Franz Rosenthal, "The Stranger in Medieval Islam," *Arabica* 44 (1997): 35–75; Thomas Bauer, "Fremdheit in der klassischen arabischen Kultur und Sprache," in *Fremdes in fremden Sprachen*, ed. Brigitte Jostes and Jürgen Trabant (Munich, 2001), 85–105.

47. Bauer, "Fremdheit," 93.

48. al-Maqdisī [under the name of ath-Thaʿālibī], *Laṭāʾif*, 229; see also Bauer, "Fremdheit," 94.

49. Muḥammad ibn ʿAbdallāh Ibn Baṭṭūṭah, *Riḥlat Ibn Baṭṭūṭah*, ed. Karam al-Bustānī (Beirut, 1960), 17.

50. Ibn Baṭṭūṭah, *Riḥlah*, 17.

51. Explicitly marked in Rosenthal, *Stranger*, 64.

52. Rosenthal, *Stranger*, 73.

53. Rosenthal, *Stranger*, 40n17, and the contributions to Jostes and Trabant, *Fremdes in fremden Sprachen*.

54. Bauer, "Fremdheit," 91n12.

55. Bauman, *Modernity and Ambivalence*, 53.

56. Bauman, *Modernity and Ambivalence*, 55.

57. Bauman, *Modernity and Ambivalence*, 55.

58. Bauman, *Modernity and Ambivalence*, 56.

59. Bauman, *Modernity and Ambivalence*, 61.

60. Bauman, *Modernity and Ambivalence*, 61.

61. Bauman, *Modernity and Ambivalence*, 64.

62. Bauman, *Modernity and Ambivalence*, 67.

63. Bauman, *Modernity and Ambivalence*, 105.

64. "Der Holocaust ist nicht einmalig," an interview with the Polish sociologist Zygmunt Bauman, in the weekly *Die Zeit*, no. 17, April 23, 1993.

65. Bauman, *Modernity and Ambivalence*, 61.

66. For the following, see Thomas Bauer, "Vertraute Fremde: Das Bild des Beduinen in der arabischen Literatur des 10. Jahrhunderts," in *Shifts and Drifts in Nomad-Sedentary Relations*, ed. Stefan Leder and Bernhard Streck, 377–400 (Wiesbaden, 2005).

67. Stefan Heidemann, *Die Renaissance der Städte in Nordsyrien und Nordmesopotamien: Städtische Entwicklung und wirtschaftliche Bedingungen in ar-Raqqa und Harran von der Zeit der beduinischen Vorherrschaft bis zu den Seldschuken* (Leiden, 2002).

68. See Bauer, "Miʿmār."

69. See Mitchell Bard, "Von Nasser vertrieben. Ägyptens Juden," *Pogrom*, no. 5–6 (2009): 21.

70. Mark R. Cohen, *Under Crescent and Cross: The Jews in the Middle Ages* (Princeton, NJ, 1994), 116.

71. Cohen, *Crescent and Cross*, 161–67.

72. Rabbi Obadya of Bartinoro, quoted in Cohen, *Crescent and Cross*, 193.

73. Cohen, *Crescent and Cross*, 193–94.

74. "Abschiebehaft," accessed January 1, 2009, Wikipedia.de, http://de.wikipedia.org/wiki/Abschiebehaft.

75. See "Vielfalt als chance," accessed July 13, 2009, http://www.vielfalt-als-chance.de.

76. "Integrieren," Synonyme, Woxikon, accessed January 1, 2009, http://synonyme.woxikon.de/synonyme/sich%integrieren.php.

77. Bauman, *Modernity and Ambivalence*, 107–110.
78. Bauman, *Modernity and Ambivalence*, 111.
79. *Geschichte des arabischen Schrifttums*, vol. 13.
80. James Montgomery, "Ibn Faḍlān and the Rūsiyyah," *Journal of Arabic and Islamic Studies* 3 (2000): 1–25.
81. Aḥmad Ibn Faḍlān, *Risālat Ibn Faḍlān*, ed. Sāmī ad-Dahhān (Damascus, 1379/1959), 155. Translated, with commentary, by Richard Frye as *Ibn Fadlan's Journey to Russia: A Tenth-Century Traveler from Baghdad to the Volga River* (Princeton, NJ, 2005), 65. See also James Montgomery's recent translation in his *Two Arabic Travel Books: Accounts of China and India and Mission to the Volga* (New York, 2014).
82. Ibn Faḍlān, *Risālat Ibn Faḍlān*, 155–56; Frye's English translation, 67–70.
83. Abū l-Ḥasan ʿAlī al-Masʿūdī, *Murūj adh-dhahab wa-maʿādin al-jawhar*, ed. Charles Pellat, 7 vols. (Beirut, 1965–1979), Section 449.
84. Ibn Faḍlān, *Risālat Ibn Faḍlān*, 130–32; Frye's translation, 46–49.
85. The expression is Olivier Roy's, *Globalized Islam*.
86. Bauman, *Modernity and Ambivalence*, 110.
87. Fuat Sezgin, "Die Entdeckung des amerikanischen Kontinents durch muslimische Seefahrer vor Kolumbus," in *Geschichte des arabischen Schrifttums*, 13:158. Translated into English as *The Pre-Columbian Discovery of the American Continent by Muslim Seafarers*, 33–34. http://www.scribd.com/doc/8710396/The-PreColumbian-discovery-of-the-American-continent-by-muslim-seafarers.
88. Sezgin, "Die Entdeckung," 160; English translation, 35.
89. Robert B. Marks, *The Origins of the Modern World: A Global and Ecological Narrative from the Fifteenth to the Twenty-First Century* (Lanham, MD, 2015), 48–50.
90. Marks, *Origins of the Modern World*, 63, with a quotation from Chaudhuri, *Trade and Civilization*.
91. al-Masʿūdī, *Murūj*, Section 274; see also Sezgin, "Die Entdeckung," 139.
92. Sezgin, "Die Entdeckung," 127–28.
93. Sezgin, "Die Entdeckung," 153–54.
94. Sezgin, "Die Entdeckung," 152.
95. Sezgin, "Die Entdeckung," 143. Juan Díaz de Solís lost his life on February 2, 1516, at the Río de la Plata.
96. Sezgin, "Die Entdeckung," 139–40.
97. Sezgin, "Die Entdeckung," 157–58.
98. First act, second scene.
99. First act, second scene. (italics T.B.)
100. Tzvetan Todorov, *The Conquest of America: The Question of the Other*, trans. Richard Howard (New York, 1984), 247.
101. Horace Bidwell English and Ava Champney English, *A Comprehensive Dictionary of Psychological and Psychoanalytical Terms*, 24, quoted from MacDonald, *Revised Scale*, 791.
102. Todorov, *Conquest*, 247–48.
103. Todorov, *Conquest*, 97.
104. See Exopolitik, accessed June 16, 2009, http://www.exopolitik.org/index.php?option=com_content&task=view&id=37&Itemid=49, italics T.B.
105. Exopolitik.
106. "SETI," Wikipedia.de, accessed June 16, 2009, http://de.wikipedia.org/wiki/SETI.
107. "Voyager Golden Record," Wikipedia.de, accessed June 16, 2009, http://de.wikipedia.org/wiki/Voyager_Golden_Record.
108. Todorov, *Conquest*, 251.
109. "SETI," Wikipedia.de.
110. Bauman, *Modernity and Ambivalence*, 98.
111. Bauman, *Modernity and Ambivalence*, 98.
112. Bauman, *Modernity and Ambivalence*, 98.

9. IN QUEST OF CERTAINTY

1. As a representative example of such accounts, one might consult Bassam Tibi's book *Der wahre Imam* (Munich, 1996), which, in the absence of any hint of knowledge of the history of Islam and Islamic law, advocates this conception. From this book, too, the meaningless expression "fiqh doctrine" is taken.
2. See for instance Griffel, *Den Islam denken*.
3. ar-Rāzī, *Maḥṣūl*, 1:200–1, with note 2.
4. See p. 108.
5. ar-Rāzī, *Maḥṣūl*, 1:392–404.
6. ar-Rāzī, *Maḥṣūl*, 1:404–6.
7. ar-Rāzī, *Maḥṣūl*, 1:407.
8. ʿAbd ar-Raḥmān Ibn Khaldūn, *al-Muqaddimah*, ed. Vincent Monteil (Beirut, 1968), 3:1027–34.
9. See, e.g., Najm ad-Dīn aṭ-Ṭūfī al-Ḥanbalī, *ʿAlam al-jadhal fī ʿilm al-jadal*, ed. Wolfhart Heinrichs (Wiesbaden, 1987); Abū l-Wafāʾ ʿAlī ibn ʿAqīl al-Baghdādī al-Ḥanbalī, *Kitāb al-Jadal*, ed. ʿAlī ibn ʿAbd al-ʿAzīz ibn ʿAlī al-ʿUmayraynī (Riyadh, 1997); al-Ghazālī, *al-Muntakhal fī l-jadal*, ed. ʿAlī ibn ʿAbd al-ʿAzīz ibn ʿAlī al- ʿUmayraynī (Beirut, 2004).
10. Bahāʾ ad-Dīn Aḥmad as-Subkī, *ʿArūs al-afrāḥ fī sharḥ Talkhīṣ al-Miftāḥ*, ed. Khalīl Ibrāhīm Khalīl (Beirut, 2001), 1:173.
11. See Hildebrandt, *Neo-Muʿtazilismus*.
12. Ignaz Goldziher, *Introduction to Islamic Theology and Law*, trans. András Hamori and Ruth Hamori (Princeton, NJ, 1981), 100–1.
13. Ahmad S. Moussalli, "Islamism: Modernisation of Islam or Islamisation of Knowledge," in *Cosmopolitanism, Identity and Authenticity in the Middle East*, ed. Roel Meijer (Richmond, VA, 1999), 98.
14. Moussalli, "Islamism," 87.
15. Marks, *The Origins of the Modern World*, 14.
16. Stephen Toulmin, *Cosmopolis: The Hidden Agenda of Modernity* (New York, 1990).
17. Toulmin, *Cosmopolis*, 80–81.
18. Toulmin, *Cosmopolis*, 53.
19. Muchembled, *Orgasm and the West*, 50–51.
20. Muchembled, *Orgasm and the West*, 78.
21. Toulmin, *Cosmopolis*, 54.
22. Toulmin, *Cosmopolis*, 55.
23. Toulmin, *Cosmopolis*, 70.
24. Toulmin, *Cosmopolis*, 72.
25. Toulmin, *Cosmopolis*, 71.
26. Toulmin, *Cosmopolis*, 75.
27. Rightly, Maḥmūd Muḥammad Shākir, in the preface to his edition of al-Jurjānī's work *Asrār al-balāgha*, 22, pronounces his indignation.
28. Toulmin, *Cosmopolis*, 153.
29. Toulmin, *Cosmopolis*, 11.
30. Muchembled, *Orgasm and the West*, 141.
31. Muchembled, *Orgasm and the West*, 22.
32. Muchembled, *Orgasm and the West*, 24.
33. Bauer, *Warum es kein islamisches Mittelalter gab*.
34. Toulmin, *Cosmopolis*, 160.
35. Toulmin, *Cosmopolis*, 167.
36. Toulmin, *Cosmopolis*, 71.
37. Alain Gresh, Philippe Rekacewicz, and Barbara Bauer, *Atlas der Globalisierung* (Paris, 2006), 54–55, 119.

38. Oskar Bie, *Die Oper* (Berlin, 1919), 9.
39. John L. Esposito and Dalia Mogahed, *Who Speaks for Islam? What a Billion Muslims Really Think: Based on Gallup's World Poll* (New York, 2007), 29–63.
40. Max Born, *Von der Verantwortung des Naturwissenschaftlers* [On the Responsibility of the Scientist] (Munich, 1965), 183.

Bibliography

ARABIC WORKS

ʿAbd al-Hādī, Ḥasan Muḥammad. *Muʾallafāt Shams ad-Dīn an-Nawājī*. Amman, 2001.

Abū Nuwās. *Dīwān*. Vol. 1–3, 5, and index 1–2 edited by Ewald Wagner. Vol. 4 edited by Gregor Schoeler. Wiesbaden, 1958–2006.

al-Būṭī, Muḥammad Saʿīd Ramaḍān. *al-Lāmadhhabiyyah akhṭar bidʿah tuhaddid ash-sharīʿah al-islāmiyyah*. Beirut, 1958. Translated in English by M. Merza et al. as *al-Lā Madhhabiyya: Abandoning the Madhhabs Is the Most Dangerous Bidʿah Threatenting the Islamic Sharīʿa* (Damascus, 2007).

adh-Dhahabī, Shams ad-Dīn Muḥammad. *Tārīkh al-Islām*. Edited by ʿUmar ʿAbd as-Salām Tadmurī. 52 vols. Beirut, 1987–2000.

adh-Dhahabī, Shams ad-Dīn Muḥammad. *Kitāb al-Kabāʾir*. Edited by Abū Ḥusayn al-Makkī. Mecca, 2004.

al-Ghazālī, Abū Ḥāmid. *Iḥyāʾ ʿulūm ad-dīn*. Edited by ʿAbdallāh al-Khālidī. 5 vols. Beirut, 1998.

Ḥājjī Khalīfah [Kātib Čelebi]. *Kashf aẓ-ẓunūn ʿan asāmī l-kutub wa-l-funūn*. 2 vols. Beirut, 1994.

al-Ḥamawī, Uways. *Sukkardān al-ʿushshāq*. Manuscript, n.d. Berlin State Library, no. 8407. See also Wilhelm Ahlwardt, *Die Handschriften-Verzeichnisse der Königlichen Bibliothek zu Berlin: Verzeichnis der arabischen Handschriften*. 10 vols. Berlin, 1887–1899.

al-Ḥarīrī. *al-Maqāmāt*. Translated into English by Michael Cooperson as *Impostures* (New York, 2020). See also Steingass, F[rancis].

al-Ḥijāzī, Shihāb ad-Dīn. *Rawḍ al-ādāb*. Manuscript, n.d. Nationalbibliothek Wien, no. 400.

Ḥusāmzādeh ar-Rūmī. *Risāla fī qalb Kāfūriyyāt al-Mutanabbī min al-madīḥ ilā l-hijāʾ*. Edited by Muḥammad Yūsuf Najm. Beirut, 1392/1972.

Ḥusayn, Ṭāhā. *Fī l-adab al-jāhilī*. Cairo, 1927.

Ibn ʿAbd al-Barr, Yūsuf ibn ʿAbdallāh. *al-Istidhkār al-jāmiʿ li-madhāhib fuqahāʾ al-amṣār wa-ʿulamāʾ al-aqṭār*. Edited by Sālim Muḥammad ʿAṭā and Muḥammad ʿAlī Muʿawwaḍ. 9 vols. Beirut, 2000.

Ibn al-Anbārī. *Kitāb al-Aḍdād*. Edited by Abū l-Faḍl Ibrāhīm. Kuwait City, 1960.

Ibn al-ʿAṭṭār, ʿAlāʾ ad-Dīn. *Adab al-khaṭīb*. Edited by Muḥammad as-Sulaymānī. Beirut, 1996.

Ibn Bassām. *Nihāyat ar-rutbah fī ṭalab al-ḥisbah*. In *K. as-Siyāsah* [. . .] *wa-yalīhi an-Nahj al-maslūk* [. . .], edited by Muḥammad Ḥasan Ismāʿīl and Aḥmad Farīd al-Mazīdī (Beirut, 1424/2003).

Ibn Baṭṭūṭah, Muḥammad ibn ʿAbdallāh. *Riḥlat Ibn Baṭṭūṭah*. Edited by Karam al-Bustānī. Beirut, 1960.

Ibn Faḍlān, Aḥmad. *Risālat Ibn Faḍlān*. Edited by Sāmī ad-Dahhān. Damascus, 1379/1959. Translated, with commentary, by Richard Frye as *Ibn Fadlan's Journey to Russia: A Tenth-Century Traveler from Baghdad to the Volga River* (Princeton, NJ, 2005).

Ibn Ḥajar al-ʿAsqalānī. *an-Nukat ʿalā kitāb Ibn aṣ-Ṣalāḥ*. Edited by Rabīʿ ibn Hādī ʿUmayr. 2 vols. (Riyadh, 1417/1996–1997).

Ibn Ḥajar al-ʿAsqalānī. *Sharḥ sharḥ Nukhbat al-fikar*. Edited by Muḥammad and Haytham Nizār Tamīm. With a commentary by Mullā ʿAlī al-Qārīʾ. Beirut, n.d. (ca 1994).

Ibn Ḥajar al-ʿAsqalānī. *Tahdhīb at-Tahdhīb*. 12 vols. (Hyderabad, 1325–1327/1907–1910).

Ibn al-Ḥajjāj, Muslim. *al-Jāmiʿ aṣ-Ṣaḥīḥ*. Edited by M. F. ʿAbd al-Bāqī. 5 vols. Cairo, 1955.

Ibn Ḥijja al-Ḥamawī, Taqī ad-Dīn Abū Bakr. *Khizānat al-adab wa-ghāyat al-arab*. Edited by Kawkab Diyāb. 5 vols. Beirut, 2001.

Ibn al-Jawzī, Abū l-Faraj ʿAbd ar-Raḥmān. *Zād al-masīr fī ʿilm at-tafsīr*. Beirut 2002.

Ibn al-Jazarī, Shams ad-Dīn Muḥammad. *An-Nashr fī l-qirāʾāt al-ʿashr*. Edited by ʿAlī Muḥammad aḍ-Ḍabbāʿ. 2 vols. Beirut, n.d. (ca. 1980).

Ibn al-Jazarī, Shams ad-Dīn Muḥammad. *Munjid al-muqriʾīn wa-murshid aṭ-ṭālibīn*. Cairo, 1996.

Ibn Juzayy, Abū l-Qasim Muḥammad. *Taqrīb al-wuṣūl ilā ʿilm al-uṣūl*. Edited by Muḥammad ʿAlī Farkūs. Algiers, 1990.

Ibn Khaldūn, ʿAbd ar-Raḥmān. *al-Muqaddimah*. Edited by Vincent Monteil. 3 vols. Beirut, 1968.

Ibn Khaldūn, ʿAbd ar-Raḥmān. *at-Taʿrīf bi-bn Khaldūn wa-riḥlatihī gharban wa-sharqan*. Edited by Muḥammad ibn Tāwīt aṭ-Ṭanjī. Cairo, 2003.

Ibn al-Muqriʾ, Ismāʿīl Ibn Abī Bakr. *ʿUnwān ash-sharaf al-wāfī fī ʿilm al-fiqh wa taʾrīkh wa-n-nahw wa-l-ʿarūḍ wa-l-qawāfī*. Edited by ʿAbdallāh Ibrāhīm al-Anṣārī. Beirut, 1417/1996.

Ibn al-Muʿtazz. *Kitāb al-badīʿ*. Edited by Ignatius Kratchkovsky. London, 1935.

Ibn Nubātah. *Kitāb sulūk duwal al-mulūk*. Manuscript, n.d. Bodleian Library, Oxford, Seld. Superius no. 29.

Ibn Rushd. *Bidāyat al-mujtahid wa-nihāyat al-muqtaṣid*. Edited by Mājid al-Ḥamawī. 4 vols. Beirut, 1416/1995.

Ibn ʿUthaymīn. *al-Khilāf bayn al-ʿulamāʾ: Asbābuhū wa-mawqifunā minhu*. n.p., n.d. http://www.ibnothaimeen.com/all/books/article_16910.shtml (Date Accessed: February 2010).

Ibn ʿUthaymīn. *al-Uṣūl fī t-tafsīr*. Ad Dammām, 1423/2002–2003. www.al-eman.com and www.ibnothaimeen.com (Date Accessed: February 2010).

Ibn ʿUthaymīn. *Tafsīr Juzʾ ʿAmma*. n.p., n.d. http://ibnothaimeen.com/all/books/printer_17863.shtml (Date Accessed: February 2010) and https://web.archive.org/web/20140312001104/http://ibnothaimeen.com/all/books/printer_17863.shtml (Date Accessed: November 2014).

Ibrāhīm al-Miʿmār. *Dīwān*. Published with German title as *Der Dīwān des Ibrāhīm al-Miʿmār (gest. 749/1348–49): Edition und Kommentar*. Edited by Thomas Bauer, Anke Osigus, and Hakan Özkan. Baden-Baden, 2018.

al-Ibshīhī, Bahāʾ ad-Dīn Abū l-Fatḥ Muḥammad. *al-Mustaṭraf fī kull fann mustaẓraf*. Edited by Ibrāhīm Ṣāliḥ. 3 vols. Beirut, 1999.

al-Jāḥiẓ, Abū ʿUthmān ʿAmr ibn Baḥr. *Kitāb al-Bayān wa-t-tabyīn*. Edited by ʿAbd as-Salām Muḥammad Hārūn. 4 vols. Cairo, 1960–1961.

al-Jāḥiẓ, Abū ʿUthmān ʿAmr ibn Baḥr. *Kitāb Mufākharat al-Jawārī wa-l-ghilmān*. Edited by Charles Pellat. Beirut, 1957.

al-Jubūrī, ʿAbdallāh. "al-Aḍdād wa-mawqif Ibn Durustawayh minhā." *al-Mawrid* 2/3 (1973): 42–48.

al-Jurjānī, ʿAbd al-Qāhir. *Asrār al-balāgha*. Edited by Hellmut Ritter. (Istanbul, 1954). Translated into German by Hellmut Ritter as *Die Geheimnisse der Wortkunst des ʿAbdalqāhir al-Curcānī* (Wiesbaden, 1959).

al-Jurjānī, ʿAbd al-Qāhir. *Dalāʾil al-iʿjāz*. Edited by Muḥammad ibn Tāwīt. 2 vols. Tetouan, n.d.

al-Juzayrī, ʿAbd ar-Raḥmān. *Kitāb al-Fiqh ʿalā l-madhāhib al-arbaʿa* (with English tr.: *Islamic jurisprudence according to the four Sunni schools*, and Muḥammad al-Gharawī, Yāsir Māziḥ, *Madhhab ahl al-bayt*). 5 vols. Beirut 1998.

Kātib Čelebī. *See* Ḥājjī Khalīfah.

al-Maʿarrī, Abū l-ʿAlāʾ. *Sharḥ Dīwān Abī ṭ-Ṭayyib al-Mutanabbī (Muʿjiz Aḥmad)*. 2nd ed. Edited by ʿAbd al-Majīd Diyāb. 4 vols. Cairo, 1413/1992.

al-Maqdisī, Abū Naṣr [erroneously published under the name of ath-Thaʿālibī]. *al-Laṭāʾif wa-ẓ-ẓarāʾif min ṭabaqāt al-fuḍalāʾ*. Beirut, 1412/1992.

al-Maqrīzī, Taqī ad-Dīn. *Kitāb as-Sulūk fī maʿrifat duwal al-mulūk*. Edited by Saʿīd ʿAbd al-Fattāḥ ʿĀshūr and Muḥammad Muṣṭafā Ziyādah. 4 vols., 12 parts. Cairo, 1934–1973.

al-Masʿūdī, Abū l-Ḥasan ʿAlī. *Murūj adh-dhahab wa-maʿādin al-jawhar*. Edited by Charles Pellat. 7 vols. Beirut, 1965–1979.

al-Māwardī, ʿAlī ibn Muḥammad ibn Ḥabīb. *al-Ḥāwī al-kabīr fī fiqh madhhab al-Imām ash-Shāfiʿī*. Edited by ʿAlī Muḥammad Muʿawwaḍ and ʿĀdil Aḥmad ʿAbd al-Mawjūd. 1 introductory vol. (*Muqaddimah*) and 19 vols. Beirut, 1999.

al-Māwardī, ʿAlī ibn Muḥammad ibn Ḥabīb. *al-Iqnāʿ fī l-fiqh ash-Shāfiʿī*. Edited by Khiḍr Muḥammad Khiḍr. Kuwait City, 1402/1982.

al-Māwardī, ʿAlī ibn Muḥammad ibn Ḥabīb. *an-Nukat wa-l-ʿuyūn: Tafsīr al-Māwardī*. Edited by ʿAbd al-Maqṣūd ibn ʿAbd ar-Raḥīm. 6 vols. Beirut, n.d.

al-Māwardī, ʿAlī ibn Muḥammad ibn Ḥabīb. *Kitāb al-Aḥkām as-sulṭāniyyah wa-l-wilāyāt ad-dīniyyah*. Edited by Aḥmad Mubārak al-Baghdādī. Kuwait City, 1409/1989. Translated into English by Qamar ud-Din Khan as *al-Māwardī's Theory of the State* (Lahore, 1983). Also translated into English by Wafaa H. Wahba as *al-Māwardī, The Ordinances of Government: A Translation of al-Aḥkām al-Sulṭāniyya wa'l-Wilāyāt al-Dīniyya* (Reading, 1996).

al-Mawdūdī, Sayyid Abū l-Aʿlā. *Tafhīm al-Qurʾān*. 6 vols. Lahore, 1949–1972. Translated into English by Abdul Aziz Kamal as *The Meaning of the Qurʾān*, 5 vols. (Delhi, 1992).

al-Muḥibbī, Muḥammad. *Khulāṣat al-athar fī aʿyān al-qarn al-ḥādī ʿashar*. 4 vols. Beirut, n.d.

al-Mutanabbī. *See* al-Maʿarrī.

an-Nafzāwī, Abū ʿAbdallāh Muḥammad. *Der duftende Garten: Ein arabisches Liebeshandbuch*. Translated by Ulrich Marzolph. Munich, 2002.

an-Nasafī, Najm ad-Dīn. *Ṭilbat aṭ-ṭalaba*. Edited by Khālid ʿAbd ar-Raḥmān al-ʿAkk. Beirut, 1416/1995.

an-Nawājī, Muḥammad. *al-Maṭāliʿ ash-shamsiyyah fī l-madāʾiḥ an-nabawiyyah*. Edited by Ḥasan M. ʿAbd al-Hādī. Amman, 1999.

an-Nawājī, Muḥammad. "Dīwān." Edited by Ḥasan M. ʿAbd al-Hādī as a PhD diss. Cairo, 1400/1980.

an-Nawājī, Muḥammad. *Marātiʿ al-ghizlān*. Manuscript, Document No. 722, Topkapı Saray, Istanbul.

an-Nawājī, Muḥammad. *Muqaddima fī ṣināʿat an-naẓm wa-n-nathr*. Edited by Muḥammad ibn ʿAbd al-Karīm. Beirut, n.d.

an-Nawawī, Muḥyī d-Dīn Yaḥyā ibn Sharaf. *at-Tibyān fī ādāb ḥamalat al-Qurʾān*. Edited by Muḥammad Riḍwān ʿArqasūsī. Beirut, 1422/2002.

an-Nawawī, Muḥyī d-Dīn Yaḥyā ibn Sharaf. *Das Buch der Vierzig Hadithe: Kitāb al-Arbaʿīn, mit dem Kommentar von Ibn Daqīq al-ʿĪd*. Translated and edited by Marco Schöller. Frankfurt am Main, 2007.

al-Qurʾān. *See* the English translation by Arthur J. Arberry.

ar-Rāzī, Fakhr ad-Dīn. *al-Kāshif ʿan al-Maḥṣūl fī ʿilm al-uṣūl*. With a commentary by Abū ʿAbdallāh Shams ad-Dīn al-Iṣfahānī. Edited by ʿĀdil Aḥmad ʿAbd al-Mawjūd et al. 6 vols. Beirut 1419/1998.

ar-Rāzī, Fakhr ad-Dīn. *al-Maḥṣūl fī ʿilm uṣūl al-fiqh*. Edited by ʿĀdil Aḥmad ʿAbd al-Mawjūd et al. 6 vols. Beirut, 1419/1998.

aṣ-Ṣafadī, Khalīl ibn Aybak. *al-Ghayth al-musajjam fī sharḥ Lāmiyyat al-ʿajam*. 2 vols. Beirut, 1395/1975.

aṣ-Ṣafadī, Khalīl ibn Aybak. *al-Wāfī bi-l-wafayāt*. Edited by Hellmut Ritter et al. 30 vols. Wiesbaden, 1962–2010.

Ṣafī ad-Dīn al-Ḥillī. *Dīwān al-mathālith wa-l-mathānī*. Edited by Muḥammad Ṭāhir al-Ḥimṣī. Damascus, 1419/1998.

Ṣafī ad-Dīn al-Ḥillī. *Dīwān*. Edited by Muḥammad Ḥuwwar. 3 vols. Beirut, 2000.

Sayyib, Khayr ad-Dīn. *al-Qirāʾāt al-qurʾāniyyah wa-atharuhā fī ikhtilāf al-aḥkām al-fiqhiyyah*. Algiers, 1428/2007.

ash-Shawkānī, Muḥammad ibn ʿAlī. *Adab aṭ-ṭalab wa-muntahā l-arab*. Edited by ʿAbdallāh Yaḥyā as-Surayḥī. Beirut, 1419/1998.

ash-Shīrāzī, Abū Isḥāq. *al-Muhadhdhab fī fiqh al-Imām ash-Shāfiʿī*. Edited by Muḥammad az-Zuḥaylī. Part 1. Damascus, 1996.

as-Subkī, Bahāʾ ad-Dīn Aḥmad. *ʿArūs al-afrāḥ fī sharḥ Talkhīṣ al-Miftāḥ*. Edited by Khalīl Ibrāhīm Khalīl. 2 vols. Beirut, 2001.

as-Subkī, Tāj ad-Dīn ʿAbd al-Wahhāb. *Ṭabaqāt ash-Shāfiʿiyyah al-kubrā*. Edited by Muṣṭafā ʿAbd al-Qādir Aḥmad ʿAṭā. 6 vols. Beirut, 1999.

as-Suyūṭī, Jalāl ad-Dīn ʿAbd ar-Raḥmān. *ad-Durr al-manthūr fī t-tafsīr bi-l-manthūr*. 5 vols. Beirut, 1983.

as-Suyūṭī, Jalāl ad-Dīn ʿAbd ar-Raḥmān. *al-Itqān fī ʿulūm al-Qurʾān*. Edited by Maḥmūd al-Qaysiyyah and Muḥammad al-Atāsī. 5 vols. Abu Dhabi, 1424/2003.

as-Suyūṭī, Jalāl ad-Dīn ʿAbd ar-Raḥmān. *Jazīl al-mawāhib fī ikhtilāf al-madhāhib*. Edited by Ibrāhīm Bājis ʿAbd al-Majīd. Beirut, 1412/1992.

as-Suyūṭī, Jalāl ad-Dīn ʿAbd ar-Raḥmān. *Rashf az-zulāl min as-siḥr al-ḥalāl*. Beirut, n.d.

aṭ-Ṭabarī, Abū Jaʿfar Muḥammad ibn Jarīr. *Jāmiʿ al-bayān ʿan taʾwīl āy al-Qurʾān*. Edited by ʿAbdallāh ibn ʿAbd al-Muḥsin at-Turkī. 26 vols. Riyadh, 2003.

ath-Thaʿālibī, Abū Manṣūr. *Also see* al-Maqdisī.

ath-Thaʿālibī, Abū Manṣūr. *al-Iqtibās min al-Qurʾān al-karīm*. Edited by Ibtisām Marhūn aṣ-Ṣaffār. 2 vols. Al-Mansurah, 1412/1992.

ath-Thaʿālibī, Abū Manṣūr. *Taḥsīn al-qabīḥ wa-taqbīḥ al-ḥasan*. Edited by Shākir ʿĀshūr. Damascus, 2006.

al-Wansharīsī, Aḥmad ibn Yaḥyā. *al-Miʿyār al-muʿrib*. 13 vols. Rabat, 1981–1983.

al-Waṭwāṭ. *Ghurar al-khaṣāʾiṣ al-wāḍiḥah wa-ʿurar an-naqāʾiṣ al-fāḍiḥah*. Beirut, n.d.

az-Zamakhsharī, Maḥmūd ibn ʿUmar. *al-Kashshāf ʿan ḥaqāʾiq ghawāmiḍ at-tanzīl wa-ʿuyūn al-aqāwīl fī wujūh at-taʾwīl*. 4 vols. Beirut, n.d.

az-Zawzanī, Abū ʿAbdallāh al-Ḥusayn ibn Aḥmad. *Sharḥ al-Muʿallaqāt as-Sabʿ*. Beirut, n.d.

FURTHER WORKS IN OTHER LANGUAGES

Abel, Carl. *Über den Gegensinn der Urworte*. Leipzig, 1884.

Abū Zayd, Naṣr Ḥāmid. *al-Imām al-Shāfiʿī wa-taʾsīs al-īdiyūlūjiyyah al-wasaṭiyyah*. Casablanca, 2007.

Abū Zayd, Naṣr Ḥāmid. "Heaven, Which Way?" *Al-Ahram Weekly*, September 12–18, 2002. https://web.archive.org/web/20120930060752/http://weekly.ahram.org.eg/2002/603/sc16-17.htm.

Adams, Charles J. *Abūʾl-Aʿlā al-Mawdūdī's Tafhīm al-Qurʾān*. In *Approaches to the History of Interpretation of the Qurʾān*, edited by Andrew Rippin (Oxford, 1988), 307–23.

Adams, Henry E., Lester W. Wright, Jr., and Bethany A. Lohr. "Is Homophobia Associated with Homosexual Arousal?" *Journal of Abnormal Psychology* 105 (1996): 440–45.

Adorno, Theodor W., Else Frenkel-Brunswik, Daniel J. Levinson, and R. Nevitt Sanford. *The Authoritarian Personality*. New York, 1950.

Ahlwardt, Wilhelm. *Die Handschriften-Verzeichnisse der Königlichen Bibliothek zu Berlin: Verzeichnis der arabischen Handschriften*. Berlin, 1887–1899.

Ahmed, Shahab. *What Is Islam? The Importance of Being Islamic*. Princeton, NJ, 2015.

Al-Azmeh, Aziz. *Die Islamisierung des Islam: Imaginäre Welten einer politischen Theologie*. Frankfurt am Main, 1996.

Al-Azmeh, Aziz. *Ibn Khaldūn: An Essay in Reinterpretation*. London, 1992.

Al-Azmeh, Aziz. *Islams and Modernities*. London, 1993.

Al-Nowaihi, Mohamed. "Towards the Reappraisal of Classical Arabic Literature and History: Some Aspects of Ṭāhā Ḥusayn's Use of Modern Western Criteria." *International Journal of Middle East Studies* 11 (1980): 189–207.

Arberry, Arthur J. *The Koran Interpreted*. London, 1964.

Assmann, Jan. "Monotheismus." In *Monotheismus*, 2nd ed., edited by Jürgen Manemann, Jahrbuch Politische Theologie 4 (Münster, 2005), 122–32.

Avenarius, Tomas. "Privater Krach, politische Folgen: Eine überraschende Ehescheidung schwächt die Opposition in Ägypten." *Süddeutsche Zeitung*, April 9/10, 2009, 9.

Bagge Laustsen, Carsten, and Bülent Diken. "Becoming Abject. Rape as a Weapon of War." *Body & Society* 11 (2005): 111–28.

Bauer, Thomas. *Altarabische Dichtkunst: Eine Untersuchung ihrer Struktur und Entwicklung am Beispiel der Onagerepisode*. 2 vols. Wiesbaden, 1992.

Bauer, Thomas. "Communication and Emotion: The Case of Ibn Nubātah's 'Kindertotenlieder.'" *Mamlūk Studies Review* 7 (2003): 49–95.

Bauer, Thomas. "The Dawādār's Hunting Party: A Mamluk Muzdawija Ṭardiyya, Probably by Shihāb al-Dīn Ibn Faḍl Allāh." In *O Ye Gentlemen: Arabic Studies on Science and Literary Culture in Honour of Remke Kruk*, edited by Jan P. Hogendijk and Arnoud Vrolijk (Leiden, 2007), 291–312.

Bauer, Thomas. "Der Fürst ist tot, es lebe der Fürst! Ibn Nubātas Gedicht zur Inthronisation al-Afḍals von Ḥamāh (732/1332)." In *Orientalistische Studien zu Sprache und Literatur: Festgabe zum 65. Geburtstag von Werner Diem*, edited by Monika Gronke and Ulrich Marzolph (Wiesbaden, 2011), 285–315.

Bauer, Thomas. "Die badīʿiyya des Nāṣīf al-Yāziǧī und das Problem der spätosmanischen arabischen Literatur." In *Reflections on Reflections: Near Eastern Writers Reading Literature*, edited by Andreas Christian Islebe and Angelika Neuwirth (Wiesbaden, 2006), 49–118.

Bauer, Thomas. *Die Vereindeutigung der Welt: Über den Verlust an Mehrdeutigkeit und Vielfalt*. Stuttgart, 2018.

Bauer, Thomas. "Fremdheit in der klassischen arabischen Kultur und Sprache." In *Fremdes in fremden Sprachen*, Übergänge vol. 43, edited by Brigitte Jostes and Jürgen Trabant (Munich, 2001), 85–105.

Bauer, Thomas. "Ibn Ḥajar and the Arabic Ghazal of the Mamluk Age." In *Ghazal as World Literature*, vol. 1, edited by Thomas Bauer and Angelika Neuwirth (Beirut, 2005), 35–55.

Bauer, Thomas. "Ibn Nubātah al-Miṣrī (686–768/1287–1366): Life and Work, Part I; The Life of Ibn Nubātah." *Mamlūk Studies Review* 12 (2008): 1–35.

Bauer, Thomas. "Ibrāhīm al-Miʿmār: Ein dichtender Handwerker aus Ägyptens Mamlukenzeit." *Zeitschrift der Deutschen Morgenländischen Gesellschaft* 152 (2002): 63–93.

Bauer, Thomas. "In Search of 'Post-Classical Literature': A Review Article." *Mamlūk Studies Review* 11 (2007): 137–67.

Bauer, Thomas. "The Islamization of Islam." In *Perspectives in Literatures and Cultures*, vol. 1 of *Ideological Battlegrounds—Constructions of Us and Them Before and After 9/11*, edited by Joanna Witkowska and Uwe Zagratzki (Newcastle upon Tyne, 2014), 1–15.

Bauer, Thomas. *Liebe und Liebesdichtung in der arabischen Welt des 9. und 10. Jahrhunderts: Eine literatur- und mentalitätsgeschichtliche Studie des arabischen Ghazal*. Diskurse der Arabistik 2. Wiesbaden, 1998.

Bauer, Thomas. "Male-Male Love in Classical Arabic Poetry." In *The Cambridge History of Gay and Lesbian Literature*, edited by E. L. McCallum and Mikko Tuhkanen (Cambridge, 2014), 107–24.

Bauer, Thomas. "Raffinement und Frömmigkeit: Säkulare Poesie islamischer Religionsgelehrter der späten Abbasidenzeit." *Asiatische Studien* 50 (1996): 275–95.

Bauer, Thomas. "Review of Majd al-Afandī's *al-Ghazal fī l-ʿAṣr al-Mamlūkī al-Awwal* (Damascus, 1994)." *Mamlūk Studies Review* 3 (1999): 214–19.

Bauer, Thomas. "Vertraute Fremde: Das Bild des Beduinen in der arabischen Literatur des 10. Jahrhunderts." In *Shifts and Drifts in Nomad-Sedentary Relations*, edited by Stefan Leder and Bernhard Streck (Wiesbaden, 2005), 377–400.

Bauer, Thomas. "Vom Sinn der Zeit: Aus der Geschichte des arabischen Chronogramms." *Arabica* 50 (2003): 501–31.

Bauer, Thomas. *Warum es kein islamisches Mittelalter gab: Das Erbe der Antike und der Orient*. Munich, 2018.

Bauer, Thomas, and Angelika Neuwirth, eds. *Transformations of a Literary Genre*. Vol. 1 of *Ghazal as World Literature*. Beiruter Texte und Studien 89. Beirut, 2005.

Bauman, Zygmunt. *Modernity and Ambivalence.* Cambridge, 1991.

Ben Naeh, Yaron. "Homosexuality in Jewish Society." In *Encyclopedia of Jews in the Islamic World,* edited by Norman A. Stillman, vol. 2 (Leiden, 2010), 431–33.

Bergengruen, Werner. *Dichtergehäuse.* Zürich, 1966.

Bernecker, Roland, and Thomas Steinfeld. "Amphibolie, Ambiguität." In *Historisches Wörterbuch der Rhetorik,* vol. 1, edited by Gert Ueding (Tübingen, 1992), 436–44.

Berque, Jacques, and Jean-Paul Charnay, eds. *L'ambivalence dans la culture arabe.* Paris, 1967.

Bie, Oskar. *Die Oper.* Berlin, 1919.

Blachère, Régis. "al-Farazdaḳ." In *The Encyclopaedia of Islam,* 2nd ed., edited by P. J. Bearman et al., vol. 2 (Leiden, 1965), 788–89.

Blanc, Haim. *Communal Dialects in Baghdad.* Cambridge, MA, 1964.

Bobzin, Hartmut. *Der Koran: Eine Einführung.* Munich, 1999.

Bobzin, Hartmut. "Translations of the Qur'ān." In *The Encyclopaedia of the Qur'ān,* edited by Jane Dammen McAuliffe, vol. 5 (Leiden, 2006), 340–58.

Bode, Christoph. *Ästhetik der Ambiguität: Zu Funktion und Bedeutung von Mehrdeutigkeit in der Literatur der Moderne.* Tübingen, 1988.

Bonebakker, Seeger A. *Some Early Definitions of the Tawriya and Ṣafadī's* Faḍḍ al-Xitām ʿan at-Tawriya wa 'l-Istixdām. The Hague, 1966.

Born, Max. *Von der Verantwortung des Naturwissenschaftlers.* Munich, 1965.

Bossaller, Anke. "Schlafende Schwangerschaft." In *islamischen Gesellschaften: Entstehung und soziale Implikationen einer weiblichen Fiktion* (Würzburg, 2004).

Bousquet, Georges Henri. "Bāh." In *The Encyclopaedia of Islam,* 2nd ed., edited by P. J. Bearman et al., vol. 1 (Leiden, 1960), 910–11.

Böwering, Gerhard. "Prayer." In *The Encyclopaedia of the Qur'ān,* edited by Jane Dammen McAuliffe, vol. 4 (Leiden, 2006), 215–31.

Brann, Ross. *The Compunctious Poet: Cultural Ambiguity and Hebrew Poetry in Muslim Spain.* Baltimore, 1991.

Brockermann, Carl, ed. *Geschichte der arabischen Litteratur,* 2 vols. and 3 supplementary vols. Leiden, 1932–1943.

Brockett, Adrian. "The Value of the Ḥafṣ and Warsh Transmissions for the Textual History of the Qur'ān." In *Approaches to the History of the Interpretation of the Qur'ān,* edited by Andrew Rippin (Oxford, 1988), 31–45.

Budner, Stanley. "Intolerance of Ambiguity as a Personality Variable." In *Journal of Personality* 30 (1962): 29–50.

Burckhardt, Jacob. *History of Greek Culture.* New York, 1963.

Bürgel, Johann Christoph. *Allmacht und Mächtigkeit: Religion und Welt im Islam.* Munich, 1991.

Bußmann, Hadumod. *Lexikon der Sprachwissenschaft.* 2nd ed. Stuttgart, 1990.

Cachia, Pierre. "The Egyptian Mawwāl." *Journal of Arabic Literature* 8 (1977): 77–103.

Caputo, John D. "In Praise of Ambiguity." In *Ambiguity in the Western Mind,* edited by Craig J. N. de Paulo, Patrick A. Messina, and Marc Stier (New York, 2005), 15–34.

Catlos, Brian A. "Washḳa." In *The Encyclopaedia of Islam,* 2nd ed, edited by P. J. Bearman et al., vol. 11 (Leiden, 2002), 159–60.

Chaudhuri, Kirti N. *Trade and Civilization in the Indian Ocean: An Economic History from the Rise of Islam to 1750.* Cambridge, 1985.

Cohen, Mark R. *Under Crescent and Cross: The Jews in the Middle Ages.* Princeton, NJ, 1994.

Condorcet, Marie Jean Antoine Nicolas Caritat de. *Esquisse d'un Tableau historique des progrès de l'esprit humain* (1795). Edited by Jean-Pierre Schandeler and Pierre Crépel. Paris, 2004. Translated in English as *Outlines of an Historical View of the Progress of the Human Mind* (London, 1795).

Crone, Patricia. *God's Rule: Government and Islam.* New York, 2003.

al-Curcānī, ʿAbdalqāhir. *Die Geheimnisse der Wortkunst.* Translated by Hellmut Ritter. Wiesbaden, 1959.

Descartes, René. *Meditations on First Philosophy*. In *The Philosophical Works of Descartes*, translated by Elizabeth S. Haldane and G. R. T. Ross, vol. 1 (Cambridge, 1911), 131–99.

Diem, Werner. "Das Kitāb al-Ǧīm des Abū ʿAmr aš-Šaibānī: Ein Beitrag zur arabischen Lexikographie." PhD diss. Munich, 1968.

Dorpmüller, Sabine. *Religiöse Magie im "Buch der probaten Mittel": Analyse, kritische Edition und Übersetzung des Kitāb al-Muǧarrabāt von Muḥammad ibn Yūsuf as-Sanūsī (gest. um 845/1490)*. Wiesbaden, 2005.

Dülmen, Richard van. *Historische Anthropologie: Entwicklung, Probleme, Aufgaben*. 2nd ed. Cologne, 2000.

Eco, Umberto. *Opera aperta*. Milan, 1962. Translated into English by Anna Cancogni as *The Open Work* (Cambridge, MA, 1989). https://www.hup.harvard.edu/catalog.php?isbn=9780644639768.

Eikelman, Dale F., and James Piscatori. *Muslim Politics*. Princeton, NJ, 1996.

El-Rouayheb, Khaled. *Before Homosexuality in the Arabic-Islamic World, 1500–1800*. Chicago, 2005.

Empson, William. *Seven Types of Ambiguity*. 3rd ed. London, 1953.

Enderwitz, Susanne. *Gesellschaftlicher Rang und ethnische Legitimation: Der arabische Schriftsteller Abū ʿUṯmān al-Ǧāḥiẓ (gest. 868) über die Afrikaner, Perser und Araber in der islamischen Gesellschaft*. Berlin, 1979.

English, Ava Champney, and Horace Bidwell English. *A Comprehensive Dictionary of Psychological and Psychoanalytical Terms*. New York, 1958.

Erasmus of Rotterdam. *De libero arbitrio*. Edited and translated into English by E. Gordon Rupp and Philip S. Watson as *Luther and Erasmus: Free Will and Salvation* (Philadelphia, 1969).

al-Fārābī, Abū Naṣr Muḥammad ibn Muḥammad. *Der Musterstaat von Alfarabi*. Translated by Friedrich Dieterici. Leiden, 1900. Also edited and translated into English by Richard Walzer as *On the Perfect State* (Oxford, 1985).

Feyerabend, Paul K. "Problems of Empiricism." In *Beyond the Edge of Certainty: Essays in Contemporary Science and Philosophy*, edited by Robert G. Colodny (Englewood Cliffs, NJ, 1965), 145–260.

Fischer, Wolfdietrich. "Die Perioden des Klassischen Arabisch." *Abr Nahrain* 12 (1972): 15–18.

Fischer, Wolfdietrich. *Farb- und Formbezeichnungen in der Sprache der altarabischen Dichtung*. Wiesbaden, 1965.

Fleischer, Heinrich Leberecht. "Literarisches aus Beirut." *Zeitschrift der Deutschen Morgenländischen Gesellschaft* 5 (1851): 96–103.

Foucault, Michel. *Folie et déraison: Histoire de la folie à l'âge classique*. Paris, 1961. Reprinted in *Dits et écrits 1954–1988*, edited by Daniel Defert and François Ewald, vol. 1 (Paris, 1994).

Foucault, Michel. *Histoire de la sexualité*. 3 vols. Paris, 1976–1984. Translated into English by Robert Hurley as *The History of Sexuality* (New York, 1978–1988).

Frenkel-Brunswik, Else. "Intolerance of Ambiguity as an Emotional and Perceptual Personality Variable." *Journal of Personality* 18 (1949): 108–43.

Freud, Sigmund. "Über den Gegensinn der Urworte"; English translation as "The Antithetical Sense of Primal Words," in Sigmund Freud, *Collected Papers*, 5th ed., vol. 4 (London, 1949), 184–91.

Fries, Norbert. *Ambiguität und Vagheit: Einführung und kommentierte Bibliographie*. Tübingen, 1980.

Gabriel, Gottfried. "Klar und deutlich." In *Historisches Wörterbuch der Philosophie*, vol. 4 (Basel, 1976), 846–47.

Gadamer, Hans-Georg. *Truth and Method*. 2nd ed. Translated and revised by Joel Weinsheimer and Donald G. Marshall. London, 1989. First published in German as *Wahrheit und Methode* (Tübingen, 1960).

Gelder, Geert Jan van. "The Conceit of Pen and Sword: On an Arabic Literary Debate." *Journal of Semitic Studies* 32 (1987): 329–60.

Gelder, Geert Jan van. "Debate Literature." In *Encyclopedia of Arabic Literature*, edited by Julie Scott Meisami and Paul Starkey, vol. 1 (London, 1998), 186.

Gelder, Geert Jan van. "*Iqtibās*." In *Encyclopedia of Arabic Literature*, edited by Julie Scott Meisami and Paul Starkey, vol. 1 (London, 1988), 396–97.

Gelder, Geert Jan van. "*Naqāʾiḍ*." In *Encyclopedia of Arabic Literature*, edited by Julie Scott Meisami and Paul Starkey, vol. 2 (London, 1998), 578.

Gelder, Geert Jan van. "*Naḳā'iḍ*." In *The Encyclopaedia of Islam*, 2nd ed., edited by P. J. Bearman et al., vol. 7 (Leiden, 1993), 920.

Gerhards, Jürgen. *Die Moderne und ihre Vornamen*. Wiesbaden, 2003.

Geries, Ibrahim. *Un genre littéraire arabe: Al-Maḥāsin wa-l-masāwī*. Paris, 1977.

Gibb, Elias John Wilkinson. *A History of Ottoman Poetry*, vol. 1. London, 1900.

Glünz, Michael. "Betrachtungen zum 'indischen Stil' in der osmanischen Dichtung." In *Ghazal as World Literature*, edited by Angelika Neuwirth and Thomas Bauer, vol. 2 (Beirut, 2005), 175–84.

Goldziher, Ignaz. *Stellung der alten islamischen Orthodoxie zu den antiken Wissenschaften*. Abhandlungen der königlichen preussischen Akademie der Wissenschaften, Jahrgang 1915, Phil.-hist. Klasse Nr. 8. Berlin, 1916.

Goldziher, Ignaz. *Vorlesungen über den Islam*. Heidelberg, 1910. Translated into English by András and Ruth Hamori as *Introduction to Islamic Theology and Law* (Princeton, NJ, 1981).

Gombrich, Ernst H. *Art and Illusion: A Study in the Psychology of Pictorial Representation*. London, 1962.

Graf, Friedrich Wilhelm. *Die Wiederkehr der Götter: Religion in der modernen Kultur*. Munich, 2004.

Green, Samuel. "The Different Arabic Versions of the Qur'ān." Answering Islam. http://answering-islam.org.uk/Green/seven.htm.

Greenberg, David F. *The Construction of Homosexuality*. Chicago, 1988.

Gresh, Alain, Philippe Rekacewicz, and Barbara Bauer. *Atlas der Globalisierung*. Paris, 2006.

Griffel, Frank. "Contradictions and Lots of Ambiguity: Two New Perspectives on Premodern (and Postclassical) Islamic Societies." *Bustan: The Middle East Book Review* 8, no. 1 (2017): 1–21.

Griffel, Frank. *Den Islam Denken: Versuch, eine Religion zu verstehen*. Stuttgart, 2018.

Gruendler, Beatrice. *The Development of the Arabic Scripts: From the Nabatean Era to the First Islamic Century According to Dated Texts*. Atlanta, 1993.

Grunebaum, Gustav Edmund von. *Medieval Islam: A Study in Cultural Orientation*. Chicago, 1946. Available online at https://oi.chicago.edu/sites/oi.uchicago.edu/files/uploads/shared/docs/medieval_islam.pdf.

Guo, Li. "Paradise Lost: Ibn Dāniyāl's Response to Baybars' Campaign against Vice in Cairo." *Journal of the American Oriental Society* 121 (2001): 219–35.

Haase, Claus-Peter, ed. *Sammlerglück: Islamische Kunst aus der Sammlung Edmund de Unger; Katalogbuch zur Ausstellung in Berlin, 27.11.2007–17.2.2008*. Museum für Islamische Kunst. Munich, 2007.

Hallaq, Wael B. "Was ash-Shafi'i the Master Architect of Islamic Jurisprudence?" *International Journal of Middle East Studies* 25 (1993): 587–605.

Hallaq, Wael B. "Was the Gate of Ijtihad Closed?" In *Law and Legal Theory in Classical and Medieval Islam*, edited by Wael B. Hallaq (Ashgate, 1994).

Haller, Dieter. *dtv-Atlas Ethnologie*. Munich, 2005.

Hasluk, Frederick William. *Christianity and Islam Under the Sultans*. 2 vols. New York, 1929 (reprint 1973).

Hawting, Gerald. "Oaths." In *The Encyclopaedia of the Qur'ān*, edited by Jane Dammen McAuliffe, vol. 3 (Leiden, 2003), 561–66.

Hees, Syrinx von. "Historische Anthropologie in der Islamwissenschaft." In *Historische Anthropologie: Ansätze und Möglichkeiten*, edited by Stephan Conermann and Syrinx von Hees, vol. 1 of *Islamwissenschaft als Kulturwissenschaft* (Bonn, 2007), 21–35.

Heidemann, Stefan. *Die Renaissance der Städte in Nordsyrien und Nordmesopotamien: Städtische Entwicklung und wirtschaftliche Bedingungen in ar-Raqqa und Harran von der Zeit der beduinischen Vorherrschaft bis zu den Seldschuken*. Leiden, 2002.

Heinz, Wilhelm. *Der indische Stil in der persischen Literatur*. Wiesbaden, 1973.

Heller, Erdmute, and Hassouna Mosbahi. *Hinter den Schleiern des Islam*. Munich, 1993.

Hildebrandt, Thomas. *Neo-Muʿtazilismus: Intention und Kontext im modernen arabischen Umgang mit dem rationalistischen Erbe des Islam*. Leiden, 2007.

Hillenbrand, Robert. "For God, Empire and Mammon: Some Art-Historical Aspects of the Reformed Dīnārs of ʿAbd al-Malik." In *al-Andalus und Europa*, edited by Martina Müller-Wiener, Christiane Kothe, Karl-Heinz Golzio, and Joachim Gierlichs (Petersberg, Germany, 2004), 20–38.

Hirsch, Helga. "'Der Holocaust ist nicht einmalig': Gespräch mit dem polnischen Soziologen Zygmunt Bauman." *Die Zeit*, April 23, 1993: 68.

Höfert, Almut. "Europa und der Nahe Osten: Der transkulturelle Vergleich in der Vormoderne und die Meistererzählungen über den Islam." *Historische Zeitschrift* 287 (2008): 561–97.

Holenstein, Elmar. *Philosophie-Atlas: Orte und Wege des Denkens*. Zurich, 2004.

Homerin, Emil T. "Preaching Poetry: The Forgotten Verse of Ibn al-Shahrazūrī." *Arabica* 38 (1991): 87–101.

Hrair Dekmejian, Richard, and Abel Fathy Thabit. "Machiavelli's Arab Precursor: Ibn Ẓafar al-Ṣiqillī." *British Journal of Middle Eastern Studies* 27 (2000): 125–37.

Huizinga, Johan. *Homo ludens: A Study of the Play-Element in Culture*. London, 1949.

al-Imam, Aḥmad ʿAlī. *Variant Readings of the Qurʾān: A Critical Study of their Historical and Linguistic Origins*. Herndon, VA, 1418/1998.

Jacob, Wilson Chacko. *Working Out Egypt: Effendi Masculinity and Subject Formation in Colonial Modernity, 1870–1940*. Durham, NC, 2011.

Jayyusi, Salma Khadra. "Arabic Poetry in the Post-Classical Age." In *Arabic Literature in the Post-Classical Period*, edited by Roger Allen and D.S. Richards, Cambridge History of Arabic Literature (Cambridge, 2006), 25–59.

Jostes, Brigitte, and Jürgen Trabant, eds. *Fremdes in fremden Sprachen*. Munich, 2001.

Kassir, Samir. *Considérations sur le malheur arabe*. Paris, 2004.

Kermani, Navid. *Der Schrecken Gottes: Attar, Hiob und die metaphysische Revolte*. Munich, 2005.

Kermani, Navid. *God Is Beautiful: The Aesthetic Experience of the Quran*. Translated by Toby Crawford. Cambridge, 2015.

Kersting, Wolfgang. *Niccolò Machiavelli*. 3rd ed. Munich, 2006.

Klauda, Georg. *Die Vertreibung aus dem Serail*. Hamburg, 2008.

Kloss, Torben, et al., *Ambiguitätstoleranz und Stereotypie*. Bericht der Fernuniversität Hagen, 2005, available at http://psychologie.fernuni-hagen.de/Sem03282/Bericht_Ambiguitaet.pdf.

Kofler, Hans. "Das Kitāb al-Aḍdād von Abū ʿAlī Muḥammad Quṭrub ibn al-Mustanīr." *Islamica* 5 (1931–1932): 241–84, 385–461, 493–544.

Krämer, Gudrun. *Gottes Staat als Republik: Reflexionen zeitgenössischer Muslime zu Islam, Menschenrechten und Demokratie*. Baden-Baden, 1999.

Kraemer, Joel L. *Humanism in the Renaissance of Islam: The Cultural Revival During the Buyid Age*. 2nd ed. Leiden, 1992.

Kraus, Karl. *Beim Wort genommen*. Munich, 1955.

Kraus, Karl. *Magie der Sprache: Ein Lesebuch*. 3rd ed. Frankfurt am Main, 1979.

Kremer, Alfred von. "Nâṣîf aljâziǧî." *Zeitschrift der Deutschen Morgenländischen Gesellschaft* 25 (1871): 243–47.

Kropp, Manfred. "Den Koran neu lesen: Über Versuche einer Vereinbarung des koranischen mit dem modernen Weltbild." In *Religion und Weltbild*, edited by Dieter Zeller (Münster, 2002), 151–78.

Kugle, Scott Siraj al-Haqq. *Homosexuality in Islam*. Oxford, 2010.

Lagrange, Frédéric. *al-Tarab: Die Musik Ägyptens*. Heidelberg, 2000.

Lange, Christian, ed. *Locating Hell in Islamic Traditions*. Leiden, 2016.

Lautmann, Rüdiger, ed. *Homosexualität: Handbuch der Theorie- und Forschungsgeschichte*. Frankfurt am Main, 1993.

Leder, Stefan. "Aspekte arabischer und persischer Fürstenspiegel: Legitimation, Fürstenethik, politische Vernunft." In *Specula principum*, edited by Angela De Benedictis (Frankfurt am Main, 1999), 21–50.

Leggewie, Claus, ed. *Die Türkei und Europa: Die Positionen*. Frankfurt am Main, 2004.

Lerner, Ralph. *Averroes on Plato's* Republic. Ithaca, NY, 1974.

Leupp, Gary. *Male Colors: The Construction of Homosexuality*. Los Angeles, 1995.

Levine, Donald N. *The Flight from Ambiguity: Essays in Social and Cultural Theory*. Chicago, 1985.

Levine, Donald N. *Wax and Gold: Tradition and Innovation in Ethiopian Culture*. Chicago, 1972.

Loos, Adolf. "Ornament und Verbrechen." In *Trotzdem: Gesammelte Schriften 1900–1930*, edited by Adolf Opel (Vienna, 1982), 78–88. Translated into English by Michael Bullock as *Programs and Manifestoes on 20th-Century Architecture*, edited by Ulrich Conrads (London, 1970).

Lübben, Ivesa. "Die Muslimbruderschaft und der Widerstand gegen eine dynastische Erbfolge in Ägypten." *Giga Focus Nahost* 5 (2009): 1–7.

MacDonald Jr., A. P. "Revised Scale for Ambiguity Tolerance: Reliability and Validity." *Psychological Reports* 26 (1970): 791–98.

Machiavelli, Niccolò. *Il Principe*. In *Opere, a cura di Mario Bonfantini*, 3rd. ed. (Milan, 1986).

Machiavelli, Niccolò. *The Prince, with Related Documents*. Translated by William J. Connell. Boston, 2005.

Mahdi, Muhsin. "Philosophical Literature." In *Religion, Learning and Science in the ʿAbbāsid Period*, edited by M. J. L. Young, John Derek Latham, and Robert Bertram Serjeant, The Cambridge History of Arabic Literature (Cambridge, 1990), 76–105.

Manemann, Jürgen. *Monotheismus*. 2nd ed. Jahrbuch Politische Theologie 4. Münster, 2005.

Marks, Robert B. *The Origins of the Modern World: A Global and Ecological Narrative from the Fifteenth to the Twenty-First Century*. 3rd ed. Lanham, MD, 2015.

Marlow, Louise. "Advice and Advice Literature." In *The Encyclopaedia of Islam*, 3rd ed., edited by Marc Gaborieau et al., vol. 1 (Leiden, 2007), 34–58.

Marschall, Veronika. *Das Chronogramm: Eine Studie zu Formen und Funktionen einer literarischen Kunstform*. Frankfurt am Main, 1997.

Martin, John Levi. "The Authoritarian Personality, 50 Years Later: What Lessons Are There for Political Psychology?" *Political Psychology* 22 (2001): 1–26.

Massad, Joseph A. *Desiring Arabs*. Chicago, 2007.

Melchert, Christopher. "Ibn Mujāhid and the Establishment of Seven Qurʾānic Readings." *Studia Islamica* 91 (2000): 5–22.

Merkel, Wolfgang. "Religion, Fundamentalismus und Demokratie." In *Fundamentalismus, Terrorismus, Krieg*, edited by Wolfgang Schluchter (Weilerswist, 2003), 61–85.

Meyerhof, Max, and Joseph Schacht, eds. *The Theologus Autodidactus of Ibn al-Nafīs*. Oxford, 1968.

Mez, Adam. *The Renaissance of Islam*. Translated by Salahuddin Khuda Bukhsh and David Samuel Margoliouth. London, 1937. German original: Heidelberg, 1922.

Montgomery, James. "Ibn Faḍlān and the Rūsiyyah." *Journal of Arabic and Islamic Studies* 3 (2000): 1–25.

Montgomery, James. *Two Arabic Travel Books: Accounts of China and India and Mission to the Volga*. New York, 2014.

Morel, Bénédict Augustin. *Traité des dégénérescences physiques, intellectuelles et morales de l'espèce humaine et des causes qui produises ces variétés maladives*. Paris, 1857.

Moussalli, Ahmad S. "Islamism: Modernisation of Islam or Islamisation of Knowledge." In *Cosmopolitanism, Identity and Authenticity in the Middle East*, edited by Roel Meijer (Richmond, VA, 1999), 87–101.

Muchembled, Robert. *L'orgasme et l'Occident*. Paris, 2005. Translated into English by Jean Birrell as *Orgasm and the West: A History of Pleasure from the Sixteenth Century to the Present* (Cambridge, 2008).

Neuwirth, Angelika. "Das islamische Dogma der 'Unnachahmlichkeit des Korans' in literaturwissenschaftlicher Sicht." *Der Islam* 60 (1983): 166–83.

Neuwirth, Angelika. "Der Horizont der Offenbarung: Zur Relevanz der einleitenden Schwurserien für die Suren der frühmekkanischen Zeit." In *Gottes ist der Orient, Gottes ist der Okzident: Festschrift für A. Falaturi zum 65. Geburtstag*, edited by Udo Tworuschka (Cologne, 1991), 3–39.

Neuwirth, Angelika. "Makkī Abū Muḥammad." In *The Encyclopaedia of Islam*, 2nd ed., edited by P. J. Bearman et al., vol. 6 (Leiden, 1991), 188–89.

Neuwirth, Angelika and Thomas Bauer. *Ghazal as World Literature*. Vol. 2, *From a Literary Genre to a Great Tradition: The Ottoman Gazel in Context*. Istanbuler Texte und Studien 4. Würzburg, 2006.

Nietzsche, Friedrich. *The Antichrist*. 3rd ed. Translated by H. L. Mencken. New York, 1927.

Nietzsche, Friedrich. *Gay Science*. Translated by Walter Kaufmann. New York, 1974.

Nietzsche, Friedrich. *On the Genealogy of Morals*. Translated and edited by Walter Kaufmann and R. J. Hollingdale. New York, 1967.

Nöldeke, Theodor. *Fünf Moʿallaqāt übersetzt und erklärt*. Vol. 1, *Die Moʿallaqa des ʿAmr und des Ḥārith*. Sitzungsberichte der Kaiserlichen Akademie der Wissenschaften, Phil.-hist. Classe 140, no. 7. Vienna, 1899.

Nöldeke, Theodor. *Geschichte des Qorāns*. 2nd ed. 3 parts. Leipzig, 1909–1938.

Norton, R. W. "Measurement of Ambiguity Tolerance." *Journal of Personality Assessment* 39 (1975): 607–19.

Omar, Sara. "From Semantics to Normative Law: Perceptions of Liwāṭ (Sodomy) and Siḥāq (Tribadism) in Islamic Jurisprudence." In *Islamic Law and Society* 19 (Leiden, 2012), 222–56.

Paulo, Craig J. N. de, Patrick Messina, and Marc Stier, eds. *Ambiguity in the Western Mind*. New York, 2005.

Pellat, Charles. "*Mathālib*." In *The Encyclopaedia of Islam*, 2nd ed., edited by P. J. Bearman et al., vol. 6 (Leiden, 1991), 828–29.

Pfaller, Robert. *Die Illusion der anderen: Über das Lustprinzip in der Kultur*. Frankfurt am Main, 2002.

Pflugfelder, Gregory M. *Cartographies of Desire: Male-Male Sexuality in Japanese Discourse, 1600–1950*. Berkeley, 1999.

Popal, Mariam. *Die Scharia, das religiöse Recht—ein Konstrukt? Überlegungen zur Analyse des islamischen Rechts anhand rechtsvergleichender Methoden und aus Sicht post-kolonialer Kritik*. Frankfurt am Main, 2006.

Reh, Mechthild. "Sprache und Gesellschaft." In *Die Sprachen Afrikas*, edited by Bernd Heine, Ekkehard Wolff, and Thilo C. Schadeberg (Hamburg, 1981), 513–57.

Reis, Jack. *Ambiguitätstoleranz: Beiträge zur Entwicklung eines Persönlichkeitskonstrukts*. Heidelberg, 1997.

Robson, James. "al-Bukhārī." In *The Encyclopaedia of Islam*, 2nd ed., edited by P. J. Bearman et al., vol. 1 (Leiden, 1960), 1296–97.

Rodinson, Maxime. *Europe and the Mystique of Islam*. Translated by Roger Veinus. London, 2002.

Rosenthal, Erwin I. J. *Averroes' Commentary on Plato's Republic*. Cambridge, 1969.

Rosenthal, Franz. "The Stranger in Medieval Islam." *Arabica* 44 (1997): 35–75.

Rosier, Irène, ed. *L'ambiguité: Cinq études historiques*. Lille, 1988.

Roy, Olivier. "Reislamisierung und Radikalisierung." *Internationale Politik* 2–3 (1999): 47–53.

Roy, Olivier. *L'Islam mondialisé*. Paris, 2002. Translated as *Globalized Islam: The Search for a New Ummah* (New York, 2004).

Rückert, Friedrich. *Die Verwandlungen des Abu Seid von Serug oder die Makamen des Hariri*. 7th ed. Stuttgart, 1878.

as-Said, Labib. *The Recited Koran: A History of the First Recorded Version*. Princeton, NJ, 1975.

Saifullah, M. S. M., Elias Karīm, and Muhammad Ghoniem. "Reply to Samuel Green's 'The Seven Readings of the Qurʾan.' Islamic Awareness. http://www.islamic-awareness.org/Quran/Text/Qiraat/green.html

Saifullah, M. S. M. "Versions of the Qurʾan?" Islamic Awareness. http://www.islamic-awareness.org/Quran/Text/Qiraat/hafs.html

Savage-Smith, Emilie. "Ṭibb." In *The Encyclopaedia of Islam*, 2nd ed., edited by P. J. Bearman et al., vol. 10 (Leiden, 2000), 452–60.

Schaade, Arthur, and Helmut Gätje. "Djarīr." In *The Encyclopaedia of Islam*, 2nd ed., edited by P. J. Bearman et al., vol. 2 (Leiden, 1965), 479–80.

Schacht, Joseph, and Clifford Edmund Bosworth, eds. *The Legacy of Islam*. 2nd ed. 2 vols. Oxford, 1974.

Scheindlin, Raymond. *Wine, Women, and Death: Medieval Poems on the Good Life*. Philadelphia, 1986.

Schmidt, Helmut. "Sind die Türken Europäer? Nein, sie passen nicht dazu." In *Die Türkei und Europa: Die Positionen*, edited by Klaus Leggewie (Frankfurt am Main, 2004), 162–66.

Schmidt, Siegfried J. *Grundriss der Empirischen Literaturwissenschaft*. Frankfurt am Main, 1991.

Schneider, Irene. *Das Bild des Richters in der "Adab al-Qāḍī"-Literatur*. Frankfurt am Main, 1990.

Schulze, Reinhard. "Die Politisierung des Islam im 19. Jahrhundert." *Welt des Islams* 22 (1982): 103–16.

Schulze, Reinhard. "Islam und Herrschaft: Zur politischen Instrumentalisierung einer Religion." In *Der Islam im Aufbruch? Perspektiven der arabischen Welt*, 2nd ed., edited by Michael Lüders (Munich, 1993), 94–129.

Sellheim, Rudolf. *Materialien zur arabischen Literaturgeschichte*. 2 vols. Verzeichnis der orientalischen Handschriften in Deutschland 17, Reihe A. Wiesbaden, 1976–1987.

Sezgin, Fuat. "Die Entdeckung des amerikanischen Kontinents durch muslimische Seefahrer vor Kolumbus." In *Geschichte des arabischen Schrifttums*, vol. 13 (Frankfurt am Main, 2007), 119–65. Translated into English as *The Pre-Columbian Discovery of the American Continent by Muslim Seafarers*. http://www.scribd.com/doc/8710396/The-PreColumbian-discovery-of-the-American-continent-by-muslim-seafarers.

Sezgin, Fuat, ed. *Geschichte des arabischen Schrifttums*. Vol. 13. Frankfurt am Main, 2007.

Shatzmiller, Maya. *Labour in the Medieval Islamic World*. Leiden, 1994.

Simon, Udo. *Mittelalterliche arabische Sprachbetrachtung zwischen Grammatik und Rhetorik: ʿIlm al-maʿānī bei as-Sakkākī*. Heidelberg, 1993.

Somekh, Sasson. *The Neo-Classical Arabic Poets*. In *Modern Arabic Literature*, edited by Muhammad Mustafa Badawi, The Cambridge History of Arabic Literature (Cambridge, 1992), 36–81.

Sommer, Volker. *Wider die Natur? Homosexualität und Evolution*. Munich, 1990.

Sonnini de Manoncourt, Charles-Nicolas-Sigisbert. *Voyage dans la haute et basse Égypte*, vol. 1. Paris, 1798. Translated by Henry Hunter as *Travels in Upper and Lower Egypt* (London, 1799).

Sprenger, Guido. *Ethnologie der Sexualität: Eine Einführung*. In *Sex and the Body: Ethnologische Perspektiven zu Sexualität, Körper und Geschlecht*, edited by Gabriele Alex and Sabine Klocke-Daffa (Bielefeld, 2005), 11–39.

Stauth, Georg. *Ägyptische heilige Orte*. Vol. 2, *Zwischen den Steinen des Pharao und islamischer Moderne*. Bielefeld, 2008.

Steingass, F[rancis]. *The Assemblies of al-Ḥarîrî*. London, 1898.

Strohmaier, Gotthard. "La longévité de Galien et les deux places de son tombeau." In *La science médicale antique: Nouveaux regards; Études réunies en l'honneur de Jacques Jouanna*, edited by Véronique Boudon-Millot, Alessia Guardasole, and Caroline Magdelaine (Paris, 2007), 393–403.

Szombathy, Zoltán. *Mujūn: Libertinism in Medieval Muslim Society and Literature*. Cambridge, 2013.

Talib, Adam, Marlé Hammond, and Arie Schippers, eds. *The Rude, the Bad and the Bawdy: Essays in Honour of Geert Jan van Gelder*. Cambridge, 2014.

Taureck, Bernhard H. F. *Machiavelli—ABC*. Leipzig, 2002.

Todenhöfer, Jürgen. *Warum tötest du, Zaid?* Munich, 2008.

Todorov, Tzvetan. *The Conquest of America: The Question of the Other*. Translated by Richard Howard. New York, 1984.

Toulmin, Stephen. *Cosmopolis: The Hidden Agenda of Modernity*. New York, 1990.

Ueding, Gert. *Moderne Rhetorik: Von der Aufklärung bis zur Gegenwart*. Munich, 2000.

Ulf, Christopher. "Ancient Greek Competition—A Modern Construct?" In *Competition in the Ancient World*, edited by N. Fisher and H. van Wees (Swansea, 2011), 85–111.

Ullrich, Wolfgang. "Grundrisse einer philosophischen Begriffsgeschichte von Ambiguität." *Archiv für Begriffsgeschichte* 32 (1989): 121–69.

Veyne, Paul. *Glaubten die Griechen an ihre Mythen? Ein Versuch über die konstitutive Einbildungskraft*. Frankfurt am Main, 1987.

Wagner, Ewald. "Munāẓara." In *The Encyclopaedia of Islam*, 2nd ed., edited by P. J. Bearman et al., vol. 7 (Leiden, 1993), 565–68.

Wagner, Ewald. "Rangstreit." In *Enzyklopädie des Märchens*, edited by Hermann Bausinger, Doris Boden, Rolf Wilhelm Brednich, and Kurt Ranke. Vol. 11 (Berlin, 2003), 194–99.

Watt, William Montgomery, and Alford T. Welch. *Islam*. 3 vols. Stuttgart, 1980.

Weiss, Bernard G. *The Search for God's Law: Islamic Jurisprudence in the Writings of Sayf al-Dīn al-Āmidī*. Salt Lake City, 1992.

al-Yousfi, Muhammad Lutfi. "Poetic Creativity in the Sixteenth to Eighteenth Centuries." In *Arabic Literature in the Post-Classical Period*, edited by Roger Allen and D. S. Richards. The Cambridge History of Arabic Literature (Cambridge, 2006), 60–73.

Yurtsever, Gülçimen. "Ethical Beliefs and Tolerance of Ambiguity." *Social Behaviour and Personality* 28 (2000): 141–48.

Ze'evi, Dror. *Producing Desire: Changing Sexual Discourse in the Ottoman Middle East, 1500–1900*. Berkeley, 2006.

Zilfi, Madeline C. *Women and Slavery in the Late Ottoman Empire*. Cambridge, 2010.

Zwettler, Michael. "Imraʾalqays, Son of ʿAmr: King of . . . ?" In *Literary Heritage of Classical Islam: Arabic and Islamic Studies in Honor of James A. Bellamy*, edited by Mustansir Mir (Princeton, NJ, 1993), 3–37.

Index

Abbasids, Abbasid era, 5, 173, 176, 209, 228, 266, 272
ʿAbd al-Ḥamīd ibn Yaḥyā al-Kātib, 155
ʿAbd al-Malik ibn Marwān (Caliph), 153f.
Abel, Carl, 163f., 292
al-Ābī, Manṣūr ibn al-Ḥusayn, 243
Abrogation (*naskh*), 46, 111f., 126f.
Abū ʿAmr ash-Shaybānī, 156
Abū ʿAmr Ibn al-ʿAlāʾ, 156
Abū Bakr Ibn ʿUthmān (Caliph), 39, 42, 63
Abū Dāwūd, 101, 113
Abū l-Fidāʾ, ʿImād ad-Dīn Ismāʿīl, 223f.
Abū Firās al-Ḥamdānī, 238
Abū Ḥanīfah, Nuʿmān ibn Thābit, 105, 113–15
Abū Ḥātim as-Sijistānī, 160
Abū Khayrah, Nahshal ibn Zayd, 156
Abū Nuwās, al-Ḥasan ibn Hāniʾ, 137, 174, 197, 210
Abū Tammām, Ḥabīb ibn Aws, 161, 176, 197, 218
Abū ṭ-Ṭayyib al-Lughawī, 160
Abū Thawr, Ibrāhīm ibn Khālid, 114f.
Abū ʿUbaydah, Maʿmar ibn al-Muthannā, 156
Abū Yaʿlā Ibn al-Farrāʾ, 220
Abū Yūsuf, Yaʿqūb ibn Ibrāhīm, 113, 115
Abū Zayd, Naṣr Ḥāmid, 60, 75, 107, 288
adilla (Pointer[s]), 107
aḍdād (words with contrary meanings), 159–64
Administration, terminology of, 163
Adorno, Theodor W., 16, 282
al-Afḍal, Nāṣir ad-Dīn Muḥammad ibn Ismāʿīl, al-Malik, 223–28
Afghanistan, 35, 191, 212
aḥkām (judgment, legal), 94–96, 104, 105, 107, 109, 118, 125
Ahmed, Shahab, xii, 281
aḥruf. *See ḥarf*
Al-Azmeh, Aziz, 290, 298
ʿAlī ibn Abī Ṭālib (Caliph), 41f., 77
Álvares Cabral, Pedro, 252
Ambiguity: crisis of, 32, 39, 96; cultural, 10–13; domestication of, xi, 12, 23, 32, 39, 56, 81, 96, 103, 182, 190, 245, 260; intolerance of, xi, 16f., 33, 128, 177, 254, 273; tolerance of, xf., 3, 11, 16f., 215, 233, 240, 251, 255, 278; training of, 172–82, 260
Ambivalence, 162, 241, 251, 273f.
Amīn, Aḥmad, 209
ʿAmr ibn Hind al-Lakhmī, 152
ʿAmr ibn Kulthūm, 152
Analogy, deduction by, reasoning according to (*qiyās*), 114
Anthology, 165, 174, 179, 197f., 296
Anthropology, historical, 4
Antiquity, 199
Antisemitism, 247, 275
Apologetic epigram, 174f., 196
Arabian Nights, ix
Arberry, Arthur J., 8, 78, 292
Aristotle, 13, 261, 271, 282
Asceticism (*zuhd*), 139, 167
al-Ashʿarī, Abū l-Ḥasan ʿAlī, 21
ʿĀṣim ibn al-Ḥasan al-ʿAṭṭār, 167
al-Aṣmaʿī, ʿAbd al-Malik ibn Qurayb, 156, 160, 285

Assessment of probability (*tarjīḥ*), 121f., 289
Assimilation, 247
Assmann, Jan, 215, 260, 297
Augustinus of Hippo, 147
Averroes. *See* Ibn Rushd
Avicenna. *See* Ibn Sīnā
Ayyubids, Ayyubid era, 6, 119, 223, 225, 227f.
al-Azharī, Abū Manṣūr Muḥammad ibn Aḥmad, 157

badīʿiyyah (rhetorical challenges tackled in poetry), 27, 177f.
bāh (sexual intercourse), 191
al-Baṣrī, Abū l-Ḥusayn, 106
al-Baṣrī, Ḥasan ibn Yasār, 98
Bauman, Zygmunt, 9, 18f., 93, 240f., 247f., 257, 283, 288, 297, 299f.
al-Bāʿūniyyah, ʿĀʾishah, 179
al-Bayāḍī, Sinān ad-Dīn, 192
Bāyezīd II (Sultan), 132
Beard, epigram on growth of, 196–98
Bedouins, 156f., 242f.
Bergengruen, Werner, 58, 286
Born, Max 1, 279, 302
Brann, Ross, 18, 168f., 283, 293
Brockett, Adrian, 58, 285f.
Budner, Stanley, 17, 169, 283
al-Buḥturī, Abū ʿUbādah al-Walīd, 176, 218
al-Bukhārī, Muḥammad ibn Ismāʿīl, 96f., 100f.
al-Bulqīnī, Badr ad-Dīn Muḥammad, 165
Burckhardt, Jacob, 172, 293
Burton, Richard, 208, 297
al-Būṣīrī, Sharaf ad-Dīn Muḥammad, 178
al-Bustānī, Buṭrus, 208
al-Būṭī, Muḥammad Saʿīd Ramaḍān, 127, 289
Būyids, 5f., 228

Caputo, John D., 14f., 30, 282, 288
Cartography, cartographers, 249, 252–54
Cevdet, Ahmet Pasha, 208
Chain of authorities on the hadith (*isnād*), 95
China, 102, 130, 150, 268
Christians, Christianity, 243–45
Chronogram, 177, 179
Cohen, Mark R., 244f., 299
Coins, 153, 234
Colonialism, colonial powers, 147, 154, 189
Colonization, 149f., 252
Columbus (Cristóbal Colón), 253, 256
Condorcet, Nicolas Marquis de, 14, 19, 282
Contradiction, contradictoriness, 111
Conversion, 251
Cornelius, Peter, ix
"counter-poems" (*naqāʾiḍ*), 173, 178

dalīl (pointer), 107f., 116, 121, 127
Darwin, Charles, 203
Decadence, 181, 191, 202f., 207f.
Degeneration, theory of, 203, 209
Democracy, 222, 236, 278f.
Descartes, René, Cartesianism, 31, 58, 60–62, 72, 77, 83, 267, 269, 271, 284
Díaz de Solís, Juan, 253
ḍidd (words with contradictory meanings), 159, 161
Dissent, scholarly, mostly legal (*ikhtilāf*), 109–11, 114, 122–26. *See also* Contradiction
Divorce, 205f.
Donne, John, 13
Double entendre (*tawriyah*), 12, 19, 176f., 227

Egypt, 7
El-Rouayheb, Khaled, 211, 296f.
Empson, William, 15, 282
Enlightenment, 32, 186, 222, 267, 274–277
Epigram, 164, 177, 194, 197f., 242. *See also* Apologetic epigram
Erasmus of Rotterdam, 74, 269f., 287
Exegesis (in particular, of the Quran), 40f., 44, 58, 85–87, 108, 234, 266
Exile. *See* Stranger(s)
Extraterrestrial(s), 256f.

Fakhr ad-Dīn ar-Rāzī. *See* ar-Rāzī
faqīh (legal scholar), 139, 219
al-Fārābī, Abū Naṣr Muḥammad, 219, 297
al-Farazdaq, Hammām ibn Ghālib, 173
Farrūkh, ʿUmar, 210
Fatimids, 6
fatwā (legal opinion), 21, 35, 116f., 142, 222f., 234, 259
Feyerabend, Paul K., 94
fiqh (jurisprudence), 104f., 121, 139, 145, 219
Fleischer, Heinrich Leberecht, 169f., 293
Foreigner(s). *See* Stranger(s)
Foucault, Michel, 183, 188, 193, 212, 294–96
Frenkel-Brunswik, Else, 16f., 282, 288
Freud, Sigmund, 164, 292

Friends, friendship, 187
Frivolous and indecent topics in poetry (*mujūn*), 194f., 207, 295
Fur, animal skin, 107f., 113–18
Fürstenspiegel. *See* Mirrors for princes

Gadamer, Hans-Georg, 92, 288
Galen of Pergamon, 133
Geographical literature, 249–54
Ghamidi, Javed Al, 67
gharīb (stranger[s]), 239f.
ghazal (love poetry), 195f., 209
al-Ghazālī, Abū Ḥāmid Muḥammad, 6, 21, 106, 190, 194, 295
ghurba (stranger[s]), 238, 245
Gilchrist, John, 67
Goethe, Johann Wolfgang von, ix
"Golden Era," 8, 202
Goldziher, Ignaz, 144f., 266, 291, 301
Góngora, Luis de, 13
"Good and bad aspects" (*al-maḥāsin wa-l-masāwi'*), 23, 174, 237f.
Grammar, grammarians, 264
Green, Samuel, 66
Griffel, Frank xii, 281, 301
Grunebaum, Gustav E. von, 136, 217, 221, 223, 290, 297

Ḥadīth criticism, 98f., 112, 121f.
Ḥafṣah (daughter of the Prophet Muḥammad), 39
al-Ḥākim an-Nīsābūrī, Muḥammad ibn ʿAbdallāh, 99f.
ḥarf (plural form *aḥruf*), 45f., 52f., 61–64, 68, 72, 87f.
al-Ḥarīrī, al-Qāsim ibn ʿAlī, 81, 197, 296
Hārūn ar-Rashīd (Caliph), 5
Hegel, Georg Wilhelm Friedrich, 202
Henry IV of France and Navarra, 269f.
Heraclitus of Ephesus, 13
al-Ḥillī, Ṣafī ad-Dīn Abū l-Maḥāsin ʿAbd al-ʿAzīz, 178, 206f., 296
Hippocrates, 133
Hobbes, Thomas, 176, 294
Höfert, Almut, 130, 290
Homonymy, 13
Homophobia, 211
Homosexuality, 188f., 196, 119f., 200f., 204, 208, 210–13
al-Hudhalī, Abū l-Qāsim, 49f.
Huizinga, Johan, 173, 179, 182, 292–94
ḥukm (judgment, legal), 104f., 117f., 123, 126f.
Humanists, 27
Ḥusāmzādeh ar-Rūmī, ʿAbd ar-Raḥmān ibn Ḥusām ad-Dīn, 27
al-Ḥusayn ibn ʿAbdallāh al-Madanī, 101
Ḥusayn, Ṭāhā, 59–65, 209, 286
Hussayn, Saddam. *See* Saddam

Ibn ʿAbbās, ʿAbdallāh, 77, 111
Ibn ʿAbd al-Barr, Yūsuf ibn ʿAbdallāh, 115f., 289
Ibn Abī l-Iṣbaʿ, ʿAbd al-ʿAẓīm ibn ʿAbd al-Wāḥid, 27
Ibn al-Anbārī, Abū Bakr Muḥammad ibn al-Qāsim, 160f., 292
Ibn al-ʿArabī, Muḥyī d-Dīn Muḥammad, 269
Ibn Bassām al-Muḥtasib, Muḥammad ibn Aḥmad, 133, 290
Ibn Baṭṭūṭah, Muḥammad ibn ʿAbdallāh, 107, 238f., 299
Ibn Durustawayh, ʿAbdallāh ibn Jaʿfar, 160
Ibn Faḍlān, Aḥmad, 249–51, 300
Ibn Ḥajar al-ʿAsqalānī, Aḥmad ibn ʿAlī, 7, 51, 98–102, 137f., 165, 196, 288, 292
Ibn al-Ḥajjāj, Abū ʿAbdallāh al-Ḥusayn ibn Aḥmad, 195
Ibn Ḥanbal, Aḥmad, 97, 101, 105, 113, 115
Ibn Ḥijjah al-Ḥamawī, Abū Bakr Taqī ad-Dīn, 177, 179, 292
Ibn Hishām, 229
Ibn Isḥāq, 229
Ibn al-Jawzī, Abū l-Faraj ʿAbd ar-Raḥmān, 82, 287
Ibn al-Jazarī, Shams ad-Dīn Muḥammad, 7, 35–39, 63–65, 72–76, 80, 87–89, 92, 124, 284–287
Ibn Juzayy al-Kalbī, Abū l-Qāsim Muḥammad, 107–10, 114, 125–27, 261, 288f.
Ibn Kathīr, ʿImād ad-Dīn Ismāʿīl, 55, 82, 144
Ibn Khaldūn, ʿAbd ar-Raḥmān ibn Muḥammad, 231–33, 236f.,265, 298f., 301
Ibn Mājah, Muḥammad ibn Yazīd, 96f., 101
Ibn Makānis, ʿAbd ar-Raḥmān ibn ʿAbd ar-Razzāq, 174
Ibn Māsawayh, Abū Zakariyyā' Muḥammad, 133
Ibn Mujāhid, Aḥmad ibn Mūsā, 48–50, 43, 59
Ibn al-Muqri', Ismāʿīl ibn Abī Bakr, 179, 294
Ibn al-Muʿtazz, Abū l-ʿAbbās ʿAbdallāh, 26, 176, 294
Ibn an-Nafīs, ʿAlā' ad-Dīn ibn Abī l-Ḥaram, 143, 220f.

Ibn Nubātah al-Miṣrī, Jamāl ad-Dīn Muḥammad, 7, 27, 174, 177, 195, 207, 219, 223–36, 298
Ibn Qutaybah, ʿAbdallāh ibn Muslim, 49, 285
Ibn Rushd, Abū l-Walīd Muḥammad ibn Aḥmad (Averroes), 108, 193, 231, 295, 298
Ibn aṣ-Ṣalāḥ ash-Shahrazūrī, Taqī ad-Dīn ʿUthmān, 98, 100, 102, 145
Ibn as-Sikkīt, Yaʿqūb ibn Isḥāq, 160
Ibn Sīnā, Abū ʿAlī al-Ḥusayn ibn ʿAbdallāh (Avicenna), 220, 261
Ibn Sinān al-Khafājī, Abū ʿAbdallāh Muḥammad ibn Saʿīd, 261–63
Ibn as-Sukkarah, Muḥammad ibn ʿAbdallāh al-Hāshimī, 195
Ibn Taymiyyah, Taqī ad-Dīn Aḥmad ibn ʿAbd al-Ḥalīm, 87, 220f., 288
Ibn Ṭufayl, Muḥammad ibn ʿAbd al-Malik, 220
Ibn ʿUthaymīn, Muḥammad ibn Ṣāliḥ, 40–42, 63, 65, 81–83, 117, 125–27, 285, 287, 289
Ibn al-Wardī, Zayn ad-Dīn ʿUmar ibn al-Muẓaffar, 174
Ibn Ẓafar aṣ-Ṣiqillī, Muḥammad ibn ʿAbdallāh, 228
iʿjāz (inimitability, of the Quran), 90f.
ijtihād (judgment, legal or theological, independent from tradition), 88, 118, 120
ikhtilāf (dissent, scholarly, mostly legal), 109f., 123f.
ʿilm (knowledge), 37, 88, 115f., 178
Imraʾalqays ibn ʿAmr, 152
Imraʾalqays ibn Ḥujr al-Kindī, 81
Inimitability (of the Quran) (*iʿjāz*), 90f.
Inspector of the markets (*muḥtasib*), 132f.
Integration, 247
iqtibās (Quranic quotation, in a secular context), 165f.
Iraq, 147–49
al-Irbilī, ʿIzz ad-Dīn al-Ḥasan ibn Muḥammad aḍ-Ḍarīr, 143f.
al-Iskandarī, Abū l-Qāsim ʿĪsā ibn ʿAbd al-ʿAzīz, 50
Islahi, Amin Ahsan, 84
Islamism, 147–50, 184, 236, 267, 276f.
isnād (chain of authorities, on the hadith), 95f., 101f., 112, 229

al-Jāḥiẓ, Abū ʿUthmān ʿUmar b. Baḥr, 174, 293
Jarīr ibn ʿAṭiyyah, 173
Jesus, 243
Jews, Judaism, 243–47
Jingiz Khān (Chengis Khan), 6
al-Jubūrī, ʿAbdallāh, 292
Judge (*qāḍī*), 117, 139–42, 166
Judgment, legal (*ḥukm*, plural form *aḥkām*), 104f., 107–10, 117, 122, 125, 216f.
Judgment, legal or theological, independent from tradition (*ijtihād*), 88, 109, 117–22, 125–28
Jurisprudence (*fiqh*), 104, 219f.
al-Jurjānī, ʿAbd al-Qāhir Abū Bakr, 26, 91, 283, 288, 301
al-Juwaynī, Abū l-Maʿālī ʿAbd al-Malik (Imām al-Ḥaramayn), 106
al-Juzayrī, 194, 295

kalām (theology), 37, 86f., 105, 135, 218, 262f.
al-Karkhī, Abū l-Ḥasan ʿUbayd Allāh ibn al-Ḥusayn, 110
Kassir, Samir, 29
Kermani, Navid, 37, 284, 288
Kersting, Wolfgang, 230–32, 298
al-Khafājī. *See* Ibn Sinān
Khārijites, 95, 218
Klauda, Georg, 211f., 295–97
Kraemer, Joel L., 5, 281
Krafft-Ebing, Richard von, 203
Kraus, Karl, 2, 12, 151, 176, 281f.
Kremer, Alfred von, 170f.

Lamarck, Jean Baptiste, 203
Language sciences. *See* Linguistics
al-Layth ibn Saʿd ibn ʿAbd ar-Rahmān al-Fakhrī, 111, 113
Legal methodology (*uṣūl al-fiqh*), 6, 86, 105–8, 121, 145
Legal opinion (*fatwā*), 116–18, 142, 222
Legal scholar (*faqīh*, plural form *fuqahāʾ*), 117, 139, 265
Legal school of thought (*madhhab*), 118–20, 125–27, 139, 220
Levine, Donald N., 19f., 282–84
Lexicography, 159
Linguistics, language sciences, 122, 157f., 164, 266
Logic, 142, 144f., 271
Loos, Adolf, 171, 293
Love poetry (*ghazal*), 167, 195–97, 209, 242

al-Maʿarrī, Abū l-ʿAlāʾ, 293
MacDonald, A. P., Jr., 17, 169, 283, 293

Machiavelli, Niccolò, 219, 222, 225, 228, 230f., 233, 269, 298
madḥ, madīḥ (panegric poetry), 120, 218
madhhab (legal school of thought), 120, 139
Magellan, Ferdinand, 253
al-maḥāsin wa-l-masāwī (good and bad aspects), 174
Makkī ibn Abī Ṭālib, Muḥammad, 50
Mālik ibn Anas, 97, 105, 114f., 124
Māmay ar-Rūmī, 27
Mamluks, Mamluk era, 6, 119, 165, 172, 174, 177, 179, 221, 223, 233, 243
al-Ma'mūn ibn Hārūn ar-Rashīd (Caliph), 201
Maqāmah, 197, 224
Marino, Giambattista, 13
Marks, Robert B., 300f.
Massad, Joseph, 211f., 295–97
al-Mas'ūdī, Abū l-Ḥasan 'Alī ibn al-Ḥusayn, 250f., 253, 300
Maupassant, Guy de, 194
al-Māwardī, Abū l-Ḥasan 'Alī ibn Muḥammad, 6, 79f., 82, 118f., 145, 216–21, 289, 297f.
Mawdūdī, Sayyid Abū l-A'lā, 63–67, 235, 286
Mayrhofer, Johann Baptist, 188
Medicine, 186f., 203f.
Melchert, Christopher, 49f., 285
Mentalities, history of, 4, 240
Merkel, Wolfgang, 222, 298
Merleau-Ponty, Maurice, 14
Metaphor, 121, 176, 264
Meyerhof, Max, 143f., 291
Mez, Adam, 5, 281, 291
al-Mi'mār, Ibrāhīm ibn 'Alī, 177, 201, 294
Mirrors for Princes (*Fürstenspiegel*), 22, 221, 223, 228, 232f.
Mission civilisatrice, 212
Modernity, modern times, modernization, 24, 248, 267–69, 271f., 274
Montaigne, Michel Eyquem de, 269
Morel, Bénédict Augustin, 203, 296
Mousalli, Ahmet S., 267f., 301
Mozart, Wolfgang Amadeus, 254f.
mu'āraḍah (counterpoem), 178
Muchembled, Robert, 270, 272, 294f, 301
Muftī, 117, 141, 222
Muḥammad (Prophet), 229
Muḥammad ibn As'ad, Abū l-Muẓaffar, 167f.
al-Muḥibbī, Muḥibb ad-Dīn Muḥammad, 192f.
muḥtasib (inspector of the markets), 132f.
mujūn (frivolous and indecent topics in poetry), 194f., 207
Muslim ibn al-Ḥajjāj, 96f., 100, 298
al-Mutanabbī, Abū ṭ-Ṭayyib Aḥmad, 27, 81, 166, 218, 263
al-Mutawakkil ibn al-Mu'taṣim (Caliph), 5
mutawātir (transmitted, as a hadith, without any gaps or errors), 52, 61, 67f., 102, 115, 264f.
Mu'tazilah, 72, 128, 190, 202, 263, 266f.
al-Muzanī, Abū Ibrāhīm Ismā'īl ibn Yaḥyā, 104
Mysticism. *See* Sufism

an-Nabhānī, Yūsuf ibn Ismā'īl, 25
Napoleon Bonaparte, 204
naqā'iḍ (contraoration), 173
an-Nasafī, Najm ad-Dīn 'Umar ibn Muḥammad, 138, 290
an-Nāṣir Muḥammad ibn Qalāwūn (Sultan), 223
naskh (abrogation), 46
Nasser, Gamal Abdel, 243
Nationalism, nationality, 246f., 251, 275f.
an-Nawājī, Shams ad-Dīn Muḥammad, 24f., 198, 207, 242, 283, 291, 296
Nietzsche, Friedrich, 14, 129, 137, 214f., 290, 297
Nöldeke, Theodor, 59, 284–87, 291
Norton, R. W., 17, 283
Nour, Ayman, 205f.

Orientalisme, 212
Orthodoxy, 143–46, 150
Ottomans, Ottoman era, 7, 120, 172, 177, 179, 272

Panegyric poetry (*madḥ, madīḥ*), 218f., 221, 223–26
Paret, Rudi, 78f., 107
Pedro I de Aragón, 230
Persians, Persia, 152, 277
Pīrī Re'īs ibn Ḥājjī Meḥmed, 253
Plato, 219, 231
Play, 163, 173, 175, 177, 179–82
Plessner, Martin, 131f., 143–46, 290f.
Poetry, 151f., 155, 157f., 264. *See also* Frivolous and indecent topics in poetry; Love; Panegyric; Rhetorical challenges; Wine
Pointer(s) in juridical procedure (*dalīl*, plural forms *adilla, dalā'il*), 107–12, 116, 121f., 126f., 263
Politics, political thought, 218
Polyvalence, polysemy of texts, 32, 77, 169, 264

Popal, Mariam, 290f.
Postmodernity, 257f.
Preacher, 140f.
Probability. *See* Assessment of probability (*tarjīḥ*)
Prohibition of foodstuff, 113
Purity/impurity, 113–19

Qāḍī (judge), 113, 119, 140f., 165
Qaddafi (al-Qadhdhāfī), Muʿammar, 205
al-Qazwīnī, Jalāl ad-Dīn Muḥammad (al-Khaṭīb), 265
qirāʾah (Quranic reading), 35f., 46f.
qiyās (analogy, deduction by, reasoning according to), 114, 145
Qudāmah ibn Jaʿfar, Abū l-Faraj al-Kātib al-Baghdādī, 26, 263
Quran: commentary (*tafsīr*), 1f., 87; recitation, 35–37, 40, 45, 47, 53; its text without diacritical dots (*rasm*), 46, 57; translation, 91–93
Quranic quotation, in a secular context (*iqtibās*), 165f., 292
Quranic reading (*qirāʾah*, plural form *qirāʾāt*), 35–39, 46f., 51, 59, 64–67, 70f., 121–23
Quṭrub, Muḥammad ibn al-Mustanīr, 159–63

Rabelais, François, 270
Racism, 275
rasm. *See* Quran, its text without diacritical dots
ar-Rāzī, Fakhr ad-Dīn Abū ʿAbdallāh Muḥammad ibn ʿUmar, 6, 106, 108, 158, 261, 263–65, 288, 291, 301
Renaissance, 199, 222, 232, 269
Rhetoric, 14, 121, 265f., 271
Rhetorical challenges tackled in poetry (*badīʿiyyah*), 27, 177, 178–80
Riddles, 177, 179
Rosenthal, Franz, 299
Rückert, Friedrich, 296
ar-Rummānī, ʿAlī ibn ʿĪsā, 26

Saddam Hussayn (Ṣaddām Ḥusayn), 147–49, 205
aṣ-Ṣafadī, Khalīl ibn Aybak, 27, 81, 177, 287, 291
Ṣafī ad-Dīn al-Ḥillī. *See* al-Ḥillī
Saḥnūn, ʿAbd as-Salām ibn Saʿīd, 113f.
as-Sakkākī, Abū Yaʿqūb Yūsuf, 26, 176, 271, 288
Saladin. *See* Ṣalāḥ ad-Dīn al-Ayyūbī
Salafists, 8, 65, 79, 82f., 125f., 136, 144, 252
Ṣalāḥ ad-Dīn al-Ayyūbī, Yūsuf ibn Ayyūb (Saladin), 6, 225
aṣ-Ṣalāḥī, Muṣṭafā ibn ʿAbd al-Wahhāb, 179
Saleem, Shehzad, 67–69, 286f.
Sasanians, Sassanian empire, 152f.
Sayyid Quṭb, Ibrāhīm Ḥusayn, 235, 276
Schacht, Joseph, 107, 120, 143f., 291
Schmidt, Helmut, 222, 298
Schöller, Marco, 103
Schubert, Franz, 188
Selim Yavuz (Sultan), 7
Seljuqs, Seljuqid era, 5
Sermonizer. *See* Preacher
Sexual intercourse (*bāh*), 190f.
Sexuality, 183–89, 193, 196, 198f., 201, 204, 206, 210f., 273
Sezgin, Fuat, 254, 292, 300
ash-Shāfiʿī, Muḥammad ibn Idrīs, 6, 21, 104–7, 113, 115, 141
Shahab, Ahmed, xii
ash-Shahrazūrī. *See* Ibn aṣ-Ṣalāḥ
Shakespeare, William, 85
Sharia (*sharīʿah*), 95, 103–7, 124, 127
ash-Shawkānī, Muḥammad ibn ʿAlī, 145, 291
Shiʿah, Shiʿites, 8, 95, 218, 259
ash-Shīrāzī, Abū Isḥāq Ibrāhīm ibn ʿAlī, 118f., 289
Sībawayh, Abū Bishr ʿAmr b. ʿUthmān, 25f., 154f., 159
Skepticism, 259–79
Slaughtering according to the *ḥalāl* regulations, 112–14
Solís, Juan Díaz de, 253, 300
"Sonderwege," 268–79
Sonnini, Charles-Nicolas-Sigisbert, 208, 296
Stoning, 35, 191–93
Stranger(s) (*gharīb*), strangeness, exile (*ghurba*), 236–58. *See also* Extraterrestrial(s)
Straton (second century AD), 197
as-Subkī, Bahāʾ ad-Dīn Abū Ḥāmid Aḥmad ibn ʿAlī, 265, 291, 301
Sufism, 85, 135, 139, 269
Sunnah, 6
"Sunni revival," 5f., 106, 168, 216, 219, 265
Syria, 7, 223
as-Suyūṭī, Jalāl ad-Dīn ʿAbd ar-Raḥmān, 7, 22, 27, 40, 53, 77, 80, 83, 86, 119f., 123–25, 283f., 287, 289

aṭ-Ṭabarānī, Abū l-Qāsim Sulaymān, 97
aṭ-Ṭabarī, Muḥammad ibn Jarīr, 62, 93, 287

tafsīr (Quran commentary), 40, 80
Taliban, 215
Tamerlan. *See* Timur Lenk
Tanning, 111–19
tarjīḥ (assessment of probability), 121f., 289
Taureck, Bernhard H. F., 225
tawātur (transmitted, a hadith without any gaps or errors), 62
tawriyah (double entendre), 12, 19, 176f.
at-Tawwāzī, ʿAbdallāh ibn Muḥammad, 160
ath-Thaʿālibī, Abū Manṣūr ʿAbd al-Malik, 174, 238, 292f.
Theology (*kalām*), 5, 37, 86, 88, 135, 144, 218, 263
Thomas More, 270
Tibi, Bassam, 301
Timur Lenk (Tamerlan), 6, 236–38
Todenhöfer, Jürgen, 148f., 291
Todorov, Tzvetan, 255–57, 300
Tolerance, 11
Totalitarianism, 274
Toulmin, Stephen, 259, 269–71, 273–75, 277, 301
Translation (in particular of the Quran), 24, 78, 91–93, 107f.
Transmitted (a hadith) without any gaps or errors (*mutawātir, tawātur*), 52, 61f., 67, 69, 102, 115, 264f.
Troll, Christian, 75f., 287
Ṭughril Beg (Sultan), 5

Ulpianus, Domitius, 139
ʿUmar ibn al-Khaṭṭāb (Caliph), 39
Umayyads, 155, 173
Universalization, ambition of, 213, 252, 254, 257
uṣūl al-fiqh (legal methodology), 6, 86, 105f., 121, 145, 263
ʿUthmān ibn ʿAffān (Caliph), 39–45, 63, 124

Vasco da Gama, 252

Wahhabites, Wahhabis, 43, 65, 252
al-Wansharīsī, Aḥmad ibn Yaḥyā, 21, 291
al-Waṭwāṭ, Abū Isḥāq Burhān ad-Dīn al-Kutubī, 174, 293
Welch, Alford T., 47f., 62
Wine: censure of, 24, 117, 130; poetry, 165–68, 224
Wittgenstein, Ludwig, 261
Wolseley, Garnet Joseph, 214
Words with contradictory meanings (*ḍidd*, plural form *aḍdād*), 151, 159–64

Xenophobia, 240

al-Yāzijī, Nāṣīf, 27, 169f., 178f.
al-Yunīnī, Quṭb ad-Dīn Mūsā ibn Muḥammad, 144

Zaheer, Khalid, 84
az-Zamakhsharī, Abū l-Qāsim Maḥmūd ibn ʿUmar, 80, 91f., 287f.
az-Zarkashī, Badr ad-Dīn Muḥammad, 86
Zayd ibn Thābit al-Anṣārī, 39, 42
Zoroastrians, 243
zuhd (asceticism), 139, 167
az-Zuhrī ibn Shihāb, Muḥammad ibn Muslim, 111, 113, 115f.

GPSR Authorized Representative: Easy Access System Europe, Mustamäe tee 50, 10621 Tallinn, Estonia, gpsr.requests@easproject.com

www.ingramcontent.com/pod-product-compliance
Lightning Source LLC
Chambersburg PA
CBHW021934290426
44108CB00012B/838
9780231170659